THE PAROCHIAL HISTORY

OF

CORNWALL,

FOUNDED ON THE MANUSCRIPT HISTORIES

OF

MR. HALS AND MR. TONKIN;

WITH ADDITIONS AND VARIOUS APPENDICES,

BY

DAVIES GILBERT,

SOMETIME PRESIDENT OF THE ROYAL SOCIETY,
F.A.S. F.R.S.E. M.R.I.A. &c. &c
AND D.C.L. BY DIPLOMA FROM THE UNIVERSITY OF OXFORD.

IN FOUR VOLUMES

VOL II

LONDON:
PUBLISHED BY J. B. NICHOLS AND SON;
AND SOLD BY

J. LIDDELL, BODMIN; J. LAKE, FALMOUTH, O. MATTHEWS, HELSTON, MESSRS. BRAY AND ROWE, LAUNCESTON, T. VIGURS, PENZANCE; MRS. HEARD, TRURO; W. H. ROBERTS, EXETER, I. B. ROWE, PLYMOUTH; AND ALL OTHER BOOKSELLERS IN CORNWALL AND DEVON

HISTORY

OF THE

PARISHES OF CORNWALL.

FALMOUTH, alias VAL-MOUTH, alias VALE-MOUTH.

HALS.

Is situate in the hundred of Kerryer, and hath upon the north Budock; east, the haven or harbour of Falmouth; south, the Black Rock and Pendennis Castle; west, Budock, and the British Channel. For the name, it is taken from the Vale river's mouth, which here empties itself into the British Ocean. And the river itself takes its name from its original fountain in Roach, under Haynes-burrow, called Pen-ta-Vale, Fenton, or Venton; that is to say, the head or chief, good or consecrated, spring or well of water, or river Valley, from thence called the Vale river. This place, in Cornish, is called Val-genow, or Fal-genne; in Saxon, Val-mune; in English, Vale-mouth, synonymous therewith.

This harbour of Falmouth, as mariners tell us, is in all respects the largest and safest haven for ships that this Island of Britain affordeth. Its mouth or entrance from the British Ocean, between the Castles of St. Mawes and Pendennis, situate in St. Anthony and Falmouth parishes, is about a mile and a half distant, the centre or middle thereof above a league, from the said mouth or entrance up the Vale river, by the Rock Island aforesaid, to Carike Road, King's Road, and Turner's Wear, south-east about two leagues from thence, still on the Vale river, a navigable arm or channel of the said harbour, extendeth itself up the country, by Trejago Creek and Castle, towards the incorporate town of Tregony, to the Bridge Place of which it formerly was navigable. [See CUBY.] And it is overlooked on the south-east side, by St. Anthony, St. Just, Philley, Ruan Langhorne, and Cuby parishes. Within the said parishes of St. Just and St. Anthony are also two navigable creeks or channels. Near the castle and incorporate town of St. Mawes, (where formerly stood a monastery of Black Canons Augustine, dedicated to the Virgin Mary, called St. Mary de Vale, for that it was situated on the Vale harbour or river, as its superior monastery is from the Plym river, in Devon, called St. Mary de Plym, whereon it is situate,) from the north-west part of this harbour of Falmouth, between the parishes of Budock, Gluvias, and Milor, another navigable channel extendeth itself up the country to the incorporate town of Penryn. And towards the north another channel or arm thereof, higher up, extendeth itself through the country from the centre about a league, and is navigable to Peran Well and Carnan Bridge. Further up, north-east, another arm or channel of Falmouth Harbour extends itself to the incorporate and coinage town of Truro, and the manor of Moris, and is navigable there about nine miles distance from the Black Rock, or island aforesaid. Lastly, another branch of this harbour extendeth itself to Tresilian Bridge, where it is navigable between the parishes of St. Erme, Probus, and Merther, about ten miles from the mouth of the haven, all which members or branches of the harbour of Falmouth are overlooked with lofty and pleasant hills and vales of land, and within the memory of man abounding with flourishing woods and groves of timber; and before that time Leland the antiquary, in his Itinerary, tells us that this river Vale in his days was encompassed about with the loftiest woods, oaks, and timber-trees that this kingdom afforded temp. Henry VII. and therefore was by the Britons called Cassi-ter, or Casse-ter, viz. wood land, from which place and haven the Greeks fetching tin, called it in in their language κασσιτερος, *cassiteros*, stanum, and the island aforesaid the Cassiteridan Island. But, alas! now this commodity tin hath made such havock of woods and timber-trees, in searching for and melting the same, that scarcely any of them are to be seen in those places; for, the woods and trees being eradicated, the hills and vales aforesaid have submitted to agriculture, and are made arable lands, which abound with cattle, sheep, corn, and pastures.

From the premises I suppose it is evident what Mr. Carew, in his Survey of Cornwall, saith of this harbour of Falmouth, that 100 sail of ships may lie at anchor within the same, and none of them see the others main tops, by reason of the steep hills and long windings of the several channels thereof. In further praise whereof take these rhymes:

> In the calme south Valubia Harbour stands,
> Where Vale with Sea doth joyne its pure hands,
> 'Twixt whome to shipps commodious port is shewne,
> That makes the riches of the world its owne;
> Ike-ta and Vale, the Britons' chiefest pride,
> Glory of them, and all the world beside,
> In sendinge round the riches of its tide;
> Greeks and Phenicians here of old have been,
> Fetchinge from thence furs, hides, pure corne, and tynn,
> Before greate Cæsar fought Cassibelynn.

The parish of Falmouth is a dismembered part of the old parish of Budock, taxed in the Domesday Roll 1087, and separated from it by virtue of an Act of Parliament made 15th Charles II. whereby that church is deprived of its rectory, the great and small tithes, as far as the boundaries of this new parish extends, on the humble petition of Sir Peter Killigrew, of Arwinike, Knt. who by his own bounty, and the charitable benevolence he had begged of others (by leave of the King and Bishop of Exeter), had built on his own land a church and cemetery, at the south end of Falmouth town, whereof he was lord and high lord, for convenience of himself, his servants, and tenants, that were far off from Budock church. This church, so built, he endowed with the tithes aforesaid, as a rectory,* and so became patron thereof, or had *jus patronatus;* reserving to himself and his heirs the right of presenting to the Ordinary a Clerk to be Rector thereof when the same should become void; and the first Rector, as I take it, that he presented to this church was Mr. John Bedford. Thus, it is evident by what ways and means men became patrons of churches, viz. patronum faciunt dos, ædificatio, fundus; the patrons of churches were either founders, builders, or benefactors thereof. Jus patronatus est potestas præsentandi aliquem instituendum ad beneficium ecclesiæ simplex et vacans. (Statute of Westminster, 13th Edward III.) This patronage or advowson Sir Peter Killigrew annexed to his manor and barton of Arwinick.

This church of Falmouth being thus built and endowed, it was consecrated according to the rights and ceremonies for consecration of a church in England by Dr. Seth Ward, Lord Bishop of Exeter, 1664. Within the chancel of which church afterwards was laid, in a vaulted grave, the dead body of its patron and founder, Sir Peter Killigrew, Knt. The present incumbent Quarm. Sir Peter Killigrew also gave the first Rector thereof, and his successors for ever, a house and garden to dwell in, for profit and pleasure; as also a very rich pulpit-cloth, with gold fringes, whereon in needlework of gold was placed the letters I. H. S. Whether it be a contraction of ΙΗΣΟΥΣ, Jesus, or to be construed as being the initial letters of Jesus Hominum Salvator, or Servator, let others resolve.

Ar-win-ike [I above said is] in this parish, [and signifies] the beloved still lake, creek, cove, or bosom of waters, according to the circumstances of the place; on part of which manor formerly stood the insular island Iktam, or Ictam, of Diodorus Siculus, before mentioned. Otherwise, if the name of this place be Ar-wynn-ike, it signifies the victorious or conquering still lake, cove, or bosom of waters;

* The Mayor of Falmouth, by Act of Parliament, pays yearly at Michaelmas three pounds to the Vicar of Budock, for the small tithes.

perhaps to be so construed with reference to Pendennis Castle, contiguous with, and built upon Arwinick lands.

This place is the chief mansion of that ancient and famous family surnamed de Killy-grewe, Killygreu, or Killygreue, from a local place in St. Herme, called Killygrew barton, downs, and hill, now in possession of Jago in fee, where Henry, the son of Maugan de Killygrew, held three parts of a knight's fee of lands, and at Trewince in Gerance, 3d Henry IV. [according to] Carew's Survey of Cornwall, p. 44. Of this family further speaks Mr. Carew, p. 150. The stock is ancient, and divers of the branches have grown to great advancement in calling and livelihood by their greater deserts.

Sir John Killigrew, knight, 1571, built the greatest part of the old house now standing here. He married Wolverston of Wolverston, and had by her issue John Killigrew, Esq.; that married Monk, who had issue by her William Killigrew, Esq. created the 585th Baronet of England, patent 22d December, 12th Charles II. 1660, with limitation to Peter Killigrew, Esq. son of Sir Peter Killigrew aforesaid, Knt. This Sir William Killigrew, Bart. by ill conduct wasted his whole paternal estate, which was valued at about 3,000*l.* per annum; and lastly, sold this manor and barton of Arwinick to his younger brother, Sir Peter Killigrew, Knt. aforesaid, who had issue Sir Peter Killigrew, Bart. aforesaid, who married one of the coheirs of Judge Twysden, and had issue by her George Killigrew, Esq. that married Ann, daughter of Sir John Seyntaubyn, Bart. and had issue by her one daughter.

This Mr. George Killigrew was afterwards, in a drunken humour, at a tavern in Penryn, slain in the chamber, in a duel, by Walter Vincent, Esq. barrister-at-law, who was tried for his life at Launceston for the fact, and acquitted by the petty jury, *through bribery and indirect acts and practices, as was generally said;* yet this Mr. Vincent, through anguish and horror at this accident, (as it was said,) within two years after wasted of an extreme atrophy of his flesh and spirits, that at length at the table whereby he was sitting, in the Bishop of Exeter's palace, in presence of divers gentlemen, he instantly fell back against the wall and died.

Sir Peter Killigrew had issue also two daughters, the one married to Richard Erisey, Esq. and another married to Martin Lister, Esq. of Liston, in Staffordshire, a captain or lieutenant in Pendenis Castle, under John Earl of Bath; upon whose issue by her Sir Peter settled much of his lands, on condition he should assume the name of Killigrew, and is now in possession of this lordship.

The country people here about will tell you, (as such are superstitious enough to do,) that this murder or manslaughter of Mr. Killigrew by Mr. Vincent, whereby the male line of that family is extinct, was a just judgment of God; for that Jane Killigrew, widow of Sir John Killigrew, Knt. aforesaid, his great-grandmother, in the Spanish wars in the latter end of the reign of Queen Elizabeth, went on board two Dutch ships of the Hans Towns, (always free traders in times of war,) driven into Falmouth Harbour by cross winds, laden with merchandize, on account (as was said) of Spaniards, and with a numerous party of ruffians, murdered the two Spanish merchants or factors on board those ships, and took from them two barrels or hogsheads of Spanish pieces of eight, and converted them to her own use.

Now, though Fleta, Liber I. chap. iii. temp. Edward II. tells us that it is no murder except it be proved that the party slain was English, and no stranger, yet afterwards, by the Statute 4 Edward III. his son, chap. 4, the killing any *foreigner under the King's protection,* out of evil design or malice, is made murder, upon which Statute those offenders were tried and found guilty at Launceston of wilful murder, both by the grand and petty juries, and had sentence of death passed accordingly upon them, and were all executed, except the said Lady Killigrew, the principal agent and contriver of the barbarous fact, who, by the interest and favour of Sir John Arundell, of Tolverne, Knt. and his son-in-law, Sir Nicholas Hals, of Pengersick, Knt.

obtained of Queen Elizabeth a pardon or reprieve for the said lady, which was seasonably put into the Sheriff of Cornwall's hands.

This Lady Jane Killigrew afterwards gave a silver cup to the Mayors of Penryn for ever, in memory of some kindness in her troubles received in that Corporation, 1612. Sir Henry Killigrew, Knt. temp. Elizabeth, was a younger brother to Sir John Killigrew aforesaid, and followed the Court for advantage, and to raise his fortunes (according to the constant genius of his family). He, as Mr. Carew in his Survey of Cornwall saith, " after embassies and messages, and many other profitable employments, both of peace and war, in his prince's service, to the good of his country, hath made choice of a retired estate, and was reverently regarded by all sorts, and places his principal contentment in himself; which to a life so well acted can no wise be wanting." He married Katherine, daughter of Sir Anthony Cooke, of Giddy Hall, in Essex, Knt. who had issue by her a daughter, married to Sir Jonathan Trelawny, of Poble, Knt.

This Sir Henry Killigrew, by the favour of Queen Elizabeth, as a boon procured Gervase Babington, Lord Bishop of Exeter, 1594, by lease and release, fine and recovery, to dismember from the church and bishopric of Exeter, the great manor, barton, and lordship of Kirton, in Devon, worth 1,000*l*. per annum, rents of assize, which had been in the possession of the Bishops of Kirton and Exeter, from the time of Edulphus, the first Bishop thereof, anno Dom. 907, being 687 years to that time; but long since this manor of land is gone out of the name and possession of Killigrew. In like manner, about that time John Coldwell, Lord Bishop of Salisbury, passed the manor of Sherburne to the Crown, by whom it was given to Sir Walter Ralegh, Knt. which is also long since gone out of his name and family.

The arms of Killigrew are, within a field Argent, an imperial eagle with two necks, within a bordure Bezanté

Sable. Which arms and bordure seem to inform us that this family was indirectly descended from Richard Earl of Cornwall, King of the Romans, by that concubine Jane de Valletorta, widow of Sir Alexander Oakeston [see Sr. STEPHEN'S BY SALTASH]. For that, as this bordure Bezanté Sable was the proper arms of Richard Earl of Cornwall, viz. 5, 4, 3,2, 1, the imperial eagle was the cognizance of the said Earl of Cornwall as King of the Romans.

Within this parish also now stands the borough town of Falmouth, which compound word is etymologized before. It was incorporated 14th Charles II by the name of the Mayor and Aldermen and Magistrates of the Borough of Falmouth, with the jurisdiction of a Court-leet, wherein plea of debt and damage is tried within its precincts. But, alas! notwithstanding its present grandeur, neither this town nor its modern name is of any great antiquity, neither being extant 500 years past; for long since that time it was known by no other appellation than that of Smith-ike, that is, the Smith's creek, leat, or bosom of waters, from a smith that lived at the creek, or cove, now in the centre thereof. And verily, I have been told by some aged persons lately living, that they remembered not above five houses standing in this place; though now, I suppose, they are increased to five or six hundred. And for its name Falmouth, it was not recorded till, at the request of Sir Peter Killigrew, it was inserted in its charter of incorporation as aforesaid. Which thing I do not mention to disparage this really good name, but to let the inhabitants of this place, and many other families now flourishing in Cornwall, know that many of them are mistaken in their antiquity and former appellations, if truly examined.

Moreover, concerning the first buildings of this town by John Killigrew, Esq. In 1613, happened a notable controversy between him and the Corporations of Penryn, Truro, and Helston, which suggested, by a petition to James the First, promoted and backed by the interest of the Burgesses thereof, viz. Sir Richard Robartes, Bart. and John Arundell, Esq. for Truro; Sir Francis Godolphin, Knt. for Helston; Richard Penwarne, Esq. for Penryn; and others, "that the erecting of a town at Smith-ike would tend to the ruin and impoverishing of the ancient coinage-towns and market-towns aforesaid, not far distant from thence; and therefore humbly prayed the King's Majesty that the buildings and undertakings of Mr. Killigrew might be inhibited for the future." Who, upon receipt and hearing of this petition in Council, ordered the Lords thereof, Egerton, Buckhurst, Hume, Marre, Sir Robert Cecil, Principal Secretary of State, and others, to write to Sir Nicholas Hals, of Fentongollon, Knt. then Governor of Pendennis Castle, to be better informed of the true merits of this case, and to know his own particular sentiments about it. Which gentleman, as soon as he received this letter, made answer, that he well approved of Mr. Killigrew's project for building a town and custom-house at Smith-ike, as being near the mouth of the harbour of Falmouth; and briefly, amongst many others, for these reasons especially.

1. For the quick and necessary supply of such ships whose occasions, or contrary winds, brought them in there, without being obliged (as then they were) to go up two miles the river to Penryn, or nine miles to Truro, in order thereto, or to take in and out their cargoes or lading, and make entries at the custom-houses at such distance, by reason of which delays of time they many times lost the opportunity of a fair wind to prosecute their intended voyages, longer than was for their advantage.

2. For the speedy supplying or reinforcing the Castle of Pendennis, contiguous therewith, with men, ammunition, and provisions, in case of any enemy's sudden invasion, or endeavouring to take the same by storm or surprise, before the country militia could be raised, or recruits brought in for that purpose.

3. For that other castles for the same reasons were

built near towns, or towns erected near them, as Dover, Portsmouth, Plymouth, Newcastle, Gravesend, and many more."

As appears more at large from the letters and reasons of Sir Nicholas Hals to the Lords of the Council aforesaid, whereof, by fees to the Clerk of the Council, or Secretary of State, copies were privately taken forth, at the special instance and request of the said Richard Penwarne, and other Members of Parliament then in London, who transmitted them, by the hands of Mr. Anthony Mundye, to the Corporation aforesaid, where the writer of these lines hath had a full view of them, amongst the papers and records of the borough of Penryn, then lodged in the chest of its town-hall. Whereupon King James, upon a full hearing of this controverted matter between the parties aforesaid, and what could be alleged on either part, gave his opinion (with which all the Council agreed) that the erecting a town at Smith-ike by Mr. Killigrew, could in no sense be prejudicial to the coinage and incorporate towns aforesaid, they standing at such considerable distances from it; but especially for that every man might lawfully do what he would for the utility and advantage of his own proper goods or lands, without the licence or approbation even of the King, or any contiguous neighbour, who had no public or private nuisance thereby done him: how much more reasonable was it, therefore, when the owners of such lands converted them to such uses as tended not only to his own, but the public good and advantage of the king and country together.

Whereupon Mr. Killigrew proceeded with his intended buildings, and his tenants, the inhabitants thereof, quickly grew rich by trade and merchandize both at home and abroad: so that in about twenty years' time the town became notably famous in respect thereof, and is now, for wealth, trade, and buildings, scarcely inferior to any town in Cornwall. It is privileged also with a weekly market on Thursdays, and with fairs upon July 27 and October 30.

The chief inhabitants of this town are Mr. Russell, Mr. Tresahar, Mr. Corker, Mr. Hill, Mr. Gwyn.

In this town his Majesty hath his custom-house collector, comptroller, customer, surveyor, sea and land waiters; and from this town the packet-boats from the Groyne, Lisbon, and America, receive their despatches from their agent, to the great advantage of this place in times of peace and war: since, as I am informed, removed to Flushing, in Mylor parish, opposite thereto.

This town also was the honorary title of Charles Lord Berkeley, Viscount Fitzhardinge, created Lord Bottetourt and Earl of Falmouth, 17th March, 16th Charles II. 1664. He was slain in the Dutch wars 1665, without legitimate issue, and gave for his arms, Gules, a chevron Ermine, between ten crosses patée, 6 and 4, Argent.

Afterwards it became the honorary title of George Fitz-Roy, third son of Barbara Duchess of Cleveland by King Charles the Second, by whom he was created Earl of Northumberland, Viscount Falmouth, and Baron Pontefract in Yorkshire; and giveth for his arms, the imperial shield of England, with a baton sinister, gobonée, Ermine and Azure. This Barbara Villiers was one of the daughters of the Lord Viscount Grandison, of the Kingdom of Ireland, and was married to Roger Palmer, Esq. created Earl of Castlemaine, in Ireland; but afterwards, when Charles the Second took a liking to this Countess, he sent the Earl her husband, with his own good liking, Governor of a Castle and Colony of the English at Surat, in the East Indies. His lady King Charles further created Countess of Southampton and Duchess of Cleveland, during life. After the death of George Fitz-Roy, in the year 1722, Hugh Boscawen, of Tregothnan, Esq. Lord Warden of the Stannaries, was created by King George, Lord Boscawen of Tregothnan, Baron Boscawen of Boscawen Ros, in Burian, and Viscount Falmouth.

In this parish, on the lands of the manor of Arwynick (the Icta and Island of Diodorus Siculus aforesaid), upon a lofty peninsula or promontory of land, stands the famous and impregnable Castle of Pendennis, for which the Crown pays annually to the lord of the manor aforesaid, out of the Exchequer, about 13*l.* 6*s.* 8*d.* rent, as I take it. For the compound name Pen-den-is Castle, it is British, and signifies that it is the head or chief man's castle, viz. the King or Earl of Cornwall. Otherwise, if the true name thereof be Pen-dun-es Castle, it signifies that it is the head or chief fort or fortress castle. This castle of old consisted only of a treble intrenchment of turf, earth, and stones, after the British and Roman manner, upon the top of the highest hill in those parts, abutting upon the west side of the mouth or entrance of the harbour of Falmouth, and containeth about twenty statute acres of ground within the lines. Repaired and indifferently fortified by Henry the Eighth, in the latter end of his reign, in the French war, with allowance of a petty garrison, whose daughter, Queen Elizabeth, in her Spanish wars, raised the new fort, and bettered the old fortification, as they are now extant; so that it is looked upon as one of the most invincible castles in this kingdom, having had in it above one hundred pieces of cannon mounted, and some thousands of foot arms. After Queen Elizabeth had thus fortified and munified the Castle of Pendennis, she placed therein a band of 100 soldiers, and over them placed as her Governor Sir Nicholas Parker, Knt. (a Devonshire gentleman, as some say, though his arms, a fess fretty or chequey,* differs from the arms of Parker of Burrington,) of whom thus speaks Mr. Carew in his Cornish Survey, p. 150: "He now demeaneth himself no less kindly and frankly towards his neighbours for the present, than he did resolutely and valiantly against his enemies when he followed the wars, wherethrough he commandeth not only their bodies by his autho-

---

* The arms of Parker of Rathon, in Sussex, were, Azure, fretty Or, over all a fess of the Second. And in the pedigree of that family Sir Nicholas Parker, Knt. is styled Captain of Pendennis Castle, Cornwall. Edit.

rity, but also their hearts by his love, to live and die in his assistance, for their common preservation and her Highness' service." He died without issue, anno Dom. 1608, and lies buried in Budock church. His successor in the government of this castle was Sir Nicholas Hals, of Fentongollan, Knt. (a domestic servant to Prince Henry, eldest son of James the First,) son of John Hals, of Efford, Esq. in Devon, who died Governor thereof in 1637; and was succeeded in that dominion by Sir Nicholas Slanning, of Marstow, in Devon, Knt. who was slain on the part of his master Charles the First against the Parliament army at the battle of Bristol, 6th July, 1643. After his death his widow (daughter of Sir James Baggs, of Plymouth, Knt.) was married to Richard Arundell, of Trerice, Esq. son of John Arundell, of that place, Esq. commonly called John of Tilbury, for that he was an officer under Queen Elizabeth when she was encamped there with her army, in expectation of the Spaniards landing, 1588.

Which gentleman, (John Arundell,) was by Charles the First made Governor of Pendennis Castle; during whose command there happened a tragical siege thereof by the Parliament army under Colonel Fortescue; wherein the besiegers and the besieged showed unparalleled valour and conduct for about six months' space, when at length it was surrendered upon honourable conditions, the soldiers going forth with their arms mounted and colours flying, more consumed with sickness and famine within the walls than destroyed by their enemies from without, having been driven to that extremity that the governor, soldiers, and many other gentlemen and ladies therein, were forced for some time to eat horseflesh, for want of other victuals; as being hemmed in by the Parliament frigates at sea on the one side, and surrounded with their army at land on the other, so that no relief of men or provisions could be brought into the garrison, whereby it was forced to capitulate and surrender as aforesaid 1647, (before which time all other castles in England, except Ragland in Wales, were yielded up to the Parliament,) and the hunger-starved soldiers of Pendennis, that came out thence, feeding too freely on victuals and drink, brought themselves into incurable diseases, whereof many died; so that here, as in many other places, it was observed that more men and women died by two frequently putting their hands to their mouths, than by clapping their hands to their swords; as the Jews did on surrender of Jerusalem to the Romans, after the siege and famine there.

After the surrender of this castle, as aforesaid, by Colonel John Arundell, he was succeeded in that dignity by Colonel Fortescue, and he was succeeded by Captain Fox; as after the restoration of Charles the Second, Fox was succeeded by Richard Lord Arundell, and he by the Earl of Bath.

One Mr. Thomas Killigrew, of this Arwinick family, was Jester or Master of the Revels to Charles the Second, who, (to give but a single instance of his wit and humour,) having been at Paris on business, went to Versailles to see the French Court for diversion; where, being well known to many French courtiers who had been in England, he was by them introduced into Louis the Fourteenth the King of France's presence, who had a long time had a desire to see him whom fame reported the wittiest man in England. But at that time Killigrew was politically out of humour, and spoke very little, out of a desire he had to hear the wisdom of the French Court, and what little discourse he had it was trivial and of no consequence; whereupon King Louis told the noblemen that gave him such encomiums of his wit, that he looked upon him as a very dull fellow. Whereupon the courtiers told him, notwithstanding what his Majesty's opinion was, assuredly he was a most ingenious and witty man. Whereupon, soon after, the King resolved to make a further trial of him, and therefore led him into a long gallery, where were many fine pictures, and asked Killigrew what they were? And amongst the rest of those draughts showed the picture of our Saviour upon the Cross; and then again asked Killigrew if he knew what it was? To which, as to the former demands, he pleaded ignorance, and answered, "No." "Why, then," said King Louis, "Monsieur Killigrew, "I will tell you what they are. The picture in the centre is the draught of our Saviour on the Cross, and that on the right hand of him is the Pope's picture, and that on the left hand of him is my own" To which Killigrew replied, "I humbly thank your Majesty for the information you have given me, for though I have often heard that our Saviour was crucified between two thieves, yet I never knew who they were till now." Which sharp repartee convinced that King of his wrong opinion of Killigrew's wit in satire and ridicule, especially it being at the time when the Pope and French King grievously persecuted the French Protestants, and either dragooned them to mass or drove them out of France.

Mr. Thomas Killigrew is further said to have put under the candlestick where Charles the Second supped, five small papers, on which he had written the word ALL. The King, on sight thereof, asked him what he meant by these five words of one signification. "Your Majesty's pardon granted, I will tell you, sir," said Mr. Killigrew; which being promised, he said, "The first All signified that the Country had sent all; the second, the City had lent all; the third, that the Court had spent all; the fourth, if we did not mend all; the fifth, that it will be worse for us all."

This was reflected on the royal family of William the Third, "That he was William Think-all; his Queen Mary, Mary Take-all; Prince George of Denmark, George Drink-all; and the Princess Ann, Ann Eat-all, which ill habit diminished her health and hastened her death."

TONKIN.

Sir Henry Killigrew, Knt. married Katherine, the second daughter and coheir of Sir Anthony Cooke, of Giddy Hall, in Essex. Her other sisters married Sir William Cecil, Lord Treasurer, Sir Nicholas Bacon, Lord Chancellor, Sir Thomas Hobby, and Sir Ralph Howlet, Knts. Which ladies were all accounted of the most learned in the kingdom, eminently skilled in the Latin and Greek tongues. To give an instance for the whole:

Sir Henry Killigrew being appointed by Queen Elizabeth, ambassador to Henry the Fourth of France, lately turned Papist, was not very fond of that employment, and would have excused himself, but knew not how: whereupon his lady wrote a letter to her sister Mildred, wife to Sir William Cecil, to try her interest with his lordship to get the Queen to excuse him, and that some other person might be appointed for that employment. The letter was these words:

> Si mihi quem cupio cures, Mildreda! remitti,
> Tu mihi, tu melior, tu mihi sola soror;
> Sin male cunctando retines, vel trans mare mittes,
> Tu mala, tu pejor, tu mihi nulla soror
> It si Cornubiam, tibi pax sit, et omnia læta,
> Sin mare—Cœcile! nuncio bella.—Vale!

Which I find thus translated by Dr. Fuller, in his Worthies, though much abated of their elegancy in Latin:

> If, Mildred! by thy care he be sent back, whom I request.
> A sister good thou art to me, yea better, yea the best;
> But if with stays thou keep'st him still, or send'st where seas may part,
> Then unto me a sister ill, yea worse, yea none thou art,
> If go to Cornwall he shall please, I peace to thee foretell;
> But, Cecil! if he set to seas—I war denounce —Farewell!

Whether this letter did procure Sir Henry Killigrew's stay, and dismission from the intended service, I am unable to resolve, although well assured I am that his daughter by this Catherine Cooke was married to Sir Jonathan Trelawney, of Poole, Knt. Sheriff of Cornwall 36th Eliz.

As for the harbour itself, it is agreed by all mariners to be one of the best for safe anchorage, large circumference, and good riding for ships, that this kingdom affords. The mouth or entrance, between the castles of Pendennis and St. Mawes, is about two miles over. The body of the harbour, from St. Mawes to Falmouth town, is about a league. From Falmouth to Turner's Weare, upon the river Vale, two leagues; from whence an arm of it goes up towards Tregony, another towards Tresilian Bridge, a third towards Truro; all which places the salt water visits every tide. Beneath Turner's Weare, on the north, another channel goes by Restrongar Passage to Carnen, and St. Perron Arworthal. From Falmouth town goeth up another creek to Penryn. Lastly, on the south there go into the country two creeks towards St. Mawes and St. Anthony. All these members or branches of the harbour are overlooked by lofty and pleasant hills, and are supplied with deep water, so that boats, ships, barges, and lighters every day, one where or another, carry and recarry goods and merchandizes to the remotest parts thereof. Hence it is that Mr. Carew says, " a hundred sail of ships may lie at anchor within the harbour of Falmouth, and none of them see the other's topmast," because of the steep hills and windings of the river.

The Killigrews are also lords of the land whereon the Castle of Pendennis stands, and receive yearly out of the Exchequer for the same 13*l*. 6*s*. 8*d*. Of all which premises take the following rhyme:

> In the calm south great Falmouth's Harbour stands,
> Where Vale with Sea doth join its peaceful hands,
> 'Twixt whom to ships commodious port is shown,
> That makes the riches of the world its own.
> Falmouth, or Vale, the Britons' chiefest pride,
> Glory of them and all the world beside,
> In sending round the treasures of her tide.
> Killigrew's the Lord both of the Fort and Town:
> Speak these the rest, to make them better known.

Arwinick signifies upon the marsh; ar being the same as war, upon, and winick, a marsh, exactly suitable to the situation of the place.

Sir John Killigrew, of this place, ought not to be forgotten; who, seeing the Parliament Army to prevail every

18   FALMOUTH.

where, with his own hands set fire to his noble house here, that they might not find shelter in it when they came to lay siege to Pendennis Castle, as they did soon after: an action which was well rewarded by Charles the Second; although the house hath not been rebuilt, a few rooms only having been fitted up just to receive the family, who have not much resided in it ever since.

THE EDITOR.

Falmouth Harbour, situated within thirty miles of the Land's End, is without all comparison the most advantageous station for packets, maintaining a regular communication with Lisbon, the West Indies, and the Mediterranean. It has also been found admirably adapted for receiving smaller ships of war; a squadron of frigates, under the command of Admiral Lord Hugh Seymour, of Admiral Pellew, &c. cruised from hence against the French during a part of the great contest following the Revolution; but, although the largest ship may enter the port, and anchor there in safety, yet it is very inferior for their accommodation either to Plymouth or to Portsmouth.

Falmouth is also a great resort of vessels coming from foreign countries, to receive orders as to their ultimate destination; and this is not only owing to the western situation of the harbour, but, in a very considerable degree, to the residence of a family which has maintained the highest reputation through a long series of years, as merchants, as men of integrity and of talent. They are said to be lineal or collateral relatives of the patriarch George Fox. On their first arrival in Cornwall, this family settled themselves at Par, near St. Austell; but afterwards removing to Falmouth, they have mainly contributed towards the prosperity of the whole county, as merchants, as manufacturers, as spirited and enlightened adventurers in mines, and in the fisheries. Among many so eminent, it would be absolute injustice not to mention particularly Mr. Robert Ware Fox, who has most successfully employed his

FALMOUTH.

leisure in the philosophical investigation of geology and of chemistry, in connexion with mechanics, not only by his own exertions, but as the judicious and liberal encourager of similar pursuits in others.

Many individuals have acquired wealth in Falmouth by a very peculiar species of commerce, carried on with Lisbon by means of the packets. The interchange of various commodities was legally prohibited, but at the same time practically allowed, by both Governments; and to such an extent did this half-contraband trade arise, that a Mr. Nowell, who kept a retail shop at Falmouth, is said to have made a fortune, by which his son became Sheriff of the county in 1787, chiefly as a carrier of these goods to and from London on packhorses; and a fortune still larger has been made by Mr. Russell, of Exeter, by conveying increased quantities in waggons over improved roads, through Devonshire and Cornwall.

It is quite impossible for such an harbour as Falmouth to have escaped the knowledge of the Phœnicians, when they came to Cornwall for tin, and strangely mistook it for a cluster of islands. The Greeks must also have known this port; and the Romans not merely encamped in various parts of the county, but having fixed stations within it, and on the very banks of the Fall, cannot have failed of noticing the longest and best roadsted and navigable river within the limits of Cornwall: but so vague and uncertain are all the descriptions transmitted to us either by geographers or by the writers of itineraries, that we are utterly unable to discriminate most places within certain limits of each other except by conjecture. It is truly a matter of astonishment that nations having made such ample progress in abstract geometry, and in astronomy itself, should have altogether disregarded latitudes which were within their reach; and even approximations towards longitudes, which might have been obtained through the medium of lunar eclipses.

jesty with the employment of Resident at the State of Venice. In his absence from this country he applied his leisure hours to poetry, and to the composition of several plays, of which Sir John Denham takes notice in his poem on our author's return from his embassy. Though Denham mentions but six, our author wrote nine plays in his travels, and two at London; all which were printed, with his picture before them, in 1664. There is, besides, "A Letter concerning some Nuns in the Nunnery of Tours," dated from Orleans in 1635, and printed in three folio sheets. Mr. Killigrew died in 1682, and was buried in Westminster Abbey. He had been twice married.

"He was a man of a very droll and uncommon vein of humour, with which he used to divert that merry monarch Charles the Second; who on that account was fonder of him than his best Ministers, and would give him access to his person when he denied it to them. It was usually said of him, that when he attempted to write he was nothing near so smart as he was in conversation: which was just the reverse of Cowley, who shone but little in conversation, although he excelled so much with his pen. Hence Denham, who knew them both, has taken occasion thus to characterize their respective excellences and defects·

> Had Cowley ne'er spoke, Killigrew ne'er writ,
> Combin'd in one, they'd make a matchless wit.

Another brother, Henry Killigrew, is mentioned in the the same work, Chaplain to James the Second while he was Duke of York, and a Prebendary of Westminster. He is there stated to have written a tragedy at the age of seventeen, called "The Conspiracy," which obtained the high approbation of Ben Jonson.

He had a daughter, Ann Killigrew, recorded as

> A Grace for beauty, and a Muse for wit.

This young lady was maid of honour to the Duchess of York, but died of the smallpox at the early age of twenty-five.

The elder brother, William, was also a poet and an author. The representative of the Killigrew family is Lord Wodehouse, in right of his late wife, Sophia Berkeley, niece of Lord Berkeley of Stratton.

Falmouth has now outgrown the property of those who originally built the town, and is extended northward, at Green Bank, into the land of Lord de Dunstanville, where the houses have all the convenience and decoration suited to modern times. The older part of Falmouth, although it dates no further back than about two centuries, is unfortunately distinguished by its narrow, crooked streets, and by every defect usually found in the smallest fishing-towns. It is, however, surrounded by beautiful villas.

Falmouth has been associated, in 1832, with Penryn, in the privilege of sending two Members to Parliament.

This parish measures 621 statute acres.

Annual value of the Real Property, as returned to Parliament in 1815:

	£.	s.	d.
The parish	10,029	0	0
The town	11,534	0	0
Poor Rate in 1831	569	1	0

Population,—	in 1801,	in 1811,	in 1821,	in 1831,
Parish	1165	1374	1982	2523
Town	3684	3933	4392	4761
Total	4849	5307	6374	7284

giving an increase on the population of the parish of 116 per cent., on the population of the town 29 per cent., in 30 years; on both together 50 per cent in the same period.

The latitude of Falmouth is given in the best tables at 50° 8′. The longitude has been ascertained by Dr. Tiarks with the greatest care (see Philosophical Transactions for 1824): the flag-staff at Pendennis Castle 20^m. 11.5^s. west. Times of high water at the new and full moon 5^h. 15′.

Present Rector, the Hon. and Rev. W. Wodehouse, instituted 1828.

ST. FEOCK.

THE GEOLOGY, BY DR. BOASE.

Hornblende rocks, both schistose and compact, such as occur near the junction of the porphyritic and calcareous series, constitute this little parish. The Castle Hill appears to belong to the latter series.

ST. FEOCK.

HALS.

Is situate in the hundred of Powdre, and has upon the north St. Kea, east and south the harbour of Falmouth towards the Vale river, west Restrongat creek, or Cainan river. As for the name Feock, or Feighe, Veage, Feage, it signifies the top of a house, or high mountain, as this parish is on, and there is still extant the lofty local place called Le Feock, Le Feage. At the time of the Domesday Tax, 20th William I. (1087), this parish was taxed by the name of Ros-carnon, now part thereof. In the Inquisition of the Bishops of Lincoln and Winchester into the value of Cornish Benefices, Ecclesia de Sancto Feoko was valued xl*s.* in Decanatu de Powdre; Vicar ejusdem xiii*s.* iiii*d.*; in Wolsey's Inquisition, 1521, and Valor Beneficiorum, the Vicarage of Feock was valued in 11*l.*; the patronage in the Bishop of Exeter, who endowed it. The incumbent Ange: and the parish rated to the 4*s.* per pound Land Tax, 1696, 126*l.* 12*s.*

St. Feock, the presidual guardian of this church, in all probability lived at the local place aforesaid, called Le-Feock, i. e. Feock's place and dwelling; but who or what his parents were, when or where born, &c. I must plead *non sum informatus.*

In the glass windows is the figure of a man in priest's robes, with a radiated or shining circle about his head and face, and under his feet written St. Feock; beneath whom, also in the glass, were painted, kneeling and bending forward, in way of adoration, the figures of a man and woman, and behind them several children, out of which figurative man and woman's mouths proceeded a label, with this inscription—" Sancte Feock, ora pro bono statu S. Trewonwoll et Elionoræ uxoris ejus." From whence I was fully satisfied that he was indeed the tutelar guardian of this church.

At Le-Feock aforesaid, temp. Charles II. was the dwelling, by lease, of Captain Thomas Penrose, whose father married Verman; originally descended from the Penroses of Penrose in Sythney. This gentleman having in his youth, temp. Charles I. been bred at sea, in the study and practice of the art of navigation, it appears from his journal that, in the year 1650, he was by the Admiral of the States of England made Captain or Commander of the Bristol frigate or man-of-war, in which he fought, together with the English fleet under command of General Blake, near Dover, against the Dutch fleet, under their General Van Tromp, who was shrewdly worsted by Blake. He was also in the engagement against the Dutch fleet under Sir George Ayscough, 1652, before Plymouth, where the victory inclined to neither side, but great losses on both. He also, 28th of October, the same year, fought in General Blake's squadron against the General of the States De Witt, who was then worsted, on one side of the North Foreland, in the Downs. Captain Penrose was also in that engagement between General Blake and Van Tromp wherein the English Fleet was worsted, and came off with great loss, so that Van Tromp sailed into the Downs in great triumph, with a broom on his main-topmast.

But, maugre his success, pride, and insolence, the States of England fitted forth their shattered ships sooner than was expected, to the number of eighty sail of men-of-war, when Captain Penrose was removed from the Bristol to the command of the Maidstone frigate. Then also were Penn and Burne discharged from command of particular squadrons, and the supreme command of the fleet was put into the hands of General Blake, General Monk, and General Dean; when soon after happened that bloody and tremendous sea-fight betwixt the English and the Dutch fleets, before Weymouth and Dungeness, wherein General Monk declared (upon the sudden death of General Dean, killed at breakfast on the deck of their ship by Monk's side, with a defiance gun-bullet shot at random by the Dutch to his destruction) that this fifth battle should put an end to the war one way or other, and gave forth strict order and command to the officers of the English fleet upon penalty of death, that they should neither take from nor give quarter to the enemy; which commands in the engagement being for a considerable time kept and observed by the English, the terror thereof so amazed the Dutch, that, after great losses of men and ships by them sustained, they declined to fight, and bore or ran away with their fleet, leaving the victory and British Channel wholly to the English fleet. In this fight, as appears from Penrose's Journal, he lost above fifty men out of the Maidstone, besides had many more wounded. Afterwards the English fleet, coasting westwards in pursuit of the vanquished Dutch fleet, were by cross winds forced into Falmouth harbour, where also for some days, as appears from Penrose's Journal aforesaid, he entertained at his house in this place of Le-Feock (opposite the harbour aforesaid) General Monk, General Blake, Sir George Ayscough, and many other officers and gentlemen of the fleet, to good content and satisfaction.

Afterwards they sent him many letters concerning the war, fleet, and ship he sailed in, and the course he should take; and in particular, amongst others, thanked him for his great valour and conduct in the several engagements aforesaid. From some of which it appears General Blake was a better soldier than scholar, as being very badly able to write the letters of his name to the letters his secretary had formed, as yet may be seen; which is not to be won-

ST. FEOCK. 27

dered at, as I am credibly informed he was at first but a man of no higher education than that of a petty mechanic, viz. a ribbon and galloon weaver in Taunton; whereof, at last, for his valour in the siege, in opposition to Charles the First, he was made governor thereof by the Parliament.

Captain Penrose fought also in the Maidstone frigate under General Monk, in the sixth and last engagement of the English at sea against the Dutch fleet, wherein Van Tromp their general was slain, and his fleet extremely shattered, sunk, and disabled, to the great terror of the United Provinces. Then also the Maidstone frigate underwent the loss of many seamen; and the Captain continued his post till the restoration of Charles the Second, when he was dismissed from his command, and another commander placed in his room; after which he retired to his country-house of Le-Feock aforesaid.

It also appears from Penrose's Journal whilst he commanded the Maidstone, that she was one of the five ships under Sir George Ayscough that was ordered by the then Parliament of England to sail into the Sound, or German Sea, to assist the King of Sweden against the Danes. But a peace being concluded betwixt those nations, soon after the arrival of those ships, nothing of action was performed by them. Nevertheless, the King of Sweden rewarded the five captains of those ships in this expedition, with so many medals and neck-chains of gold, with the King of Sweden's face on one side of the medal, and the several arms of those gentlemen on the other, weighing about eighteen ounces each together with the chain. Penrose's medal is yet to be seen with his daughter.

In the year 1664, when another Dutch and French war broke out between them and Charles the Second, and able sea-officers were wanted for the fleet, Penrose (who as aforesaid for several years had been displaced) had divers letters sent to him from James Duke of York, and the Duke of Albemarle (formerly General Monk), by order of

Charles the Second, requesting in this time of need that he would come up to London, accept of the command, and take the charge of the Monk frigate, in the Dutch war; which at length with some reluctance he accepted. In which post he discharged the place with such care and faithfulness as before he had done in the Parliament service. And, moreover, in the three sea-fights which the Duke of York and the Duke of Albemarle had with the Dutch fleets, (in all which he was commanded, though but a third-rate ship, to follow the admiral or general's ships,) he behaved himself with such prudent valour and conduct (though with the loss of several hundreds of his men) that he preserved his ship, to the admiration of all that saw her, from destruction, though often boarded and surrounded with enemies.

In brief, those matters are so abundantly set forth in the several letters of thanks, after those engagements, from the said Dukes and their Secretaries to Penrose, that if I should take the pains to transcribe them, they would only be thought a romance, as containing in them almost unparallelled adventures and dangers, which he most valiantly and successfully passed through, in the midst of seas, slaughter, fire, and bullets, were not the originals yet extant, and to be seen.

Lastly, it appears from letters, and his Journal, which he kept daily for eighteen years' space, which he spent at sea in the public service of his country, that in the year 1667 he was by Charles the Second made Admiral of a squadron of ships of sixteen men-of-war, which were ordered to cruise between Harwich and Newcastle towards the coasts of Holland, to watch the motion of the enemy. Where he received many letters by King Charles's order from the Secretaries of State, War, and Admiralty, as also from the Dukes aforesaid (yet to be seen), containing thanks for his good service, and further desiring the continuance of his care, conduct, and watchfulness against the enemy, whensoever they should put out to sea again: in the mean time to observe such further orders as should be sent him.

In this kind of post he remained till his death, 1669, King Charles then owing him for his salary or pay above 1,500*l.* of which neither he nor his heir or executor ever received a farthing. His death was thought to be hastened through grief and vexation (being scarcely fifty-six years old when he died), and the occasion thus:—His ship, the Monk, being all manned with Cornish men in those three last engagements with the Dutch, who for the love and respect they bore him, their countryman, were all volunteers without being impressed for the public service; now it happened that, in the year 1668, peace being concluded betwixt King Charles and the States of Holland, the greatest part of our English fleet were hauled up, the officers, seamen, and soldiers disbanded, without satisfaction, wages, or pay for their service; and amongst them Captain Penrose's ship and squadron underwent the same fate. So that soon after, he happening to be at London upon some occasions, his disbanded company of Cornish men from the Monk, being far from home, were very troublesome and tumultuous with him about their pay, and so clamorous as to tell him that he, by his fair promises, had cajoled them into the public service, and that now they could get nothing for their labour and the hazard of their lives.

The Captain answered for himself, as well as he could, that it was his own case, as well as many other officers' and theirs, at this exigence to want his money, and therefore desired their patience till the King was better provided with cash for their satisfaction. But the Cornish men being more and more dissatisfied with him by those delays, and their wants and necessities pressing hard upon them, they formed a petition, setting forth the premises, to his Majesty, and with the same came to the Captain's chamber, and endeavoured (after words would not prevail) to constrain or compel him in person to present it to the King's Majesty, which he refusing to undertake, a scuffle happened at the top of the stairs between him and the petitioners; in which conflict one Lampeer, of Truro, by thrust of Penrose's hands, his feet and hands failing, was thrown over the stairs, and so much bruised with the fall that soon after he died.

Whereupon Penrose was apprehended, held upon bail, and afterwards indicted before the grand jury of Middlesex or Westminster, and found guilty of murder or manslaughter, and afterwards was tried for his life, and by the grand and petty jury found guilty of manslaughter: that is to say, the unlawful killing of a man without premeditated malice, (which is felony, because wilful — but admits of the benefit of clergy for the first crime,) whereupon Penrose was condemned to death, and put into Newgate, where forthwith he received a reprieve or pardon of this offence from Charles the Second, under the broad seal of England, yet to be seen. Nevertheless, for the drawing, sealing, or procuring this pardon, the clerks and officers through whose hands it passed extorted from the Captain 200*l.* before he could get out of their hands to show it to the Sheriff of Middlesex.

This unhappy accident so troubled Penrose, that, to put off the thoughts thereof, he kept company more than ordinary with gentlemen and officers of the fleet and others; so that at length, by excess of drinking healths, and otherwise, he fell into a malignant fever, whereof he died, leaving issue one only daughter, his heir, named Martha, married to James Hals, of Merther, Gent.

Tre-gew, alias Tregue, in this parish, synonymous words, signifying the spear or javelin town, is the dwelling of Henry Edmunds, Gent. originally descended from the Edmunds of Middlesex, whose ancestor, being a person well qualified for the purpose, temp. James I. was sent from London by the Company of Pewterers to inspect and try the Cornish tin, then corrupted by the blowers thereof, before it was coined, that so the bad metal might be examined and taxed before it was coined, proportionable to

ST. FEOCK.

the badness. In which assay-master's office he thrived so well, that at length he became a tin-factor himself, grew rich, and bought this place, and other lands near, as also the manor of Truro, of Sir Bevill Grenvill, Knt. But he and his security failing in paying the consideration money, he was cast into prison, where he died without further satisfation to his said creditor; notwithstanding which, those lands descended to his heir, now in possession thereof, except the manor of Truro, sold to Samuel Enys, Esq.

The Cornish tongue was retained in this parish by the old inhabitants thereof, till about the year 1640. Mr. William Jackman, then Vicar thereof, Chaplain of Pendennis Castle, at the siege thereof by the Parliament Army, was forced for divers years to administer the Sacrament to the communicants in the Cornish tongue, because the aged people did not well understand the English, as himself often told me. Now because it may not be unacceptable to the curious to know the Cornish words then used in administering the bread and wine to the communicants, I will here set them down, for their satisfaction:

The Body of our Lord Jesus Christ which was given
An Gorfe ay agan Arluth Jesus Chrest toan fe ry
for thee, preserve thy body and soul unto eternal life;
rag thy, gwetha tha gorfe hag eneff, warthe Ragnaveffera;
take and eat this in remembrance that Christ died
kemera hag dybbery henna en predery may Chrest marnans
for thee, and be thankful.
rag thy, hag be grassylen.

Again:

The blood of our Lord Jesus Christ, which was shed for
An goyse ay agan Arluth Jesus Chrest toan the fowle rag
thee, preserve thy body and soul unto eternal life, drink
thy, gwetha tha gorfe hag eneff warthe Ragnaveffera; evah
this in remembrance that Christ's blood was shed for
henna in predery may Chrest's goyse be towle rag

thee, and feed on him in thy heart by faith and *tha, hag dybbery wor ren en tha gollon ryb creignans hag* thanksgiving.
grassylen.

Mr. John Lanyon, of this parish, a sea sand-barge daily labourer, had a son named John Lanyon, who having had his education under Hugh Boscawen, Gent. Master of Arts, who kept a school at St. Michael Penkivell Church, became afterwards a steward to Trefusis, St. Aubyn, Coryton, and lastly came into the service of Brook Lord Chandos, and having by these services accumulated considerable riches, he gave lands, and built and endowed an almshouse for poor people.

TONKIN.

Mr. Tonkin does not make any addition to the history of this parish, except by stating that James Hals, who married Martha Penrose, the only child of Captain Thomas Penrose, was "an elder brother of the author; and that their eldest son, then about fourteen years of age, was engaged in the pursuit of his grandfather's profession, by serving as one of the King's scholars, or gentlemen volunteers, on board the Sunderland, Captain Tudor Trevor commander, receiving about 30*l.* per annum of his Majesty."

THE EDITOR.

Trehsick is now the most splendid feature of this parish. The situation, beautiful in all other respects, commands a view of the whole inland sea constituting Falmouth Harbour. The House was built about the middle of the last century, by Mr. John Laurence, a captain in the county militia, during the Seven Years' War, still remembered for his good-nature, convivial habits, and wild eccentricities. It is perhaps deserving of notice that the architect was Mr. Davy, grandfather of the celebrated chemist.

ST. FEOCK. 33

The property became divided on Mr. Laurence's decease; and it was purchased, about the year 1800, by the late Mr. Ralph Allen Daniell; other lands were added to the domain, and the whole became a handsome seat suited to the natural advantages of the place.

Still further additions and decorations have been made by his son, Mr. Thomas Daniell; but this gentleman choosing to quit Cornwall, has sold the whole to Lord Falmouth, the proprietor of Tregothnan, a still more magnificent seat, and removed from Trelisick only a few miles further up on the Truro river.

Mr. Thomas Daniell, the grandfather, was chief clerk to Mr. Lemon, and having married Miss Elliott, niece of Mr. Allen, of Bath, he found himself enabled to take the whole of Mr. Lemon's great concerns off the hands of his executors in 1760; and soon after to build the house in Truro, remarkable not only on account of its being the largest and most decorated mansion in that very splendid town, but as being constructed of Bath Oolite, the gift of Mr. Allen, from Prior Park.

Mr. Daniell continued throughout his whole life to conduct most extensive concerns as a general merchant, as a tin smelter, and, above all, as a spirited adventurer in mines on the largest scale. He left one son and one daughter.

The daughter married the Rev. John Napleton, a dignitary in the church of Hereford, and previously tutor at Brasenose college, Oxford; where he is well known as the author of a work ("Elementa Logicæ, subjicitur Appendix de Usu Logicæ et Conspectus Organi Aristotelis") which has been adopted into the lectures of every college throughout the University. The son, Mr. Ralph Allen Daniell, continued most of his father's concerns, adding to them a large smelting-work for copper in Glamorganshire; and so successful were his mining speculations, that he is said to have gained, in the course of a very few years, above a hundred and fifty thousand pounds from Wheal Tower alone.

thee, and feed on him in thy heart by faith and *tha, hag dybbery wor ren en tha gollon ryb creignans hag* thanksgiving.
grassylen.

Mr. John Lanyon, of this parish, a sea sand-barge daily labourer, had a son named John Lanyon, who having had his education under Hugh Boscawen, Gent. Master of Arts, who kept a school at St. Michael Penkivell Church, became afterwards a steward to Trefusis, St. Aubyn, Coryton, and lastly came into the service of Brook Lord Chandos, and having by these services accumulated considerable riches, he gave lands, and built and endowed an almshouse for poor people.

TONKIN.

Mr. Tonkin does not make any addition to the history of this parish, except by stating that James Hals, who married Martha Penrose, the only child of Captain Thomas Penrose, was "an elder brother of the author; and that their eldest son, then about fourteen years of age, was engaged in the pursuit of his grandfather's profession, by serving as one of the King's scholars, or gentlemen volunteers, on board the Sunderland, Captain Tudor Trevor commander, receiving about 30*l.* per annum of his Majesty."

THE EDITOR.

Trelisick is now the most splendid feature of this parish. The situation, beautiful in all other respects, commands a view of the whole inland sea constituting Falmouth Harbour. The House was built about the middle of the last century, by Mr. John Laurence, a captain in the county militia, during the Seven Years' War, still remembered for his good-nature, convivial habits, and wild eccentricities. It is perhaps deserving of notice that the architect was Mr. Davy, grandfather of the celebrated chemist.

ST. FEOCK.

The property became divided on Mr. Laurence's decease; and it was purchased, about the year 1800, by the late Mr. Ralph Allen Daniell; other lands were added to the domain, and the whole became a handsome seat suited to the natural advantages of the place.

Still further additions and decorations have been made by his son, Mr. Thomas Daniell; but this gentleman choosing to quit Cornwall, has sold the whole to Lord Falmouth, the proprietor of Tregothnan, a still more magnificent seat, and removed from Trelisick only a few miles further up on the Truro river.

Mr. Thomas Daniell, the grandfather, was chief clerk to Mr. Lemon, and having married Miss Elliott, niece of Mr. Allen, of Bath, he found himself enabled to take the whole of Mr. Lemon's great concerns off the hands of his executors in 1760; and soon after to build the house in Truro, remarkable not only on account of its being the largest and most decorated mansion in that very splendid town, but as being constructed of Bath Oolite, the gift of Mr. Allen, from Prior Park.

Mr. Daniell continued throughout his whole life to conduct most extensive concerns as a general merchant, as a tin smelter, and, above all, as a spirited adventurer in mines on the largest scale. He left one son and one daughter.

The daughter married the Rev. John Napleton, a dignitary in the church of Hereford, and previously tutor at Brasenose college, Oxford; where he is well known as the author of a work ("Elementa Logicæ, subjicitur Appendix de Usu Logicæ et Conspectus Organi Aristotelis") which has been adopted into the lectures of every college throughout the University. The son, Mr. Ralph Allen Daniell, continued most of his father's concerns, adding to them a large smelting-work for copper in Glamorganshire; and so successful were his mining speculations, that he is said to have gained, in the course of a very few years, above a hundred and fifty thousand pounds from Wheal Tower alone.

Mr. Daniell was twice Member for West Looe. He married the only daughter of the Rev. Mr. Pooley, Rector of Ladock, and has left a numerous family. His eldest son has married Miss Osbaldeston, and they have several children.

Killiganoon, probably the grove by the downs, is next to be noticed in Feock.

The place was entirely created by Mr. Richard Hussey. This gentleman was the son of an attorney at Truro, who died insolvent, leaving a widow with one son, and three or four daughters. The son is represented to have exerted himself with efforts proportional to the embarrassments in which he found the affairs of his family, and he became in consequence one of the most distinguished lawyers of the time. He had the honour of being appointed Attorney General to the Queen; and he was Counsel to the East India Company, and Member of Parliament, I believe, for Michael. Mr. Hussey died in the year 1770, under sixty, and divided his fortune among his sisters. One had married the Rev. Mr. Vivian, and her grandson is the distinguished officer, General Sir Hussey Vivian. Another sister married Mr. Walker, of Lanlivery, and left an only son, the Rev. Robert Walker, Vicar of St. Winnow. A third sister married Mr. Ustick, of Penzance.

Mrs. Mary Hussey, widow of Mr. Hussey of Truro, married, secondly, Mr. William Davies of St. Earth, a half-brother of the Editor's grandfather, where she continued to reside; and her funeral appears on the parish register September 18th, 1750.

Killiganeen was sold after Mr. Hussey's decease, and passed into the hands of Mr. Dagge. Two brothers of that name went to London from Bodmin to seek their fortunes. One became the manager of Covent Garden Theatre; the other pursued the law, to which both were probably educated, and ultimately retired to this place. It has since become the property of Admiral Spry, who improved and enlarged the house and the plantations; and it belongs at

ST. FEOCK.

this time to his son, Samuel Thomas Spry, Esq. M.P. for Bodmin.

A coarse part of this parish remained uninclosed till within a few years, and was known by the name of Feock Downs. The surface appeared to be more smooth and even than any other piece of open ground in the west of Cornwall; consequently, when local political dissensions were at a great height, about sixty years ago, this place was selected by one party for establishing races, in rivalship of others conducted by their opponents at Bodmin. These races fell, however, with the temporary feeling which gave them birth, and the ground is now inclosed.

A small village in this parish is distinguished by the name of "Come-to-Good;" a name probably given to it at first in ridicule, because there was established the earliest Quakers' meeting in that part of Cornwall. And, for some reason now quite forgotten, the first Sunday in August became designated all over that populous mining district as "Come-to-Good Sunday," when several thousand persons continued to assemble, till the very prudent Society to whom the house belongs, adopted the expedient of discontinuing their meeting on that particular day.

This parish measures 2,580 statute acres.

	£.	s.	d.
Annual value of the Real Property, as returned to Parliament in 1815	2871	0	0
Poor Rate in 1831	457	19	0

Population,— { in 1801, 696 | in 1811, 968 | in 1821, 1093 | in 1831, 1210

giving an increase of 74 per cent. in 30 years.

GEOLOGY.

Dr. Boase remarks on this parish, that the rocks are similar to those of Falmouth.

FOWEY, FOY, or FOYS.

HALS.

Is situate in the hundred of Powdre, and hath upon the north Glant, east the haven or harbour of Fowey, south the British Channel. For the name, it is taken from foys-fenton, i. e. the walled well or spring of water, rising about Alternun, St. Cleather, or Temple Moors.

In the Domesday Tax, 20th William I. (1087,) this place or parish was rated under the jurisdiction of Tywardreth. Neither was there any endowed church here extant at the time of the Inquisition of the Bishops of Lincoln and Winchester (1294), unless (what can hardly be supposed) Ecclesia *de Funum* appropriata domui de Tywardreth, in Decanatu de Powdre, be a corruption of Faoi, or Foy-town. In Wolsey's Inquisition, and Valor Beneficiorum, the Vicarage of Foye is rated 10*l*. The patronage formerly in the Prior of Tywardreth, who endowed it, now Treffry. The incumbent Trubody. The parish and town rated to the 4*s.* per pound Land Tax, 1696, 195*l*. 14*s*. The rectory, sheaf, or impropriation, in . . . .

In the ancient chapel at Foy, now the minister's chancel, was inscribed temp. Edward III. the name of Fisart Bagga, a famous sea commander in the then French wars, a native of this town of Foy. [Carew's Survey of Cornwall, p. 135.] This church and town I take to be under the tutelary guardianship of St. Catherine, whose history is misplaced under Lanteagles by Fowey.

[Mr. Hals's history of St. Catherine is lost. It may, therefore, be sufficient to give the following short statement of her legend.

In the Μηνολογιον, the *Menology*, (the Monthly Register, synonymous with Martyrology,) of the Emperor Basil, said to be composed by himself, but certainly written under his own inspection, St. Catherine is stated to have sprung from one of the families which in those times obtained a transient possession of the imperial throne.

She was probably born at Alexandria, and suffered martyrdom there under the reign of Maximus the Second, about the year 310.

Her learning, abilities, and zeal were so great, that, having been ordered to dispute with several of the most able philosophers, she confuted them all, and even converted some among them to the Christian faith. These new proselytes are said to have been instantly hurried to the flames, but that the Saint herself was reserved for a still more cruel fate, the persecutors of religion having contrived a wheel set round with hooks and spikes, for the purpose of tearing and lacerating its victim. The legends, however, go on to say that this horrible engine was dashed in pieces by angels, just as the tormentors were about to use it against the Saint, whom they nevertheless decapitated, unawed by the recent miracle, and no longer interrupted by any supernatural interference.

The body of St. Catherine was found five hundred years afterwards, when the Saracens had possession of Egypt, although it is not recorded by whom the discovery was made, nor how the identity was proved. A subsequent great event, however, placed that most important circumstance beyond all doubt; for it having been resolved to translate the body from the immediate power of the Mahometans to a monastery built on Mount Sinai by St. Helena, and augmented by Justinian, a company of angels, probably the very same who destroyed the wheel, conveyed the relics to Mount Sinai through the air.

Some recent martyrologists have endeavoured to explain away the latter miracle, by asserting that angels meant monks, who on account of the purity of their morals, the sanctity of their divine duties, and the eminent utility of their lives, are frequently confounded with the inhabitants of heaven.—It is almost needless to add that St. Catherine's Wheel has uniformly reference to the intended instrument of her martyrdom, and never to a spinning-wheel, of which the Saint is sometimes supposed in England to have been the inventor. EDITOR.]

But for the church and tower of Foy, as it now stands, it was built about the year 1466, towards which Richard Neville, Earl of Warwick, was a great benefactor; as appears from his badge, or cognizance, viz. ragged staves, yet to be seen cut in many parts of the stones of the said church and tower thereof.

The town of Foys is the voke lands of an ancient lordship by prescription, which the Prior of Tywardreth held of the ancient Earl of Cornwall's manor of Pow-valletcoyt, now Lostwithiel, or Restormel Castle, under the rent of . . . . ; from whom also they had their privilege of sending two members to sit in the Commons' House of Parliament. It was incorporated by Charles the Second, by the name of the Mayor, Recorder, Portreeve, eight Aldermen, and a Town Clerk. Notwithstanding which, by ancient custom, the members of Parliament were elected by the freemen, (viz. scot and lot men, that pay rates and taxes) and the precept from the Sheriff for the writ for election of them must be thus directed: Præposito et Senescallo Burgi de Foy, in Comitatu Cornubiæ, salutem, &c. As also the writ for removing any action at law depending in Foy court-leet to a superior court, must be directed to the Portreeve and Town Clerk or Steward.

The arms of this town are, a ship in full course, with sails expansed, on the waves of the ocean. It is further privileged with a weekly market on Saturdays, and fairs annually, on Shrove Tuesday, May 1st, and September 10th. This town hath also added to its privileges some of the liberties and freedoms of the Cinque Ports, which other towns or harbours have not: what they are, the inhabitants there best know. Those privileges were first granted only to the ports of Hastings, Hythe, Dover, Romney, and Sandwich, in Kent, by Edward the Confessor; afterwards much increased in the days of the three Edwards, the First, Second, and Third. which in this place are too long for me to recite. Mr. Carew tells us, that in Edward the Third's days sixty tall ships did belong to this harbour; and that the town of

Foys did assist that King with forty-seven sail of men-of-war and transport-ships, anno Dom. 1347, in order to the siege of Calais; whereupon that King granted commissions to the chief commanders of those Foy ships to take French prizes, during his wars with those people, or French nation; so that in few years those Foy men were grown so rich and formidable, by taking French prizes, that by force and arms they would enter many ports of that kingdom, and carry with them all ships they could conquer, and what they could not, would use means to set them on fire in the places where they lay. In fine, when French prizes grew scarce, (I speak upon the authority of Mr. Carew,) they scrupled not to turn sea-robbers, or pirates, taking, plundering, and destroying all ships they could master, of what country soever, not sparing the sailors' lives. By which means the townsmen grew unspeakably rich and proud and mischievous, which occasioned the Lord Ponmer, and other Normans, to petition John, King of France, to grant them a private commission of marque and arms, to be revenged on the pirates and thieves of Foy town, which accordingly they obtained, and carried their design so secretly that a small squadron of ships, and many bands of marine soldiers, were prepared and shipped without the Foymen's knowledge or notice, who accordingly put to sea out of the river Seine, in the month of July 1457, in 35th Henry VI. and with a fair wind sailed thence across the British Channel, and got sight of Foy harbour, where they lay off at sea till night, when they drew towards the shore and dropped anchor, and in the night landed their marine soldiers and seamen, and at midnight approached the south-west end of Foy-town, where they killed all persons they met with, set fire to the houses, and burned one half thereof to the ground, to the consumption of a great part of the inhabitants' riches and treasures, a vast deal of which was gotten by their piratical practices; in which massacre and conflagration, the women, children, and weakest sort of people, forsook the place, and fled for safety into the hill country.

But others of the stoutest men, under conduct of John Treffrye, Esq. fortified themselves as well as they could in his then new-built house of Plase, yet extant, where they stoutly opposed the assaults of their enemies: whilst the French soldiers plundered that part of the town which was unburned, without opposition, in the dark. The news of this French invasion in the morning flew far into the country, and the people of the contiguous parts as quickly put themselves in arms, and in great multitudes gathered together, in order to raise the siege of Foy; which the Frenchmen observing, and fearing the consequence of their longer stay, having got sufficient treasures to defray the charge of their expedition, as hastily ran to their ships as they had deliberately entered the town, and as privately returned into France as they had clandestinely come into England, with small profit and less honour.

The town of Foy being thus consumed by fire, and plundered by the French soldiers and seamen, the inhabitants' former wealth and glory reduced to poverty and contempt, they politically cast themselves at the feet of Richard Nevill, Earl of Warwick (aforesaid), who, pitying their distressed condition, and being Lord High Admiral of England, granted some of them new commissions for privateering and taking French ships, on promise of their just and righteous proceedings, and renouncing the trade of piracy (for which reason their former commissions were revoked); whereupon in few years they plied their sea-business so effectually, that they increased their riches to such degree that they began to repair and rebuild their damnified houses, and in the stones of many of them, in memory of the Earl of Warwick's favour and bounty towards them, there is cut his arms, badge, and cognizance, as aforesaid.

Nevertheless (so hard it is for those to do well who are accustomed to do evil, as for a blackmoor to wash himself white) those Foy men, not content with lawful privateering, fell again to their old trade of piracy, robbing and killing the seamen of all nations whose ships they could conquer; of which they were again detected 18th Edward IV. 1478, who thereupon sent a messenger or serjeant-at-arms to Foy, to apprehend some of those delinquents, and bring them up to London to be tried for those crimes, in order to receive condign punishment. But, instead of obeying the King's command and officer, in contempt of his authority they barbarously cut off his ears, and so dismembered sent him back to his master King Edward; at which affront the King was so distasted, that soon after he sent down Commissioners to Lostwithiel, under pretence of raising able seamen to go in war against the French, and that such amongst them as appeared most fit and able should have command of some of the King's best ships. At this news a great part of the freemen and seamen of Foy were drawn to Lostwithiel; where they no sooner came, but immediately they were apprehended and taken into custody for the crimes aforesaid, their ill-gotten goods and chattels seized by the Sheriff and King's officers, and one Harrington, a most notorious pirate, executed; and the chain of their harbour was removed to Dartmouth. (Carew's Survey of Cornwall, p. 135.)

The harbour of Foy aboundeth with deep and navigable waters for ships of the greatest burthen, overlooked with winding and lofty hills, and, though narrow, extends itself in several branches three or four miles up the country, and is navigable to Lanlivery and Lostwithiel, St. Wenow and Laranbridge, and abounds with all sorts of fish proper to that country, as salmon, peal, trout, plaice, soal, millet, bass, eels, congers, pullocks, &c. here daily sold at a cheap rate. At the mouth or entrance of this harbour, are two petty bulwarks, or blockhouses, the Polman, or Porth-Eran on the Lanteglos side, the other at St. Catherine's, under Foy town, most famous for a fight they had with a Dutch man-of-war of seventy guns, doubly manned, that was sent from their main fleet of ships of eighty sail, that lay at anchor and cruised before this haven, 16th July, 1666, then in pursuit of our Virginia fleet of eighty sail, which, escaping their cognizance, safely got some hours before them into this harbour, and, on notice given of the war, sailed up the branches thereof as far as they could, and grounded themselves on the mud lands thereof.

Notwithstanding which, this Dutch frigate resolved to force the two forts or fortresses aforesaid, and to take or burn our said Virginia fleet. Accordingly, it happened on that day, a pretty gale of wind blowing, this ship entered the haven, and as soon as she came within cannon-shot of those forts, fired her guns upon the two blockhouses with great rage and violence; and these made them a quick return of the like compliment or salutation. In fine, the fight continued for about two hours' time, in which were spent some thousands of cannon-shot on both sides, to the great hurt of the Dutch ship, in plank, rigging, sails, and men, chiefly because the wind slacked, or turned so adverse, that she could not pass quick enough between the two forts up the river, so as to escape their bullets, but lay a long time a mark for them to shoot at, till she had opportunity of wind to tack round, turn back, and bear off at sea to their fleet, to give them an account of her unsuccessful attempt and great damage as aforesaid, to the no small credit and reputation of Foy's little castles, manned out with gunners and seamen from the ships of the Virginia fleet for that purpose, who all, by reason of the walls and intrenchments thereof, were preserved from death, notwithstanding the continual firing of the cannons of the Dutch man-of-war upon them; whereby the contiguous lands by the bullets were ploughed up, to the terror and astonishment of all beholders.

After this engagement, the cargo of the whole Virginia fleet was landed at Foy, (its owners at London fearing the hazard of the sea in time of the Dutch war, to transport it there by water,) and gave opportunity to the townsmen to buy much tobacco at a very cheap rate, which instantly, upon the conclusion of the peace between England, France, and Holland, was sold in this kingdom, France, Spain, and Holland, at a dear rate, and much enriched the townsmen thereby, as Mr. Major, one of those merchants, informed me.

The chief place in this town is Plase, in British a palace, which is the dwelling of John Treffrye, Esq. so called from some of the many local places passing under that denomination in Cornwall, and compounded of treu or tref frye, synonymous words, signifying the free or manumitted town. He was the son of John Treffrye, of Rooke, Esq. that married Vivian of Truan; the which John Treffrye succeeded to the patrimony or lands of the Treffrys of this place, more for similitude of name than consanguinity or affinity of blood, by the will, devise, or entail of the last gentleman that died without issue in this house. The present possessor, as aforesaid, is John Treffrye, Esq. my very kind friend and kinsman, Member of Parliament for the town of Foy, whereof comparatively he is lord and high lord. He married Stephens. His predecessors in this place were gentlemen of great fame and estates, and have served their country in the several capacities of Parliament men for this town, justices of the peace, and sheriffs of Cornwall; particularly John Treffrye, Esq. was Sheriff of Cornwall 1st Richard III. 1482. He was a great benefactor towards building the present church of Foy, as appears from his arms being cut in divers places of the stones and tower thereof. Sir John Treffrye, Knt. (probably his son), was Sheriff of Cornwall 5th and 15th Henry VII.; William Treffrye, Esq. was Sheriff of Cornwall 16th Hen. VII. 1501, when Richard Whiteleigh, of Efford, was Sheriff of Devon. The arms of those gentlemen are, Sable, a chevron between three hawthorns Argent (i. e. summer thorn, hau, haw, in British is summer).

The chief inhabitants of this town, besides Mr. Treffrye, are Mr. Pomeroy, Mr. Goodall, Mr. Major, Mr. Toller, Mr. Tyncombe, and others.

In this town Philip Rashleigh, Esq, temp. Charles I. built and endowed a hospital with the garb or tithe sheaf of the parish of St. Wen for ever, towards the relief of six poor widow women, two of the said parish and four from from another parish, who receive weekly 15*d*. in money, and suits of apparel yearly, with other privileges, but are prohibited from begging the country, or any parish stipend. [See TYWARDRETH.]

This gentleman got great riches by trade and merchandize, and sea adventures; more particularly by a small ship or frigate, of about eighty tons, bearing about sixteen cannons or demi-culverins, besides small arms, and 60 men, for defence thereof; the commander of which ship had a commission from Queen Elizabeth as a privateer, in her wars with the Spaniards, to take all Spanish ships it should meet with at sea, and make them prizes for him, his adventurers, and the Queen's advantage, which said privateer, or man-of-war, was so successful and fortunate in its adventures at sea for some years, and in traffic, and merchandizes, and prizes, that those gentlemen accumulated and laid up great riches thereby; and in remembrance and memory of this ship, caused the figure in memory of it to be to be perpetuated in a small ship, about five feet long, made and formed by a ship carpenter, of timber, with masts, sails, ropes, guns, and anchors, and figures of men thereon; which is hanged up to the roof, or planking, with an iron chain, in their old house in this town, of which ship those gentlemen have often given me ocular observation, as well as told me the above history of the premises, in the time of Charles the Second.

TONKIN.

Mr. Tonkin has not any thing of the least importance but what is copied from Mr. Hals.

THE EDITOR.

I have retained the whole of what is stated by Mr. Hals respecting the proceedings at Fowey, in the periods of its greatest prosperity and of its subsequent fall, given partly on the authority of Mr. Carew, (p. 313, &c. of Lord Dunstanville's edition,) and in part from what he himself had heard. It must, however, be remembered that tradition always exaggerates facts, more especially such as bear unfavourably either on individuals or on communities, and that the times of Edward the Third were essentially different from those of order, protection, and impartial administration of justice, in which we have the happiness to live; nor can the license or excesses imputed to some adventurers at Fowey, be more abhorrent to our feelings than the mean artifice of a feeble government, practised to entice men from Fowey to Lostwithiel, under a pretence of enabling them to assist their country in the prosecution of a war, but really with the view of arresting them as criminals.

The fact of this port having sent forty-seven ships, with seven hundred and seventy mariners, to the siege of Calais in 1346-7, would exceed all belief, were it not established by national records; and Mr. Carew relates their vanquishing, in a private feud, the naval armaments of Winchelsea and Rye, two members of the Cinque Ports (p. 315). But these two ancient towns, and the Five Ports themselves, exhibit a contrast scarcely less remarkable than Fowey, between their actual appearances and the relative importance they must have once attained; except that Hastings is enlarged for the temporary residence of strangers, and Dover from the like cause, in addition to its being the well-known station for packets.

It is quite certain that the Priory of Tywardreth exercised considerable feudal authority over Fowey, which, however, not only fell into disuse after the general dissolution of monasteries, but, in all probability, was greatly diminished by the subsequent incorporation of the town.

The right of voting for Members of Parliament, up to the period when it discontinued to send any, in 1832, was vested jointly in resident payers of scot and lot, and in copyhold tenants of the manor taken from Tywardreth by Henry the Eighth, and annexed by him to the Duchy of Cornwall.

This manor was purchased by the late Mr. Philip Rashleigh, about the year 1800, under the powers created by the Land Tax Redemption Act. This gentlemen and his ancestors had long represented Fowey, and he was succeeded by his nephew, Mr. William Rashleigh, who subsequently sold the manor, and the whole borough property, to Mr. George Lucy, of Charlecot, near Stratford-upon-Avon. Mr. Lucy, in consequence, represented Fowey, and retained what he had purchased till in 1832 it became quite useless for all election purposes.

Mr. Joseph Thomas Austen is the present representative of the ancient and distinguished family of Treffry, one of the most spirited adventurers in mines, and of the most judicious and enlightened managers, that Cornwall has witnessed for many years. Mr. Austen has diverted a river for the use of machinery; and he has sat the first example of bringing a canal to mines, for the purpose of conveying coal and other heavy articles, from the sea-coast, and of taking down the ores, which are then exported from a harbour of his own construction.

Mr. Lysons gives an account somewhat different from that of Mr. Hals, respecting the final repulse of the French from Fowey. He attributes the achievement to one of Mr. Austen's female ancestors; and, quoting from Leland, adds that after this event "Thomas Treffry builded a right fair and strong embattled tower in his house, and embattling the walls of the house, in a manner made it a castle, and even to this day it is the glory of the town buildings in Fowey." The present possessor has, however, added considerably to the beauty of this "right fair" mansion, by completely restoring whatever might be defective in the existing parts, and by completing, or perhaps by improving, the original plan.

The late Mr. Philip Rashleigh, who represented Fowey

during the greater part of a long life, added to his character of a most respectable country gentleman, the well-deserved reputation of a skilful and zealous naturalist, more especially in the department of minerals, to which, as a Cornish man, his attention would be more particularly directed. Mr. Rashleigh led the way in Cornwall as a collector, on a large scale, of the interesting and curious products of the mines, and left at his decease perhaps the most valuable collection of minerals belonging to any individual throughout England. Geology had not acquired the semblance of a regular science when Mr. Rashleigh directed his attention to the metallic ores, and to the chrystallography, not of Cornwall alone, but of all parts of the known world. He has given to the public two volumes of coloured engravings from his choicest specimens.

Mr. Rashleigh attained a good old age, with the satisfaction of witnessing the progress through life, in various lines, of the younger branches of his family, with the highest credit to themselves, and of leaving his ample property to a nephew in all respects worthy of receiving it.

For various further details respecting Fowey, the Editor must refer to the recent Histories of Cornwall.

Mr. Lysons gives an ample account of the descents or alienations of manors; and a very curious letter from Lord Thomas Cromwell to the Prior of Trewardreth, dated on the 21st of May, but without the insertion of any year, probably, however, not long before the dissolution. See p. 109 of Lysons's Magna Britannia, vol. iii. Cornwall.

A considerable property was accumulated about the middle of the last century by two brothers, natives of this town, of the name of Lamb. One filled the office of Collector of the Customs at Fowey, the other practised medicine at St. Austell; both left their fortunes to an only sister, who after their deaths, and late in life, married Mr. Graham, a gentleman from London; through whom the property has passed to his nephew, Thomas Graham, Esq. Sheriff of Cornwall in 1806, a magistrate for the county, and resident within the limits of Fowey, where he has built a new and handsome house.

The parish of Fowey measures 1,726 statute acres.

	£.	s.	d.
Annual value of the Real Property, as returned to Parliament in 1815	4,856	0	0
Poor Rate in 1831	473	16	0

Population,— | in 1801, | in 1811, | in 1821, | in 1831, |
| 1155 | 1319 | 1453 | 1767 |

giving an increase of 53 per cent. in 30 years.

Present Vicar, the Rev. John Kempe, instituted 1818.

Latitude of the Windmill near Fowey 50° 20′ 7″. Longitude 18^m. 30^s. west. High water at the full and change of the moon 5^h 20^m.

THE GEOLOGY, BY DR. BOASE.

This parish appears to be situated entirely in the calcareous series, near its junction with the porphyritic; and thus its rocks are very similar to those at the entrance of Falmouth Harbour.

FARABURY.

HALS.

Is situate in the hundred of Lesnewith, and has upon the north St. George's Channel, or the Irish Sea, east Minster, west Trevalga, south Lantegles. For the name it is Saxon ꝼapa buꞃẏ, i. e. the far off hiding or burying-place, being a promontory of land shooting far out into the sea. Otherwise Fara-bury may be interpreted as a fair or beautiful burying-place. (See BURYAN.)

In the Domesday Roll it was taxed either under the jurisdiction of the Botterell, now Botreaux, or Tollcarne, now

FARABURY.

Minster. In the taxation of Benefices made by the Bishops of Lincoln and Winchester, 1294, Ecclesia de Farabury, in Decanatu de Trigminorshire, was valued xxs. In Wolsey's Inquisition, 1521, 4*l*. 12*s*. 8*d*. The patronage formerly in the Prior of Hartland, Lancells, or Minster, who endowed it, and passeth in presentation and consolidation with Minster. The patronage now in Amye; the incumbent Amye; and the parish rated, together with Minster, to the 4*s*. per pound Land Tax, 1696, 98*l*. 7*s*. 4*d*.; of which parish, in the first Inquisition (1294), I thus read: Abbas de Hartiland percepit de Eccles. Farabury p' an. viis. Prior de Morton (percepit) per annum in eadem vis.

TONKIN

thinks that this name means fare bury. The patronage in Edward Amy, Esq. as heir of Sir John Cotton. The incumbent James Amy, his brother.

THE EDITOR.

This is the least extensive parish in Cornwall. It probably owes its existence to the monastic establishment in the adjoining parish of Minster, with which, as a benefice, it has long been consolidated. The church is situated very near to the sea, and commands an extensive view of the romantic cliffs forming that iron-bound coast, with Lundy Island in the horizon. The name is sometimes written, and I believe always pronounced, Fotherbury.

This parish measures 432 statute acres.

	£.	s.	d.
Annual value of the Real Property, as returned to Parliament in 1815	859	0	0
Poor Rate in 1831	81	10	0

Population,	in 1801,	in 1811,	in 1821,	in 1831,
	140	212	223	358

giving an increase of 156 per cent. in 30 years.

GEOLOGY, BY DR. BOASE.

This little parish is formed by a belt of high and precipitous hills, and is principally composed of a very interesting rock. It is of a dark colour, does not alter in the streak, and abounds in iron pyrites; it is a kind of shale, and in the cliff, not far from the church, contains a layer of some carbonaceous mineral, to the intimate diffusion of which the colour of this rock appears to be owing. The section of the hill by the road side, from the church to Valancey Bridge, exhibits the layers of this rock convoluted and contorted in a most extraordinary manner; and the same appearance is beautifully illustrated in the cliffs at the entrance of Boscastle harbour.

GERANS, GERANCE, or GERRANS.

HALS.

Is situate in the hundred of Powdre, and hath upon the north St. Just in Rosland, east Verian, west St. Anthony, south the British Channel. For the modern name, Gerans, whether it be so called in memory of Geruncius, a king of the Britons, successor of King Rimo, that lived a hundred years before King Lud, according to Galfridus' Chronicle, or if from Ferint ab Erbyn, one of King Arthur's admirals at sea, I cannot determine; especially for that, in the Domesday Tax in Cornwall, 20th William I. 1087, this district, St. Just, and St. Anthony, all passed under the name of Ros-land, or Tre-gara-due, now the Bishop of Exeter's manor of Tregare (of which more under) and Elerchy.

In the Taxation of Benefices in Cornwall aforesaid, 1294, Ecclesia de Sancto Gerando, in Decanatu de Penryn, is rated x*l*. porcionis Rectoris in eadem xlvi*s*. viii*d*.; porcionis Prioris Sancti Antonii in eadem xlvi*s*. viii*d*. From whence it is evident that the Bishop of Exeter, lord of Penryn, and the Prior of St. Anthony endowed this church, the one half as a Rectory, the other as a Vicarage, viz. that of the Prior's part. For the name of this church in the Inquisition aforesaid, St. Gerandus, whether it may not possibly relate to one St. Gereon, a Roman whose feast is October 12. In Wolsey's Inquisition, 1521, it is valued 15*l*. 6*s*. 0½*d*. by the name of Gerens. The patronage in the Bishop of Exeter; the incumbent Fowler; and the parish rated to the 4*s*. per pound Land Tax, 1696, by the name of Gerance, 156*l*. 16*s*. 4*d*.

Tregeare, in this parish, was the voke lands of the Bishop of Bodmin, now the Bishop of Exeter's great lordship, so called. In the Domesday Book for Cornwall, 20th William I. 1087, it is named Tregara-an, id est, the town of the friend, or lover, of God. Concerning the possession of this manor, by virtue of the Bishop of Exeter's lease, there happened a costly and troublesome suit, both in law and equity, between Edward Nosworthy, Esq. then in possession thereof, and Hugh Trevanion, of Treligan, Esq. in the latter end of the reign of Charles the Second, James the Second, and part of the reign of William the Third (as I was informed). The case being thus:

The tenure of those lands being copy of Court Roll, or freehold for life, the Bishop of Exeter, the lessor, grants to the lessee a fee-farm lease of the said manor, for three lives absolute: and so, by custom and law, each of these lives named in the said lease are entitled to the land successively after each other's death, and have power successively in like manner to grant copies of court roll to the under-tenants of those lands absolute for three lives, to succeed each other. Now it happened that Trevanion bought the remainder of one of those lives, in reversion, of

Nosworthy or some other first life named in the Bishop's lease; after the death of whom, Trevanion's right by custom commenced; who accordingly delivered ejectments upon the lands and tenements of the said manor, by consent and approbation of the Bishop of Exeter for the time being, and brought down a trial at Launceston on the same, where the issue passed for Trevanion.

Thereupon Nosworthy filed his bill in chancery, prays a writ of injunction to stop further proceedings at common law, and to be relieved in the premises; where, after many commissions for examination of witnesses, and hearing of the merits of the cause in favour of Nosworthy's title, it passed for him. The plaintiff Trevanion thereon prays that another issue at law might be directed out of Chancery to try this matter; which accordingly being granted, upon the issue it again passed for the plaintiff, and afterwards, as before, upon all hearings in Chancery it passed against him, by the universal opinion and judgment of the Lord Chancellors and Lord Keepers for the time being: " That it was contrary to equity and good conscience that any person, who was only named a life on the bishop's lease, to the farmer of the manor, or the lives named on the farmer's lease, or copy of court roll, to under-tenants, without ever paying a farthing consideration of money, should sell or carry away the original lessee's estate, who pays a valuable consideration for it, or from his heirs or assigns after his death." So that, in fine, Nosworthy's title was confirmed by a decree in Chancery. But, as I said before, the cost of this controversy pro and con lasted so long, and proved so chargeable, as was very conducing to the ruin of both those gentlemen's estates, (vide Cargoll in Newland,) Nosworthy absconding into Holland, and Trevanion procuring himself to be made one of the Poor Knights of Windsor.

It was the happiness of Cornwall, in the latter end of the reign of Charles the Second, to behold Mr. Justice Dolben, appointed for two or three Assizes one of the Judges Itinerant for this county, who so discouraged the injustice, delay, and frivolousness of many Cornish law-suits, and so uprightly and succinctly, upon proof of matters of fact and law, directed the jury as to their verdict, that there was little or no occasion for the wrangling and jangling arguments of counsel at the bar. He further told the people in general, that he admired how they should be so weak in judgment, as to be persuaded into so many lawsuits in this province, wherein was nothing but pride, heat, mistakes, or malice, by the advice and direction of lawyers and attornies, whose trade and occupation was only to get money, without regard had to the merit or success of their causes longer than their client could dispense with cash. Upon those and the like arguments of this upright and conscientious judge, the number of our Cornish trials was much abated, and fell from a hundred and sixty *venire facias* brought to about seventy; so that it was generally hoped by this means we should have had as few lawsuits depending in this as in other countries, or that all controversies would be ended by references amongst ourselves, and that it would be said of the Court of Common Pleas by commission transmitted to Launceston, as was said of the Court of Chancery when Sir Thomas More was Lord Chancellor thereof, tempore Henry VIII., who by his upright judgment, and discouragement of trivial Chancery suits, had ended all causes depending therein, so that the clerks and counsel had no more business there to do; whereupon one made this rhyme:

> When More some time had Chancellor been,
> No more suits did remain:
> The like will never more be seen,
> Till More comes back again.

But, alas! this good Judge Dolben soon after, by the attornies and lawyers of the Western Circuit all in confederacy together, as the shrine-makers of Diana at Ephesus against St. Paul, prompted a petition to Charles the Second against him, suggesting that the overhasty proceedings of this judge, and his discouraging lawsuits, tended not only to the damage of his Majesty's revenues proceeding from lawsuits in those parts, but to their great prejudice, hurt, and damage, in point of their support and livelihood, as having little else besides their profession and practice of law to subsist by; which petition Charles the Second taking into further consideration, against the next assizes he ordered the clerk to leave Judge Dolben's name out of the commission of oyer and terminer, and then he was never more seen in those parts. Since which time the judges that come this circuit are content to hear with great patience the loud, reflective, perplexed arguments of counsel upon trials of small moment and concern, if not to suffer themselves to be at some times imposed upon in point of law and evidence therein, by the importunate arguments of topping serjeants-at-law, according to the magnitude of the fees they receive from their clients; so that it is become a proverb among those men in this province, it matters not what the case be so the client hath store of money.

Tre-ligan, or Tre-ligon, in this parish, (i. e. the legate, nuncio, or ambassador's town, perhaps the rector's,) is the dwelling of the said Hugh Trevanion, Gent. a branch of Caryhaye's family. He married Crossman, the relict of Courtney of Penkivell, and had issue by her . . . . . Trevanion, Gent. his son and heir, whose estate being greatly depressed by his father's debts and lawsuits aforesaid, hath sold his patrimony, and is by Hugh Boscawen, Esq. Privy Councillor to William the Third, promoted to be one of the Poor Knights of Windsor as aforesaid.

Ros-teage, in this parish, (i. e. the valley house, or fair valley,) is the dwelling of Nicholas Kempe, Gent. that married Sprye; his father Williams of Probus; his grandfather Budge. Ther arms, Gules, within a bordure engrailed three garbs Or.

At Tre-wince, i. e. the under town, or town exposed to the weather,) is the possession of Nicholas Hobbs, Gent. that married Kempe; his father Prouse; and giveth for his arms, three eagles displayed Purple.

TONKIN.

Most of the lands in this parish, if not the whole, are either part of the manor of Tregear, or are held from it. This hath been, ever since the first erection of the see, in the Bishop of Cornwall, and in the united bishopric seated at Exeter. It has for many ages been held by different gentlemen under the Bishops, on leases for lives.

The family of Nosworthy held it for some time; the last of which family, Edward Nosworthy, Esq. assigned it, a few years before his death, to Henry Vincent, of Trelevan, Esq. but Mr. Nosworthy, who was the last life, dying suddenly at Dunkirk in 1701, it fell into the Bishop's hands, then Sir Jonathan Trelawny, who granted a new lease of it in trust for his own family, with whom it now resteth. But the barton was separated from the manor and granted apart, as it was in the time when Nosworthy held the manor, to the Trevanions of Trelegar, between whom and the Nosworthys arose a great lawsuit, as is related by Mr. Hals.

Near to this barton is Trewithian, that is, the town of peace. In this village Mr. Edward Cregoe hath lately built a good house. He married Sarah, the daughter of John Foot, of Treleyassick, Gent. and is lately dead, leaving a young widow and three sons, of which the eldest is christened Friend.

To the south of this is Trelegar, the downy town. This is likewise a large village, at one end of which stood the seat of a younger branch of the Trevanions of Carhays. Hugh Trevanion, who was engaged in the expensive lawsuit with Mr. Nosworthy, had a son, Hugh Trevanion. This gentleman was so reduced as to become Governor of the Poor Knights of Windsor. The father sold Trelegar, in the latter end of Charles the Second's reign, to Stephen Johns, Esq.

Between Trelegar and Trewithian is a double round Danish intrenchment, which being very high, the middle serves for a beacon, by which name of Beacon it is called.

To the westward of Trewithian is Tregalravean, that is the small miry dwelling; and such it really is. This place has recently been leased by copy of court roll from the manor of Tregear, to Edward Hobbs, Gent.

Roseteage. This is rightly interpreted by Mr. Hals, the fair or beautiful valley; and its delightful situation doth fairly entitle it to this appellation.

This place, in the reign of Elizabeth, and of James the First, was the seat of Reginald Mohun, Esq. a younger brother to Sir William Mohun, of Hall, and a captain under Sir Walter Raleigh. This gentleman never marrying, sold the barton (which is held from the manor of East Greenwich, in Kent, by the payment of three peppercorns yearly when demanded,) with the royalty of wreek, and in November 1619, the 19th year of James the First, to Nicholas Kempe, Gent. who was the younger brother of Humphrey Kempe, of Lavethan, in Blisland, Esq. who is the chief of that name in Cornwall.

THE EDITOR.

Since the splendour of the Bishop's residence has disappeared, if it ever existed, Roseteague has been, without all comparison, the leading place in this parish, and indeed few more beautiful situations can any where be found. It continued in the family of Mr. Kempe from the year 1619 till about 1780, when Roseteague was purchased by Mr. Harris, of Rosewarne, in Camborne, and given by him to Mr. Richard Harris, one of his younger sons; but this gentleman having remained single, the estate has reverted to the only daughter and heiress of the eldest son, William Harris, Esq. Sheriff of Cornwall in 1773, married to Henry Winchcombe Hartley, Esq. of Berkshire.

Trewince, situated on a hill northward of Roseteague, and separated from it by a deep valley, is also a place well deserving of notice. An extremely good house was built here about the year 1750, by the grandson or great-grandson of the gentleman who made the purchase of Trelegar from Mr. Trevanion, and it is now inhabited by his grandson.

The church commands an extensive prospect from an elevated piece of ground, and contains a splendid monument to the family of Hobbs; and near the church still exists a public bowling-green. Bowling appears to have been the favourite amusement of gentlemen residing in the county up to a later period than the middle of the last century. A weekly meeting used to be here numerously attended during the summer, but as most landed proprietors then occupied a portion of their own estates, it was an invariable rule to discontinue their pastime when the appearance of a single Arrish Mow, indicated the more important avocations connected with harvest.

Mr. Hals has noticed that a Bishop of Exeter endowed this church, the one half as a rectory, the other as a vicarage. This division was effected in a very unusual manner, although in one not quite without example. Instead of apportioning the tithe of corn to the rector, and all other portions, as small tithes, to the vicar, the whole has here been divided into equal shares; so that Mr. Johns, of Trewince, the lay impropriator, is entitled to one-twentieth of every thing titheable, and the incumbent to another twentieth.

On the coast eastward of the church town is a village called Polskatho, or Porthskatho, the boat-harbour; and here an extensive fishery is carried on, more especially for mackarel. This place, with the manors of Pettigrew and Nanquitty, belongs to J. S. Enys, of Enys, Esq. and they have been long possessed by this very ancient and respectable family.

The barton of Tregeare was purchased in 1712 of the Hoblyns of Bradridge, by Samuel Kempe, Esq. of Carclew. In 1765 it was leased by Frederick Bishop of Exeter, on lives, to Nicholas Kempe, Esq. of Rosteague, of whom it was purchased in 1767 by his cousin Nicholas Kempe, Esq. of Chelsea, and it remained in 1823 in the possession of John Kempe, Esq. of Newington, Surrey. The Kempes sold Rosteague to John Harris, Esq. in 1780.

Trewithian is now vested in Matthew Garland Cregoe, Esq. who married Anna Coryton Kempe, eldest daughter of the late Arthur Kempe, Esq. Admiral of the White.

The Kempes of Cornwall were derived from the knightly family of Kempe, of Olantigh, in Wye, in Kent; Richard Kempe, Esq. grandson of Sir William Kempe, Sheriff of Kent 20 Henry VIII. is the first of the family recorded to have settled at Lavethan, in Blisland.

Gerans measures 2,460 statute acres.

	£.	s.	d.
Annual value of the Real Property, as returned to Parliament in 1815 .	3487	0	0
Poor Rate in 1831	387	9	0

Population,—	in 1801,	in 1811,	in 1821,	in 1831,
	771	698	732	766

giving the unusual result of a diminution, although extremely small, on the population, 5 on 771, or about ¾ per cent. in 30 years.

GEOLOGY, BY DR. BOASE.

The rocks of this parish belong to the same series as those of St. Anthony in Powder. On the eastern side of Porthskatho Cove the blue slate is very much curved and contorted; and is intersected by innumerable quartz veins, which are exceedingly irregular, and partake much of the same arrangement as the laminæ of the slate. Here also occur, interstratified with the slate, beds of a compact blue rock, which is very hard, and effervesces with acids, occasioned by particles, and minute veins or strings, of calcareous spar. In the cliff also may be seen a small patch of conglomerates, and red sandstone of the most recent formation, such as is common on these shores.

ST. GERMAN'S.

HALS.

Is situate in the hundred of Eastwellshire, and hath upon the east Landrak and Saltash, north Menhynet, west Morvall, south Shevyock, and the British Channel; as for the name of this parish it is derived from the tutelar guardian of the church, St. German, Bishop of Anticiodorum in Gallia, now France, anno Dom. 425. Whether this name be derived from the Latin Germanus, i. e. come of the same stock, very like or natural; or the adverb Germaine, brother or a very brother; or from ʒapnan or ʒepnan, Saxon German, signifying altogether a man, or a complete and entire man; I must leave to others to resolve.

At the time of the Domesday Tax 20 William I. 1087, this district was taxed either under the jurisdiction of Abbe Tone, i. e. Abbey Town, or Cudan-woord, of which more under. In Liber taxationum omnium beneficiorum in Cornubia, folio 148, Ecclesia Sancti Germani, in Decanatu Sancti Germani, by the Bishops of Lincoln and Winchester 1294, was valued towards the Pope's Annates 10*l.*; Vicar ejusdem xl*s*. But before the statute 15th of Richard the Second, against wholly impropriating vicarages, the revenues of this church were wholly impropriated by the convent, and only 14*l. per annum* deducted towards maintenance of two vicars to serve the cure, for which reason it is not named in Wolsey's Inquisition 1521. The patronage formerly in the King of England, afterwards in the Abbat and Prior of St. German's. The incumbent Kendall, the rectory or sheaf in possession of Glanvill, and the parish rated to the 4*s*. in the pound land tax 1696, 649*l.* 6*s.* 8*d.* The now minister's chancel of this church was a chapel, founded and endowed by King Athelstan, at such time as he was in Cornwall, anno Dom. 930 (see Burian and Bodman) and dedicated to St. German, of which fact thus speaks Roger Hoveden, a priest of Oxford, in his Annals of the Kings of England, anno Dom. 1200, p. 160.

"Rex Athelstanus in potestatem Anglorum dedit unum mansionem Deo, ad fundandum monasterium pro monachis, et Sancti Germani fratribus canonicis ibi famulantibus in Cornubia, anno Dom. 930," i. e. King Athelstan, being in full possession of all England, gaue to God one mansion, tarrying, or abiding place, for laying the foundation of a monastery of monks, and for St. German's canonical brothers and servants in Cornwall. He also enriched with jewels, money, or lands, every considerable abbey in this land. Baker's Chron. p. 10.

This Abbey of St. German's was afterwards endowed with larger revenues by King Canute, anno Dom. 1020, who turned it, after ninety years continuance in monkery, to a collegiate church of secular canons, which might marry wives, converse in the world, as not tied to a monastic life, first introduced by St. Berinus, Bishop of Dorchester, anno Dom. 635: that is to say, a society or corporation of religious men, under the government of a dean, warden, provost, and master, to whom belonged clerks, chaplains, singing men, or choristers. Of those men, the gloss upon the Canons Clementine tells us, that secular priests have no certain order or fashion of apparel appointed them, forasmuch as there is no express mention made in any canon, neither of the colour or form thereof, by which two differences the other several orders of religious men and women are distinguished or discerned.

In this Abbey of St. German's, anno Dom. 986, Bishop Stidio placed the see or seat of his Cathedral Church, (for Bodman was before burnt by the Danes,) which he and his successors enjoyed till the year 1032, at which time Livignus, first a monk of Winchester, afterwards Abbat of Tavistock, then made Bishop of Kirton, by King Canutus, who after the death of Berwoldus, the thirteenth Bishop of Cornwall, prevailed with that King to annex the bishopric

ST. GERMAN'S.

of St. German's, thus translated there, to his bishopric of Kirton, and turned this college of secular priests into a priory of Black Canons Augustine, from whence afterwards Leofrick, chaplain to King Edward the Confessor, 1049, by licence, consent, and approbation of that King, removed both those bishoprics to Exeter. And this fact of Kirton is more manifest from the missal or mass book of the said Leofrick, given to the church of Exeter.

This Monastery or Abbey of St. German's, founded by King Athelstan, was as aforesaid by King Canute turned into a collegiate church of secular canons, over which a prior was governor or ruler, who, after he had endowed the same with lands and revenues, King Ethelred the Second having before given Bishop Sidio, to recompense his loss by the Danes, the great lordship of Cunan Boake, still pertaining to the Bishop of Exeter (see Prince's Worthies of Devon, p. 9) he ordained many good laws which sound thus in English:

" We will and command that God's Ministers, the Bishops, Abbats, Priors, &c. do in especial manner take a right course and live according to rule, that they call to Christ night and day much and oft, and that they do it earnestly; and we further command that they hearken to God, and love chastity; full truly they wit that it is against the right to meddle with women." Canute's Laws, No. 6.

The word abbat is derived from the Hebrew abba, pater, for that he is the father or governor of his monks, who together make up a spiritual society or corporation. Some abbats were elective by the convent, others presentative, and under this title also was comprehended other corporations spiritual, as a prior and his convent, friars, canons, and such like; and as there were lord abbats so there were lord priors, who had exempt jurisdiction, and were lords of parliament, and what consecration is to a bishop, the same is benediction to an abbot or prior, but in different respects, for a bishop is not such before consecrated, but an abbat or prior, being elected or confirmed, is properly such before benediction.

Some abbats were mitred from the pope, and so exempt from the bishop's jurisdiction, as having granted them from him episcopal authority; and if either abbats or priors were called by the King's writ as barons to parliament, they were called abbats and priors sovereign; see statute 9th Richard II. chap. 4. But, alas! neither this Abbat of St. German's, nor the Prior of Bodmin, nor any other in this province, was either a baron of Parliament or a mitred man, but were all subject to the visitation and spiritual government of the Bishop of Exeter, till 23d Henry VIII. when all those orders of religious men were dissolved.

In this abbey of St. German's, anno Dom. 1040, in the time of Lurginus Bishop of Kirton, lived Hucarius, commonly called the Levite, as Bale and Pits, in their writings of Britain, tell us; either for that he assisted the priest at the altar as the Levites of old did, and was more excellent, or did excel all others in that particular; otherwise, by the appellation Levite we must understand him a priest, and that he was universally famous in performing his function of preaching and divine service. Certain it is, he was a holy and learned man, (according to the laws of King Canutus aforesaid,) as the 110 homilies or sermons, and many other books which he wrote, declare; but whether he was a native of this province or not, I know not.

This Priory of Canons Augustine was dissolved 26th Henry VIII. and its revenues valued per annum 243*l*. 8*s*. according to Speed and Dugdale's Monasticon Anglicanum.

This borough town of St. German's, as Mr. Carew saith, mustereth many inhabitants, and sundry ruins, but little wealth; occasioned either by abandoning their fishing-trade, as some conceive, or their being abandoned of their religious people, as others imagine. It appears to have been the yoke lands of a manor before the Norman Conquest; since it is rated in Domesday Roll, 20th William I. 1087, by the name of Abbytone, i. e. abbey-town, (for that before that time it was a monastery or abbey of monks,) and consists of a Portreeve and forty Censors; and the Portreeve yearly chosen, in the manor court, by the major part of the Censors. And the Members of Parliament are in like manner elected by the major part of them, and the precept from the Sheriff for their election, (as also to remove any action at law depending in this to a superior court,) must be thus directed: " Præposito et Seneschallo Burgi nostri de St. Germano, in Comitatu Cornub. salutem," &c. Note, that in old British, reve, reeve, is rent, tithes, or revenues. Port-reeve is the bearer or gatherer of the gate or borough rent.

The arms of this priory are only the letters G. P.

It is further privileged with a weekly market on Friday, and a fair yearly, August 1.

The history of St. German. He was a native of Gaul, about the year of our Lord 380, born of wealthy, rich, and Christian parents, by whom he was bred up and baptized into the Christian religion After which he followed the study of the liberal arts and sciences, and so profited therein that he was generally noted for a very learned man. But that which made him most famous was his piety and virtue; wherein he so far excelled most other men of his time, that he could not be at rest, or have peace in himself, till he made known his propensions to a religious course of life. Whereupon he was admitted into deacon's orders, then into priest's, and lastly advanced to the dignity of Bishop of Antiscidorum, or Auxerre, in France, anno Dom. 425.

After he took upon him the office of a bishop, he discharged the same with great justice and piety, admitting none into orders within his jurisdiction, but such as were men of great learning and sound faith, but especially such as were neither Arians nor Pelagians. For about that time the Christian church was grievously pestered with two heretics; the one Arius, born and bred at Constantinople; the other an inhabitant of Britain, viz. Pelagius.

But the doctrines of Pelagius manifesting themselves throughout this land, to the great disturbance of the orthodox faith and churches thereof, after great heats and animosities between Catholics and heretics about those doctrines, it was at last agreed upon between those parties that a General Council of the Clergy in Britain should be convened at St. Alban's, in Hertfordshire, and those tenets further examined and discussed. But the British Catholics, knowing the interest, skill, and subtlety of the heretics to be great, thought it not safe for religion, and the orthodox faith, in this convention to trust alone to their own skill and learning, therefore concluded on this expedient, viz. against the day of meeting to send for some foreign divines for their coadjutors or helpers in this controversy; and accordingly applied to St. German, Bishop of Antiscidorum aforesaid, or Auxerre, in Gallia, now France, a city situate upon the river Auxona, now called Le Disne, and Lupus, Bishop of Troyes, in that country, for their counsel and assistance, who gladly granted their request: and accordingly against the day, and at the place appointed, met the British Clergy on both sides; where the tenets and doctrines being heard, and particularly examined, chiefly by the skill and learning of St. German, were all refuted and condemned, according to the sense of the General Councils, as impious and heretical, to the great satisfaction of the orthodox clergy.

After this dispute and council ended, St. German, as a good bishop, resolved, though out of his country and diocese, whilst he stayed here, to preach the Gospel publicly, and to that end caused a pulpit to be set up in an open place at St. Alban's, (so called from St. Alban, the Briton, martyred there under Dioclesian, anno Dom. 303,) anciently Verulam; where on set days he preached to the multitude there assembled, and first began to handle the doctrine of Pelagius against original sin, taking for his text the words of St. John the Evangelist. " If we say that we have no sin we deceive ourselves, and the truth is not in us." Upon which subject he shewed that the doctrine of Pelagius was contrary to the writings and doctrines of Moses and the Prophets.

These and the like words and preachings of St. German seemed so angelical and full of power to the Britons, that generally they were convinced of Pelagius's errors, and abandoned their former opinions; and in testimony of their unfeigned respect and remembrance of him, in the very place where he preached at St. Alban's, they erected a chapel, and dedicated it to the honour of God, in the name of St. German; which chapel was extant (and still bears his name) tempore James I. though misapplied to profane uses. (See Camden, in Hertfordshire.) After St. German had thus preached down Pelagianism at St. Alban's, he travelled through Britain, Wales, and Scotland, on the same account, as our chronologers tell us; and that, in the place where Oxford stands, he preached six months against the heresies aforesaid. That he was in Cornwall upon the same account I doubt not, since there is still extant in this parish whereof I treat, a large church bearing his name. He was in Wales, for Camden, in Flintshire, informs us a field bearing his name, called Mars Garman, i. e. German's field, in memory of a battle there obtained by the Welch over the Picts, on the prayers of St. German, and by crying Hallelujah! To him also is ascribed the building or augmenting Landaff cathedral there, and dedicating it to St. Delyan, if there be not a mistake in the chronology thereof, St. German, as appears to me, being dead before Delyan.

That he preached in Scotland, is evident from his meeting and converse with Patrick, born at Bluisdale, in that country, who became his disciple, and afterwards the apostle of Ireland.

This priory-house, before its dissolution, was called Porth-Prior, or Port-Prior, synonymous words, signifying either the prior's creek, cove, or haven. It is now, after the name of its owner, transnominated to Port or Porth-

Eliot, who derives his title thereto from Champernowne, as he did by a boon from King Henry the Eighth.

These gentlemen I take to be of Scots original, and so denominated from the local place of Eliot, near Dundee, in Scotland, and their descent of later time from the Eliots of Devonshire, Berkshire, or Cambridgeshire, of which last county one Sir Thomas Eliot, Knt. was Sheriff 24th Henry VIII. also in 36th. This gentleman wrote a book called Defensorium bonarum Mulierum, The Defence of good or virtuous Women. But that which made him most famous was, (to the disgrace of the critics and clergy that get their livings by the liberal arts and sciences, he being only a layman,) he wrote and composed the first Latin and English Dictionary that ever was seen in England, about the year 1540. Upon whose stock and foundation Bishop Cooper and others built and grafted all the Latin and English dictionaries now extant in Britain. He died in Suffolk, 1546; and upon the foundation, rules, and observation of this my Parochial History of Cornwall, it will be very easy for any other person to make a better and more perfect History thereof.

Those gentlemen settled here about the middle of Queen Elizabeth's reign, and there ever since flourished in this place in genteel and worshipful degree, serving their king and country in the several capacities of Justices of the Peace and Members of Parliament for their Borough of St. German's; and amongst them, in particular, it were great injustice to forget the memory of that worthy patriot Sir John Eliot, Knt. for his bold asserting the prerogative and privilege of Parliament, the freedom and liberty of the subject, in the House of Commons, against the arbitrary and despotic power of the British Monarch, then exerted and setting up by the Attorney-general Noye and others, temp. Charles I. as before it had been done by Cecil Earl of Salisbury temp. James I.: for which reasons and arguments of law he was committed prisoner to the Tower of London by order of that King, where he died, without payment of the 2,000*l.*

fine laid upon him, but not without suspicion of poison, about the year 1638.

Edward Eliot, Esq. is now in possession of this estate. He married the daughter of Craggs.

Bake, in this parish, is the dwelling of the ancient and gentle family of the Moyles; so called, I presume, from the local place of Moyle, in or about St. Minvor, who have flourished here for several generations in worshipful degree, ever since they married with the sole inheretrix of this name and place; originally descended, as I am informed, from the Moyles of Tresurans, in St. Colomb, or the Moyles of Bodmin. The present possessor, Sir Walter Moyle, Knt. son of John Moyle, Esq. Sheriff of Cornwall 22 James I. that married Morrice, giveth for his arms, in allusion to their name, Gules, a moyle (or mule) passant Argent.

I take Thomas Moile, Esq. Speaker of Parliament 34th Henry VIII. 1543, ancestor of the Moyles of Oxford and Kent, whose name, blood, and estate is terminated in the Finches, to be a younger brother of this family, or those of his.

Colt-dryn-ike, in this parish, i. e. dry neck lake, leate, or riveret of waters, (perhaps so called from some lake or leate that intermits its current in summer season,) is the dwelling of Jonathan Trelawney, Esq. one of his Majesty's Commissioners of the Peace, a younger branch of the Trelawneys of Poole and Trelawne houses, and therefore giveth the same arms which they do. Since the writing hereof this gentleman is dead without issue; and his second brother, my very kind friend, Major John Trelawney, Fort Major of the royal citadel of Plymouth, succeeded to his estate.

Millin-ike, alias Melin-ike, i. e. the mill lake, leate, or bosom of waters, (so called from some river and a mill heretofore thereon,) was the dwelling of William Scawen, Esq. that died without issue.

The name Scawen is local, and signifies a place where

skawan or elder trees grow, (as I have said before,) and is derived from the Japhetical Greek, σκοβιεμ, sambachus, ebulus, the elder-tree, who, suitable to his name, gives for his arms, Argent, a scawen or elder-tree Vert. This is an ancient and mere British family of gentlemen, as their name implies.

Hendre, in this parish, (i. e. the old or ancient town,) is the dwelling of the gentle family of the Hancocks; particularly William Hancock, Esq.

Catch-French, in this parish, was the seat of the Keckwitches, originally descended from the Keckwitches of Essex, gentlemen heretofore also of considerable estates in those parts, now by ill conduct wasted, so that this barton was sold by John Keckwitch, Esq. temp. Charles II. to Hugh Boscawen, Esq. who settled it upon his daughter Bridget, married to Hugh Fortescue, of Filley, Esq. now in possession thereof. George Keckwitch, Esq. of this house, was Sheriff of Cornwall 17th of Elizabeth, as was also his son George Keckwitch, Esq. 33d of Elizabeth. He was also a Commissioner of the Peace temp. James I. who gave for his arms, Argent, two lions on a bend Sable, coticed Or.

TONKIN.

The town of St. German's lieth to the southward of Port Eliot, but adjoining with it, and between that and Cuddenbeck: but as Browne Willis, in his Notitia Parliamentaria, has given a particular description of this town and parish, of which he was the most capable, having married his lady out of it, I shall here insert what he has said thereof:

"Its first return of Members to serve in Parliament, was in the session held by proclamation in the 5th year of Queen Elizabeth, A. D. 1562, at which time their having Representatives was questioned; however, Mr. Speaker declared in the House that the Lord Steward agreed that they (i. e. the two Members) should resort there with all convenient speed to show their letters patent, whereby they be returned. In this indenture the returning officer is called the Mayor, but in the next, and in all other records, the Portreeve; which magistrate is yearly nominated and chosen at the lord's court-leet, held about Michaelmas by his steward, who impannels a jury for that purpose. As to the choice of Members of Parliament, all the inhabitant householders have votes, that have lived a year within the borough, the bounds of which do not extend very far, and only comprehend about fifty or sixty houses lying near the church, and not the whole vill of St. German's, great part of which is without the borough, as is the rest of the parish. It is styled in some writings Cuddenbeck Borough; a privilege which it might perhaps have obtained from Walter Bishop of Exeter, temp. Henry III. when Penryn seems to have been made a borough; and from this example the Prior, with the assistance of the Bishop, might also have dignified in like manner the vill of St. German's, though neither of them, anno 30th Eliz. when they certified respecting their liberties, and claims of privilege, as of markets, fairs, &c. styled this place otherwise than the manor of St. German's; nor have I met with it under any other denomination than till Queen Elizabeth's time, or seen any record mentioning its incorporation, nor any other charter of privileges granted thereunto; though the inhabitants have a tradition that they had an ancient charter, which was unfortunately stolen from them by a person imprisoned by the Portreeve, who is by prescription bailiff of the town, and may make what house he pleases within the borough, his prison. As to a description of this borough, called by Carew 'a church town,' it mustereth, as that author tells us, sundry ruins, but little wealth."

Browne Willis gives the following account of the Priory:

"After the removal of the bishoprics from Crediton and from this place to Exeter, A. D. 1050, Leofric, the first Bishop of Exeter, changed the seculars of this collegiate church, founded by King Athelstan, and endowed by

King Canute, into Black Canons, between whom, and his new-erected episcopal see, the manor of this town was divided; and it stood upon that establishment at the time of the Norman invasion, as appears from Domesday Book, which informs us, that the manor or parish of St. German's consisted of twenty-four hides, whereof the Bishop of Exeter had twelve, and the Canons of that place twelve also. What belonged to the Bishop was valued at 81s. per annum, and what belonged to the Canons at 100s. Domesday also shews us, that in this manor there was then a market on the Lord's Day; but it became reduced to nothing, by reason of that of the Earl of Morton's being very near, which I conceive might have been kept at Trematon, that Earl having privilege of a market at his castle there. That such was the state of this town and parish at the time of the Conquest, is plain from the above-stated record; and the division into two manors continues to the present day, the Bishop's moiety being held by lease for three lives by Edward Eliot, Esq. proprietor of the other manor; whose predecessors have probably ever since the dissolution of the monasteries been farmers, or lessee tenants, to the See of Exeter, by virtue of which lease, as this manor is vested in them, so the other, belonging to the Priory, has thus descended since the surrender thereof, dated March the 2d, anno 30th Henry VIII. when Robert Swimmer, the last Prior, with seven Monks, yielded up the same into the King's hands, who not long after, by letters patent dated March the 10th, anno regni 33, A. D. 1542, granted to John Champernoun, John Ridgeway, and Walter Smith. Among other lands, the site, &c. of this priory, upon partition, came to John Champernoun's share, whose heir sold it, about thirty or forty years afterwards, to Richard Eliot, Esq. my wife's ancestor, in which family both those manors yet continue: which place, soon after Mr. Eliot had made the purchase, was named Port Eliot, since when this appellation has so far prevailed that Port Eliot has been inserted in maps, as if it was a particular vill. This family flourished for eight or ten generations in Devonshire, before their transplanting themselves hither, and had matched into several considerable families in that county, as the Sigdons, Cotlands, Bonvilles, Sumasters, Fitzes, Careswells, &c. Walter Eliot was returned among the gentlemen of Devonshire anno 1433, temp. Henry VI. And to this family, as it should seem by the arms, was allied Sir Richard Eliot, made by King Henry the Eighth one of the Justices of the King's Bench, who was, as I take it, father to the famous Sir Thomas Eliot. Richard Eliot seated himself here, where he lived (as Carew tells us) in great hospitality. He left issue John Eliot, born and baptized here April 20, 1592. This John, A. D. 1607, became a gentleman commoner of Exeter College, Oxford, which place leaving about two or three years after, he went to the Inns of Court, and May the 10th, 1618, received the honour of knighthood, and was all his lifetime after a member of the succeeding Parliaments, in one of which, 3d Charles I. he was chosen knight of the shire for Cornwall. He was a very plausible speaker in the House of Commons, as his speeches published testify, but, being a virulent enemy to the Court, often suffered confinement, and died in custody in the Tower of London; and, as appears by the inquisition on the 27th of November, 8th Charles I. A. D. 1632, leaving issue John, his son and heir, then twenty years old. This John was born at Port Eliot, and baptized October 18th, 1612, where he died and was buried March the 25th, 1685, leaving an only son, Daniel Eliot, my father-in-law, who departed this life about the sixtieth year of his age, and was buried among his ancestors October 28th, 1702. This gentleman, in regard that he had only one daughter, named Katherine, bequeathed his estate, in order to keep up the name of his family, to Edward Eliot, grandson to Nicholas Eliot, fourth son to Sir John Eliot, Knight, aforesaid."

Mr. Browne Willis then goes on to state respecting the remains of the monastery.

"The Priory fronts the river, now called, as above

noted, Port Eliot. It is a handsome large building, containing several spacious rooms, and has a court before it, adorned with a strong pier by the present proprietor, Edward Eliot, Esq. who has much beautified the whole building." Since Mr. Willis wrote the above, almost the whole of the ancient building has been taken down, so that except the refectory, now called the gallery, very little remains.

In the 26th year of the reign of King Henry the Eighth, this place had an honour bestowed on it (little taken notice of, if not altogether forgotten), by being established by Act of Parliament the see of a suffragan bishop for the county of Cornwall, in the diocese of Exeter.

The advowson of this church, together with the impropriate rectory, late the possessions of the priory, valued at 61*l*. 13*s*. 4*d*. per annum, were granted by King Edward the Sixth to the Dean and Chapter of Windsor, in whose hands they now continue.

THE EDITOR.

St. Germanus is among the most celebrated saints of the fourth and fifth centuries, having gained his reputation by furiously opposing the unpopular doctrines of Pelagius; at the same time that he adopted all the brutalizing austerities, which in those days conveyed power, influence, and reputation to all who practised them.

Pelagius maintained that Almighty God has been pleased to bestow on mankind, from their births, power and inclination to execute his will, and to render themselves acceptable in his sight; while the orthodox supported, on the contrary, a doctrine more analogous to the practices of earthly despots and tyrants, by declaring that such powers were capriciously given, by little and little and from time to time, branding their opponents with an accusation, well suited to the understanding of those from whom distinction could then be obtained, namely, that Pelagius set up man as independent and in opposition to God; forgetting or concealing that the free gift was and must have been the same in both cases, differing only in the manner after which it is bestowed. Perhaps the arbitrary disposition of fiefs, commencing about that period, afforded an additional analogy for assimilating the practices in heaven to those on earth, while appeals to the capricious exercise of arbitrary power afforded evidently the most ample field for vehement declamation. The saint is stated in his legend to have sprung from an illustrious family, and, while the appellation implied a real office, to have been made Duke of a Roman province, and in that capacity to have been leader of the troops, with whom he obtained repeated victories, and acquired the just reputation of an able warrior. He also excelled in the chace, but neither his skill in military stratagems nor in the devices of the field, could protect him against falling into an ambuscade laid by St. Amator, Bishop of Auxerre, who, having learnt from a dream, that the young Duke should succeed to the bishopric, enticed him into the church, and then, securing the doors and passages, imposed on him the tonsure, with the order of a deacon. Germanus appears to have submitted with perfect resignation to this important change in the whole tenor of his life, and adopting the line afterwards pursued by Sir Thomas of Canterbury in regard to spiritual matters, and that in respect to his wife, which enrolled King Edward the Confessor in the list of saints, he soon obtained a reputation so high as to point him out as the most proper person, first to succeed St. Amator, as Bishop of Auxerre, in fulfilment of the dream, and then to go on a spiritual crusade against the Pelagians of Britain. He accordingly embarked, accompanied by St. Lupus, in the midst of winter, and soon encountered a violent storm, raised, it would seem, on purpose to evince the divine mission of these two saints, for, on their throwing some holy water into the sea, it immediately subsided.

Saint Germanus and St. Lupus not only preached with

such power as to astonish and to convince whole congregations, too large for any building to contain, but they gave sight to the blind, cast out devils, and raised the dead. St. Germanus was even induced to assist the faithful in the way of his original profession; for a Pagan army of Northmen and Picts invading the Christian provinces, the saint took the command of such persons as he found willing to defend their country, and having selected a place suited to his purpose, either by naturally possessing an echo, or by receiving it miraculously from his prayers, he there awaited the enemy, and on their approach shouting three times ALLELUIAH, and the whole army joining with their utmost might, the divine sounds, repeated and enforced by the reverberation on all sides, so terrified the assailants as to drive them into immediate flight, with the casting away of their arms, who were, in consequence, readily and safely pursued with great slaughter, through the whole space separating them from their fleet, none being spared but such as had the grace instantly to acquiesce in a method of conversion so clear, so powerful, and so coercive.

St. Germanus and St. Lupus soon afterwards left Britain, in the full confidence of having suppressed the heresy; but so obstinate and perverse were the people, that it broke out with increased violence, the circumstance of Pelagius being their countryman having probably more weight with the inhabitants than the arguments on either side, as in modern times all German Protestants are followers of Luther, as those of France are invariably of Calvin.

On receiving this intelligence, St. Germanus made a second voyage to Britain, armed with a small box of relics, suspended round his neck by a leathern string, which acting in aid of his own inherent sanctity, produced a train of miracles more wonderful even than those of the first expedition. Success of course attended him; and when the work of conversion was complete, he deposited the box of relics in the shrine of St. Alban, to be preserved for future use, if the seeds of heresy should again vegetate, taking in exchange some ashes of the British protomartyr. He then finally left Britain, returning to his diocese of Auxerre, on the confines of Burgundy; but on the way he encountered a second Pagan army, employed by the Christian Emperor of Rome to ravage the saint's province, in revenge for some popular insurrection. The saint succeeded, however, in converting the general, with all his forces, and then proceeded to Ravenna, in Italy, to obtain a pardon for the offenders. In this he was also successful; but having now filled the measure of his earthly services, and, as was usual in such cases, having predicted the hour of his own dissolution, he expired at Ravenna, in the odour of sanctity, on the last day of July, A. D. 448. His remains were brought back to France, with all the honours due to the successful leader of any party, spiritual or temporal, and they were finely enshrined in the oratory of St. Morice, which he had founded at Auxerre, and where an abbey has since been built. Various places in Britain were dedicated to him as to their tutelar saint. Of these the abbey of Selby was on the largest scale, and the priory in Cornwall distinguished by his own name, held the next place; although a chapel near the church of St. Alban, where he had triumphed in a general disputation with the heretics, became most celebrated, multitudes flocking there, as to St. Mary of Walsingham, for remission of their sins.

The ancient Priory of St. German's has again assumed a new form since the time of Mr. Tonkin, in consequence of Mr. Richard Eliot having greatly increased his fortune by marrying Harriet, daughter of James Craggs, Secretary of State in the time of King George the First. This gentleman, and still more his son, Mr. Edward Craggs Eliot, who obtained an hereditary seat in Parliament, after representing Cornwall in the House of Commons, added so much to the place, by enlarging the house, by embanking against the sea, and by laying out the grounds, as to make it one of the first among gentlemen's seats in the West of England. The statute referred to by Mr. Tonkin, for conferring the honour of a suffragan see on this town, in the 26th Henry VIII. c. 14, passed in the year 1534, by which it is declared that Thetford, Ipswich, Colchester, Dover, Guilford, Southampton, Taunton, Shaftesbury, Molton, Marlborough, Bedford, Leicester, Gloucester, Shrewsbury, Bristow, Penrith, Bridgewater, Nottingham, Grantham, Hull, Huntingdon, Cambridge, Pereth, Berwick, St. Germain's, and the Isle of Wight, shall be taken and accepted for sees of Bishops Suffragans, to be made in this Realm. This statute appears to have been very little if at all acted on; but two of the towns, Gloucester and Bristol, as is well known, became the seats of independent bishoprics.

At Bake lived Mr. Walter Moyle, of whom Cornwall has reason to be proud. He represented Saltash in the reign of King William; but, notwithstanding several successful efforts in the House of Commons, Mr Moyle retired to his family seat, and past the remainder of his time in learned leisure, where he died in 1721, not having completed his fiftieth year. Most of his works were published separately, but in 1727 came out in London, " Works of W. Moyle that were published by himself; with some account of his life and writings, by Anthony Hammond, Esq. 8vo." His works were principally:

An Argument, showing that a Standing Army is inconsistent with a free Government.

Translations from Xenophon.

The Miracle of the Thundering Legion explained.

A Charge to the Grand Jury at a Sessions in Liskeard.

Letters to Dr. W. Musgrave, of Exeter, on subjects of Criticism and Antiquity.

A Dissertation upon the Age of Philopatris, a Dialogue commonly attributed to Lucian.

Letters to and from Mr. Moyle on various subjects.

Remarks on Prideaux's Connection of the Old and New Testament.

Democracy Vindicated; an Essay on the Constitution of the Roman Government.

Bake now belongs to Sir Joseph Copley, whose grandfather, a brother's son of Mr. Walter Moyle, having married the heiress of Copley, of Sprotborough, in Yorkshire, assumed her name.

Aldwinnick is the property of Mr. Charles Trelawny, son of Mr. Edward Trelawny, who acquired it under the will of Mr. Charles Trelawny, who died in 1764, the last male descendant of their branch of the family. Mr. Edward Trelawny's original name was Stephens.

Catchfrench was till lately the residence of Mr. Francis Glanville, Member some time for Plymouth. This gentleman's ancestors purchased Catchfrench from the Fortescues more than a century ago. Mr. Glanville has given it up to his son, and on quitting the county he has carried with him the regret of every one in it.

Much obloquy having been cast upon Sir John Eliot, by a misrepresentation on the part of his political adversaries, of an affair in which sudden passion very probably caused him to act in a manner different from what would have been his conduct under other circumstances, I will add a narrative of the occurrence, taken from Lord Nugent's Life of Hampden.

" In a letter in the possession of Miss Aikin, written by an ancestor of one of the most respectable families in Devonshire, the cause and course of the quarrel are given, as described by the daughter of Mr. Moyle himself, a witness not likely to be unjustly partial to Sir John Eliot.

" Mr. Moyle having acquainted Sir John Eliot's father with some extravagancies in his son's expenses, and this being reported with some aggravating circumstances, young Eliot went hastily to Mr. Moyle's house, and remonstrated.

" What words passed she knew not; but Eliot drew his sword, and wounded Mr. Moyle in his side. On reflection," continues Mr. Moyle's daughter, " he soon detested the fact, and from thenceforward became as remarkable for his private deportment, in every view of it, as his public conduct. Mr. Moyle was so intirely reconciled to him, that no person in his time held him in higher esteem."

The editor cannot induce himself to believe that an English gentleman, a patriot, and ultimately a martyr in the cause of national freedom, could have formed and endeavoured to execute a plan for deliberate assassination; he is, moreover, unwilling perhaps to believe it of one who married the heiress of his own paternal family. It would be unfair, however, not to state that Mr. D'Israeli,* one of the most intelligent and candid of modern writers, and of the highest authority, has found in the course of his miscellaneous researches, various documents placing this transaction in a point of view much less favourable to Sir John Eliot, than would be inferred from Lord Nugent's account of it. The editor, however, continues to hope that these documents are coloured, at least, by the party spirit of times immediately preceding civil war, when all occurrences, private as well as public, receive their tincture from contending factions.

St. German's measures 9,029 statute acres.

	£.	s.	d.
Annual value of the Real Property, as returned to Parliament in 1815 .	15,283	0	0
Poor Rate in 1831	1,822	12	0

Population,—	in 1801,	in 1811,	in 1821,	in 1831,
	2030	2139	2404	2586

giving an increase of about 27½ per cent. in **30** years.

* For the extraordinary " Apology of Sir John Eliot" regarding this " hasty and unpremeditated act of violence," as Lord Eliot has judiciously described it, see Mr. D'Israeli's " Commentaries on the Life and Reign of Charles the First," vol. iv. p. 512. It must be also observed, that the fact was published by Echard, in the life-time of Dean Prideaux, who had communicated it to that historian. For other particulars hitherto unknown respecting the interesting character of Sir John Eliot, the reader may be referred to an historical pamphlet, entitled " Eliot, Hampden and Pym," by the author of the " Commentaries."

GEOLOGY, BY DR. BOASE.

This extensive parish is entirely situated within the calcareous series. On the northern part it touches the serpentine of Clicker Tor; and from thence to the sea-shore it exhibits many repetitions of clay slate, of calcareous schist, and of black limestone. An extensive quarry of the latter rock, near Trerule Foot, shews the nature of this limestone. It is of a dark-blue colour, compact, and rather hard; and in some parts of the mass it is very glittering, in consequence of the numerous shining facets of calcareous spar disseminated throughout. This rock abounds also in veins of calcareous spar, and the whole may be traced passing gradually into the adjacent calcareous schist.

In this tract beds of compact, and of schistose hornblende rocks, are also found, such as are common in this series of rocks at Saltash, at Padstow, Veryon, and at various other places.

St. GERMOE, alias GARMOW.

HALS.

Is situate in the hundred of Kerryer, and has upon the north St. Erth; south and east St. Breage; west St. Hilary. In the Domesday Tax (20 Will. I. 1087), it was rated under the jurisdiction of Lan-migell, i. e. Michael's Temple or Church, now St. Michael's Mount. In the Inquisition of the Bishops of Lincoln and Winchester, 1294, Ecclesia de Sancto Gordon in decanatu de Kerryer, is valued viii *l*. In Wolsey's Inquisition, 1521, it is valued, together with Breock, Cury, and Gonwallow, in all 33*l*. The patronage formerly, as I take it, in the Prior of St. Michael's Mount, who endowed them. The Incumbent Trewinard. The rectory or sheaf in the possession of ——; and the parish, rated to the 4*s*. per pound Land Tax, 1694, 40*l*.

In this parish stands Godolphin-Ball. This is that inexhaustible mountain, or tin-work, which for some hundreds of years hath afforded its owners or lord, the Lamburns, Stephens, Navas, now Godolphins, and other adventurers, several thousand pounds worth of tin.

TONKIN.

In this parish stands Godolphin, or Godolphin-Ball, from whence the lands thereof were denominated de Godolphin; who for many ages have had a considerable augmentation of their paternal estate by the casualties of tin from thence issuing. The same is a barren mountain, of pretty large extent and great height; and, although wrought for tin at the least during three hundred years, seems still, like the widow's cruise of oil and barrel of meal, to increase in the using, for, notwithstanding the incredible quantities of tin that have been taken thence in former ages, it still affords employment, and pays the wages, with some overplus, of at least three hundred men throughout the year.

The name of this parish is derived from its patron, St. Germow, or Germach, said to be an Irish king, who came over with St. Breage. St. Germow is there buried, and his tomb or chair is still to be seen in the churchyard.

THE EDITOR.

Mr. Hals has given the history of St. Gordian at very great length, to whom, without the slightest authority, he assumes this church and parish to have been dedicated. I have omitted the whole, as entirely unconnected with Cornwall, and because the very existence of such a saint is at the least doubtful. The writers of legends now content themselves with stating that some one of that name was beheaded at Rome in the year 362, as appears from the ancient Martyrologies; that his body lay many centuries in a cave, together with the remains of St. Epimachus, brought there from Alexandria, and that both relics are preserved in the Benedictine Abbey of Kempton, in the diocese of Ansbury.

The tradition of St. Germoe having been a king in his native country, is cherished by the inhabitants up to the present time, and they point to his tomb or shrine in the churchyard, with an evident feeling of their being elevated by his dignity.

But, on whatever grounds the ancient claims of this parish may rest to a canonized or to a royal patron, the village of Bojil has in modern times bestowed more real honour on the whole district, than could be derived from regal missionaries or from legendary saints.

In the parish register of Breage may be seen the following entry: "William, the son of William Lemon, of Germo, was baptized the 15th day of November, 1696."

I have endeavoured, but without much success, to collect

information respecting this very extraordinary man. It appears that his father and mother, whose maiden name was Rodda, were in a situation of life raised above the common level, and that they bestowed on their son the best education easily attainable, who on his part became eminently distinguished among his companions. If young Lemon ever, therefore, employed himself in executing the inferior labours usually performed by mining boys, as some have alleged with the view of increasing the wonder of his subsequent progress, and others impelled by less laudable motives, it is clear that they must have been undertaken from a desire of making himself practically acquainted with all the details of perhaps the most delicate operations in metallurgy.

His bodily strength and firmness of mind seem to have been commensurate with those abilities, which displayed themselves most conspicuously in after life. Within my recollection, the people of Breage and Germoe were fond of relating that Squire Lemon in his youth made the foremost link of a living chain, which, connected only by the grasp of their hands, extended itself into a tremendous surf, and rescued various human beings from a watery grave.

At a very early age, Mr. Lemon became one of the managers of a tin-smelting house at Chiandower, near Penzance; and the career which he pursued with so much ability and success, was traced for him at this place.

The ancient mining of Cornwall, like that of Banka in the present day, had been confined for a long succession of ages to merely collecting diluvial deposits of tin ore, which, from its great specific gravity, is always found beneath every other debris, and immediately incumbent on the solid rock, or unmoved strata, provincially called "the Fast." As the first operation invariably consists in washing away the lighter ingredients, by agitating the whole in streams, which never fail of gliding through the vallies where alone these deposits are found, the name "stream-work" has been adopted, to distinguish these sources of tin from mines which descend on the lodes themselves.

Mines invariably grew out of the stream-works, but with a progress so very slow as scarcely to be imagined by persons conversant only with the rapid improvements of modern times. Pits were at first sunk on the backs of lodes, till the presence of water impeded the work. Shallow adits, or drains, were obviously used in favourable situations, and the windlass, with its bucket and rope, must be of great antiquity. To this succeeded the rack and chain pump, identical with those still used in large ships; but the span beam and cage, moving on a perpendicular axis, by which the labour of horses became applicable to what had previously been done by the human arm, are so very modern, that the Editor remembers a carpenter who used to boast that he assisted in making the first whim ever seen westward Hayle.

A new era had, however, now commenced. The steam-engine, which consists essentially in a piston alternately sliding through a cylindrical vessel, invented by Mr. Newcomen, of Dartmouth, had been used at least on one mine, called the Great Work, in Breage, when Mr. Lemon came forward, gifted with the ability and the energy which enabled him to anticipate, by nearly half a century, everything that could add to the wealth and to the prosperity of his native county.

Mr. Lemon first associating himself with Mr. George Blewett, of Marasion, and with Mr. Dewen, commenced working a mine on a farm called Trowel, in the parish of Luddvan, the property of Lord Godolphin, and named Whele Fortune, where the second steam-engine was used. Capital was of course requisite for the undertaking, and that is said to have been supplied to Mr. Lemon by his marriage. It appears, from the register of Gulval, that "William Lemon and Isabel Vibert were married April the 22d, 1724." The Viberts were among what are termed the good lines in Gulval parish, and Mrs. Lemon had recently succeeded by will to the property of Mrs. Elizabeth Noles her godmother, and probably relation, who had acquired a fortune by some business at Chiandower.

But fortune, except perhaps for its timely supply of capital, was the least of Mrs. Lemon's recommendations; uniform report has represented her as entirely worthy of the very extraordinary person to whom she was united.

Mr. Lemon is said to have gained from Whele Fortune ten thousand pounds; and, thus enabled to execute more extensive plans, he removed to Truro, and commenced working the great Gwennap mines, on a scale never witnessed before, and perhaps never contemplated, in Cornwall. Cañon Adit was either actually commenced, or at the least was effectually prosecuted, by Mr. Lemon; a work unrivalled for extent or for utility in the mines of England, and his exertions increasing as his means enlarged, Mr. Lemon soon became the principal merchant and tin-smelter of Cornwall. But the energies of his mind were not limited to these undertakings, great as they were; he cultivated a taste for literature, and, what is extremely unusual, acquired, amidst business, and at a middle age, the power of reading the Classic authors in their original language. In the year 1742, we find his name in the list of Sheriffs. He became one of the magistrates of Truro, and might have represented the borough in Parliament. He obtained from Government a drawback of the duty on coal used in mines, when Sir Robert Walpole, then at the head of public affairs, complimented him on the clear and able manner in which he had made every statement; and a present of silver plate from Frederick Prince of Wales, as Duke of Cornwall, is preserved in his family.

About the same time he was mainly distinguished as "the great Mr. Lemon;" but, above all, so strongly were the impressions received of his abilities, his exertions, and general merit, that a progress so rapid and unexampled does not appear to have excited envy, or any of those bad passions which usually alloy the enjoyments of prosperity.

Mr. and Mrs. Lemon had but one son, and no daughters. Mr. William Lemon, Jun. married Ann, only daughter of Mr. John Willyams, of Cannerton, near St. Colomb, and sister of the late Mr. John Oliver Willyams, many years Colonel of the Cornwall Militia. He died at an early period of life, and several years before his father, who lived to the 25th of March 1760, and is buried in Truro church, where he had built by far the largest and most decorated house in the town. He had also purchased and improved Carclew, since become the family seat.

The younger Mr. William Lemon left two sons and a daughter. The elder of the sons, Sir William, represented the County of Cornwall in Parliament during fifty years, and commanded the regiment of militia. The second son, John, became a Colonel in the Guards, represented Truro, and commanded the Miners' Militia. The daughter married Mr. John Buller, of Morval, near Looe.

As instances of the respect paid to the commanding genius of Mr. Lemon, the people of Truro are said to have drawn back from their doors or windows as he passed through the street. And the Rev. Samuel Walker, a respectable although a fanatical clergyman, exhorting the children to be circumspect in the presence of Almighty God, incautiously added, "Only think, my dear children, how careful you would be if Mr. Lemon were looking upon you."

The parish of Germow measures 1,062 statute acres.

	£.	s.	d.
Annual value of the Real Property as returned to Parliament in 1815 .	1,373	0	0
Poor Rate in 1831	180	11	0

Population,—	in 1801,	in 1811,	in 1821,	in 1831,
	629	735	830	1175

giving an increase of 87 per cent. in 30 years.

GEOLOGY, BY DR. BOASE.

The geology of this parish is identical with that of Breage, of which in fact it forms a part, occupying only a segment of the Godolphin Hills.

ST. GENNYS.

HALS.

Is situate in the hundred of Lesnewith, and hath upon the north the Irish sea, west St. Juliot, east Jacobstow, south Otterham.

In Domesday Roll, 20 William I, 1087, this district was taxed under the jurisdiction of Otterham. In the taxation of benefices, made by the Bishops of Lincoln and Winchester, 1294, into the value of benefices in Cornwall, Ecclesia de Sancto Genesy, in Decanatu de Trigmajorshire, is rated c.s.; Vicar ejusdem £iiii. vis. viiid. In Wolsey's Inquisition and Valor Beneficiorum, St. Genis is taxed £8. The patronage in   The incumbent Crew. The rectory or sheaf in possession of
       and the parish rated to the 4s. per pound Land Tax, 1696, £160. 6s.

TONKIN

has not added any thing to the little said by Mr. Hals.

THE EDITOR.

It seems to be quite uncertain to whom this parish is dedicated.

There was a St. Genesius, or St. Genes, of Auvergne in France; he exterminated heresies and founded monasteries. His festival is kept on the third of June, and he is said to have died in the year 662. Such were the heroes of those days, and therefore he may possibly have been selected as patron of this church.

Mr. Lysons states that Treveeg, formerly a seat of the Yeos, is now the property of Lord Eliot, and that the great tithes, with the advowson of the vicarage, have passed to him with the priory of St. German's.

The Yeos were persons of consequence in the north of Cornwall and of Devonshire; they bore arms, Argent, a chevron Gules, between three birds.

Mr. Lysons further states that the manor of St. Gennis was for some time the property of Treise, from whom it passed by marriage to Morshead. It must since have been sold in the general wreck of that family.

Lord Rolle has also a manor in this parish. And another manor, called Treworgy, (a name common in Cornwall, and meaning a house or village on a stream,) belonged to the Priory of Canons of the Order of St. Augustine, founded at Launceston by William Warlewast, Bishop of Exeter from 1150 to 1159, in the time of King Stephen and of Henry the 2d.

Treworgy appears among the lands of this priory in the roll of 31 Henry VIII. preserved in the Augmentation Office; where it is stated as then paying the following sums, £4. 13s. 7d., £3. 17s., and 6s. 8d.

This is one of the manors given to the Duchy of Cornwall, in exchange for the manor of Wallingford, and it has been held for a long time under the Duchy by the family of Braddon.

One of this family, Captain William Braddon, was an officer of some distinction on the Parliamentary side in the Civil War. He is buried in the chancel of this church, where some verses to his memory begin with these lines:

> In war and peace I bore command,
> Both gown and sword I wore.

Henry Braddon, his son, or grandson, has the following verses:

> In peace I lived, and in peace did die,
> And now translated am to peace on high;
> Where I in peace perpetual shall remain,
> Until the Prince of Peace return again

This parish is said to afford an excellent specimen of the

romantic scenery distinguishing many portions of the north coast, from Cornwall, through Devonshire, to Somersetshire. The cliffs are bold, and the land is intersected by deep narrow vallies.

The parish of St. Gennys measures 5350 statute acres.

	£.	s.	d.
Annual value of the Real Property as returned to Parliament in 1815	2,562	0	0
Poor Rate in 1831	308	2	0

| Population, — | in 1801, 597 | in 1811, 658 | in 1821, 680 | in 1831, 761 |

giving an increase of $27\frac{1}{2}$ per cent. in 30 years.

The Rev. John Symmons, Vicar, was presented by Sir W. Molesworth in 1783.

THE GEOLOGY, BY DR. BOASE.

The whole of this parish is situated on the massive and schistose varieties of Dunstone, which are so prevalent in the northern parts of Cornwall and Devon. The Dunstone is in general very silicious, and it thus constitutes high and barren hills. A very curious variety of this rock occurs at Tresparret Down. It is in a state of decomposition, but when it is broken numerous hard rounded nodules fall out, having uniformly small crystals of pyrites in their centres. The same rock, in an unaltered state, forms the cliff on the left side of Crackington Cave, near the church, where it is inclined at an angle of 40°, having the entire surface covered with projecting nodules, which give it a blistered appearance not unlike that of hæmatites.

GLANT, GOLANT, or ST. SAMPSON'S.

HALS.

Is situate in the hundred of Powdre, and hath upon the north Lanlivery, east part of Foye Harbour, south Foye town, west Tywardreth.

GLANT. 89

At the time of the Norman Conquest this district was taxed under the name of Tywardreth, or Lan-tine. In the taxation of benefices made by the Bishops of Lincoln and Winchester, 1294, in this province, the church is not named, probably it was not then extant, or not endowed; neither is it mentioned in Wolscy's Inquisition 1521, or Valor Beneficiorum, so that I take it to be wholly impropriated under Tywardreth. However, 24 Henry VI. St. Sampson's was rated to the Cornish clergy's fifteenths 35s. Carew's Survey of Cornwall, page 91. It was endowed by the prior of Tywardreth. The patronage now in Barret, the curate or vicar Hosken, the sheaf or rectory in Barrett. The parish of St. Sampson's was rated to the 4s. per pound Land Tax, 1696, temp. William III. £103. 2s.

Pen-coit, alias Pen-coid, alias Pen-quite, all synonymous words, signifying head or chief wood, or head of the wood, is a name given and taken from the once natural circumstances of the place, from whence was denominated an ancient family of gentlemen, surnamed de Pencoit. And here lived John de Pencoit, temp. Henry III. and Edward I. who held one acre of land in Lamellyn of 5s. price, (that is to say a Cornish acre, consisting of 60 statute acres) for making and keeping the king's grey coat when he came into Cornwall, due out of Cabulion, from Peter, the son of Orger. [Carew's Sur. Corn. p. 45. See also Pengelly in St. Breock, Pyder, and Warliggan.]

This barton is now the dwelling of John Barret, esq. Sheriff of Cornwall 3 William III. whose ancestor is said to have come out of Normandy with William the Conqueror, 1066, an ensign under Colonel Henry de Ferrers, commonly called Henry Earl Ferrars, son of Wakelyn; to whom the Conqueror gave the castles of Tutbury in Staffordshire, and Oncomb in Rutlandshire. Since which time this gentle family of Barrets have flourished in this county in good fame and reputation for above twenty descents. The present possessor of Pencoit married Kendall of Medroff, and giveth for his arms, Gules, a bend Varry.

90 GLANT.

In this parish is the dwelling of Reginald Couch, gent. Attorney at Law, that married Vincent of Creed; his father, Hawkey of St. Wenowe.

TONKIN.

How these names of Glant or Golant prevailed over that of St. Sampson I am not able to determine, unless perhaps it was the primitive name thereof before the parish church was erected, consecrated, and endowed to God under the name of St. Sampson. For in Cardinal Wolsey's Inquisition, and in Carew's Survey, it is called St. Sampson.

The name Golant is obviously compounded of Gol, holy, and of lan, a church. (Mr. Whitaker remarks that Y-Gol, by the Holy One, is still an oath in Cornwall.)

THE EDITOR.

Mr. Hals has given a very long and uninteresting account of St. Sampson, the patron saint of Golant, involving a dissertation on the antiquity of archbishops.

He is reported to have commenced his ecclesiastical career by the practice of ascetic observances, in due time he became the chief of a monastic institution, from whence he was taken to be Archbishop of York; but the north of England being at that time ravaged by the northern pirates, he was driven from thence, and going over into Brittany he founded a monastery at Dal, and became the first Bishop of that place, where a see was created at his request by Pope Pelegius the First, who honoured him moreover personally with the pallium or pale. He was present at the Second Council of Paris, held in 557, and died about the year 564. His remains were enshrined at Dal, but when the Normans began in the tenth century to invade and pillage Neustria, these barbarians, equally hostile to the saint alive or dead, obliged his brethren to remove the relics to Paris, where they are supposed to have been preserved up to the period of the great revolution.

Penquite was acquired by purchase about the beginning or towards the middle of last century from the Prestwoods, by Mr. Rashleigh, of Menwhilly, by whom a perpetual lease was soon after granted in favour of a relation, which has since passed through various hands.

Mr. Lysons says that the manor of Lentyon in this parish, belonged to the Montacutes Earls of Salisbury.

It appears from Dugdale's Baronage that this property was seized by king Henry VIII., on his judicial murder of the last Plantagenet, Margaret Countess of Salisbury. It now belongs to Mr. William Rashleigh, who is impropriator of the great and small tithes, and appoints the perpetual curate, in right of the monastery of Tywardreth.

A castle is said to have belonged to this manor, but no traces of it remain; the appellation seems indeed to have been very loosely applied in the latter part of our feudal times, so as frequently to indicate no more than the residence of a chief.

The village round the church, or, according to the expression used in Cornwall, "the church town," is always called Golant. The houses are situated in a romantic cross valley, nearly where it terminates in Fowey River.

The inhabitants boast that in this village was established the first boarding-school for young ladies that appeared in Cornwall, and they call the attention of visitors to these peculiarities connected with this church :—" That it has a fire-place within it; that a well of water flows over in the porch; and that a tree in the churchyard o'ertops the tower."

This parish measures 1340 statute acres.

	£.	s.	d.
Annual value of the Real Property, as returned to Parliament in 1815 .	1874	0	0
Poor Rate in 1831	185	5	0

Population,—{ in 1801, | in 1811, | in 1821, | in 1831
               164 | 186 | 248 | 314

giving an increase of 86 per cent. in 30 years.

The Rev. Thomas Pearse was presented to St. Sampson's chapel in 1815, by W. Rashleigh, Esq.

THE GEOLOGY BY DR. BOASE.

The rocks of this parish are intermediate between those of the porphyritic and calcareous series: on the northern part passing into the former, which are better developed as they pass on towards the granite in Tywardrath; on the southern part the rocks begin to assume the character of the calcareous series, which is complete in Fowey.

GLUVIAS.

HALS.

Is situated in the hundred of Kerryer, and hath upon the north Peran-Arwothan, east Mylor, west Mabe, south Budock. Here was an endowed church or chapel, or place of jurisdiction, before the Norman conquest; for in the Domesday Roll, 20 William I. 1087, Gluvias is rated as such. In the taxation of benefices in Cornwall, made by the Bishops of Lincoln and Winchester, 1294, Ecclesia de Sancto Gluviano, in Decanatu de Penryn, is rated xls. In Wolsey's Inquisition, 1521, it is valued together with Budock, in 21l. 16s. 9d.; before which time it seems those churches were united and consolidated by the Bishops of Exeter, the patrons and endowers thereof; the incumbent Collyer; the rectory, or sheaf, in possession of

Enys; and the parish rated to the 4s. per pound Land Tax, 1696, 132l. 11s.

Roscrow is the dwelling of Alexander Pendarves, Esq. that married the Lady Dorothy Burke, daughter of the Earl of Clanricarde, and afterwards the daughter of Colonel Granville; his father Carew, his grandfather St. Aubyn, his great-grandfather (Roberts of Truro); viz. Samuel Pendarves, Esq. Sheriff of Cornwall, 19th James I. who gave for his arms, Sable, a falcon rising between three mullets Or; originally descended from the Pendarves of Pendarves, or Constenton, as I am informed.

Roscrow gave name and origin to an old family of gentlemen surnamed Roscrow, whose heir, about the time of Richard II. was married to one of the Seneschalls of Holland, where John de Seneschall held by the tenure of knight's service part of a knight's fee of land, 3 Henry IV. (See CAREW's Survey of Cornwall, p. 40.) from whence it appears also that Luke, the son of Bernard Seneschallus, was by letters mandatory, or a mandamus, made one of the Barons of the Exchequer, by King Richard I. (See his arms under GWENDRON.)

Innis, Enys, Ennis, is an island or place encircled with water, in this place to be construed as a river island; where two rivers in their confluence meet, and shape the land between them in form of a corner, or triangle; from which place was denominated an old British family of gentlemen now in possession thereof, surnamed Enys; particularly John Enys, Esq. that married the inheritrix of Gregor of Truro, his father Pendarves, his grandfather Winifred, daughter and coheiress of Thomas Price, of Trewardreva; and giveth for his arms, Argent, three water enets Vert, creatures frequently seen in the rivers by which those lands are insulated.

A great number of places, or lands, in Cornwall, under the like circumstances, are from thence denominated Enys, Ennis, and Ennys in St. Erme, Roach, Luxsilian, Peransand, taken some times with other words.

Gosose river, in this parish (the slow-wood river), situate upon Gosose creek of the sea: from whence was denominated Gosose tenement, the native place of Captain Henry Carverth (i. e. rock-strength, or car-veth, rock-grave), who being bred to sea affairs and navigation in his youth, was taken into the service of King Charles II. in the beginning of his Dutch and French war, 1665, to whom he gave the command of a frigate, in the several engagements of the Dukes of York and Albemarle in their sea-fights with those nations; wherein he demeaned himself so well in point of valour and conduct, that after those wars were ended he was chosen one of the standing Captains under the Earl of Ossory, for which he received about 300*l*. per annum salary, during his life, which ended about the year 1684, when he had a military interment in this church: who dying without legitimate issue, left his brother, Thomas Carveth, of this place, gentleman, his heir and executor, who giveth for his arms, Argent, a chevron between three talbots Sable. Those gentlemen, from living at Carveth, or Carverth, in Mabe, were transnominated from Thoms to Carverth; as another family of those Thomses, from living at Carnsew, in the said parish, were transnominated to Carnsew; and there are some deeds yet extant dated tempore Henry VIII. which will evidence the truth of this fact, as Mr. Carverth told me.

Between the parishes of Budock and Gluvias, on a promontory of land shooting into the sea creek of Falmouth harbour, between two vales and hills, where the tide daily makes its flux and reflux, stands the ancient borough of Penrin, or. Penryn, a name given and taken from the natural circumstances of the place; and by the name of Penrin it was taxed as the voke lands of a considerable manor in Domesday Roll, 20 William I. 1087. (See BRIN, BRYN, in WITHELL.)

. This place I take to be the Οκρινυμ (Ocrinum) of Ptolemy. The town was a privileged manor, with a court leet, before the Norman Conquest; and in the year 1230

GLUVIAS. 95

King Henry III. granted a charter to William Brewer, Bishop of Exeter, then lord thereof, as his successors still are, in right of the bishopric of Bodman, or Cornwall, long before annexed to Exeter. (See more in LANWHITTON.) It was also incorporated by King James I. by another charter, consisting of a Mayor, Recorder, and Portreeve, eleven Magistrates, and twelve Assistants; with liberty to send two of its members to sit in the Commons' House of Parliament, to be elected by the majority of those that are freemen, and pay rates and taxes. It is also, amongst many other things, appurtenanced with markets weekly, upon Wednesdays and Saturdays; fairs on May 1, July 7, December 21; and of old had free warren in all the King's lands. The arms of this town are a Saracen's head couped at the shoulder, and crowned, or environed, with a laurel.

The precept from the Sheriff on the Parliament writ, as also to remove an action at law depending in this leet to a superior court, must be thus directed: " Majori et Burgensibus Burgi sui de Penrin in Comitatu Cornubiæ salutem," otherwise, " Proposito, Ballivis, et Burgensibus Burgi sui de Penryn;" and to remove an action from the court leet of Penryn foreign: " Senescallo et Ballivis manerij de Penrin forreigne salutem."

But, alas! notwithstanding all its privileges, our Cornish historian, Mr. Carew, in his time, tells us that on the top fo a creek Penrin town hath taken up its seat; rather passable than notable for wealth, buildings, or inhabitants. Though now, *tempore* Charles II. I take it to be much altered for the better in these particulars, and to be parallel with, or equal therein, with any other town in Cornwall. And, moreover, I look upon it as the most commodious, pleasantly situated, and healthful borough within that province, it being situated upon a hill, and having continually passing through its streets a useful river of water, and through the gardens and orchards of the town, behind the street-houses on each side, pass two considerable mill-leats, or rivers of water, met daily by the flux and reflux of the sea.

Where, on the south of this town, on one of those rivers, Walter Brounscomb, Bishop of Exeter, 1260, at a place called Glasnith, or green-ford, so named from the estuaries, or ebbing and flowing of the sea under it, founded and endowed a collegiate church of Black Canons, or Canons Augustine, that could not marry wives, consisting of twelve prebends and a dean; " Clerici tresdecem, personæ discretæ," are the very words of the leger book of its foundation; and then endowed and confirmed all by a charter in these words, as translated from Bishop Brounscomb's original Latin.

" To give to God, the blessed Virgin Mary, and St. Thomas of Canterbury, in Budock, Penryn, and Glasnith College, and his thirteen canonical brothers and their successors, all lands, woods, meadows, waters, pastures, mills, laws, rents, and courts, and all things to the same pertaining, to possess, have, hold, and enjoy for ever. This agrees with the register,

ROBERT MICHELL, Register, 1611."

Afterwards this collegiate church, thus founded and endowed, and dedicated to the Virgin Mary and Thomas Becket, Archbishop of Canterbury, received a greater augmentation of wealth, lands, aud revenues from John Grandison, Bishop of Exeter, 1358, who had persuaded all rich priests of his diocese to make him his heir and executor, in order to build and endow churches with their riches; which trust, in a great measure, he performed to his lasting credit and renown; so that at length, amongst others, this collegiate church's yearly revenues, at the suppression, 26 Henry VIII. was valued at 205*l*. 10*s*. 6*d*. according to Speed and Dugdale's Monasticon Anglicanum, now worth 1200*l*.

This collegiate church is now entirely demolished. Since the beginning of this century there was one of its towers standing, but it is lately pulled down, and a dwelling-house built in the place where it stood.

Bishop Brounscomb died 1280, and lies buried in his cathedral church of Exeter.

The chief inhabitants of this town of Penrin are Mr. Hallamore, Mr. Worth, Mr. Hearle, Mr. Kempe, Mr. Bloyse, Mr. Melhuish, Mr. Vellhuish.

The Lady Jane Killigrew, of Arwinick (see FALMOUTH), for some protection and favour shewn her in her troubles by the Mayor of this town, gave a silver cup and cover to the Mayor of this town and his successors for ever, containing about three quarts, and about 12*l*. value, whereon is this inscription: " From Mayor to Mayor, to the town of Penryn, when they received me in great misery.

JANE KILLYGREW, 1613." (of which before).

TONKIN.

After transcribing, with little variation, what has been stated from Mr. Hals, Mr. Tonkins adds,

Enis, in this parish, gave name to an old family of gentlemen from thence, denominated de Enis; that is to say, of this island; for innis, ennis, enys, signify in Cornish, an island, and also a tongue of land where two rivers meet.

John Enys, Esq. acquired a great flow of wealth by his marriage with Ann, only daughter of Mr. Henry Greys of Truro. His son, Samuel Enys, is the present possessor of the estate; he married Dorothy, daughter of Thomas Willis, of London, merchant, and has lately succeeded to a considerable fortune by the decease of her two brothers, Sir Thomas and Sir William Willis, of Fen Ditton, in Cambridgeshire, Baronets, the last in the year 1733. This gentleman is in the commission of the Peace, and was Sheriff of Cornwall, 8 Anne, A.D. 1709. He has expended large sums of money in the improvement of his seat, as well by enlarging the house as by making beautiful gardens.

Roscrow means clearly the valley cross; although the house stands on a very elevated station.

The family of Pendarves settled here, have far outstripped all the other branches in estates, and have served their country as Members of Parliament, Commissioners of the Peace, Sheriffs, and Deputy-Lieutenants. The arms of Pendarves are, Sab. a falcon rising Arg. between three mullets, Or. I cannot refrain from making some remarks on Alexander Pendarves, Esq. the last of this family.

He was Surveyor-general of the Crown and Duchy lands in Cornwall to Queen Anne, and a Member of Parliament the greatest part of his life. He married Mary, eldest daughter of the Honourable Bernard Grenville, brother of Lord Lansdowne, a beautiful young lady, but she did not bring him any children. He died in 1726, very suddenly, at his house in London, being then a burgess for the town of Launceston. His death was a great surprise to all his friends, and especially to me, with whom I had taken a hearty breakfast that very morning at my aunt Vincent's, at Chelsea. I must add, that on the Sunday before he and I bore up the pall to John Goodall, of Fowey, Esq. buried in St. Margaret's, Westminster; and that on the Sunday fortnight after, I had the misfortune to bear up his in St. Mary's, Savoy. He was the last male of the family of Pendarves in this place, which, with the rest of his property, has devolved to his niece, Mary, the only daughter and heiress of his brother, John Pendarves, clerk, Rector of Drews Teignton, in Devonshire, and relict of Francis Basset, of Tehidy, Esq.; and this lady is now the possessor, paying an annuity of £.400 a-year to her uncle's widow. But before I leave this place I must not forget to give this just character of my deceased friend, with whom I had the honour to serve as burgess for Helston, in Queen Anne's last Parliament; that for good humour, good sense, for a true and sincere adherence to the interests of his country, and for a harmless merry disposition, he hath left not many his equals, and none that exceed him, in this county.

This parish takes its name from the saint to whom the church is dedicated.

THE EDITOR.

Mr. Hals gives a very improbable etymology for the name of this parish, deriving it from the Cornish verb, *glewas*, to hear, which he quotes from the 12th stanza of Mount Calvary.

<pre>
An ger a Du maga del wrei neb vynno tro glewas.
Lavar   Du maga del wrei neb a vyuno y glewas.
The word (of) God feed so will do (he) who is willing to hear,
</pre>

The first line is transcribed from Mr. Hals, the second is the line as it stands in the MS. from which the editor of this work has printed Mount Calvary.

The Editor has not been able to find any traces of St. Gluvias, but these may have easily disappeared amidst the throng of our provincial hierarchy.

The borough of Penryn, with enlarged limits, has been united with Falmouth in sending two Members to Parliament under the constitution of 1832. Of the principal inhabitants noticed by Mr. Hals, the Hearles had risen into most importance. They were the younger branch of a family said to have migrated into Cornwall, and to have settled at Prideaux, in Luxulian, and afterwards at Trelawn, in Pelynt, usually written Trelawny, since it was purchased by a gentleman of that name. The last Mr. Hearle, of Penryn, married the heiress of Paynter, of Trelisick, in St. Erth; and having lost an only son, his daughters became coheiresses, who married Mr. Rodd, of Trebartha, the Rev. Henry Hawkins Tremayne, and Captain Wallis of the R. N.

Enys is now the property of John Samuel Enys, Esq. where his family are ascertained, by authentic documents, to have been seated from times far back in the reign of the Plantagenets, and probably from periods antecedent to them. Samuel Enys represented Penryn in the first Parliament of Charles II. and they appear in every page of our list of Sheriffs. Mr. Enys has built an excellent new house on the foundation of the old; and very recently (1834) he has married Catherine Gilbert, the Editor's eldest daughter.

The manor of Cosawis, or Gosose, was a part of the large possessions taken from the Bodrugons by Henry VII. and given by him to Sir Richard Edgecumbe, whose descendant, Lord Mount Edgecumbe, parted with it to the late Sir William Lemon.

But a farm called Bohelland has for two centuries continued to excite great curiosity and attention on account, of its having been the place where events occurred in real life more horrible than the most heated and gloomy imagination could well invent. Mr. Lysons refers to a small pamphlet of eight leaves, printed in black letter, and accompanied with several wood-cuts, entitled, "News from Perin, in Cornwall, of a most bloody and unexampled Murder, &c." but not having given any clue for finding it, the Editor has examined several public libraries without success. The following narrative has, however, been extracted from a work entitled "The Reign and Death of King James, of Great Britain:"

"He had been blessed with ample possessions and fruitful issue, unhappy only in a younger son, who taking liberty from his father's bounty, and with a crew of like condition, that wearied on land, they went roving to sea, and in a small vessel southward, took boot from all they could master, and so increasing force and wealth, ventured on a Turk's man in the Streights; but by mischance their own powder fired themselves, and our gallant, trusting to his skilful swimming, got on shore upon Rhodes, with the best of his jewels about him; where offering some to sale to a Jew, who knew them to be the Governor's of Algier, he was apprehended, and, as a pirate, sentenced to the gallies among other Christians, whose miserable slavery made them all studious of freedom, and with wit and valour took opportunity and means to murther some officers, got on board of an English ship, and came safe to London; where his misery, and some skill, made him servant to a surgeon, and sudden preferment to the East Indies. There, by this means he got money; with which returning back, he designed himself for his native county, Cornwall. And in a small ship from London, sailing to the west, was cast away upon that coast. But his excellent skill in swimming, and former fate to boot, brought him safe to shore; where, since his fifteen years' absence, his father's former fortunes much decayed, now retired him not far off to a country habitation, in debt and danger.

"His sister he finds married to a mercer, a meaner match than her birth promised. To her, at first, he appears a poor stranger, but in private reveals himself, and withall what jewels and gold he had concealed in a bow-case about him; and concluded that the next day he intended to appear to his parents, and to keep his disguise till she and her husband should meet, and make their common joy complete.

"Being come to his parents, his humble behaviour, suitable to his suit of clothes, melted the old couple to so much compassion as to give him covering from the cold season under their outward roof, and by degrees his travelling tales, told with passion to the aged people, made him their guest so long by the kitchen fire, that the husband took leave and went to bed. And soon after his true stories working compassion in the weaker vessel, she wept, and so did he; but compassionate of her tears, he comforted her with a piece of gold, which gave assurance that he deserved a lodging, to which she brought him; and being in bed, shewed her his girdled wealth, which he said was sufficient to relieve her husband's wants, and to spare for himself, and being very weary fell fast asleep.

"The wife, tempted with the golden bait of what she had, and eager of enjoying all, awakened her husband with this news, and her contrivance what to do; and though with horrid apprehension he oft refused, yet her puling fondness (Eve's enchantments) moved him to consent, and rise to be master of all, and both of them to murder the man, which instantly they did; covering the corpse under the clothes till opportunity to convey it out of the way.

"The early morning hastens the sister to her father's house, where she, with signs of joy, enquires for a sailor that should lodge there the last night; the parents slightly denied to have seen any such, until she told them that he was her brother, her lost brother; by that assured scar upon his arm, cut with a sword in his youth she knew him; and were all resolved this morning to meet there and be merry.

"The father hastily runs up, finds the mark, and with horrid regret of this monstrous murther of his own son, with the same knife cuts his own throat.

"The wife went up to consult with him, where in a most strange manner beholding them both in blood, wild and aghast, with the instrument at hand, readily rips herself up, and perishes on the same spot.

"The daughter, doubting the delay of their absence, searches for them all, whom she found out too soon; with the sad sight of this scene, and being overcome with horror and amaze of this deluge of destruction, she sank down and died; the fatal end of that family.

"The truth of which was frequently known, and flew to court in this guise; but the imprinted relation conceals their names, in favour to some neighbour of repute and kin to that family. The same sense makes me therein silent also."

These dreadful events have been wrought into a drama by Lillo, the author of George Barnwell; and if terror and pity form the essential bases of tragedy, the "Fatal Curiosity" is built on a most ample foundation; the sister, of course, changes her character to heighten the effect, but in other respects the play scarcely differs from the actual course of events.

The celebrated Mr. Harris of Salisbury, has given the following account of this drama in his last work, entitled, " Philological Inquiries."

"A long lost son, returning home unexpectedly, finds his parents alive, but perishing with indigence.

"The young man, whom from his long absence his parents never expected, discovers himself to an amiable friend, his long-loved Charlotte, and with her concerts the manner how to discover himself to his parents.

" It is agreed that he should go to their house, and there remain unknown till Charlotte should arrive and make the happy discovery.

" He goes thither accordingly, and having by a letter of Charlotte's been admitted, converses, though unknown, both with father and mother, and beholds their misery with filial affection; complains, at length, he was fatigued (which, in fact, he really was), and begs he may be admitted for a while to repose. Retiring he delivers a casket to his mother, and tells her it is a deposit she must guard till he awake.

" CURIOSITY tempts her to open the casket, when she is dazzled with the splendour of innumerable jewels. Objects so alluring suggest bad ideas; and poverty soon gives to those ideas a sanction. Black as they are, she communicates them to her husband; who, at first reluctant, is at length persuaded, and for the sake of the jewels stabs the stranger while he sleeps.

" The fatal murder is perpetrating, or at least but barely perpetrated, when Charlotte arrives, full of joy, to inform them that the stranger within their walls was their long-lost son.

" What a discovery? What a revolution? How irresistibly are the tragic passions of terror and pity excited?

" It is no small praise to this affecting fable that it so much resembles the Œdipus Tyrannus of Sophocles. In both tragedies, that which apparently leads to joy, leads in its completion to misery; both tragedies concur in the horror of their discoveries, and both in those great outlines of a truly tragic revolution, where (according to the nervous sentiment of Lillo himself) we see

> ———————— the two extremes of life,
> The highest happiness and deepest woe,
> With all the sharp and bitter aggravations
> Of such a vast transition

It is a very curious circumstance that the name of these wretched people, having been kept back at first from compassion towards their relatives, it is now actually unknown.

This parish has been peculiarly fortunate in its succession of clergymen. The Rev. John Penrose, who died in 1776, after being thirty-five years Vicar, has left the reputation of learning, of piety, and of all the virtues which adorn a clergyman. Mr. Temple bore a very high reputation as a man of letters; Mr. Howell was universally esteemed; and the present vicar, Mr. Sheepshanks, ranked in the first lists of science and of literature at Cambridge, and became a distinguished tutor in a college, which continues to support the rank bestowed upon it by the greatest of philosophers.

The town, lying on the back of a sharp ridge of land dividing two deep vallies, has great beauty of situation, and deserves in other respects the praises bestowed by Mr. Tonkin. To travellers, however, all the circumstances are quite different; the main street descending with the ridge is scarcely safe for carriages; and the great road from London through Truro to Falmouth, passing directly across the ridge, has to go up and then down through streets so steep and narrow, and in parts so turned, as to make the safe-passage of the mail-coach a matter of wonder; these defects have been, however, completely remedied by a road carried round the point and accommodated with a drawbridge; thus reducing the road to a level, and preserving the communication by water; this improvement was made about the year 1830.

GORAN.

This parish measures 2,271 statute acres.

Annual value of the Real Property as returned to Parliament in 1815,

	£	s.	d.			
The Parish £.3951	0	0	}	9068	0	0
The Town 5117	0	0				

Poor Rate in 1831,

The Parish 584	3	0	}	1746	11	0
The Town 1162	8	0				

Population,—	in 1801,	in 1811,	in 1821,	in 1831,
The Parish	624	714	745	969
The Town	2324	2713	2933	3521
	2948	3427	3678	4490

giving an increase on the Parish of $55\frac{1}{2}$, on the Town $51\frac{1}{4}$, on both $52\frac{1}{4}$,—per cent. in 30 years.

Present Vicar, the Rev. John Sheepshanks, collated by the Bishop of Exeter in 1824.

THE GEOLOGY, BY DR. BOASE.

The western side of this parish skirts along the boundary of the granite of Mabe; but it does not extend on this rock, with the exception of a small triangular space near Chywoon, at its northern corner. The rest of the parish lies on felspar rocks, both slaty and massive; some of which contain hornblende, whence it passes into green stone.

These felspar rocks, when they are disintegrated, afford a soil which is covered with luxuriant vegetation, forming a striking contrast with the utter barrenness of the adjacent granite.

GORAN.

HALS.

Is situate in the hundred of Powdre, and hath upon the north St. Ewe, east Mevaguisey, south the British Channel. By this name it was taxed in Domesday Roll, 20th William I. 1087. Also in the Inquisition of the Bishops of Lincoln, &c. into the value of Cornish benefices, 1294, Ecclesia Sancti Goran in Decanatu de Powdre, was valued in vi*l*. xiii*s*. iiii*d*. Vicar ibidem, xxvi*s*. viii*d*. In Wolsey's Inquisition, 1521, it was rated by the same name of Goran at 20*l*. The patronage in the Bishop of Exeter, who endowed it; and when it was made a Vicarage reserved to him and his successors 100*l*. per annum rent out of the garb, or sheaf, which is in the possession of Ratcliff. The Incumbent Shapter. And the parish rated to the 4*s*. per pound Land Tax, 1696, temp. William III. by the name of Goran, 317*l*. 14*s*. This, undoubtedly, was an endowed church before the Norman Conquest, or, at least, a privileged manor, since it appears from that time to this it hath not admitted of any mutation of name.

Goran-hoane, in this parish, signifies Goran-haven, bay, winding of the sea, or harbour. A place much frequented by ships, boats, barges, and lighters, for fishing and carrying and re-carrying fish, goods, and merchandizes; and wherein is a convenient quay, or landing-place, for that purpose, made secure by a considerable promontory of land that shoots far out into the sea on the west side thereof, commonly called (for what reason I have not learned) the Dead-man; which forms a large bay, or winding bosom of the sea, on the east, betwixt it and Ram Head, twenty miles distant; and such another west, to the Lizard Point, at a like distance, all notable and well-known places, and sea-marks to such mariners as navigate the British Channel in those parts. In this haven town is still extant the ruins of an ancient free chapel, wherein God was duly worshipped in former ages by the inhabitants of the place.

The barton of Bo-drig-ham, or Bod-rig-an, also Botrigan (for in British *d* and *t* are indifferently used and pronounced for each other) gave name and origin to an old family of gentlemen surnamed de Bodrigham, or Bodrigan, also

Bodrigan, who flourished here in great fame, wealth, and reputation for several descents; and in particular here lived Otho de Bodrigan, temp. 17th Edward II. of whom we read in Carew's Survey of Cornwall, p. 51: viz. " Otto de Bodrugan peregrinatus est ad San. Jacobum licentia Domini Regis;" i. e. Otho de Bodrigan, by license of our Lord the King, is gone a pilgrimage to St. James; that is to say, to the apostle St. James's Church, at Compostella, in Spain; who had for his fellow-traveller Radolphus de Belloprato, " qui peregrinatus est cum Ottone de Bodrigan, cum licentia Regis, pro se et duobus valectis;" that is to say, Ralph of the fair meadow, who by license of the King for himself and two servants, or young gentlemen, is gone a pilgrimage with Otho of Bodrigan. And of those it follows, in the same page, " isti prænominati habent 40 libras terræ et redditus per ann. ;" that is to say, held by the tenure of knight's service.

This Otho de Bodrigan, Sheriff of Cornwall, 3d Richard II. anno Dom. 1400, gave for his arms (as appears yet on the door of this house), Argent, three bends or bendlets Gules. And as a further testimony thereof, Nicholas Upton, in his Latin Manuscript of Heraldry, written before printing was invented (now in my custody), said of his son, 1440, " Monsieur William Bodrigham port de Argent trois bends de Gules;" who dying without issue, his two sisters became his heirs; the one married to Champernowne, of Halewin, or Haleworth, who in her right held in this place by the tenure of knight's service, 3d Henry IV. a Knight's fee of land (Carew's Survey of Cornwall).

His other sister, as tradition saith, was married to Trenowith, who thereupon discontinued his own paternal name and arms, viz. in a field Argent, on a fess Sable, three chevrons transverse (to the dexter) of the Field; and assumed those of Bodrigan. He had issue by her Henry Trenowith, or Bodrigham, temp. Henry VI. who married Jane, sixth daughter of William Herbert, Earl of Pembroke, slain 8th Edward IV. 1469, the relict of Thomas Viscount Lisle, and by her had issue. He was knighted by King Edward IV. or King Richard III. by the name of Sir Henry Bodrigham; who siding with King Richard III. at the battle of Bosworth Field (where he, the said King Richard, was slain by the Earl of Richmond's soldiers), he was therefore, with many others, attainted of treason against King Henry VII.; and in order to shun justice he made his escape after the battle aforesaid, and secretly repaired to this place, where he was kept close for a season, but not so private but King Henry's officers got notice thereof, and at an appointed time beset the same in quest of him; which he understanding, by a back-door fled from thence, and ran down the hills to the sea cliff near the same, the officers pursuing so quick after him that he could not possibly make his escape. As soon therefore as he came to the cliff, about a hundred feet high, he leaped down into the sea, upon the little grassy island there, without much hurt or damage; where instantly a boat which he had prepared in the cove, attended him there, which transported him to a ship that carried him into France. Which astonishing fact, and place, is to this day well known and remembered by the name of Harry Bodrigan's leap, or jump. But notwithstanding his own escape beyond the seas, this lordship and his whole estate were forfeited and seized by King Henry VII. for attainder of treason; and the greatest part thereof he settled upon Sir Richard Edgcumb and his heirs for ever; whose posterity are still in possession thereof. This Sir Richard Edgcumb, not long before, on suspicion of being confederated with the Earl of Richmond against King Richard III. (as tradition saith), was shrewdly sought after and pursued by means of this very Sir Henry Bodrigan, in order to be taken into custody, who from his house at Cotehele, made also a wonderful escape thence, and got into France, to the Earl of Richmond; of which see more in Carew's Survey of Cornwall, p. 114 (p. 270,

GORAN. 109

Lord Dunstanville's edition), so unavoidable a thing is fortune or destiny.

Tradition tells us that there was great discord and variance between the families of Bodrigan and the knightly family of the Haleps of Lammoran, either upon account of private affronts or grudges, or upon the different interests or factions, and wars between the houses of York and Lancaster, wherein they were associated and engaged against each other, so that as often as they met between themselves and servants some combat or battle ensued, whereby blood was shed and the peace broken; and they often came to each other's gates armed in defiance on horseback.

At Tre-garden lived John de Tregarthyn, temp. Edward I. how long before I know not; after which his posterity in this place married with the great inheritrixes of Pever, Chamberlayne, and Hendower, of Court, in Branell, by which last, by the Cornwalls of that place, they were lineally descended from Richard Earl of Cornwall, King of the Romans, by his concubine, Joan de Valletort, widow of Sir Alexander Oakeston. (Vide St. Stephen's.) Certainly this was an ancient, rich, and famous family in those parts, for it appears by their seats, or pews, in Goran church, they had the precedence or right hand of the seats pertaining to the great family of Bodrigan, as is yet to be seen. Thomas Tregarthyn, Esq. was Sheriff of Cornwall, 7 Henry VII. 1492, who married Hendower aforesaid, and removed to Court, in St. Stephen's, in Branell. He had issue by her, John Tregarthyn, Esq. and two daughters; Margaret, the eldest, married to Richard Whiteleigh, of Efford, in Devon, Esq. Sheriff of that county 16th Henry VII.; from whose two daughters and heirs the Grenvilles of Stowe, and the Halses late of Efford aforesaid, and Fentongallan, in Cornwall, are lineally descended. Catherine, the second daughter of Thomas Tregarthyn, was married to John Carmenow, of Fentongollan, Esq. Sheriff of Cornwall 5th Henry VIII. whose posterity are extinct.

John Tregarthyn, Esq. aforesaid, son of Thomas, married Jane, daughter of Thomas Trethyrfe, Esq. and had issue by her four daughters that became his heirs; Mary married to Degory Grenvill, of Penheale, Esq.; Jane to Tripcony, who passed those lands to Richard Trevanion, Esq. (ancestor to Richard Trevanion, now in possession of this place); Margaret, married to George Tanner, of Cullumbton, Esq. to whose share and partage the manor of Court and Branell, in St. Stephen's, fell; Joan married to John Kellaway, of Egge, in Devon, Esq.; after his death to Wadham of Merryfield, in Somerset, as appears from her tombstone in Branscombe church, Devonshire, where is to be read and seen those words:

"Here lyeth the body of a virtuous and ancient gentlewoman, descended of the ancient house of the Plantagenets, some time of Cornwall, namely, Joan, one of the daughters and coheirs of John Tregarthin, of Tregarthyn, Esq.; she was first married to John Kellaway, Esq. who had by her much issue. After his death she was married to John Wadham, of Meryfield, in the county of Somerset, Esq. by whom she had children. She lived a virtuous and godly life, and died in an honourable age, in the year of our Lord 1581." Now because this dark phrase, "descended of the house of the Plantagenets," needs a clavis to unlock it, let the reader view the history of St. Stephen's in Branell, and St. Stephen's by Saltash, and he shall find one that will do it effectually. The arms of Tregarthin, whose name and whole family is now extinct, were, Argent, a chevron between three escallops Sable.

The present possessor of this barton is Richard Trevanion, Esq. that married Bond, of Earth; who had issue by her one only daughter, married to Peter Major, of Foye, merchant, now in possession thereof, whose names are the same as the Trevanions of Caryhayes.

Trewoola, Tre-wolla, or Tre-wole, gave name and origin to an old family of gentlemen surnamed de Trewolla; who, in allusion to their names, gave for their arms, Sable, three owls. This estate, in the latter end of the reign of

Charles II. was sold to Charles Trevanion, of Cary-Hayes, Esq. for 900*l.* by John Trewolla, gentleman, attorney-at-law, which was the last parcel of land Trewolla had to sell of a considerable estate elsewhere, formerly sold by his ancestors; and this place was so depressed with mortgages, statutes, and judgments, that the whole consideration-money fell much short of paying his creditors, and the incumbrances that were upon it; so that, in order to make a clear title to the purchaser, several of Trewolla's creditors came to a loss, and in particular, James Hals, of Merthyr, Gent. and Martha his wife, who had a statute staple for 700*l.* on those lands, who, to comply with Trewolla's bad circumstances, on Mr. Trevanion's paying them 250*l.* he and his wife levied a fine thereon, and executed a deed, then declaring the uses thereof to be for the only use of the said Charles Trevanion, Esq. his heirs and assigns for ever.

In this parish, at   , was the dwelling of my very kind friend Dr. James Gibbs, third son of James Gibbs, Vicar of this parish, who had his education in Exeter College, as a servitor to his kinsman Mr. Davis, son to Dr. Davis late of Plymouth; where, after he had taken his Bachelor's degree, he declared for the study of physic in Oxford; and soon after, to better his study and experience, went with the said Mr. Davis into France, and fixed at Montpelier, where he practised physic (and also surgery in an hospital, as himself informed me) for several years; afterwards in the College of Physicians there took his degree of Doctor of that science; and, lastly, returned to this place, where he practised physic with admirable care, skill, and success, and through multitudes of patients and moderate fees, hath purchased a considerable estate. Since the writing hereof this gentleman, to the great grief and loss of his country, departed this life of the hemorrhoides sickness; and before his death (who for many years had been his patient, to the great benefit of my health, by God's blessing, after the endeavours of all other physicians proved ineffectual,) left me this legacy,—that if I myself or friends were sick, and had occasion to make use of physic, that we should in all distempers make use only of the common, plain, and natural remedies.

Anthony Wills, of this parish, Gent. farmer of the sheaf thereof, having by misfortune much incumbered his estate with debts, quitted the same at such time as the Prince of Orange landed with his forces at Torbay, and presented himself and his six or seven sons to that Prince, for soldiers of war in his army; which proposal was graciously accepted; and they were all posted as officers of command in his bands, or troops. And after the Coronation of this Prince, King William III. they followed him in all his Flanders and Irish wars against King James II. and King Lewis XIV. and discharged their trusts with such great care, faithfulness, valour, and conduct, that (as I am informed,) before their deaths they all arrived to the dignities of Captains, and some of them to the authority or commands of Majors, Colonels, and one of them to become a standing Major-General of the field. Who afterwards, about the year A.D. 1714, being made principal commander of the army and troops of horse of King George the First, against the Pretender's (James Henry Edward Stewart,) army at Preston, in Lancashire, where, after a furious, violent, and bloody battle with them, he obtained the victory over that pretended Prince's forces; for which fact, and other noble deeds, he was created a Baronet of England, and is since made General of all the land forces in England next the King, his salary amounting to 7000*l.* per annum, as reported.

TONKIN.

For the name, I take it to be a contraction of St. Gordian, pronounced in Cornwall St. Gorian, who having been, like St. Paul, a violent prosecutor of the Christians, became a proportionably zealous convert, and was beheaded at Rome in the year 341.

GORAN.

A tradition in the parish, nevertheless, assigns the guardianship of this church to St. Gorien, or Coren, one of the missionaries from Ireland who accompanied St. Perran.

The name of Trevennen, or Tremenen, probably the town of birth, in reference to its fertility, belonged to the Priory of Tywardrith, and formed a part of the lands given by Henry VIII. to the Duchy in exchange for the manor of Wallingford.

Adjoining to Trevennen, and within the manor, is Trevasens, which was long the seat of a family of the same name, but passed to the Hoblyns of Nanswydan, in St. Columb, through an heiress.

Polgorror was heretofore a country residence of the Provost of Glasnith College, at Penryn, to which the great tithes were impropriated. This place, with the great tithes and the advowson of the vicarage, now belong to the bishopric of Exeter.

Adjoining to this is Treveor, the great town, or dwelling, formerly the seat of Treveors; and the parishioners still talk of Sir Henry Treveor, who lived here; and a part of his house is yet standing.

Pennore, or Penarth. I take nore to signify the same as in Saxon, a promontory; and that it is here applied to a point jutting out into the sea, namely, to the Dead-man, which is separated from the village by a double intrenchment, yet pretty entire, running from cliff to cliff, and cutting off about an hundred acres of coarse ground. The intrenchment is about twenty feet broad and twenty-four feet high in most places; but the outer wall is the least high. The people call it Thica Vosa, which is the Vallum, and the Hack and Cast, fabling it to be the work of a giant, who performed the whole in one night. They show also a hole in the cliff which opens into a hollow below, formed by the sea; and the people relate that this giant growing unwell, applied to a physician, who, that he might rid the world of such a monster, bled him near this spot, and recommended him to let the blood flow into this hole till it became full. The giant did so, and bled himself to death, when his body fell over on a rock, still called the giant's house. The hole thus attempted to be filled with blood is denominated from the immense quantity of ivy growing round it.

The church is placed very conveniently in the middle of the parish. It is well built, with a handsome square tower of hewn moor stone, with four tunable bells; and by reason of its high situation this church is seen from a great distance. It consists of a large lofty nave, one south aile of the same length, and two cross ailes to the north, of which one is but small. In the chancel, near the north wall, before the communion table, is a plain marble stone, on which are seen the hollows where the figure of a woman kneeling, with arms, inscription, &c. must have been inlaid. Tradition calls it the tomb of Lady Brannell, but who this Lady Brannell was is unknown, although some conjectures are formed of her belonging to the family of Tregarthen.

Against the eastern wall, by the window, is a comely monument of black marble, to Richard Edgecombe, of Bodrigan, Esq. son of Sir Richard Edgecombe, of Mount Edgecombe, Knight, who died Nov. 5, 1755.

THE EDITOR.

The manor of Trevascus belongs by purchase to Mr. Slade Gulby, who resides on the barton of Trevenion, which has been in his family since the time of the Tudors.

Treveor belonged to the late Rev. Dr. Wynne, and was given by him to Mr. Pendarves. On this barton may be seen one of those round entrenchments usually denominated castles in the West of England. It is at least doubtful in most cases whether any permanent dwelling was ever connected with them.

The barton of Bodrigan has descended in the family of Edgecombe since the time of Henry VII.

It is generally apprehended that Sir Henry Bodrigan was present at the battle of Bosworth Field; and that, having escaped from thence to Cornwall, he endeavoured to defend his property in a private house against Edgecombe and Trevenion, who, in despoiling and endeavouring to take his life, did no more than he would have done, had the fortune of arms inclined the other way; or than what he actually did against Sir Richard Edgecombe a few years before at Cotehele. Such are the effects of civil wars, when—

> Lance to lance, and horse to horse!
> Long years of havoc urge their destined course,
> And through the kindred squadrons mow their way.

Bodrugon's property was mainly divided between Edgecumbe and Trevanion, who are also believed to have fought against King Richard in Bosworth Field, and then to have attacked Sir Richard Bodrugon near his own house after the defeat at that place. He effected his retreat to a vessel by the extraordinary effort already mentioned, and left the shores of England never to return. He had a brother settled in the north of Devon, but his line became soon extinct.

Goran measures 4,596 statute acres.

	£.	s.	d.
Annual value of the Real Property, as returned to Parliament in 1815	3487	0	0
Poor Rate in 1831	950	0	0

Population, —	in 1801, 1009	in 1811, 1116	in 1821, 1203	in 1831, 1205

giving an increase of somewhat less than $19\frac{1}{2}$ per cent. in 30 years.

Present Vicar, the Rev. David Jenkins, collated by the Bishop of Exeter in 1824.

GEOLOGY, BY DR. BOASE.

This parish forms a continuation of the calcareous series of St. Ewe. At the Deadman point the rock is for the most part siliceous, affording an example of the quartz rock of Dr. Macculloch.

GRADE.

HALS.

Is situate in the hundred of Kerryer, and has upon the north Ruan Major, west Mullyan, east Ruan Minor, south Landawidnick. At the time of the Norman conquest this district was taxed under the jurisdiction of Lisart.

In the taxation of benefices in Cornwall, towards the Pope's annats, made by the Bishops of Lincoln and Winchester, 1294, Ecclesia Sancti Grade in decanatu de Kerryer, was valued lxs. in Wolsey's Inquisition, 1521, 11*l*. 1s. 5d. The patronage in the Bishop of Exeter; the incumbent Symons; and the parish rated to the 4s. per pound Land Tax, 1696, 58*l*. 12s.

TONKIN.

This parish takes its name from its titular female saint, St. Grada. In the taxation of 1294, in the 20th year of Edward I. it is valued by the name of Ecclesia Sanctæ Gradæ.

THE EDITOR.

The etymologies offered by Mr. Hals appear so very improbable that they are omitted. If any such person as St. Grade ever existed, she must have been among the tribe of early missionaries, of whom no traces are left except that of their names being affixed to churches.

This parish has within its limits the manor and barton of Erisey, the seat of a very respectable family bearing the same name, who gave for their arms, Sable, a chevron between three griffins segreant Or. The name has been extinct above a century, and the barton belongs by purchase to Lord Falmouth. Several monuments of different members of the family remain in the church.

The advowson of the living belongs by purchase to Mr. Rogers, of Penrose. The parish feast is kept on the nearest Sunday to St. Luke's day. The family of Lord Wodehouse, through his marriage with Sophia Berkeley, niece of Lord Berkeley, of Stratton, are supposed to represent the Eriseys.

This parish measures 2,005 statute acres.

	£.	s.	d.
Annual value of the Real Property, as returned to Parliament in 1815	1357	0	0
Poor Rate in 1831	208	2	0

Population,—
in 1801,	in 1811,	in 1821,	in 1831.
320	306	355	306

giving a decrease of nearly 4¼ per cent. in 30 years; but with unusual anomalies in intermediate enumerations.

Present Rector, the Rev. John Peter, instituted in 1818.

GEOLOGY, BY DR. BOASE.

The portion of this parish around the church, and the various insulated portions, are situated on magnesian rocks; the most abundant variety of which is serpentine. This rock is generally of a red colour, but this is evidently in some cases derived from a partial chemical change. In its perfect state this serpentine is generally of a dark-green, with shining scales of diallage, which are commonly of a bronze colour, and at other times of a fine green. The serpentine at Cadgwith may be seen to pass gradually into a schistose rock of a dark bottle-green, and very glassy and spangled on the surface of its lamellæ. This slate is generally called greenstone, but it differs therefrom, and consequently requires a distinct appellation. At Cagar there is a quarry in the serpentine; and at Kennick Cove adjoining, many varieties of these rocks may be obtained.

GULVAL.

HALS.

Is situate in the hundred of Penwith, and hath upon the north Ludgvan, south the Mount's Bay, west Maddaran, east St. Hilary.

In the time of William the Conqueror's survey of lands, anno Dom. 1087, this parish, I suppose, passed in tax under the jurisdiction of Ludgvan. In the Inquisition and Taxation of Benefices in Cornwall, by the Bishops of Lincoln and Winchester, 1294, Ecclesia de Laneseley, in decanatu de Penwith, appropriata priori Sancti Germani, is valued lxvis. viiid. Vicar ibidem, xxs. At which time it seems it was but a Vicarage church; the garb impropriated, though since restored. Neither was the name of Gulval then mentioned. However, in Wolsey's Inquisition, 1521, it is rated by the name of Gulval, also Laneseley, 6l. 11s. 0¼d. The patronage was formerly in the Prior of St. German's, now in the crown. The incumbent Penhellick; and the parish rated to the 4s. per pound Land Tax, 1696, by the name of Gulval, 120l.

This manor of Laneseley, in this parish, was, in the time of Richard I. and King John, the lands of the family surnamed De Als, now Hals, so called from the barton and dismantled manor of Als, now Alse and Alesa, in Buryan, as tradition saith, or Beer Alseton, Alston, in Devon, in possession of Trevanion and others, whereof they were lords; and in particular William de Als, in the beginning of the reign of King Henry III. that married Mary, the daughter of Francis de Bray, was possessed thereof; father of Simon de Alls, who lived at Halsham, in Yorkshire (from him denominated), that married Jane, daughter of Thomas de Campo Arnulpho (now Champernown), Sheriff of York second, third, sixth, and seventh years of King Henry III. Anno Dom. 1222, as appears from the catalogue of those Sheriffs, and the Hals's allowed pedigree, 1483; from which also it is manifest, by an authentic deed or record therein, yet legible, that the said Simon for the health and salvation of his soul, his wife's, his ancestors, and other relations, gave the said manor of Laneseley to the Prior of St. German's, his canonical brothers, and their successors for ever, in these words.

In nomine Domini, &c. Ego Simon de Als, pro salute animæ meæ, et Janæ uxoris meæ, et parentum meorum, dono et concedo manerium de Laneseley, in comitatu Cornubiæ, Priori Sancti Germani, et fratribus canonicis, et successoribus eorum, cum dominicis redditibus, &c. et omnibus ibidem appendentibus, terra, sylva, pratos, et aquam, &c. ut habeant, teneant, et possideant in perpetuum, &c.; dat vicesimo sexto die Augusti, anno regni nostri Regis Henrici tertii post conquestum octavo. Hiis testibus, Thoma de Tracye, Henrico de la Pombre, Reginaldo de Valtorta, Roberto de Cheni, Radolpho de Esse. This grant, or donation, was in the year 1266. (See Lelant.)

By virtue whereof the Prior of St. German's and his successors were possessed of this manor from that time till the 26th Henry VIII. 1536, when that Priory was dissolved, and the lands thereof vested in the crown. At which time King Henry VIII. gave the lands thereof to Champernown, Beaumont, Barry, and others; and to Beaumont's and Barry's share fell this manor of Laneseley; who parted with it either by purchase or in marriage with his daughter, to John Tripcony, about the year 1565; whose son, John Tripcony, having by riot and excess comparatively wasted his paternal estate, mortgaged this manor of Laneseley to Sir Nicholas Hals, of Fentongollan, knight, about the year 1620, who was lineally descended from Simon de Als, aforesaid, and died seised thereof about the year 1637. After his decease his unthrifty son and heir, John Hals, became possessed thereof, who assigned the mortgage thereof for 500*l.* to one Mr. Downes, A.D.

1655; and soon after, having spent his whole paternal estate elsewhere, went beyond the seas, and was never since heard of to this day; leaving issue, by Jane Arundel his wife, Major Thomas Hals, of Hals's Savana, in Clarendon parish and province, in Jamaica, who had issue Thomas Hals, Esq his son and heir.

After the departure of the said John Hals beyond the seas, the said Mr. Downes assigned over the mortgage of the premises to one Mr. Collwell, a scrivener of London; who dying soon after, his son, Thomas Collwell, became seised thereof; and after his death his widow, who by her last will and testament (as executrix of her said husband,) conveyed the said manor to Charles Bonython, Esq.—Spur, Longeville, and others, in trust, now in possession thereof, 1700; before which time, between the said Downes and Collwell, on pretence of the equity of redemption reserved in Downes, John Hals being beyond the seas, and that the mortgage money to Collwell was satisfied out of the profits of these lands; and a cross bill of Collwell's against Downes, alleging the contrary, and to foreclose him; happened so many tedious and costly Chancery suits as comparatively undid them both. But, maugre all their endeavours, the old titles of Tripcony and Hals were foreclosed by a decree in Chancery, betwixt Downes and Collwell, in Hillary term 1689, yet extant and to be seen.

This manor of Laneseley, for goodness of land, jurisdiction, court leet, fishing craft, and royalties over all that part of the sea of the Mount's Bay, between Longbridge and Chiandower, near Penzance, may equal, if not surpass, any other manor in those parts of its value, which is now scarcely worth 300*l*. per annum, though in former ages it was of far larger extent; for in the survey of Cornish acres, tempore Edward II. (Carew's Survey of Cornwall, p 46, p. 131, of Lord Dunstanville's edition), it was numbered in the Exchequer to contain twenty-eight acres, that is, about six thousand statute acres;* every ancient Cornish acre being

---

* Surely sixteen or seventeen hundred. ED.

sixty statute acres of land; the contents of the whole now not exceeding a thousand statute acres, which lies in Gulval and Ludgvan.

In Fosses Moor, part of this manor of Lanesely, in this parish, is that well-known fountain called Gulval Well. To which place great numbers of people, time out of mind, have resorted for pleasure and profit of their health, as the credulous country people do in these days, not only to drink the waters thereof, but to inquire after the life or death of their absent friends; where, being arrived, they demanded the question at the well, whether such a person, by name, be living, in health, sick, or dead; if the party be living, and in health, the still quiet water of the well-pit, as soon as the question is demanded, will instantly bubble or boil up as a pot, clear christaline water; if sick, foul and puddle waters; if the party be dead, it will neither bubble, boil up, or alter its colour or still motion. However, I can speak nothing of the truth of those supernatural facts from my own sight or experience, but write from the mouths of those who told me they had seen and proved the veracity thereof. Finally, it is a strong and courageous fountain of water, kept neat and clean by an old woman of the vicinity, to accommodate strangers for her own advantage, by blazing the virtues and divine qualities of those waters.

TONKIN.

After copying from Hals, Mr. Tonkin adds of Lanistley manor :—It extendeth throughout the parish of Gulval from the Moreps to the Gundrons; that is to say, from above the sea to the Down Hills; it extendeth also through a part of the parish of Ludgvan.

At Kenneggy is the dwelling, by lease (the fee being in his elder brother, William Harris, of Hayne, Esq.), of Christopher Harris, Gentleman, an attorney-at-law, who married a daughter of John Foote, of Truro, Esq. His elder brother, who married the daughter of John St. Aubyn, Esq. of Clowance, in the parish of Crowan, is now in possession of Hayne, near Lifton, in Devonshire, having succeeded to it on the decease of Sir Arthur Harris, jun. the last heir male of the elder branch. On removing to Hayne he leased Kenneggy to his younger brother aforesaid; who, by reason of the elder brother's yet want of issue, is likely to become his heir. The arms of Harris are, Sable, within a bordure three crescents Argent.

Mr. Edward Llwyd, in his letter to me, would have this parish to take its name from the inscription on the stone in Maddern parish, " Riolabran : Cunoval : Fil : " and that Cunoval is turned by corruption into Guloval, for that he found many such instances in Wales.

I should be glad to agree with so great a critic, but since there is a saint, or bishop, whose name comes very near to this—St. Gunwall, whose memory the church celebrates on the 6th of June, I cannot forbear fancying, especially the humour of the country being considered, that he is the patron and the namer of this parish.

THE EDITOR.

There cannot be any reasonable doubt of St. Gunwall having bestowed his name on this parish, more especially when the prophetic well is taken into account, since saints scarcely ever failed of imparting some supernatural quality to their favourite streams.

St. Gunwall was, moreover, a Briton, and is stated to have been in Cornwall.

Saint Gudwall, or Gunwall, was born in Wales about the year 500. Being entirely devoted to God, he collected eighty-eight monks in a little island called Plecit, being no more than a rock surrounded by water. For some reason, however, he abandoned this establishment, and passed by sea into Cornwall; and from thence he went into Devonshire, where he betook himself to the most holy, perfect, and useful state of a solitary anchorite; at length, however, again emerging, he sailed into Britany, and there succeeded St. Malo, as Bishop of that see, although he is said even then to have dwelt in a solitary cell, and to have died there at a very advanced age. His relics have been widely distributed, and various places in France have been called by his name.

Mr. Whitaker explains the ancient name of this parish, Lanisley, by Lan and Ishei, low, or lower, the low church, which appears to agree very well with the situation.

The great tithes certainly belonged to the Priory at St. German's, for in the returns made to Henry VIII. of the property belonging to them, appears—

Gulval, decimæ Garbarum, £10. 6s. 8d.

These tithes, since the law-suits mentioned by Mr. Hals, have passed by purchase into the possession of the Beauchamps of Gwenap, and now belong to the two daughters and coheiresses of the late Mr. John Beauchamp.

The vicarage, although it has risen into one of the most valuable to be found in that district, in consequence of modern improvements, and of its being situated near Penzance, is yet rated under twenty pounds a-year in the King's Books, and therefore passes by the presentation of the Lord Chancellor. Two Mr. Pennerks, father and son, held this living in succession. It was then given, in 1789, to Mr. John Cole, afterwards Doctor in divinity and Rector of Exeter College, and his successor is the present Vicar, the Rev. Robert Dillon.

Kenegie passed from Mr. William Harris, of Hayne, accordingly as Mr. Tonkin had conjectured, to the family of his brother, Mr. Christopher Harris; and the family becoming extinct in the male line by the death of this gentleman's grandson in 1775, by much the largest part of the estate went, under the provisions of a will, to Mr. William Arundell, then resident at Crane, in Camborne, who assumed the name of Harris; but his grandson choosing to fix his permanent residence at a very handsome seat of his own creating near Lifton, parted with all his Cornish property; and Kenegie now belongs, in fee, to the farmer, who had occupied it at an annual rent. This place having formerly belonged to the family of ——— Tripcony, who bore for their arms, Argent, three rabbits passant Sable, and kynin and kyninger being the Cornish names for a rabbit, I cannot but suspect that kynneggy, or kenegie, must have some relation to the name of Tripeney.

Trevailer is the place next of importance in this parish. It has been long the residence of a very respectable family, the Veales. They are said to have come from Gloucestershire, their ancestor having been the first Protestant Vicar of Gulval. The Reverend William Veale, the present possessor, has rebuilt the house; the second brother of his grandfather, Mr. George Veale, made a large fortune at Penzance, by the practice of the law and by success in mines, which became divided between three daughters who married Hichens, Baines, and Jenkins. Mr. William Veale has married the only daughter of the Rev. Richard Gerveys Grylls, of Helston.

But the most beautiful place in this parish, and one of the greatest ornaments to the whole neighbourhood, is Rosemorron, the Vale of Blackberries, formed by Mr. George John. This gentleman having married Jane, the eldest daughter of Mr. Arundall, who assumed the name of Harris on succeeding to the large fortune of that family, and having been for many years at the head of his profession in Penzance, has at length retired to this delightful spot in the summer months. Nor have his decorations of the country been confined to one situation; he has shewn, by extensive plantations at Try, that the most elevated and barren tracts, even on a granite soil, may be rendered useful and decorative by the growth of trees.

The lower part of the parish, adjoining to the sea, is fertile in the highest degree, from the village of Chiandower (the house by the water), through Pendrea to the Church Town. And the vallies, abounding in trees, rival those of any country. Chiandower is also become a place worthy of the adjacent scenery, through the taste and the exertions of Messrs. Bolitho, who, in making ample fortunes, have benefited the country still more than themselves by promoting every species of productive industry. The parish feast does not certainly corroborate the supposition of the patron saint; it is held on the nearest Sunday to the 12th of November, the day of St. Martin, the first Pope of that name, a native of Todi, in Tuscany, and elected Pope in the year 649. He assembled in the same year the sixth council of Lateran, where the heresy of the Monothelites was condemned; but the schismatic Emperor, Constans, sent Olympius, his chamberlain, to Rome, to support the obnoxious sect, who arrived there while the council were deliberating; and failing in his attempts to divert them from supporting the orthodox faith, he suborned a person to murder the Pope, but in attempting to execute the atrocious deed the assassin was miraculously struck blind. Yet, nevertheless, Constans persevered in his speculative errors and in his wicked conduct, by causing St. Martin to be seized, and after suffering many casualties, to be banished to the Tauric Chersonesus, where he died in 655.

His relics were afterwards brought to Rome, and deposited in the church of St. Martin of Tours, on the 12th of November, which, from thenceforward, was observed as a festival to his honour.

The day of St. Martin of Tours, the popular patron of beggars, happens to be on the day before, and several parishes give their feasts on the nearest Sunday to November the 11th, but Gulval alone honours the Pope and Saint.

Gulval measures 3950 statute acres.

	£.	s.	d.
Annual value of the Real Property, as returned to Parliament in 1815	5170	0	0
Poor Rate in 1831	406	8	0

Population,— { in 1801, | in 1811, | in 1821, | in 1831,
                 1076 | 1224 | 1353 | 1467
giving an increase of nearly 36½ per cent. in 30 years.

GEOLOGY, BY DR. BOASE.

The northern part of this parish rests on granite, which is for the most part a coarse crystalline rock, containing very large porphyritic crystals of felspar. The granite is, however, in some places very fine-grained, and near its juncture with the slate abounds in shorl. The schistose rocks composing the southern part of the parish, have a basis of compact felspar, assuming various appearances according as it is more or less siliceous; those rocks are often beautifully marked with crystalline patches and veins of actynolite, as may be seen in the rocks on the sea shore, and they are traversed here and there by beds of felspar porphyry, into which they gradually pass.

GUNWALLO.

HALS.

Is situate in the hundred of Kerryer, and hath upon the north the Loopoole and part of Mawgan, east Cury, south Mullyan, west the British Channel, or Ocean.

At the time of the Norman Conquest this district was taxed either under the jurisdiction of Lisart, now Lisard, or Trevery. In the value of Benefices towards the Pope's Annates made by the Bishops of Lincoln and Winchester, 1294, Ecclesia Sancti Winwalli, i. e. the church of the holy, victorious, or conquering Wallo, in decanatu de Kerryer, was rated iiii*l.* iii*s.* iiii*d.* In Wolsey's Inquisition, 1521, it goes in value and consolidation with Breock, Germo, and Cury, by the name of the Vicarage of Wynnanton, i. e. the conquering, or victorious town; all doubtless referring to the conquests of King Gunwallo, or Dun-

GUNWALLO. 127

wallo. The patronage, I take it, was formerly in the Prior of St. Michael's Mount, or the Duke of Cornwall, who endowed it. It is now in the King, or Duke; the incumbent Trewinard, and parish rated to the 4s. per pound Land Tax, 1696, temp. William III. 53l. 9s. 8d. by the name of Gunwallo.

The manor of Gunwallowinton, a lordship in this parish, claimeth the royalty and jurisdiction, by sea and land, over the whole parish, and was formerly the lands of Carmenow, now of Arundell of Lanhearne, by match with one of the daughters and heirs of that name.

TONKIN.

In this parish stands a circle of rude unwrought stones in the shape of a wall heaped together, and called Earth.

THE EDITOR.

Mr. Whitaker remarks in a note on Hal's MS. that the name of this parish is clearly derived from its patron saint, Winnwallo.

I find that Winwallo was the son of a petty Prince in Wales; who, flying with his family from the Saxons, went into Britany, where he acquired the habit of undergoing monastic austerities under the guidance of St. Budock. He ultimately founded a monastery called Landevenech, about three miles from Brest. He became the first Abbat, and died on the 3d of March about the year 529. His body was buried at Landevenech; but in after ages, when the northmen extended their ravages to this part of the Continent, his relics were removed to places of greater safety; and as an effectual security against an entire loss, portions were preserved at St. Peter's, at Blandinberg, at Ghent, at Montreuil, and at other places.

The Celtic name has given origin to various pronunciations, and to as many corresponding orthographies; the G and W at the beginning of words are well known to take each the place of the other almost without discrimination. In Picardy, where he is esteemed the patron, Winwallo is changed into Vignevaley and Walovay; in Britany into Guignole and Vennole; in other parts of France into Guingalois.

It is the more probable that St. Winwallo may be the patron saint of this parish, and that he may have given it his name, since a parish in the neighbourhood stands in that relation towards his teacher St. Budock. The parish feast, however, is held on the last Sunday in April, although St. Winwallo is honoured in the Roman calendar on the third of March.

Mr. Lysons says that the manor of Wynyaton, or Winington, called by Mr. Hals Gonwallowinton, was given about the year 1235, by Roger Earl of Cornwall, in exchange for Bossiney, to Gervase de Harnington; from whom it passed by an heiress to the family of Trevanthians, and again in the same way to Roskymers. It ultimately belonged to the Arundells till the general sale of all Lord Arundell's property in Cornwall, when this manor was purchased by Mr. John Rogers, of Penrose, near Helston.

The church is situated among sandbanks, and very near the sea. In those banks Captain Avery, the celebrated buccaneer, is reported to have buried several chests of treasure previously to his leaving England on the voyage from which he never returned. So strongly has this opinion prevailed, that Mr. John Knill, collector of the customs at St. Ives, procured, about the year 1770, a grant of treasure trove, and expended some money in a fruitless search.

This gentleman is still remembered on account of his singularities, and his having erected a pyramid on a hill near the town where he had long resided.

In the churchyard of Gunwallo is a tombstone with the following conceit:

> We shall die all,
> Shall die all we,
> Die all we shall,
> All we shall die.

GWENAP.

The parish measures 1175 statute acres.

	£.	s.	d.
Annual value of the Real Property as returned to Parliament in 1815	1,405	0	0
Poor Rate in 1831	150	14	0

Population, — { in 1801, | in 1811, | in 1821, | in 1831,
216 | 206 | 252 | 284

giving an increase of $31\frac{1}{2}$ per cent. in 30 years.

GEOLOGY, BY DR. BOASE.

This parish runs parallel with the sea shore from Poljew Cove to Loo Bar. The shore, where the land lies low, is covered with banks of siliceous sand, which near the church form an extensive down. At the Cove the rocks consist of a blue glassy slate, and of a compost rock of the same colour which decomposes into a white clay. Nearly the whole of the cliff is a diluvial mass; the lower part of which, just above high-water mark, is consolidated into a conglomerate sandstone, apparently through the cementing medium of a solution of carbonate of iron, derived from the percolation of rain-water through the bed of ferruginous clay that forms the upper part of this deposit.

GWENAP.

HALS.

Is situate in the hundred of Keryer, and hath upon the north, part of Redruth, east Peranwell and Key, south Gluvius, west Stithians. That this church was extant before the Norman Conquest is plain from the name thereof, for in the Domesday Tax, 20th William I. 1087, it is rated by the name of Gwenap. In the Inquisition into the value of Cornish Benefices made by the Bishops of Lincoln and Winchester, 1294, Ecclesia Sancti Wenap in decanatu de Kerrier, is rated at vii*l*. Vicar ejusdem xxvi*s*. viii*d*. In Wolsey's Inquisition, 1521, the Vicarage of Wenap is valued 16*l*. 18*s*. 9*d*. The patronage in the Bishop of Exeter, who endowed it. The incumbent Bishop; and the parish rated to the 4*s*. per pound Land Tax, 1696, 148*l*. 3*s*. by the name of Gwenap. The garb, or rectory, in Wright or Nicholls.

Trefyns (i. e. the springs of water, or fountains town,) came to Beauchamp by marriage with the heiress of this name and land, where they have ever since flourished in gentle degree. The present possessor, William Beauchamp, Esq. that married Courtney of Trehane, his father Boaden, his grandfather Tregoze, giveth for his arms, Vairy Argent and Azure. The first progenitor of the tribe and name of Beauchamp came into England a soldier under William the Conqueror, and probably some of his posterity were planted in this province, from whence those gentlemen are descended; especially if the name, Stephen de Bellocampo, 40th Henry III. who held in Cornwall by tenure of knight's service 15*l*. per annum land and rents, may be interpreted the same as Beauchamp (Carew's Survey of Cornwall, p. 40), for otherwise verily I know not from what family of gentlemen those Beauchamps are descended; since none other of that name give the same arms as these do; for Guy de Beauchamp, Sheriff of Devon, 12th King John, gave for his arms, Gules, a fess between three crosses bottony Or; from whom are descended the Beauchamps of Bletsho and Hatch, in Wiltshire. Beauchamp Earl of Warwick gave for his arms, Gules, a fess between six cross-crosslets Or. William Beauchamp, Sheriff of Devon 18th Henry VI. that married the inheritrix of Henry de Ties, lord of Alverton and Tywarnhayle, summoned to Parliament as a Baron temp. Henry IV. gave for his arms, Gules, a fess between six martlets Or; from whence I gather there were diverse families of those Beauchamps heretofore in England, no way related in blood to each other. Query, whether the arms of those gentlemen living in this place be not the arms of Bochym, as I have been informed they are, which is Vaire Argent and Azure.

Notwithstanding this place of Trefyns was heretofore denominated from springs of water abounding there in winter season, yet I assure you now in summer time, by reason of the tin-mines and subterranean adits near it that carry those springs of water invisibly under ground, water is very scarce and much wanting in those lands. It is also called Trevense, and Trewince.

St. Dye chapel in this parish was heretofore a chapel of ease to Gwenap; the tutelar guardian whereof is St. Dye, of Gaul, very famous in that country for his piety and holy Christian living about the fifth century, who held the faith in opposition to Arianism and Pelagianism, then raging in the church. And there is a church in the province of Lorraine still bearing his name. If it were as easy for the Vicar to attend and perform divine service in this remote quarter of the parish where this chapel is, as it is convenient to his parishioners in the town of St. Dye, it had been doubtless still applied to the end and use for which it was erected.

Not far from this place is that unparalleled and inexhaustible tin-work called Paldys; i. e. the top or head of St. Dye's Town, which for above forty years' space hath employed yearly from eight hundred to a thousand men and boys, labouring for and searching after tin in that place, where they have produced and raised up for that time yearly, at least twenty thousand pounds worth of that commodity, to the great enriching of the lords of the soil, the bound owners, and adventurers in those lands.

Of those miners, or searchers for metals, hath Ovid written elegantly in Latin verse, which sounds thus in English, tempore Augusti:—

> Men deep descend into the earth
> With mattock, shoul, and spade,
> And wicked wealth is digged up,
> Which mischiefs all hath made,

> Dame Nature did it hide and put
> Where gristly ghosts do dwell;
> So that the hurtful iron and
> The glittering gold from hell
> Produced is, more noisome than
> The other metal vile,
> Through foul desire whereof for aye
> Is virtue in exile.
> Shame, truth, and faith, are put to flight;
> Their place do those uphold,
> Both fraud, deceit, fell force, and wiles,
> And wicked love of gold,
> For which the laws are sold.
> *Metamorph.* Lib. i. p. 138—150.

MEMORANDUM.—On Friday, 19th September, 1707, about four of the clock in the afternoon, happened in those parts divers flashes of lightning and cracks of thunder, which not only terrified the inhabitants thereof, but after one of those cracks a ball of fire, or Jupiter's thunderbolt (as the Greeks called it), entered by the window into the house of one John Kent, a carpenter of this parish, where he was working, the windy force thereof instantly struck him dead on the place, scalded his wife and two children in that room, then passed out through the chimney wall, and so shattered the same that a great part of it instantly fell to the ground.

TONKINS.

In this parish, on the top of a lofty mountain called Carne-mark, are two or three stone tumuli, under which are doubtless interred the bodies of some distinguished persons.

The right name of this parish is St. Wenep, a female saint, to whom the parish is dedicated.

THE EDITOR.

Saint Wenep is, I believe, only remembered by the dedication of this parish; but St. Dye is a personage o' more consequence. He was a native of France, and in the year 655 became Bishop of Nevres; but St. Dye happened to live at a period when the prevalent fanaticism induced persons to believe that the Author of all good was most gratified by beholding the misery of his rational creatures, accompanied by their voluntary debasements through ignorance and solitude below the level of the brute creation. With this persuasion, St. Dye resigned his bishopric, and founded a house for monks at a place called Jointures, but retired himself to an anchorite cell. He is said to have died on the 19th of June, 680.

The chapel, dedicated to St. Dye, in Gwenap, had long been in ruins; but since the eager contest has grown up between the Establishment and Dissenters for retaining or acquiring power through the media of extensive education and proselytism, and Chapels, Meeting Houses, and Schools have arisen all over England, St. Dye has seen a new and spacious building displace the ruins that remained from former times.

The Beauchamps had removed from Trewince to Pengreap; where the family became extinct in the male line about the year 1818, by the decease of Mr. Joseph Beauchamp, who had lost his only son a few years before, and the estate is now divided between the two daughters of his elder brother, Mr. John Beauchamp.

Cornmarth has been already mentioned. Mr. Whitaker says that the true name is Cornmarke, and that it means the Knight's barrow.

On the southern declivity of Cornmarth is a large excavation, supposed by some to have been made long ago for the exhibition of games, but by others to owe its general form to the accidental running together of an old mine. It is, at all events, admirably adapted to the purpose of enabling a speaker to address an extremely large assembly; and the late Mr. John Wesley has been distinctly heard by many thousands at a time in Gwenap pit.

Scornier, which a few years since exhibited the appearance of a small village, has now become perhaps the chief place in this parish. Mr. John Williams, one of the most extensive and most successful managers and adventurous miners of the present time, built here an excellent house, and adorned it with the finest collection of Cornish minerals ever brought together. Mr. Williams, after making a large fortune, has retired at an advanced age, leaving several sons engaged in the same pursuits with equal advantage to themselves and to the public; one of whom has added a second splendid house to the village.

It is quite impossible for me to enter fully into a description of the mines, which have continued in work on the most extensive scale from the period when Mr. Leman commenced the modern system up to the present time. It is said that no district of the same extent in any part of the world ever produced so much riches.

Poldice was worked for tin about the commencement of the last century by Mr. Hearle, of Penryn. The mine happened to have very little water, and this was exhausted by rack and chain pumps moved by human labour.

Copper seldom appears near the surface, as is the case with tin; but tin lodes out of granite frequently produce copper in depth. All the lodes in Gwenap have done so, and in some places the mines have gone to the depth of two hundred and thirty or forty fathoms from the surface, more than two hundred fathoms under the level of the sea, assisted by steam engines having working-cylinders ninety inches in diameter and ten feet long.

The freehold of the land containing those mines is possessed in undivided shares between several persons; Mr. Hearle had one-third, that is now divided again into thirds between the descendants of three daughters, Mr. Tremayne, Mr. Rodd, and Mr. Stephens.

The church in Gwenap is large in every dimension, but, what is very unusual, the tower stands apart. One of our late historians very justly complains of what he terms the "mangling of modern Vandalism," in alterations of the church; Venetian frames have been substituted for stone mullions; windows of painted glass bearing the figures of saints have been removed; and the screen, or rood-loft, of beautiful workmanship has disappeared; modern deal seats have been introduced throughout the church, and a glare of light on the white-washed walls has completed the overthrow of very thing venerable.

The interior is divided into a nave, a chancel, and two side ailes, supported on each side by seven handsome columns.

The burial-ground contains a monument of fine marble in memory of the Beauchamps.

There is a tradition in the parish of monks having been established in the church tower, and that a house now converted to an inn, was a part of the building. No notice whatever is taken of such a monastery in any authentic work. If therefore this tradition rests on any fact, the house cannot have been more than an hostelry for friars.

The parish measures 5,289 statute acres.

	£.	s.	d.
Annual value of the Real Property as returned to Parliament in 1815	18,273	0	0
Poor Rate in 1831	3,329	9	0

Population, —	in 1801,	in 1811,	in 1821,	in 1831,
	4594	5303	6294	8539

giving an increase of 86 per cent. in 30 years, and a numerical increase of three thousand nine hundred and forty-five persons.

Present Vicar, the Rev. W. Marsh, presented by the Dean and Chapter of Exeter in 1825.

GEOLOGY, BY DR. BOASE.

Gwenap has long been one of the most important mining districts of Cornwall. Its western part rests on the same patch of granite as the eastern part of Cornborne, the one stretching to the east and the other to the west. The slate is also similar to that of Cornborne, and like that it is traversed by numerous beds of porphyry, some of which, in the vicinity of Burncoose, are of the most beautiful description, containing well-defined crystals of felspar and of quartz.

GWENDRON.

HALS.

Is situate in the hundred of Kerryer, and hath upon the north Camburne, south Maugan in Meneage, east Stithiany, Constantine, west Sithney.

In the taxation of benefices in Cornwall, as aforesaid, 1294, Ecclesia Sancte Wendrone (I suppose together with Helston, its daughter church,) in decanatu de Kerryer, is valued xviil. vis. viiid. In Wolsey's Inquisition, 1521, it is valued, together with Helston, at 26l. 19s. 3d. The patronage formerly, as I am informed, in the Hospital and Prior, or Governor, of St. John the Baptist, at Helston, or the College of regular Canons at Glasnith, or Abbat of St. Michael's Mount; now Jago, and the Incumbent Jago. The rectory, or sheaf, in Boscawen. And the parish rated to the 4s. per pound Land Tax, 1696, 174l. 8s. 4d.

Trenithike, in this parish (i. e. the town of the bridge or ford, leate or lake of waters). It is the dwelling of Sampson Hill, Esq. one of his Majesty's Commissioners for the Peace, that married Callmady, the relict of Silly, and giveth for his arms, Or, a fess between two chevrons Sable, which is the coat-armour of the ancient family of the Seneschalls of this place, whose daughter and heir was married to the gentleman's ancestor now in possession thereof, as I am informed.

Query, whether these arms are not the same as given by Sir John Lisle, knight, one of the first founders of the noble order of the Garter, lord of the manor of Wilbraham, in the county of Cambridge, whose posterity enjoy, as I take it, those lands and his arms to this day, viz. in a field Or, a fess between two chevrons Sable.

In this parish, by the post road, or highway, are set up, in perpendicular manner, about ten feet asunder in a line, nine large moor stones commonly called the Nine Maids, or Virgin Sisters; probably set up in memory of so many sister nuns heretofore interred there.

TONKIN.

This church, although a Vicarage, is endowed with the sheaf over all the southern part of the parish, which most abounds in grain. It carries with it Helston in the same presentation. The patronage in Mr. William Iago. The Incumbent Mr. John Jago. The sheaf not endowed in the possession of Mr. Hugh Boscowen, of Tregothnan.

At Trenithike is the dwelling of Sampson Hill, Esq. a Commissioner of the Peace, who married a sister of Joseph Colmady, of Longdon, in Devonshire, and widow of Heale of Battlesford.

All the lands in this parish lie within the great duchy, lordship, and manor of Helston in Kerrier, as it is named for distinction from Helston in Trigg. The church is certainly called Wendron, from its female patroness.

Bodilly I interpret the house by the church, from ilis, the same as eglis, a church, from which it is not far distant. There are two houses adjacent so called, Bodilly Veor and Bodilly Vear, the great and the little. Bodilly Veor was the seat of Thomas Tresilian, Gent. descended from the Tresilians of Roughtra, who, having mortgaged it to Sir Peter Killigrew, sold the freehold to Mr. William Glynn, and younger brother to Mr. Thomas Glynn, of Polkinhorne.

At Trenere there is an arched vault of moorstone adjoining to the house, said to have been a cellar, and this place a hunting seat to the ancient Dukes of Cornwall.

THE EDITOR.

It appears that the vicarage of Wendron, and perhaps the endowed portion of the great tithes, belonged to Rewley Abbey, near Oxford, founded by Edmund Earl of Cornwall, in compliance with an injunction of his father Richard Earl of Cornwall; although Richard himself seems to have commenced the foundation, for a manuscript history in the Cotton Library says,

" Frater enim hujus regis (Henrici tertii) Ricardus primus Comes Cornubiæ, post Rex Alemaniæ et Semper Augustus, fundavit Abbatias monachorum Cisterciensis ordinis de Royal alias Rewley Oxoniæ, et de Hayles in Comitatu Gloucestriæ, ubi honorifice est sepultus. Cor tamen suum Oxoniæ in choro fratrum minorum, sub sumptuosa et mirandi operis pyramide humatum est."

The Charter of his son Edmund begins,

" Sciant præsentes et futuri, quod nos Edmundus, claræ memoriæ Domini Ricardi regis Alemannii filius, et Comes Cornubiæ, dedimus concessimus et hac præsenti carta nostra confirmavimus Deo, et ecclesiæ beatæ Mariæ de Regali Loco in North Oseney juxta Oxon, et abbati inibi commoranti et quindecim monachis capellanis ordinis Cisterciensis ibi professis, pro anima Ricardi quondam regis Alemanniæ patris nostri, divino celebrantibus, et eorum successoribus ibidem commorantibus Deo servientibus et in perpetuum servituris, omnes terras et tenementa quæ habuimus in North Oseneye prope Oxon et (inter alia) unam acram terræ, secundum Angliæ consuetudinem mensuratam, de dominico nostro in terra de Bel juxta Roslyn, cum advocatione ecclesiæ de Sancta Wendrova, et aliis pertinentiis suis in hundredo de Kerier in Cornubia."

And in the schedule returned to King Henry VIII. after the dissolution of property belonging to Rewley Abbey,

Com. Cornub.

Wendromo et Stadyon, firma Rector' .... £.22.

This advowson had passed through various hands till it was assigned by Mr. Matthew Wills, of Helston, on whose decease, in 1782, it came to his son, Mr. Thomas Wills. This gentleman, although not intended for the church, had received his education at Winchester and Oxford, and the living happening to become vacant just at the period of his father's death, Mr. Wills was induced to take holy orders, and he is now (1834) the Incumbent; but the advowson has been transferred to Queen's College, Oxford, for its Michell or new foundation ; thus returning almost to the very spot where it was bestowed almost six hundred years before.

The barton of Trenethick is traced back to the family of Seneschalls, from whom it came by a marriage to the Hills; the last of whom, Mr. John Hill, gave it by will, about seventy years since, to a family long seated in Constantine, of the same name, but, from their bearing different arms, probably not related.

Nansloe, the vale leading to the lake, is beautifully situated in a valley near the Loo. It has been for some time the seat of the Robinsons, since they removed there from Bochim in Cury. The last representative of this family in the male line was the late Reverend William Robinson, Vicar of Crowan.

Trelil belonged to Mr. Rowe, steward to Lord Godolphin. his only daughter and eventual heiress married Mr. William Harris, of Rosewarne, in Camburne, Sheriff of Cornwall in the year 1773 ; and their only daughter, married to Winchcombe Hartley, Esq. of Berkshire, is its present possessor.

This parish has for ages been one of the most productive

of tin in the whole county; and before the improved operations of smelting had placed all ores nearly on the same level as to the quality of their products, the neighbourhood of Porkellis boasted of producing the best tin in Cornwall.

The church is situated nearly at one extremity of this immense parish, and has nothing to distinguish it but a monument to the memory of Warin Penhallinyk, a prebendary of the monastery at Penryn, Rector of St. Just, in Roseland, Vicar of Wendron and of the adjoining parish, Stithyans. The Vicarage-house is a mere hovel. The parish feast is on the nearest Sunday to October the 28th, St. Simon and St. Jude.

Mr. Jago, Vicar of Wendron, was perhaps the last clergyman in the west of Cornwall supposed to exercise supernatural powers; various anecdotes were current about him sixty years ago, and then generally believed; all I apprehend to his credit, being such as laying spirits, discovering thieves, &c. mixed up, however, with frivolities, as seems ever to have happened in those popular legends. Whenever parson Jago got off from his horse he struck the ground with his whip, and a demon immediately appeared to hold or take care of his horse till he wanted it again. The Rev. Francis Vyvyan Jago Arundell is descended either from this gentleman or from his father.

This parish measures (including Helston) 12,317 statute acres.

	£.	s.	d.
Annual value of the Real Property, as returned to Parliament in 1815, Helston included	8870	0	0
Poor Rate in 1831, The Parish £1766 8 0 Helston . 889 17 0	2656	5	0

GWINEAR. 141

Population,—	in 1801,	in 1811,	in 1821,	in 1831,
Wendron	3006	3555	4193	4780
Helston	2248	2297	2671	3293
	5254	5852	6869	8073

giving an increase on the Parish of 59, on the Town 46½, on both together 53½,—per cent. in 30 years.

THE GEOLOGY, BY DR. BOASE.

About two-thirds of this extensive parish is situated on granite, which is the same as that of Camborne, Crowan, and Sithney adjoining; the other third, which forms the southern part of the parish, is composed of slate rocks, which near the granite are felspathic, and clearly referrible to the porphyritic series; but as the sea is approached, the character of these slates becomes obscure, such as they generally are whenever the porphyritic and calcareous series pass into each other.

GWINEAR.

HALS.

Is situate in the hundred of Penwith, and hath upon the north Gwythian, west Phelack, south Crowan and St. Erth, east Camburne.

In the Domesday Tax this district passed under the jurisdiction either of Caerton in Crowan, Lewellen in Gwythian, or Hella in Camburne. In the Inquisstion of the Bishops of Winchester and Lincoln into the value of Cornish Benefices, 20th Edward I. 1294, Ecclesia de Sancto Winer in decanatu de Penwid, was valued cxiiis. iiiid. In Wolsey's Inquisition, 1521, it is valued 12l. by the same name of Winer. The patronage in the Bishop of Exeter, who endowed it. The Incumbent Thomas

Paynter. The Rectory, or garbe sheaf, in possession of Howell, under lease from Exeter College, Oxford. And the parish rated to the 4s. per pound Land Tax, 1696, 147*l.* 7*s.* 2*d.* by the name of Gwiniar.

Lanyon, in this parish, a seat of the Lanyons, the first propagators of this family in Cornwall, came, with many other French gentlemen, into England, with Isabella, wife of King Edward II. and settled themselves in those parts; amongst which Lanyon's posterity have ever since flourished in gentle degree in Cornwall; and for further proof of this matter, that originally they came from the town of Lanyon, situate upon a sea-haven, or harbour, in France, they give still the arms of that town for their paternal coat armour, viz. in a field Sable, a castle Argent, standing on waves of the sea Azure, over the same a falcon hovering with bells. The present possessor, Tobias Lanyon, Gent. that married Pineck; his father Reynolds.

Polkinhorne, in this parish (eminent or notable iron head). From this place was denominated an old family of gentlemen surnamed Polkinhorne, who gave for their arms, Argent, three bars Sable; whose only daughter and heir, temp. Charles II. was married to Thomas Glynn, Gent. a younger branch of the Glynns of Glynn, whose father giveth for his arms, Argent, a chevron between three salmon-spears handled and barbed Sable, two in chief, and one in the base part, with points downwards.

Coswin, in this parish (i. e. the white wood or fair) gave name and original to an old family of gentlemen surnamed De Coswyn, who lived reputably in this place for several descents, till John Coswyn, temp. Charles II. by ill husbandry, wasted his paternal estate, and sold this little barton to the person now in possession thereof.

TONKIN.

The right name of this parish is St. Wynnier, a corruption of St. Wymer, its tutelar saint, by which name it is called in the Taxatio Beneficiorum, Ecclesia Sancti Wymeri.

The great tithes of this parish are believed to have been bestowed on Exeter College, by its founder, Walter de Stapledon, Bishop of Exeter, A.D. 1318.

A younger brother's daughter of Coswin, who squandered the property, married Peter Pendarves, gent. and brought Bodrigge in Thellark into that family.

THE EDITOR.

The parish of Gwiner has been extremely productive in copper. Herland Mine, usually called the manor, produced so large a return to Mr. Hobbin, only part proprietor of the land, as paid for the building of Nansewidden in St. Columb, about the middle of the last century. It has been since wrought on a most extensive scale, and to a great depth.

Whele Alfred, Whele Trelistion, and others, have been very productive; but at present they are all discontinued.

The family of most consequence connected with this parish is that of Lanyon.

The first syllable certainly implies an inclosed place, from which it has become specifically applied to a church, to a castle, and even to a town. Mr. Hals' conjectures as to the termination of the name, appear to be so utterly groundless that they are omitted.

Mr. Whitaker believes that Lanyon in Normandy bears only a castle for its cognisance, and that the falcon has been added on account of the similarity in sound of Lanyer to Lanner, the favourite bird in falconry.

It must be observed however that Lanyon is always in Cornwall pronounced La-nine.

The Gwinear and Madern branches of the Laryon family were together possessed of extensive property in the adjacent parishes; combinations of unfortunate circumstances have diminished their possessions, but hopes may be entertained that the Lanyons of Gwinear, who have never lost the sense of what is due to the memory of their ancestors, may again resume the former station of their family.

The Rev. Malachy Hitchins, Vicar of St. Hilary, held this living for almost thirty years.

Gwinear measures 3,882 statute acres.

	£.	s.	d.
Annual value of the Real Property, as returned to Parliament in 1815	5185	0	0
Poor Rate in 1831	800	18	0

| Population,— | in 1801, 1651 | in 1811, 1952 | in 1821, 2383 | in 1831, 2728 |

giving an increase of 65 per cent. in 30 years.

Present Vicar, the Rev. John Thomas Wilgress, collated, by the Bishop of Exeter in 1813.

GEOLOGY, BY DR. BOASE.

This parish, like those adjoining, Camborne and Crowan, has been long celebrated for its mines, but it does not resemble them by reposing in part on granite, being confined entirely to rocks of the slate series.

The porphyritic courses are not so common here as in Gwennap; but they often assume a very interesting form, occurring as insulated masses, which in some cases are perfectly granitic, and at the same time afford every indication of their having been formed contemporaneously with the slate. The most curious geological phenomenon of this parish is to be met with in Relistion Mine, where one of the lodes, (metalliferous veins) at a considerable depth, is composed of rounded pedules, cemented together in a hard solid mass; at first sight it would be pronounced to be a decided conglomerate of derivative origin; but on a more close examination it is found to have the spheroidal structure, which is common to many rocks, and which in regard to this mineral was probably coeval with its original formation.

GWITHIAN.

HALS.

Is situate in the hundred of Penwith, and hath upon the north the Irish Sea, or St. George's Channel, and that creek or cove called Gwithian Bay, east Illigan, west Phelack, south Gwynuar.

The entry occurs, Rex tenet Canardi-tone, in the Domesday tax 20 William I. 1087.

For in this parish is the voke lands of the great and privileged manor of Coner, or Conner-ton, which claims by prescription not only the royalties and jurisdiction within its limits, but also over the whole hundred of Penwith (id est, the head tree). Hence it is that this manor of Connerton is privileged not only with the jurisdiction of a Court Leet or Baron for the whole hundred of Penwith, within which two courts are tried all matters of debt and damage between party and party within the same, (life, land, and limb excepted,) wherein heretofore infinite number of causes have been depending, by reason of its being the most remote part of the kingdom from the Courts of Westminster; the steward or judge of which courts, (which offices commonly are vested in one person,) takes his deputation from the now lord of the manor, viz. Sir John Arundell, of Lanherne, Knight, and not from the King or Duke of Cornwall's stewards, as other bailiwicks do.

For in the time of King Henry III. this manor was the King of England's or Earl of Cornwall's lands, who, by letters patent, yet to be seen at Lanherne, passed it over, together with the bailiwick of the said hundred, to Simon Pincerna, or Butler, lord of Lanherne, in consideration that he the said Simon had enfeoffed the said King Henry, his heirs and successors, with the lordship and manor of St. James at Westminster, in the county of Middlesex. After which exchange or settlement, Pincerna and his heirs enjoyed this manor for several descents, till Edward III's days. At which time one of the two daughters and heirs of Pincerna was married to Arundell of Trenibleth, the direct ancestor of Sir John Arundell of Lanherne, Knight, now in possession of both those lordships. The other daughter to Umphravill.

To remove an action at law depending in those Courts, the writ must be thus directed: " Senescallo et Ballivo hundredi et libertatis suæ de Penwith in Comitatu Cornubiæ salutem."

In the Inquisition of the Bishops of Lincoln and Winchester into the value of Cornish benefices, 1294, " Ecclesia de Sancto Gwyth-ran, in decanatu de Penwidh," is valued cxiii*s.* iiii*d.* It seems at the time of this inquisition this church was not consolidated into Phillack; but before Wolsey's Inquisition, 1521, it past in consolidation and value together with it, at 45*l*. 10*s*. 8*d*. The patronage was formerly in the King of England, who endowed it; now Arundell of Lanherne. And the parish is rated to the 4*s*. per pound Land Tax, 1696, 58*l*. 2*s*. by the name Gwith-ran.

TONKIN.

This church is a rectory, daughter to Phillack, together with which it is rated in the King's Books, and passeth in the presentation. The patronage is in Arundell of Lanherne, the incumbent Mr. Jasper Phillips. This gentleman is since deceased, and has left the next presentation, held by lease under the Arundells, to his nephew Mr. Gregory, who has presented his brother-in-law, Mr. Edward Collins, son of Mr. Collins, of Treworgy in St. Erm (great-grandfather to the Editor).

This parish takes its name, like many others, from the

Saint to whom the church is dedicated, called by Mr. Carew, St. Gothian.

THE EDITOR.

Mr. Hals's derivation is again so utterly improbable as to be omitted.

The Arundells, being Catholics, leased the advowson of Phillack and Gwithian on lives, to prevent its lapsing to the University of Oxford, under an Act of Parliament. On the death of Mr. Edward Collins it did so lapse, and the University presented Mr. William Glover, of Worcestershire, first of Balliol College and then a chaplain of All Souls. A lease was then granted to Mr. Hoŝkin, of Gwithian, and his son the Rev. Richard Hoŝkin succeeded Mr. Glover, who on the general sale of all the Arundell property in Cornwall, purchased the freehold, so that his son is now patron and incumbent of the united parishes.

Mr. Lysons says that the advowson of these united parishes belonged to the Priory of St. James in Bristol, and I find a charter of King Henry II.

" Henricus Dei gratia Rex Angliæ, et Dux Normanniæ et Aquitaniæ, et Comes Andegaviæ, Archiepiscopis, &c. salutem. Sciatis me concessisse et præsenti carta mea confirmasse ecclesiæ sancti Jacobi de Bristow omnia subscripta, quæ Willielmus comes Gloecestriæ ei rationabiliter concessit et dedit in perpetuam elemosinam, scilicet inter alia et omnes ecclesias quæ sunt de feodo jam dicti comitis in Cornubia cum capellis et cum omnibus pertinentiis suis; scilicet Ecclesiam de Eglosiek, Ecclesiam de CONORTON, Ecclesiam de Eglasheil, Ecclesiam de Eglossant, Ecclesiam de Egloscraweyn, et Capellam de Bennartona, Ecclesiam de Melioton, et Ecclesiam Sancti Germoch.

It is understood that the manor of Conorton had in some way been connected with the honour of Gloucester before the Conquest. William certainly gave it with that honour to Alan Earl of Britanny. Rufus had it again to bestow, and under his grant it descended to the Earls of Gloucester, originating in an illegitimate son of King Henry I. William, the second of these earls, endowed the Priory of St. James.

Mr. Lysons says that Robert Earl of Gloucester, son of this Robert, gave Conorton to Richard Pincerna in 1154, but he is clearly mistaken, for the date proves it to be done by the same William. Pincerna is a word used by writers mediæ et infimæ Latinitatis for butler. Qui vinum convivis miscet, a Græco πινειν κιρνα. Ducange.

> Mihi sapit dulcius vinum in taberna,
> Quam quod aqua miscuit Præsulis Pincerna.
> WALTER DE MAPES.

The son of this Pincerna took the name of Conorton, as was usual in those times, and settled at Lanherne; from this family it passed with Lanherne to the Arundells, by marriage, in whom it continued till the general wreck above referred to, when being reduced to a mere royalty it was bought by the late Sir Christopher Hawkins, and since his decease in 1829 the royalty has been purchased by an attorney, for the purpose in all probability of holding the courts.

There is a tradition, supported by the authority of Leland, that a town so large as to contain two churches stood on this manor, which has been destroyed by sand; but the tale must at the least be a very great exaggeration.

The account given by Mr. Hals of the exchange of the manor of Conorton for St. James' in Westminster, can scarcely be made to quadrate with the above account, which appears to be authentic, and it is still further opposed by the history of St. James's Hospital, as given by Tanner and Dugdale, they say:

"At a distance from the city, in the fields near Westminster, some well disposed citizens of London, beyond the memory of man, and (as some think) long before the Conquest, founded a hospital for the reception of fourteen leprous women, to whom were afterwards added brethren, to minister divine service. This house was dedicated to St. James, and rebuilt in the time of King Henry III.

It was under the government of a master (although the Abbat of Westminster claimed a jurisdiction over it) till King Henry VI. granted the perpetual custody of it to Eton College, who surrendered it to King Henry VIII. anno Regni 23, (A. D. 1531) when it was valued at 100*l.* per annum, in exchange for Chattisham in Suffolk. On or near the place where this hospital stood has been since built the present Royal Palace of St James.

Mr. Lysons has been so fortunate as to obtain from the late rector some information respecting the inundation of sand, which has devastated a large portion of these two parishes, extending its ravages wherever the coast is low, throughout the whole northern space of Cornwall, from the Land's End to Devonshire. There has always existed a traditional account of this inundation, corroborated by the ecclesiastical valuations, which are far too high for the actual extent of land, and also said to be confirmed by documents preserved in the Arundell family, carrying back the commencement of the evil nearly to the period of their acquiring the property.

With respect to more recent inundations, Mr. Hoskin stated to Mr. Lysons, that the barton of Upton, one of the principal farms, was suddenly overwhelmed; that his great-grandfather remembered the occupier residing in the farmhouse, which was nearly buried in one night, the family being obliged to make their escape through the chamber windows; and that in consequence of the wind producing a shifting of the sand, in the winter of 1808-9, the house, after having disappeared for more than a century, came again to view.

The rector further stated that he himself remembered two fields lost at Gwithian, and that they are now covered with sand to the depth of ten or twelve feet, and that the church-town would have been also lost, if the parish officers had not promptly resorted to an expedient, which, simple as it may seem, has every where proved to be the most efficacious in arresting this gigantic evil, that of planting rushes; these stop completely the progress of sand, and greatly facilitate the growth of other vegetation on the surface, so as to create a thin turf. The hillocks of sand exhibit a model in miniature of the Alps.

This sand is entirely calcareous, being a mass of comminuted shells, and immense quantities are carried away for manure, more especially in the cultivation of strong clay lands; but no method sufficiently cheap for practice has yet been invented for burning this shell sand into lime, as the fine powder chokes the fuel in any kiln, and a reverberatory furnace is much too expensive.

On the opposite coast of Cornwall the sand is siliceous.

Godrery belongs to Lord De Dunstanville, a bold promontory distinguished by an island beyond it, and by a dangerous reef extending far into St. Ive's Bay.

Other lands are much divided. Mr. Hoskin the present rector, and his relations, are considerable proprietors, and several resident farmers live on their own freeholds, Mr. Veal, Mr. Phillips, and others.

Notice has been taken of a very large fig tree growing in the churchyard; the wonder is much diminished by knowing that this tree was planted by the late rector; but as chalk is of all soils the most favourable to figs, it is not improbable that calcareous sand may participate in the same quality.

The parish feast is held on the nearest Sunday to the first of November, All Saints Day.

This parish measures 2,249 statute acres.

	£.	s.	d.
Annual value of the Real Property as returned to Parliament in 1815,	1,110	0	0
Poor Rate in 1831	92	2	0

Population, — { in 1801, 329 | in 1811, 372 | in 1821, 412 | in 1831, 539 }

giving an increase of about 64 per cent in 30 years.

GEOLOGY, BY DR. BOASE.

The rocks of this parish are well exhibited at Godrery Point, they consist of a fine blue and fissile slate, and of a thick lamellar and somewhat compact rock. They are not metalliferous, and resemble those of Trevaunance in St. Agnes. The greater part of the parish is covered with hillocks of calcareous sand, as is common on many parts of the north coast.

HELLAND.

HALS.

Is situate in the hundred of Trigge, and hath upon the north St. Mabyn, East Blissland, and part of Bodmin parish; south, Bodmin Town; west, part of St. Mabyn and Egleshayle. The name refers to the church, and signifies the hall college, temple, or church.

That there was an endowed rectory church here before the Norman Conquest I make no doubt, since in the Domesday Roll it is taxed by the name of Henland, and also in the Inquisition of the Bishops of Lincoln and Winchester into the value of Church Benefices in Cornwall, 1294, " Ecclesia de Hellan in decanatu de Trigminorshire," is valued xl*s*. In Wolsey's Inquisition, 1521, 9*l*. 13*s*. 4*d*. The patronage formerly in the Prior of Bodmin, who endowed it; after in Heale and Bulteel; now in Robins, or Tress, or Trelawny; and the parish rated to the 4*s*. per pound Land-Tax, 1696, by the name of Helland, 84*l*. 17*s*. 4*d*. The incumbent White.

At Bo-cuny-an, in this parish, is the dwelling of my very kind friend Dr. Robert Heart, who married Moles-

152   HELLAND.

worth and Hawkey; originally descended from the Hearts of Tencreek, of Mynhyniet, or St. German's, and giveth for his arms, Gules, on a chief Argent three human hearts Proper.

Note further, that whosoever is possessed in fee of the barton of Helland, (for Bara-ton, i. e. the Bread Town lands in this parish,) is legal patron of the same, paying only 40s. to the Rector Incumbent for the time being, in full satisfaction for all the great and small tithes of the said barton, according to an ancient pact or composition made between the first Rector thereof and the Prior of Bodmin, who endowed it. Which sum of 40s. per annum at the time of the Inquisition aforesaid, was the value of the tithes of the whole parish.

Note further, wherever the word barton occurs in this history, it being Cornish British, it must be interpreted either as the barred, bolted, or fenced towne, or as a contraction of the word Bara-ton aforesaid, for as bara is bread in British, so ton or tone is a town or village, a manor, parish, tenement, or part thereof; the place where commonly the lord of the land had a well bolted or barred house to dwell in; or else a town or house which was notable for keeping or dispensing freely of bread for support of man's life.

TONKIN.

The words Hel or Hale are at least the Cornish pronunciation of the English hall, atrium, and this word was applied to churches as well as to gentlemen's houses in various parts of England, as Helldon Rectory in Norfolk Halling, Kent, &c., and see the 140th stanza of Mount Calvary.

> Pylat eth yn mes ay hell yn un lowarth an gevo
> Pylat went out of ye hall into a garden wch he found,

But after all, if we may believe the parishioners, the name

is a contraction for Helen's Land, the church being dedicated to St. Helena, the mother of Constantine.

In this parish lived the old family of the Giffords, who married one of the inheritrixes of the Esses, or Vanstorts, in the time of Henry VI. as Gifford's heiress was married to Nicholls of Penrose.

THE EDITOR.

Mr. Whitaker has observed, in a note on what Mr. Hals says on the word barton, a term now almost indiscriminately applied to all large farms, although in former times it was probably restricted to what Mr. Hals denominates the yoke land of a manor.

Barton in English is Bere-ton, as Berwick, and signifies primarily a farm-house distinguished by the corn generally raised, once bere, or barley; and from the house the term has been transferred to the estate annexed. Baraton here means the same as bara, bread or corn, bara pill the corn harbour, bara-Llan, barton (Cornish) a cornfield, and barn (as in English) a corn-house.

Mr. Lysons mentions several manors in this parish, but they do not appear ever to have possessed any importance or curiosity, except that the manor of Penhargard belonged to the unfortunate Chief Justice Trevilian, and that the barton of Brades or Broads was for some time the seat of a younger branch of the Glynns.

Robert Glynn, Esq. residing there, married in 1711 Lucy Clobery, and their only son was Doctor Glynn, a Fellow of King's College, Cambridge, well known and distinguished for his abilities, learning, and philanthropy, and in some degree also for occasional eccentricities. He obtained not merely one of the University prizes, but great reputation by a Latin Poem on the Day of Judgment, in the year 1757; and in illustration of other parts of his character, having attended as a physician on the family of some agricultural labourer near Cambridge, and restored them to health, the man's wife lamented their poverty, but begged of the Doctor to take a tame bird in their possession, as the only thing in their power to bestow. Doctor Glynn accepted the present, but declared that he could not keep his bird in a college room, and that therefore they must keep it for him, at an allowance of half a crown a week.

To be invited by Doctor Glynn to drink tea at his room was always considered as an honour by the younger members of the University, and the Editor remembers to have heard that Mr. Pitt, then at the head of the government, and just elected into a seat more flattering than any office the crown could confer, expressed himself pleased by the repetition of these invitations from Doctor Glynn.

Helland measures 2,053 statute acres.

	£.	s.	d.
Annual value of the Real Property, as returned to Parliament in 1815	1,588	0	0
Poor Rate in 1831	102	0	0

Population,—
in 1801,	in 1811,	in 1821,	in 1831,
221	223	264	285

giving an increase of 29 per cent. in 30 years.

Present Rector, the Rev. Francis J. Hext, presented in 1817, by William Morshead, Esq.

GEOLOGY, BY DR. BOASE.

The geology of this parish is similar to that of the western part of Bodmin. It is however worthy of remark that in the road from Bodmin to Camelford several beds of granitic elvan are exposed to view. The first at the top of the hill near Smith's, resembles a coarse granitic sandstone, and at its junction with the slate both rocks are perfectly distinct, not having any appearance of transition, which circumstance is in favour of its being a derivative rock. This subject, however, requires further examination. The other elvans are more compact and porphyritic, and contain hornblende, resembling those of Carraton Hill, near Liskeard, situated within the granite.

HELSTON.

HALS.

Is situate in the hundred of Kerryer, and hath upon the east Gwendron, west Sythney and the Loopoole, south Maugan and Gunwallo.

That this was a privileged place, and the voke lands of a manor, with court leet, before the Norman Conquest, I make no doubt, since the whole hundred of Kerryer, in King Alfred's days, was in chief denominated from it. Besides this testimony, in Domesday Roll 20 William I. 1087, we read that by the name of Henliston, it was then taxed. Moreover, Brooke, York Herald, tells us temp. James I. in the Catalogue of Cornish Earls, that the privileges of this town or manor were concerted into a charter, and incorporated by Richard Plantagenet, Earl of Cornwall, 3d son of King Henry II. surnamed Cur-lyon, from his lion-like heart, in the name of Helleston, as appeared from the charter, which he had then in his custody, to the seal whereof was affixed a lion rampant. It was also made one of the four coinage towns by King Edward I. in his charter to the Tinners, by the same name (See the charter under Luxilian). As also incorporated into the Duchy of Cornwall, by the same name 1336, when King Edward III. to his son the Black Prince promoted or translated the Earldom of Cornwall into a Duchy or Dukedom.

Whereby this town is also confirmed to be the voke lands of the manors or stanneries of Helston and Kerryer, (id est, Hall, Broad Town, and Lover,) and privileged with a Court Leet, wherein all pleas of debt and damage, between party and party, concerning tin matters, are tried by a jury of six men, before the Vice Warden and Steward of the Stanneries, (under the Lord Warden thereof,) life, land, and limb excepted. It is also privileged with a Court

Leet before the tribunal of the Mayor and Aldermen, and Quarterly Sessions of the Peace, and sending two members to Parliament; markets weekly on Saturday; fairs on August 29, October 28, Saturday before Midlent Sunday, Saturday before Palm Sunday, Whitsun Monday, and two fairs before St. Thomas à Becket's day. Moreover, these privileges were confirmed and enlarged by charters temp. Queen Elizabeth and King Charles I. by the name of the Mayor and Burgesses, who consist of a Mayor (who is a Justice of the Peace for the Borough, the year succeeding his Mayoralty), and four Aldermen, who elect as many Common Councilmen as make their number twelve. Their Members of Parliament are elected by the majority of the freemen, and returned by the Mayor, to whom the precept on the writ for election must be thus directed, as well as that for removing an action depending in the Leet of Helston to a superior Court:

"Majori et Burgensibus Burgi nostri de Helleston in Comitatu Cornubiæ, salutem."

Not far from this town stands the ruins of an old camp, or intrenchment, called Castle Weire, or Wera, an old fort or citadel to defend it from its enemies' invasion. The arms of which town are Argent, a castle, or house, garreted on the top thereof, between two watch-towers, the Archangel St. Michael fighting with a dragon, or the devil.

That King Edward I. frequented this place for delight or pleasure, or designed so to do, upon the death of his uncle Richard Earl of Cornwall, King of the Romans, when the Earldom of Cornwall reverted to himself, in right of his Crown of England, Anno Dom. 1272, is evident from his granting lands by the tenure of grand sergeantry to William de Treville, on condition of bringing a fish-hook and a boat and net, at his own proper costs and charges, for the king's fishing in the lake of Helston, whensoever the King should come to Helston, and as long as he should tarry there. See the copy of this enfeofment deed in Sythney parish.

HELSTON.

The chief inhabitants of this coinage town for tin are Mr. Penrose, Mr. Polkinhorne, Mr. Hooker, attorney at law, Mr. Williams, Mr. Rawe, Mr. Burges, Mr. Pinock, and others.

In the Inquisition of the Bishops of Lincoln and Winchester, into the value of Cornish Benefices, 1294, the church of Helston is not named, but passed then under the title of its mother or superior church, Gwendron, into which it was consolidated, 17*l.* 6*s.* 8*d.*; in Wolsey's Inquisition, by the names of Wendron and Helston, 26*l.* 19*s.* 3*d.*; both endowed, I suppose, by the Master or Governor of St. John's Hospital at Sythney, who were patrons thereof till the 6th Henry VIII. when it was dissolved, now Jago; the incumbent Jago; and the town or parish of Helston rated to the 4*s.* per pound Land Tax, 1696, 181*l.* 9*s.* 4*d.*

In the year 1727 happened in those parts astonishing claps of thunder and lightning, which in fine broke down and tore in pieces the greatest part of this town's church and tower, and did it damage to the value of two or three hundred pounds in repair thereof.

TONKIN.

This church is a Vicarage, endowed, and passeth in the presentation with Gwendron.

Mr. Carew, in his Survey of Cornwall, tells us that within this town was an hospital, but gives no further account of it; so that it is unknown to me whether it were a spital erected for the relief of pilgrims from abroad, or for the use of sick impoverished people within the town. Most assured I am that near this place there was a priory erected to the name of St. John the Baptist.

THE EDITOR.

I have omitted some paragraphs from Hals and from Tonkin respecting several derivations of the name " Helstone," as all the circumstances of the place seem to point at one so decidedly as to exclude all consideration of the others. No doubt this one transgresses an arbitrary rule confining the themes of all derivations to a single language; but the instances in contradiction are so numerous throughout all England, as to render this circumstance of no importance.

The spot long used as a bowling-green is acknowledged on all hands to have been the site of an ancient castle. It must therefore have been the nucleus of the town; and the marsh extending from the Loo Pool along the valley, passes under the scarped rampart of the castle.

Hellas is well known to signify a marsh in the Celtic dialect used in Cornwall, and the termination Ton, the origin of our general word town, signified, in the Saxon,— more especially a walled town, or fortress; Helleston is therefore the fortress on the marsh.

The first charter of incorporation given to Helston, at least from the supreme feudal chief, is said to have been by King John. It is, however, highly probable that privileges of guild may have been bestowed long before by the Princes of Cornwall, vassals from the time of Athelstan. Various other charters were granted, till, in the early part of the reign of George III. the number of corporators became so reduced that the remainder were incapable of performing any corporate act; a new charter was in consequence obtained, and at the next general election the individuals named in it returned two members; but six persons remaining of the former party did the same: and so strong at that period was the feeling for chartered rights, in consequence of the conduct pursued by King Charles II. and his successor, that a committee of the House of Commons determined the right to remain in this fragment, incapable of performing any other civil act. And songs were made on the occasion, comparing these heroes with Eustace de St. Pierre and his companions.

> When Edward set down before Calais,
> Replete with rage and with malice,
> Not the six famous burghers
> More courage displayed
> Than the six men of Helston

One, if not two more returns were made in the same manner, till the number being fallen down to two very old men, they were induced to wave their privilege, partly, it is said, from an apprehension entertained that the maxim of Roman law, tres faciunt collegiam, might be effectually urged against them.

A custom had grown up at Helston, from early times, and by no means peculiar to that place, in compliance with which the patron, a well known and definite appellation, paid all the parochial rates; but an opinion may be formed of their small amount at no distant period, from the following statement. The Editor being on a Committee of the House of Commons, to consider and report on the poor laws soon after the conclusion of the late war, laid before the Committee a copy of a poor rate made for a parish in the west of England in the year 1704: it amounted to four pounds and some few shillings, while in the current year it exceeded six hundred pounds.

This practise in Helston became the ground of a petition after the general election of 1812; and, opinions having now changed, the matter was taken up so seriously in the House of Commons, as to induce the passing of a bill for disfranchising the borough. The other branch of the legislature, however, considered the practice, although wrong in itself, yet a delictum sine crimine, in this particular instance, as it most clearly appeared that some leading gentlemen, possessed of such influence as would have enabled them to make great lucrative advantages for themselves other ways, were benefited in so slight a degree by these payments, as to make it quite evident that self-interest had not been the motive of their conduct. The bill did not pass into a law, and the town became regularly assessed like other places. The well-known connection usual in such cases had long subsisted between this town and the neighbouring family of Godolphin.

At the period of the last heraldic visitation in 1640, the signatures to the return of arms, &c. were,

The mark × of John Roe Moyes.	William Robinson.
	Thomas James.
Thomas Seyntaubyn.	John Herbert.
Dated October 9, 1640.	

And the members of the corporation are stated to be,

BURGESSES.	
John Rowe Moyes.	Thomas James.
Thomas St. Aubyn, Gent.	Robert Cock.
William Robinson.	William Penhaluwick.
Alexander Bolytho.	Daniel Bedford.
John Harbert.	William Trewin.
John Alexander.	Patrick Pesseme.
Thomas Godolphin, of Godolphin, Esq. Recorder.	John Cock.
	Thomas Randall, Steward of the said Town and Corporation.

In the Parliament preceding that, the Editor's great-great-grandfather, William Noye, afterwards Attorney-General, represented Helston; and he himself had the same honour in the Parliament following the Union with Ireland. On the total change of the parliamentary constitution in 1832, the limits of Helston were extended so as to include a large portion of Wendron and the entire parish of Sithney. And the whole was reduced to sending one Member, or, according to a familiar expression, it was placed in Schedule B.

On that occasion a letter was addressed to a gentleman of the town, in return for a present of some delicacies, so full of wit and humour that the Editor, having been favoured with a copy, is induced to insert it.

"Your very obliging present made its appearance this day, together with your note of the 2d instant; pray, accept my best thanks for the same, the quality of which will, I have no doubt, on trial fully justify the favourable impression already made by their fragrance.

"Under the melancholy circumstances of affliction in which your town must be plunged by the announcement of the intended spoliation of a moiety of its electoral privileges, it is most pleasing to recognise a disposition in the leading citizens to impart of their good things to others; and although I should at all times have been much delighted by any mark of your friendly remembrance, yet it is doubly gratifying at a period like the present, when public embarrassments might naturally be supposed to absorb every other feeling, and to leave little room for indulging a spirit of individual philanthropy.

"Allow me, however, to express the hope, that as, when Hercules broke off the horn of the river god Achelous, it became the medium through which the golden gifts of the Genius of Plenty were showered down, so the ancient and patriotic borough of Helston, although shorn of a part of its long-enjoyed honours, and mutilated as to one of its protectors, may still flourish with a cornucopia of abundance and of prosperity.

2671. (φυε, φυε, οττοτοι, παπαι, αι, αι) 2671.

quoth the Population Return for 1821.

"For which slight numerical deficiency, and for no earthly offence imputable to the inhabitants, save that of a practical application of the principle ' non numero, sed honore valemus," the long-standing privileges of loyal men are scandalously invaded, and a body of independent electors declared incapable of exercising more than one half of their prescriptive rights.

"I seem to hear an indignant voter of Helston exclaim, 'Why this measure of penal severity, accompanied at the same time with an apparent mitigation and lemency? Political annihilation had been a milder doom; extermination from the lists of suspected corruption had been far better than thus to suffer mutilation from the pruning knife of reform, beneath the wound inflicted by which the gangrene of dissatisfaction will still lurk and fester for ever.

——— Mene Iliacis occumbere campis
Non potuisse!

Happier were it to have sunk amidst the ruins of Sarum, or to have perished in the plains of Gatton,

Sævus ubi Æacidæ telo jacet Hector, ubi ingens
Sarpedon———

than to be thus sent adrift, single-masted and disabled, on the doubtful sea of political adventure. They who now fall,

Sumptis apud Ilion armis

will meet no inglorious fate; under the banners of Peel, or the shield of Wetherall, it will be honourable to be conquered; and the page of history will supply a never-dying splendour for the illustrious patriots whose destinies were sealed by the Parliament of 1831. But to be denied this noble privilege, to remain a still-enduring monument of the wrongs inflicted, and of the mercies awarded! to be held up as an example of the wisdom of half-measures, and the policy of semi-destruction! to be denied the consolation of despair! and to be snatched from the gulph of ruin to an acuter sensation of helplessness!

Σκληροκαρδιος αρ' ειη
'Οτῳ ταδ' ου μελησει.

The remainder of this classic dirge, or ælinon, no less remarkable for the purity of its diction than for the fine flow of feeling and tone of patriotism by which it is characterised, is intended to form a part of a great national work, to be printed at the Clarendon press, and to be sent forth into the world,—Ihadum lachrymas inter* justasque querelas.

" But I find that I must come to a hasty conclusion; trusting therefore that you will pardon my adventuring to meddle with any thing so sacred as a venerable borough in affliction, and begging you will present my unfeigned condolence to all parties interested to whom I have the honour of being known, I remain, &c."

The old church is said by Mr. Hals to have been greatly injured by a thunder-storm in 1727. It appears never to have been thoroughly repaired; and in 1763, Lord Godolphin, the patron, built a large church and a lofty tower, nearly on the site of the former. The church is without pillars, and capable of containing a numerous congregation; but the whole is strongly characteristic of the bad taste prevalent at the period when it was erected.

Just over the bridge leading to the westward stood the hospital dedicated to St. John, and founded by a member of the Killegrews. The spot is still marked by a large upright stone near the bridge, bearing the sword with its crosletted hilt, the cognizance of the military order of St. John. Little, however, is known about it. Dugdale states that at the dissolution in the 26th of Henry VIII. the total annual revenue of the house amounted to 14*l*. 7*s*. 4*d*. and the actual receipts to 12*l*. 16*s*. 4*d*.

About the year 1805 the town received a very considerable improvement by the removal of the Coinage Hall from the middle of the principal street leading south-west from

* " An old scholiast upon this passage proposes to read meritas; but says little in defence of his suggestion, beyond adverting to divers suicidal acts of the ultra Tories, as he calls them, which are said to have been perpetrated by them on various occasions."

the middle of the town. The Editor at that time represented Helston, and had the good fortune to assist materially in promoting the negociation with the Duchy officers, in consequence of his acquaintance with Mr. Sheridan, and with others whose consent was necessary to be obtained. The Market-house is a venerable monument of former times; yet, if this also could be removed, the improvement would equal that effected by the former.

Helston, in great measure unconnected with trade or with a sea port, little of a thoroughfare before the turnpike road was made, surrounded by the residences of ancient, respectable, and wealthy families, and inhabited by gentlemen of a similar description, has ever been celebrated for the superior quality of its social manners, and at the same time for an easy and familiar intercourse between all the people in their various stations; the inferior experiencing the truth of what all the histories of all nations have confirmed from the earliest periods of Greece to the recent events of our own time,

Αρχαιοπλουτων δεσποτων πολλη χαρις·
'Οι δ' ουποτ' ελπισαντες, ημησαν καλως,
Ωμοι τε δουλοις, παντα και παρα σταθμην.

And the reverse of

Απας δε τραχυς, όστις αν νεον κρατῃ.

These circumstances account for the continuance of old manners and of old customs longer here than in other places.

All towns appear to have adopted, on one day at least in the year, practices similar to the Roman Saturnalia; in most places, the lines of society having become broad and strongly impressed, their observances descended to the more vulgar, or rather perhaps to the vicious; and changing their character from harmless amusements to practices of outrage and violence, they have been discontinued or suppressed: but in Helston an ancient observance of this kind, refining with the refinement of the age, still continues in activity.

The origins of all these customs are obscured or totally lost in their remote antiquity. That of Helston corresponded, however, precisely with its name—" a foray," locally corrupted into furray; the young people rushed out of the town into the country early on the eighth of May, when, entering all houses without leave or ceremony, they appeared to seize whatever they wanted, and from the real nature of the transactions, whatever they wanted was sure of being found; and ultimately they returned to the town in triumph, dancing and decorated with flowers, where the scenes of the morning were, in some degree, repeated. All these practices, however, are less and less persevered in from year to year, so that the whole is rapidly tending towards the single entertainment of a ball; and if the ladies had succeeded in a classical fancy, which, some how or other, got possession of their minds, the very memory of this festival would have been lost.

Not intimately acquainted, one may presume, with the true history of the patroness they had selected to sanction their gaieties, the goddess Flora was made to preside over a foray, instituted, as some assert, before the Norman conquest, and in commemoration of a victory obtained over the Saxons, who had landed at a cove still called Perth-sasnac; but the utter absurdity of the substitution, and the popularity given to the word FORAY by Sir Walter Scott's Poems, have restored the ancient and true appellation.

Causes similar to those which have retained the foray, have also kept up the practice of bowling; so that in Helston alone can one now see the principal gentlemen of the town assembled on the bowling-green, enjoying at once exercise, fresh air, and agreeable intercourse, free from any

166 HELSTON.

spirit of gambling and from the slightest indulgence of a habit more common and less excusable.

The word faddy is used to express the dance, the air, or both, used in celebrating the foray; the origin of this term is quite unknown.

The air is preserved by Edward Jones in his Musical and Poetical Relics of the Welsh Bards. He has also printed some lines which were sung by the dancers; they are, however, so entirely devoid of sense, or even of antiquity, that I shall not transcribe them.

The air is supposed to be a remnant of British music; one very like it, if not identically the same, has been found in Ireland, and according to report in Scotland. It may therefore be justly esteemed a curiosity.

The measurement of Helston is included in Gwendron; and the value of Real Property is not distinguished in the returns to Parliament from the parish.

The Poor Rates and Population have been given under Gwendron (Wendron), but they are here repeated.

Poor Rate in 1831, £889. 17s.

Population,	in 1801,	in 1811,	in 1821,	in 1831,
	2248	2297	2671	3293

giving an increase of $46\frac{1}{2}$ per cent in 30 years.

GEOLOGY, BY DR. BOASE.

The northern part of this parish, approaching the granite of Wendron, is composed of felspar and hornblende rocks; the southern so much abounds in some parts with siliceous varieties of rock as to form barren downs, which stretch from Love Bar to the vicinity of Gweek.

ST. HILARY.

Mr. Hals begins his account of this parish with a long history of the patron saint, including all the controversies or disputed points of doctrine in which he was engaged; all this, extending through many pages, is omitted.

St. Hilary was born at Poictiers, in France, about the end of the third or the beginning of the fourth century.

He was descended from an illustrious family, and received an education suited to his station in life, by which he was initiated into all the secular learning of those times; but finding the Pagan mythology utterly absurd, and the prevalent system of philosophy quite unsatisfactory, he examined the Christian writings, and became a convert. He seems never to have adopted the brutalizing austerities so prevalent in those ages, but to have employed his talents, his acquired eloquence, and his learning, against the Arians and in defence of the Nicene creed. Several of his works are extant, and have gone through many editions. The whole were printed by the Benedictine Monks of Paris, "St. Hilarii Opera omnia per Monachos Benedictinos edita; Gr. et Lat. Parisiis, 1693, Fol." Erasmus published the works of St. Hilary in 1544, and says in his Preface, "Quicquid ingenio, quicquid eloquentia, quicquid sacrarum literarum cognitione posset:" and his contemporary, St. Jerome, says of him, "Hilarius, meorum Confessor temporum, et Episcopus, duodecim Quintiliani libros et titulo imitatus est et numero;" referring to his twelve books on the Trinity.

In the judgment of modern critics his style at least is not thought worthy of all the praise bestowed on it by St. Jerome; for, although it is stated to be lofty and noble, and moreover beautified with rhetorical ornaments and figures, yet it is too much studied and lengthened in many periods, so as to be obscure and even unintelligible.

The following passage on singleness of heart, has been cited by various authors.

"Christ teaches that only those who become again, as it were, little children, and by the simplicity of that age cut off the inordinate affections of vice, can enter into the kingdom of heaven. Those follow and obey their father, love their mother, are strangers to covetousness, ill-will, hatred, arrogance, lying, and are inclined easily to believe what they hear. This disposition of affection opens the way to heaven. We must therefore return to the simplicity of little children, in which we shall bear some resemblance to our Lord's humility." From his commentary on the Gospel of St. Matthew.

St. Hilary, previous to his conversion, had married, and his family consisted of one daughter; he immediately separated himself from them; his wife retired into a religious society. And after the saint had been consecrated Bishop of Poictiers in the year 355, he learned with the utmost horror and affright that his daughter was about to take on herself the unholy bonds of matrimony. His prompt and impassioned remonstrances conveyed in a letter which is printed among his works, conjuring her by the God of heaven not to act so unworthy a part, were successful; the marriage was broken off, and he had the gratification of seeing his daughter, a spouse of Christ, expire not long after at his feet.

St. Hilary composed a treatise which might in ordinary times have conciliated him to every sect then in existence. He there maintained that errors on speculative points of abstruse doctrine, were more sinful in the sight of God than any conduct the most atrocious; but controversy ran so high, and St. Hilary had taken a part so violent against the Arians, that even this merit could not save him from banishment, when that equally poised division of the church obtained some temporary preponderance in a synod, or succeeded in acquiring to their party the temporal chief; who, without using the form of words, prac-

ST. HILARY. 169

tically evinced that he was " over all persons and over all causes, ecclesiastical as well as civil, within those his dominions supreme."

The saint, however, died at Poictiers in the year 368. St. Augustine relates many miracles wrought at his tomb; but the relics are said to have been removed to the Abbey of St. Denis, near Paris; and his festival is kept on the 14th of January, although it is not certain either that he died, or that his relics were translated on that particular day.

HALS.

Hilary is situate in the hundred of Penwith, and hath upon the north St. Earth, west Gulval, [Ludgvan EDITOR,] east Germow, south and west the Mounts Bay and Peranuthno. As for the name Hilary, it is derived from the tutelar guardian and patron of this church, viz. St. Hilary, Bishop of Poictiers in Gaul, the maul and hammer against the Arians, whose fame is eternized in the Roman agonals and festivals, though his memory and day is not celebrated as a martyr, but as one of the principal confessors of the Roman church; that is to say, one of those that suffered great persecution for the name and Gospel of Christ Jesus.

In Domesday book this district, or parish, was taxed under the jurisdiction of Lanmigall, i. e. Michael's church or temple; now St. Michael's Mount and Tremarastell, i. e. the market hole or cell, of which more under.

In the Taxation, or value, of Cornish Benefices aforesaid, made by the Bishops of Lincoln and Winchester, 1294, Ecclesia de Sancti Hilary in decanatu de Penwith, appropriata Priori Sancti Micaelis, is rated to first fruits lxxiiis. iiii*d*. In Wolsey's Inquisition and Valor Beneficiorum, St. Hilary Vicarage is valued 11*l*. 6*s*. 0*d*. The patronage formerly in the Abbat or Prior of St. Michael's Mount, who endowed it. After its dissolution, 26th Henry VIII. it fell to the crown, and was sold to Militon, whose six daughters and heirs invested their husbands and purchasers therewith; the patronage now alternately in Erisey, Godolphin, Buller, and others (or Roberts); the garb, or rectory, in possession of Pennock. The parish of St. Hilary was rated to the 4s. per pound Land Tax, of 1696, at 120l.

Tregumbo, also Tregimbo, is the dwelling of Captain John Pinneck, Deputy-Governor of the Island of Scilly, under Sir William Godolphin, Knight, salary about 13l. per annum; who married Davies.

Treveneage, in this parish, was formerly the lands of Sir Thomas Arundell, of Tolverne, Knight, who sold this barton and manor to Sir Nicholas Hals, of Fentongallan, knight, whose son and heir, John Hals, sold it to Walker of Exeter; from whose heirs it came by purchase to Sir Joseph Tredinham, Knight, now in possession thereof.

On the confines of this parish is situate the ancient manor and borough of Marazion.(a)

In Domesday Roll, 20th William I. 1087, this place was taxed by the name of Tremarastoll; that is to say, the cell, chapel, or hole market-town; situate in a remote corner, vallum, or pit, upon the seashore of St. Michael's Mount. At which time, no doubt, the Abbat or Prior of St. Michael's Mount (as they were afterwards till 26th Henry VIII. when that Abbey was dissolved), were lords and high lords thereof; when it was privileged with the jurisdiction of a court leet; as afterwards, temp. Henry II. with sending two of its members to sit in the Commons' House of Parliament. But, as appears from the Parliament Rolls in the Tower of London, after the dissolution of the Abbey or Priory aforesaid, this town neglected to send its Members, "for that it could not conveniently pay its burgesses their daily wages, propter paupertatem, which are the words of the record.(b) It is also privileged with a fair, or mart, on July 11th, November 30th, Good Friday, and Palm Monday; and a market weekly on Saturdays.

ST. HILARY.

And as a further mark of its ancient grandeur, I take it still to be an incorporate mayor or portreeve town; but more sure I am, that, as some other petty corporations' names in Cornwall are adjectives merged or fallen in or upon the parishes wherein they are situate, as Camelford, Mitchell, &c. this town is a noun substantive, and stands charged by itself in the Exchequer to the 4s. per pound Land Tax, 1696, by the name of the borough of Maraszeyan, 76l. 12s. 6d.

In the beginning of the reign of King Henry VIII. (1514) when war had been proclaimed against the French King, a fleet of French men of war, consisting of thirty sail, with some marine regiments of soldiers therein, coasting in our British Channel, at length came into this Mount's Bay, and there dropped anchor; when soon after they landed a considerable number, or quantity, of seamen and soldiers, and marched in hostile manner towards this town. Which the inhabitants observing, they forsook their houses, and fled to the hill country; whereby the Frenchmen became peaceably possessed thereof, and plundered the same for some days, till they understood that John Carminow, of Fentongollan, Esq. was coming or marching towards them, with his posse comitatus, to give them battle; when instantly they set the town on fire, and the houses on the contiguous part of the country, and burnt the same totally to the ground, to the great loss and damage of the inhabitants, and forthwith fled to their ships for safety and protection; and thereupon their ships hoisted anchors and put forth to sea again. Where they had not long been till Sir Anthony Oughthred, King Henry VIII.'s Admiral at sea, with a squadron of thirty men of war, met and gave them battle, to their great loss of men and some ships of war, whilst the rest of their fleet ran away, and fled into the haven of Brest for safety and protection.

THE HISTORY OF ST. MICHAEL'S MOUNT.—PART I.

So called, for that our ancestors, the Britons, apprehended the appearance of the Archangel St. Michael, about the year of our Lord 495, was in this place, though the Italians say it was upon Mount Garganus, in their country, and the Frenchmen tell us that it was upon their Mount St. Michael, in Normandy; such difference amongst writers is about it; and verily this matter of fact is worth contending for, since the etymology of Michael is "sicut Deus," i. e. as God, as I have shewn elsewhere under other churches to him dedicated. It appears from the history of the church of Landaff, as Mr. Camden hath observed, that this mount was called Dinsill, and Dinsull, but what those words should signify he could not tell.(c)

Mr. Carew, in his Survey of Cornwall, p. 154, tells us, that beside those religious appellations that were given to it, it was called in British, Cara cowz in clouz, which he interprets as the Grey rock in the flood, a corruption of Carra clo gris en an coos; i. e. rock-clo-grey in the wood.(d) Of this place Mr. Carew, and Mr. Camden that trode in his steps, tells us, that it was the Ocrinum, Οκρινυμ, or Ocrinium of Ptolomy and Atticus, the Greek geographers; and yet Camden, in another place, fixes that name on the Lizard Point.

This Mount is comparatively a pyramidal crag, containing about seven acres of land in compass; at the foot whereof, towards the land, is a level piece of ground covered with grass, where there is a wharf, or key, for landing goods and merchandize from the sea; also some dwelling-houses and fish-cellars, and a cemetery for burying the dead. To this Mount the sea daily makes its flux and reflux, and affords safe riding and anchorage to boats, barks, and barges, with some winds. And that which tends more to the convenience and security of this place, that at low water it is all part of the insular continent of Britain, and

ST. MICHAEL'S MOUNT. 173

at full sea an island of itself. To which purpose thus speaks Mr. Carew out of the Cornish Wonder Gatherer:

> Who knows not Migell's Mount and chair,
> The pilgrim's holy vaunt;
> Both land and island twice a day,
> Both fort and port of haunt.

For to this Mount and chapel of St. Michael devout Christians in former ages came as pilgrims from the furthest part of this land, with rich offerings and oblations to St. Michael's altar, Abbat, or Prior; also tradition tells us that in former ages this mount was parcel of the solid lands of this parish of St. Hilary, and severed or disjointed from it by some earthquake, terrestrial concussion, or inundation of the sea; and to prove this, it is alleged that in the Mount's Bay, after some great tempests, the bodies and roots of oak-trees have been discovered in the sand, broken up by the surges of the sea, the like observation is made by Camden and Lhuyd on the sea shores of Pembrokeshire, and I myself, and many others, in the moors of Calestock Veor, Calestock Rule, Rheese, and Polgoda in Peransand, have seen and found, deep under ground, far from the sea, in the fens and turf lands, the bodies and roots of several oak trees, the hearts whereof were firm and solid. But whether those seas were formerly dry land, and the fens aforesaid the places where these trees grew (none in those parts being now to be seen there), let others resolve; or rather whether they are not subterraneous trees, that grew or are generated there, as some philosophers hold and teach, under the earth.

From the foot of Mount St. Michael you ascend the hill or rock through a narrow, crooked, craggy path to the outer portal or gate; a considerable height on the one side, by the way in the rock, is a small spring of water, that falls into pits made in the stones to lodge the same, for the lower or bottom inhabitants' use, which water never intermits its current. Above the second gate there is another spring of water issuing out of the rocks, that makes a pretty confluence for six or seven winter months, and then intermits, which renders the portage of it upwards much the easier for the inhabitants' use in that season. After you pass through this second gate, betwixt a winding and crooked path, artificially cut in the rocks on the north side thereof, and follow the same, you arrive to the top of this Mount, where towards the north-west is a kind of level plain, about four or six land-yards, which gives a full prospect of the Mount's Bay, the British Ocean, Penzance town, Newlyn, Moushole, Gulvall, Maddarn, Paul, and other parishes, over a downright precipice of rocks towards the sea, at least twenty fathoms high. From this little square or plain, there is an artificial kind of ascent also going towards the east, which offers you a full sight of the outer walls of the castle, and brings you to Porth-Horne, (i. e. the Iron Gate) part of which is yet to be seen. This little fortress comprehendeth sufficient rooms and lodgings for the captain or governor and his soldiers to reside in, to which adjoining are several other houses or cells, heretofore pertaining to the monks that dwelt here; all admirable for their strength, buildings, and contrivance, on the top of a rock naturally fortified: so that a small number of soldiers, having provision and ammunition, might defend themselves against the greatest armies in former ages, though I confess now, since the art of war is grown to greater perfection in mischief and destruction, a few cannon or bombs from the opposite hills would soon shatter it to pieces.

On this Mount, King Edward the Confessor, anno Dom. 1044, founded and endowed an Abbey or Priory of Benedictine Monks, that is to say Augustines reformed, with a little chapel yet standing, and dedicated the same to the Archangel St. Michael, part whereof is now converted to a dwelling house, in which there is yet to be seen cut in stone three or four coats of arms, one of which was, as I remember, a Chevron between three fleurs-de-lis.

ST. MICHAEL'S MOUNT.

That it had at that time considerable revenues belonging to it I make no question, since in the Domesday Book, 20 William I. 1087, Lan-migell was then taxed, that is to say Michael's church or Temple, as aforesaid. But that which renders this place most famous is the present church or chapel and tower, cemetery, and cells cut in the rocks for hermetical monks of the order aforesaid; built and further endowed by William Earl of Morton and Cornwall, yet extant and kept in good repair, with pews; to whose father, Robert Earl of Morton, King William the Conqueror had given the lands of many rebels in those parts, and in particular this Mount, with its appurtenances, (dedicated as aforesaid) and created him Earl of Cornwall, whose successors held the same by tenure of Knight Service till temp. Charles II. Of which sort of tenures there were lately extant, in the hundred of Penwith, thirteen knight's fees.—Carew's Survey of Cornwall, p. 39. And in other hundreds three hundred more in Cornwall.

Upon the tower of this church or chapel, for it is bigger than many other Cornish parish churches, is that celebrated place called Kader Migell, i. e. Michael's Chair, viz. a kind of seat artificially made or cut in the stones on the top of its tower, very dangerous in the access and tremendous to behold.

Contrary to this description, Mr. Carew, in his Survey of Cornwall, p. 154, tells us that St. Michael's Chair is a bad seat, in a craggy place without the castle, dangerous for the access and therefore holy for the adventure; so that I conceive he had this report by hearsay, not ocular demonstration. In this chapel are yet to be seen the tombstones of several persons there interred, in the rocks, (with a small quantity of earth, though without the chapel there is a bank of earth, brought there by art for burying the dead,) but the inscriptions on those tombstones are so obliterated with dust and time, that I had not leisure much to examine them. The roof and timber of this temple is yet so firm and uniformly kept in repair, that no decay, moth, or spider's web are to be seen in the roof thereof, which gives occasion to a conjecture that the same was all built of Irish oak, which drives that poisonous creature the spider from it. Certes, this fabrick is not only an evident proof of the great skill which former ages, in William the Conqueror's days, had in the art of architecture, but that many other such of much later erection can hardly equal the same, though it has stood firm above six hundred years.

This abbey or priory of Benedictine Monks of St. Michael, after the donation thereof by the Conqueror to his nephew Robert Earl of Morton aforesaid, was by him annexed and made subject for religious matters to the Abbey of Mount St. Michael in Normandy, under which circumstance it stood till the French wars, temp. Henry V. 1414, when the Statute, made 1380, in the reign of King Richard II. was put in force, for suppressing alien priories (who secretly communicated the state affairs to foreigners). King Henry V. or VI. then gave this Alien Priory of St. Michael to Sion Abbey in Middlesex, under which rule and jurisdiction it remained till 26 Henry VIII., 1533, when it was dissolved; when, I take it, it passed in value with Sion, since the Monasticon Anglicanum does not mention it separate.

The Mount is now in possession of Sir John Saintaubyn, (formerly Bassett) who for melancholy retirement dwelleth here. It is still privileged with royalties over the Mount's Bay, as far north as Long Bridge in the manor of Lanesely, with wrecks, anchorage of ships, quayage or wharfage of goods, and with keeping annual fairs on the sea shore near it, September 29, Monday after Midlent Sunday. Round this Mount, for two leagues space, is an indifferent safe road for anchorage of ships, when the wind is proper for it; and here, as Froissart saith, landed Sir Robert Knollys, a valiant commander of the Black Prince's in the French wars temp. Edward III. (who drew the traitor Sir Perducas D'Albert from the French to the English army, to

ST. MICHAEL'S MOUNT. 177

which afterwards he returned again most perfidiously,) where he had been highly instrumental in taking the forts of Froyns, Roach, Vandower, Ville Franck, and other places for the English; from hence he went to London by land, was graciously received and plentifully rewarded for his good services by King Edward III.

PART II.

This Mount, from the time of King Edward the Confessor to the middle of the reign of King Richard I. for the space of 150 years, was a sacred nursery of religion; but then, notwithstanding the sanctity thereof, and the guardianship of St. Michael, it was seized by one Henry de la Pomeray, Lord of Berry-Pomeray in Devon, and Tregony Pomeray in this county, being distasted at the government of King Richard I. as many others were, by reason of the Pope's request he engaged in the Holy War, and forsook his kingdom, leaving for his vicegerent William Longchamp, a Norman Bishop of Ely; who had extorted great sums of money from the people in his absence, without a Parliament; and moreover so insulted over the nobility and gentry of this kingdom in his office, that he discontented the greatest part of them; and to countenance his grandeur he seldom rode abroad with less than a thousand attendants. Those and others his exorbitances gave occasion to John Earl of Cornwall and others to fall into treasonable practices, and of this number it seems this Sir Pomeray was one, who not only informed the King beyond the seas of these topping, magisterial, and illegal practices of Longchamp at home, but that by reason thereof King Philip of France, in those distractions, took occasion with a great army of soldiers to invade Normandy, and had taken the town of Guisors and many other places by force and arms, and would reduce the whole province in short while (if not resisted) to his dominion. Whereupon the King, in answer, by his letters patent, deposed Longchamp from his authority, and placed the Archbishop of Rouen in his place, when soon after Longchamp, in women's apparel, made his escape into his own country, but was detected and shrewdly beaten with rods before his departure out of England, by the women there.

Longchamp, as tradition saith, having notice that de la Pomeray was in confederacy with Earl John, who under pretence of opposing his vice-government, designed the usurpation of King Richard's Crown, (though he had told him that in case his brother should die, before he returned into his kingdom, without issue, that the right of succession was in Arthur Duke of Britany, his elder brother's son, not him,) sent a sergeant at arms to the castle of Berry Pomeray in Devon, where he then resided, in order to arrest and take him into custody, which he no sooner did but Pomeray stabbed him to the heart, of which wound he instantly died. Upon which tragical accident the murderer fled into Cornwall, where he had great possessions in lands, and besides twelve lordships held by the tenure of knight service. And there cast himself upon his amicus, John Earl of that province, who as tradition saith secretly supplied him with divers men at arms to secure his person against his enemy the Viceroy, which accordingly they did till Longchamp was displaced.

Afterwards, notice being given that King Richard was taken prisoner coming from the Holy War, 1194, by Leopold, Archduke of Austria in Germany, and cast into his prison called Trivalis, in which no man before was known to be put that escaped with life, this news prompted Pomeray from the sin of murder to that of rebellion; resolving to reduce this Mount of St. Michael to Earl John's dominion, and to place himself therein for better safety. In order to which he found out this expedient, to go with his guard of armed men that daily attended him in disguise to that place, under pretence of visiting a sister that he had amongst the religious people there;(e) who upon discovering who he was, and the occasion of his coming, had the gates opened, where he entered with his followers, who soon after discovered under their clothes their weapons of war, and declared their design was for reducing the Mount to the dominion and use of John Earl of Cornwall, and that if any person opposed them therein, they would revenge it upon him to the loss of their lives; whereupon, he commanded the Prior and his monks to deliver him the keys of the gates, and possession of the houses thereof for common uses, though therein they much discommoded the monks with their soldiers. Nevertheless, for fear of greater damage, they patiently submitted to his pleasure; who thereupon with his soldiers fortified the place, and so made it comparatively impregnable, and so there lived in great pomp and triumph for some time, not expecting ever to hear that King Richard was in the land of the living, or delivered from prison, it being for some time reported he was dead. But, alas! many times common fame is a common liar, and all men are apt to believe such matters and things as they would willingly have come to pass, or stand well affected to.

But contrary to the expectation of Pomeray and his confederates, King Richard, after fifteen months' durance in prison, was ransomed for one hundred thousand pounds, and returned safe to London; when he found his brother John formidable, and making way to his crown, having got possession of the castles of Lancaster, Marlborough, Nottingham, St. Michael's Mount, and other fortresses, into which he had placed governors and soldiers. Whereupon, in order to reduce those places, King Richard raised a considerable army; at the news whereof Earl John fled into France, and was by his brother deprived of all his possessions in England: notwithstanding which, the garrisons aforesaid stood firm to Earl John's interest, till at the siege of Vernoil in Normandy, he fled from the French army to that of his brother, threw down his arms and submitted to his mercy; whereupon he was restored to all his lands and dignities, both in Normandy and England.

But notwithstanding this concord and agreement between King Richard and his brother John, the castles aforesaid stood out, and would not surrender for some time after, especially this Mount, which Pomeray commanded. Whereupon King Richard commanded Richard Revell, then sheriff of Cornwall, with his posse comitatus, to assist Hubert Walter, Archbishop of Canterbury, Chief Justice and Lord Chancellor of England, whom he had sent as his general into Cornwall to besiege St. Michael's Mount, and reduce Pomeray to his duty and allegiance; which army of men, and bands of soldiers, no sooner approached the same (as Hoveden saith) and gave him summons, but the sight of the numerous army he was to contend with so affrighted Pomeray and his confederates, that forthwith, without resistance, he surrendered the garrison on mercy to the said Walter, for the use of King Richard, 1194, at the consideration of which and his other facts, through trouble of mind he soon after died, as despairing of pardon.

Mr. Carew, in his Survey of Cornwall, tells us, by report of some of his posterity, that he made his will and bequeathed part of his lands to the monks of St. Michael's Mount, others to the Knights of St. John of Jerusalem, to pray for his soul; the remainder descended to his heir (which we have no reason to doubt of, since Henry de la Pomeray, one of his posterity, 3 Henry IV. at Tregony, held twelve knights' fees of land in Cornwall, id. Mr. Carew); having so done, he caused himself to be blooded to death, to make his bequests good and valid in law; after his death King Richard restored the prior and his monks to the full possession of their cells, revenues, and chapel; and in de la Pomeray's fort, he placed a small garrison of soldiers, to defend the same against sudden invasion of enemies; and in this condition St. Michael's Mount remained from the year 1196 to the year 1471, 275 years, manned out with carnal and spiritual soldiers.(*f*)

PART III.

Richard de Vere, the eleventh Earl of Oxford, married Alice, one of the daughters and coheirs of Sir Richard Sergeaulx, knight, Lord of Collqnite and Killygarth, widow of Guy Seyntaubyn, Sheriff of Cornwall 22 Richard II. 1399; but she passed her lands from her son by her first husband, to her second husband the Earl of Oxford, who had issue by her John de Vere, the 12th Earl of Oxford, who married Elizabeth, daughter of Sir John Howard Knight; the which John, the 12th Earl, was the chief of those barons that opposed the precedence in parliament of the Lords Spiritual, temp. Henry VI. the which Parliament roll in the Tower of London, is thus endorsed:

MEMORANDUM.—The Lords Spiritual alleged that, forasmuch as they were spiritual Barons, they ought to have the right of precedence of the Lords Temporal, for it was well known how far things spiritual exceeded carnal or temporal. To which this Earl of Oxford replied on behalf of the Lords Temporal, that whatsoever right or privilege they had or could challenge, [see Brooke on Oxford, Earl,] it came from them and their ancestors, and their almsdeeds, who had been the worthy founders and benefactors of the Lords Spiritual; and further said it was an unseemly thing for masters to be inferior to their servants, who were descended of regal, honourable, and noble families, which most of the Spiritual Barons were not; which matter being fully understood, and indifferently heard, the Lords Temporal, by means of the logic and rhetoric of this Earl, had then the precedence of place in Parliament given them. But, alas! this bold demand, question, and argument of his, at that time, was a project rather pitied than admired by his best friends, for though it succeeded well in one Parliament, it got him many enemies in another. So that in the Parliament, held 2d November, 1462, tempore Edward

IV., this Earl, and his son Aubrey, were attainted of treason against that King, on the behalf of Henry VI., and both beheaded without trial or answer.—(Baker's Chronicle, page 204.)

Whereupon John, his second son, succeeded, and was the 13th Earl of Oxford, who married Margaret daughter of Richard Nevill, Earl of Salisbury, who, as his father had done before, adhered to the interest of King Henry VI., against Edward IV., and was at the battle of Barnet Heath 1471, and had, with the Marquess Montacute, the command of the right wing of King Henry's horse, under Richard Earl of Warwick, general of his army; and when in the battle, it appeared the vanward of King Henry's horse had somewhat worsted King Edward's party, by the valour of the Earl of Oxford, the news presently fled to London that Warwick had obtained the victory; but, alas! Fama est mendax; for immediately after a strange misfortune befel the Earl of Oxford and his men in the latter part of this encounter They having a star with streams on their liveries, as King Edward's soldiers had the sun, the General Warwick's men, by reason of a great mist, (raised as was thought by the magic art of Friar Bungey) mistaking the badges, shot at the Earl of Oxford's men, which were of their own party, to their great hurt and destruction; whereupon the Earl, seeing how matters went, cried out treason, and forthwith fled with 800 men, whose departure gave King Edward opportunity to obtain a total victory over his enemies.

Whereupon the Duke of Somerset and this Earl of Oxford fled to Jasper Earl of Pembroke, in Wales, for safety and protection; from whence Oxford, and a convenient number of men of arms, shipped themselves from Milford-haven, and with a fair wind sailed down St. George's Channel, turned the Land's End, and came safely at anchor in this Mount's Bay. Where, as soon as the Earl and his men had disguised themselves in pilgrims' and friars' apparel, under which all had lodged a small sword and a dagger, they went on shore, pretending that they were pilgrims that had come a long pilgrimage from the remotest part of this kingdom, to perform the penance imposed upon them by their father confessors, and to perform their vows, make orisons and oblations to the altar of St. Michael, who presided there; upon which pious pretext the monks and inhabitants opened their gates and let them into the castle, where they were no sooner entered, but, as de la Pomeray had done before, they shewed their weapons, discovered their impious fraud, and made known who they were, and their designs to kill all persons that made resistance or opposed King Henry VI. for whom the Earl of Oxford was come to take possession of this Mount, and would keep it to his use; whereupon, the monks and the small garrison were necessitated to comply with their demands, and yield them a quiet possession thereof; which forthwith the Earl put in better repair, and by the interest of King Henry and the Earl's friends and relations in those parts, his grandmother as aforesaid being Sir Guy St. Aubyn's widow and Sergeaulx's coheir, he soon got ammunition, provision, and soldiers sufficient for their defence.

As soon as King Edward IV. heard of the surprise of St. Michael's Mount by the Earl of Oxford, he issued forth his proclamation, proclaiming him and all his adherents traitors, and then consulted how to regain both to his obedience; and in order thereto he forthwith sent to Sir John Arundell of Trerice, Knight, then Sheriff of Cornwall, to reduce and besiege the same by his posse comitatus; which gentleman, pursuant to his orders, and by virtue of his office, soon rose a considerable army of men and soldiers within his bailiwick, and marched with them towards St. Michael's Mount, where being arrived he sent a trumpeter to the Earl with a summons of surrender of that garrison to him for King Edward upon mercy; especially for that in so doing, in all probability, he would prevent the effusion of much Christian blood.

To this summons of the trumpeter the Earl sent a flat

denial; saying further, that rather than he would yield the fort on those terms, himself and those with him were all resolved to lose their lives in defence thereof. Whereupon the Sheriff commanded his soldiers, being very numerous on all parts, to storm the Mount, and reduce it by force; but, alas! maugre all their attempts (of this kind) the besieged so well defended every part of this rocky mountain that in all places the Sheriff's men were repulsed with some loss; and the besieged issued forth from the outer gate and pursued them with such violence, that the said Sir John Arundell and some others were slain upon the sands at the foot of the Mount, to the great discouragement of the new-raised soldiers, who quickly departed thence, having lost their leader; leaving the besieged in better heart than they found them, as much elevated at their good success as themselves were dismayed at their bad fortune. This Sir John Arundell, as Mr. Carew, in his Survey of Cornwall, tells us, p. 119, had long before been told by some fortune-teller that he should be slain in the sands; wherefore, to avoid that destiny, he removed from Efford, near Stratton on the sands, where he dwelt, to Trerice, far off from the sea-sands, yet by this misfortune fulfilled the prediction in another place.

King Edward, upon news of this tragical accident, forthwith ordered letters patent to be drawn for making John Fortescue, Esq. Sheriff of Cornwall, in the place of Sir John Arundell, slain as aforesaid; who being accordingly sworn in that office, received the same commands, and took the same measures for reducing the Mount as the former Sheriff had done, by summons and assault, but was always, and in all places, repulsed with dishonour and loss, the same being as stoutly defended within as it was assaulted without; the fort thus appearing invincible. All which circumstances being transmitted to King Edward by Mr. Fortescue, the Sheriff, the King, for prevention of further bloodshed, ordered him to have a parley with the said Earl of Oxford, and know what his designs and expectations were; who thereupon sent a messenger to him for that purpose; from whom he received this resolute and desperate answer,—that, if the King would pardon the offences of him and his adherents, and grant them their lives, liberties, and estates, that then he would yield up the fort to his use; otherwise they would fight it out to the last man. Which answer being sent up to the King, he granted their request; and forthwith ordered a proclamation of free pardon to be made unto them, under the broad seal of England; which, with all convenient speed was sent down, and by Mr. Sheriff Fortescue delivered to the Earl, to the great quiet and content of all parties. Whereupon the fort was yielded to him for the King's use; and the Earl of Oxford was soon after sent prisoner to the castle of Hamms, in Normandy, where he was continued a prisoner till the first year of King Henry VII. 1485, with whom he came into England, and led the vanward of his army at Bosworth Field against King Richard III. where he was slain. After the death of this Earl's first wife, he married Elizabeth, daughter of Sir Richard Scrope, Knight, widow of William Lord Beaumont, by whom he had no issue; so that, he dying the 4th Henry VIII. left John, the son of George Vere his brother, his heir and successor, and the fourteenth Earl of Oxford, who gave for his arms, Gules, escartellé de Or, le premier brisé d'un molette de Argent.

King Edward attributed this ineffectual long siege of St. Michael's Mount either to the cowardice or disloyalty of the Sheriffs and country people of Cornwall; but there was no just cause for this conjecture, since Sir John Arundell and several of his men lost their lives about it: at other times, he would say the inhabitants were more affected to the house of Lancaster than that of York; whereupon, when the said Mr. Fortescue went out of his office after four years' service, he made his brother Richard Duke of Gloucester Sheriff of Cornwall during life; for that he was often heard to say he looked upon Cornwall only as the back-door of rebellion; so that those several persons set down in the catalogue of Sheriffs of Cornwall after Fortescue, were not absolute Sheriffs, but Deputies under the said Duke, viz. Daubeny, Carnesew, Willoughby, Naufon, Grenvill, Fullford, Treffry, Terrill, and Houghton, who stiled themselves Vicecomes, and their under Sheriffs Sub-Vicecomes.

PART IV.

About the year of our Lord 1496, when James IV. King of Scotland, upon a truce with King Henry VII. of England, had expulsed from Scotland that counterfeit sham Prince, Perkin Warbeck (the pretended Richard of Shrewsbury, youngest son of King Edward IV. who had before been murdered in the Tower), to whom he had given in marriage his near kinswoman the Lady Katherine Gordon; he, together with his wife and family, sailed from thence over into Ireland, to seek friendship there of the rebels and all others well affected to the House of York; where being arrived, and fortune favouring him according to his expectation, news was brought him there that the Cornish rebels were ready to renew their former hostility, and venture their lives in battle upon the title of the house of York against that of Lancaster, had they a valiant and able General to lead them, notwithstanding Flammock and his confederates under the same engagement were defeated and executed in 1495.

These tidings were very acceptable to Perkin; who thereupon consulted his privy councillors, Hearn, Astley, and Skelton, a mercer, a tailor, and a scrivener, all bankrupts; these all agree, nemine contradicente, that his four ships of war should forthwith be rigged and manned for an expedition into Cornwall; which accordingly being prepared, himself with his lady, and 120 soldiers, embarked thereon, and being favoured with a fair wind, took his leave of his Irish friends, and in the month of September, 1499, 15th Henry VII. (Carew's Survey of Cornwall,

p. 98,) came safely to anchor in St. Michael's Mount's Bay; where soon after he landed, and went up to the Mount, and made himself known to the monks and other inhabitants, publishing himself to be the true and real Richard of Shrewsbury aforesaid, the true heir of the House of York; which the monks, greatly affected to that title, were so very ready to believe, that they yielded the Mount and garrison without resistance into his hands; who presently renewed the old fortifications, and put the same into a better posture of defence.

Which having done, himself with a band of soldiers marched from thence to Bodmin (where the rendezvous of Flammock's rebels in those parts formerly was,) in which place, by false words and promises, he so prevailed with the discontented rebels of that town and contiguous country, that he soon got together, without money or reward, at least three thousand men that could bear arms; these he divided into companies, and bands, and regiments, under Captains, Majors, and Colonels expert in war to instruct them in military discipline, till at length his army grew to six thousand well-armed soldiers. Whereupon King Henry VII. having notice of Perkin's landing and formidableness in these parts, ordered Sir Peter Edgecombe, Knight, then Sheriff of Cornwall (whose father, Sir Richard Edgecombe, Knight, was one of that King's Privy Councillors, and had comparatively been raised to his great estate by his boon and favour), that he should forthwith, by virtue of his office, raise the country, and give battle to this counterfeit Richard of Shrewsbury and his confederate rebels. Whereupon, the Sheriff did as he was commanded, and raised an army of twenty thousand men, as tradition saith, and led them towards Bodmin; but when they approached near, and saw Perkin entrenched at Castle Keynock, on the east hill of Bodmin Downs, with the body of his army, and divers troops of horse and bands of foot placed towards Lanhydrock and the roads from Cardenham, in order to resist and oppose the Sheriff, his men resolved to march no further, but to return from whence they came without giving battle. Which accordingly they did (notwithstanding the Sheriff's threats and commands to the contrary), in great terror and confusion and astonishment; but whether this fear proceeded from the cowardice of the Sheriff and his men, or their disaffection to the Lancastrian dominion of King Henry, is uncertain, for the like fact was committed two years before by the posse comitatus of John Basset, of Tehidy, then Sheriff, which he had raised to suppress Flammock's rebellion.

Upon news of this flight and disbanding of the Sheriff's men, Perkin was saluted by his soldiers and confederates as King of England; and soon after, not only in his camp, but in divers places of Bodmin town, was proclaimed by a trumpeter and others, King of England and France, and Lord of Ireland, with great shouts and acclamations of the people, and bonefires, by the name of Richard IV. And it is reported he assumed majesty with such a boon grace and affable deportment, that immediately he won the affections and admiration of all who made addresses unto him; in which art of kingship he had long before been educated and instructed by his pretended aunt, Margaret Duchess of Burgundy, sister to King Edward IV. which he had also acted to the good liking of all that saw him in Burgundian, Irish, Scots, and French courts. And, moreover, besides his magisterial port and mien, being an incomparable counterfeit, natural crafty, liar and dissembler, " Qui nescit dissimulare, nescit regnare," as the old proverb saith; so that in short time he grew to be so popular and formidable about Bodmin that no power durst oppose him there. But, alas! this Cornish regniculum gave him not content, for his pride and ambition put him upon further expedients, viz. to get possession of the whole kingdom of England, and reduce it also to his obedience; in order to which, with a well-prepared army of four thousand men and two thousand of other sorts, he marched out of Cornwall into Devon, where met him also great numbers of volunteers of that county and Somerset, that joined with his forces; the dread whereof so terrified James Chudleigh, Esq. then Sheriff of Devon, and the power of his bailiwick raised to stop his march to Exeter, that they durst not give him battle or obstruct his passage till he came before that city, pitched his camp, and laid siege thereto

Upon whose approaches the citizens shut their gates and prepared to defend themselves; when soon after he sent a message or summons to them in the name of Richard IV. King of England, commanding them to surrender the same to him upon their allegiance: but the citizens so ridiculed his pretended title, and slighted his summons, that by his own messenger they gave him defiance; at which time Dr. Richard Redman was Lord Bishop of Exeter; William Burgoigne, Esq. Recorder; William Frost, Mayor; Francis Gilbert, Sword-bearer; John Bucknam, William Wilkinson, John Doncaster, and Richard Howse, were Stewards, or Bailiffs; John Clodworthy, John Bonifant, Philip Bullock, John Wilkin, Nicholas Auburne, John Atwell, William York, Thomas Lanwordaby, Philip Binks, John Slugg, Thomas Andrews, Thomas Oliver, and others, Aldermen. See Isaack's Memorials of Exeter, 1499.

Soon after this defiance given, Perkin and his soldiers surrounded the city walls, and attempted to scale the same in several places daily for some time, but always were repulsed with considerable loss by the valour of the citizens. During which siege they sent to King Henry for his aid and assistance in this great distress; whereupon the Lord Daubeny was ordered to raise forces and march towards Exeter therewith, in order to remove the siege thereof; but before he came, Edward Courtenay, sixteenth Earl of Devon, and the Lord William his son, accompanied with Sir Edmund Carew, Sir Thomas Fulford, Sir William Courtenay, Sir John Halwell, Sir John Croker, Walter Courtenay, Peter Edgecombe, William St. Maur, Richard Whiteleigh of Efford (Sheriff of Devon the year after),

Richard Hals of Kenedon, John Fortescue of Vallapit, James Chudleigh aforesaid, and other gentlemen of those parts, had raised a considerable army of soldiers, with which they marched towards the rebels. At the sight of whose approach Perkin and his host were as much dispirited then as they were elevated before; whereupon he called a council of war, in which it was unanimously agreed upon, that it was not advisable to give them battle, being at least ten thousand fighting men, but to dislodge from their trenches, and leave the siege of that place, and forthwith to march into Somersetshire, a country better affected to King Perkin, where he might raise more soldiers. Accordingly, this order of council was observed and put in practice, so that the night after Perkin and all his army marched towards Taunton; where he mustered his men as if he intended to give battle; but when, by the muster-roll, he saw what numbers of men had deserted him in his nightly march from Exeter, falling then much short of six thousand, and further, notice being brought him that King Henry was in pursuit of him with a much greater army, he foresaw the worst, and doubted that fortune would favour him no longer in his military and regal practices; and therefore contrived, for the preservation of himself, with sixty horse troopers, to forsake his army by night, and fly to the Abbey of Beauley, in Southampton, as resting upon the name and privilege of the place, where he took sanctuary. As soon as King Henry understood Perkin had deserted his soldiers and had taken sanctuary at Beauley, he forthwith ordered a band of soldiers to guard and surround that Abbey to prevent his escape beyond the seas (from whence it appears that at that time the privilege of sanctuary was allowed to traitors). So that Perkin, despairing of getting thence, submitted to the King's mercy, and was committed prisoner to the Tower of London; from whence he made an escape, and fled to the Priory of Sheen, at Richmond; where, on condition of making a true confession who he was, in a pair of stocks set before Westminster Hall door, and true answer make to such questions as should be demanded of him, the Prior got the King's pardon for him. And accordingly, he sat in the stocks a whole day before Westminster Hall door, afterwards on a scaffold in Cheapside, openly reading, declaring, and giving manuscripts under his own hand, wherein he told his parentage, the place of his birth, the passages of his life; that he was a cheat, an impostor, and by what ways and means he was drawn into those treasonable and bloody attempts and practices, &c. After which he was again committed to the Tower of London, where endeavouring to make an escape, he was afterwards, with others, executed at Tyburn.

After Perkin took sanctuary at Beauley, his soldiers from about Taunton and elsewhere, were all brought to Exeter; where King Henry, in St. Peter's church-yard, pardoned them all, on their promise of being good subjects afterwards. But some of them were not so good as their word. King Henry also then sent the Lord Daubeny to St. Michael's Mount for Perkin's wife, the Lady Katherine Gordon, whom he brought to King Henry; who commiserating her youth, birth, and beauty, bestowed a competent maintenance upon her, which she enjoyed during that King's life and long after, to her dying day.

PART V.

This Priory, or Abbey, being dissolved by act of Parliament, and given to the King, 33d Henry VIII. 1542, he gave the revenues and government of the place to Humphry Arundell, Esq. of the Lanherne family, who enjoyed the same till the first year of King Edward VI. 1549; at which time that King set forth several injunctions about religion: amongst others, this was one, viz. that all images found in churches, for divine worship or otherwise, should be pulled down and cast forth out of those churches; and that all preachers should perswade the people from praying to saints or for the dead; and from the use of beads, ashes, processions, masses, dirges, and praying to God publicly in an unknown tongue; and least there should be a defect of preachers as to those points, homilies were made and ordered to be read in all churches. Pursuant to this injunction one Mr. Body, a commissioner for pulling down images in the churches of Cornwall, going to do his duty in Helston church, a priest, in company with Killtor of Kevorne and others, at unawares stabbed him in the body with a knife; of which wound he instantly fell dead in that place. And though the murderer was taken and sent up to London, tried, found guilty of wilful murder in Westminster Hall, and executed in Smithfield, yet the Cornish people flocked together in a tumultuous and rebellious manner by the instigation of their priests in diverse parts of the shire or county, and committed many barbarities and outrages in the same; and though the justices of the peace apprehended several of them, and sent them to jail, yet they could not with all their power suppress the growth of their insurrection; for soon after Humphry Arundell aforesaid, Governor of this Mount, sided with those mutineers, and broke out into actual rebellion against his and their Prince. The mutineers chose him for the General of their army, and for inferior officers as Captains, Majors, and Colonels,—John Rosogan, James Rosogan, Will. Winslade of Tregarrick or St. Agnes at Mithian, John Payne of St. Ives, Robert Bochym of Bochym, and his brother, Thomas Underhill, John Salmon, William Segar; together with several priests, rectors, vicars, and curates of churches, as John Thompson, Roger Barret, John Woolcock, William Asa, James Mourton, John Barrow, Richard Bennet, and others, who mustered their soldiers according to the rules of military discipline at Bodmin, where the general rendezvous was appointed But no sooner was the General Arundell departed from St. Michael's Mount to exert his power in the camp and field aforesaid, but diverse gentlemen, with their wives and families, in his absence possessed themselves thereof; whereupon he dispatched a party of horse and foot to reduce his old garrison; which quickly they effected, by reason the besieged wanted provision and ammunition, and were distracted with the women and children's fears and cries, and so they yielded the possession to their enemies on condition of free liberty of departing forthwith from thence with life, though not without being plundered.

The retaking of St. Michael's Mount by the general Arundell proved much to the content and satisfaction of his army at Bodmin, consisting of about six thousand men, which they looked upon as a good omen of their future success, and the first-fruits of the valour and conduct of their general. Whereupon the confederates daily increased his army with great numbers of men from all parts, who listed themselves under his banner, which was not only pourtrayed, but by a cart brought into the field for their encouragement, viz. the pyx under its canopy, that is to say, the vessel containing the Roman host, or sacramental sacrifice, or body of Christ, together with crosses, banners, candlesticks, holy bread and water, to defend them from devils and the adverse power; (see Fox's Martyrology, p. 669,) which was carried wheresoever the camp removed; which camp grew so tremendously formidable at Bodmin, that Job Militon, Esq. then Sheriff of Cornwall, with all the power of his bailiwick, durst not encounter with it during the time of the general's stay in that place, which gave him and his rebels opportunity to consult together for the good of their public interest, and to make out a declaration, or manifesto, of the justice of their cause, and grounds of taking up arms; but the army, in general, consisting of a mixed multitude of men of diverse professions, trades, and employments, could not easily agree upon the subject matter and form thereof. Some would have no justice of the peace, for that generally they were ignorant of the laws, and could not construe or English a Latin bill of indictment without the clerk of the peace's assistance, who imposed upon them, with other attornies, for gain, wrong sense, and judgment; besides, in themselves, they were corrupt and partial in determining cases; others would have no lawyers nor attornies, for that the one cheated the people in wrong advice or counsel, and the other of their money by extravagant bills of costs; others would have no court leets, or court barons, for that the cost and expense in prosecuting an action at law therein was many times greater than the debt or profit. But generally it was agreed upon amongst them, that no inclosure should be left standing, but that all lands should be held in common; yet what expedients should b found out and placed in the room of those several order and degrees of men and officers, none could prescribe.

However, the priests, rectors, vicars, and curates, the priors, monks, friars, and other dissolved collegiates, hammered out seven articles of address for the King's majesty; upon grant of which they declared their bodies, arms, and goods should all be at his disposal, viz.

1. That curates should administer baptism at all times of need, as well week days as holy days.

2. That their children might be confirmed by the Bishop.

3. That mass might be celebrated, no man communicating with the priest.

4. That they might have reservation of the Lord's body in churches.

5. That they might have holy bread and water in remembrance of Christ's body and blood.

6. That priests might not be married.

7. That the six articles set forth by King Henry VIII. might be continued at least till the King came of age.

Now those six articles were invented by Stephen Gardiner, Bishop of Winchester (who was the bastard son of Lionel Woodvill, Bishop of Salisbury, by his concubine, Elizabeth Gardiner; the which Lionel was fifth son of Richard Woodvill, Earl Rivers, 1470), and therefore called his creed, viz.

1. That the body of Christ is really present in the sacrament after consecration.

2. That the sacrament cannot truly be administered under both kinds.

3. That priests entered into holy orders might not marry.

4. That vows of chastity entered into upon mature deliberation, were to be kept.

5. That private masses were not to be omitted.

6. That auricular confession was necessary in the church of God.

To those demands of the Cornish rebels the King so far condescended as to send an answer in writing to every article, and also a general pardon to every one of them if they would lay down arms. (See Fox's Acts and Monuments, Book ix. p. 668.) But, alas! those overtures of the King were not only rejected by the rebels, but made them the more bold and desperate; especially finding themselves unable longer to subsist upon their own estates and money, or the bounty of the country, which hitherto they had done. The general therefore resolved, as the fox who seldom chucks at home, to prey upon other men's goods and estates further off, for his army's better subsistence. Whereupon he dislodged from Bodmin, and marched with his soldiers into Devon, where Sir Peter Carew, Knight, was ready to obstruct their passage with his posse comitatus. But when they saw the order and discipline of the rebels, and that their army consisted of above six thousand fighting men, desperate, well-armed, and prepared for battle, the Sheriff and his troops permitted them quietly to pass through the heart of that country to Exeter, where the citizens, upon notice of their approaches (as formerly done), shut the gates, and put themselves in a posture of defence. At which time Dr. John Voysey was Bishop of Exeter, viz. 10th July, 1549, John Blacaler was Mayor, William Tothill was Sheriff, Lewis Pollard, Recorder, William Beaumont, Sword-bearer; John Drake, Geffery Arundell, Henry Maunder, and John

Tooker, were Bailiffs or Stewards; Thomas Prestwood, John Maynard, John Webb, William Hals, Hugh Pope, William Hurst, Nicholas Limmet, Robert Midwinter, Henry Booth, John Berry, John Britnall, John Tuckfield, John Stawell, Edward Bridgman, Thomas Grigg, John Drake, Thomas Skidmore, John Bodley, and others (all which had before that time been Mayors), Stewards or Bailiffs of the city.—See Isaack's Memorials of Exeter, p. 122.

Things being in this posture, the general Arundell summoned the citizens to deliver their town and castle to his dominion; but they sent him a flat denial. Whereupon, forthwith he ordered his men to fire the gates of the city, which accordingly they did; but the citizens on the inside supplied those fires with such quantities of combustible matter, so long till they had cast up a half-moon on the inside thereof, upon which, when the rebels attempted to enter, they were shot to death or cut in pieces. Their entrance being thus obstructed at the gates, they put in practice other expedients, viz. either to undermine the walls or blow them up with barrels of gunpowder, which they had placed in the same; but the citizens also prevented this their design, by countermining their mines and casting so much water on the places where their powder barrels were lodged, that the powder would not take fire. Thus stratagems of war were daily practised between the besieged and besiegers, to the great hurt and damage of each other.

King Edward being informed by his council of this siege, and that there was little or no dependance upon the valour and conduct of the Sheriff of Devon, and his bailiwick, to suppress this rebellion or raise the siege of Exeter, granted his commission to John Lord Russell, created Baron Russell of Tavistock by King Henry, and Lord High Admiral and Lord Privy Seal, an old experienced soldier who had lost an eye at the siege of Montrueil in France, to be his general for raising soldiers to fight those rebels; who forthwith, pursuant thereto, raised a considerable army and marched with them to Honiton; but when he came there he was informed that the enemy consisted of ten thousand able fighting men armed; which occasioned his halting there longer than he intended, expecting greater supplies of men, that were coming to his aid under conduct of the Lord Grey; which at length arrived and joined his forces, whereupon he dislodged from thence and marched towards Exeter; where on the way he had several sharp conflicts with the rebels with various success, sometimes the better and sometimes the worse; though at length, after much fatigue of war, maugre all opposition and resistance of the rebels, he forced them to raise their siege, and entered the city of Exeter with relief, 6th August, 1549, after thirty-two days' siege; wherein the inhabitants had valiantly defended themselves, though in that extremity they were necessitated by famine to eat horses, moulded cloth, and bread made of bran; in reward of whose loyalty King Edward gave to the city for ever the manor of Evyland, since sold by the city for making the river Exe navigable.

After raising the siege as aforesaid, the general Arundell rallied his routed forces of rebels, and gave battle to the Lord Russell and the King's army, with that inveterate courage, animosity, and resolution, that the greatest part of his men were slain upon the spot, others threw down their arms on mercy, the remainder fled, and were afterwards many of them taken and executed. Sir Anthony Kingston, Knight, a Gloucestershire man, after this rebellion was made Provost Marshal for executing such western rebels as could be taken, or were made prisoners in Cornwall and Devon, together with all such who had been aiders or assisters of them in that rebellion; upon whom, according to his power and office, he executed martial law with sport and justice (as Mr. Carew and other historians tell us); and the principal persons that have come to my knowledge, over whose misery he triumphed, was Boyer the Mayor of Bodmin; Mayow of Clevyan, in St. Columb Major, whom he hanged at the tavern sign-post in that town, of whom tradition saith his crime was not capital; and therefore his wife was advised by her friends to hasten to the town after the Marshal and his men, who had him in custody, and beg his life. Which accordingly she prepared to do, and to render herself the more amiable petitioner before the Marshal's eyes, this dame spent so much time in attiring herself and putting on her French hood then in fashion, that her husband was put to death before her arrival. In like manner the Marshal hanged one John Payne, the Mayor, or Portreeve of St. Ives, on a gallows erected in the middle of that town, whose arms are still to be seen in one of the fore-seats in that church, viz. in a plain field three pine apples. Besides those he executed many more in other places in Cornwall, that had been actors, assisters, or promoters of this rebellion. Lastly, it is further memorable of this Sir Anthony Kingston, that in Sir John Heywood's Chronicle he is taxed of extreme cruelty in doing his Marshal's office aforesaid. Of whom Fuller, in Gloucestershire, gives us this further account of him: that afterwards, in the reign of Queen Mary, being detected, with several others, of a design to rob her exchequer, though he made his escape and fled into his own country, yet there he was apprehended and taken into custody by a messenger, who was bringing him up to London in order to have justice done upon him for his crime, but he being conscious of his guilt, and despairing of pardon, so effectually poisoned himself that he died on the way, without having the due reward of his desert.

After the death of Humphrey Arundell, Governor of St. Michael's Mount, executed for treason as aforesaid, King Edward VI. sold or gave the government and revenues thereof to Job Milton, Esq. aforesaid, then Sheriff of Cornwall, during his life; but his son dying without issue male, the government, by what title I know not, devolved upon

ST. MICHAEL'S MOUNT. 199

the Bassets of Tihidy, from some of whom, as I am informed, it came by purchase to Sir John St. Aubyn, Bart. now in possession thereof.

In the month of July, 1676, at St. Michael's Mount, about four of the clock in the afternoon, came from the British ocean, or sea, a ball of fire, seen by the inhabitants and fishermen at sea, which struck against the south moorstone wall of this Mount's church or chapel; where, meeting resistance from the wall, it glanced through the stones thereof with some rebounds, making a path, or strake, through the same, in some places about four inches broad and two inches deep, from one end of the long side wall almost to the other; and from thence, by another rebound, it struck the strong oak durns of the dwelling-house entry, and broke the same in two or three pieces, and so flew into the hall, where it fell to the ground, having spent its force and strength as aforesaid, and then brake asunder in pieces, by the side of Mrs. Catherine St. Aubyn, without doing her any manner of hurt, leaving a sulphurous smoke behind it in the room; which ball of fire then appeared to consist of a black-blue metally matter, congealed or melted by fire like as coal and cinders may be, as Sir John St. Aubyn, the elder, and other spectators told me.

TONKIN.

Mr. Tonkin has not any thing in addition to Mr. Hals, except an uninteresting dissertation to prove that St. Michael's Mount is not the Ocrinum of Ptolemy.

WHITAKER.

Mr. Whitaker has given several notes and comments on the narrative of Mr. Hals, which will here be placed, together with references to the passages to which they relate.

P. 170. (*a*) The name is Mara-zion, or zien, on the sea, I

believe, and Market-Jew is merely a similar appellation in English. A Jew, in Cornish language, is Ethow, and Edheuon, Ethchan, are Jews.

P. 170. (*b*) This corrects Mr. Willis, in ii. 3, who there says of the Market-Jew, and other towns expressly, " none of them ever sent Members to Parliament, or were ever summoned so to do." Yet it coincides exactly with what Dr. Brady remarks in his very valuable treatise on Boroughs, p. 57, 59, and adds one more to his few returns, and instances of very many more which might have been produced " if needful," p. 59.

P. 172. (*c*) Sel, sil, or sul is merely a view, or prospect, from the Welsh sylly, to look or behold, and the Armorick sell, a look or sight; and din-sil, or din-sul, means only the hill of prospect.

(*d*) The real name of St. Michael's Mount in Cornish is this, Carreg luz en kuz, a hoary rock in a wood. Borlase's Scilly Isles, p. 94.

P. 178. (*e*) This notice, unobserved by the noticer himself, lets us into a part of the history of this Mount, which has never been unfolded yet. There was plainly a nunnery here, as well as a monastery. Accordingly we find before what this circumstance alone explains, that there were two chapels upon the Mount. One is described before as " a little chapel yet standing, and dedicated to the Archangel St. Michael, part whereof is now converted to a dwelling house." The other is thus, as " that which renders this place most famous, the present church or chapel, yet extant, and kept in good repair with pews; upon the tower of this church or chapel, for it is bigger than many other Cornish parish churches, is that celebrated place called Kader-Migell, i. e. Michael's chair." So distinct are these chapels! The monastery I apprehend to have been, " where, towards the north-west, is a kind of level plain about four or six landyards," with " a downright precipice of rocks towards the sea, at least twenty fathoms high." And where, about the greater chapel, are " cells cut in the rocks for hermitical monks of the aforesaid order." And the nunnery I suppose to have been where, "from this little square, or plain, there is an artificial kind of ascent going towards the east, which offers you a full sight of the outer walls of the castle, and brings you to Porth Horne (Hourn), part of which is yet to be seen."

Thus do we get a glimpse of a nunnery that is invisible from every other point. Tanner, that witness for all other authors upon monastic notices, gives us no intimation from any of them concerning this nunnery. Yet Leland confirms what I have observed in Mr. Hals before, the existence of two churches, or chapels, upon the summit of the Mount. "The way to the church," he says, concerning the ascent to the top, "entereth at the north side from half ebb to half flood, to the foot of the Mount, and so ascendeth by steps and grices westward, and thence returneth eastward to the utterward of the church," or Mount. Within the said ward is a court strongly walled, " wherein on the south side is the Chapel of St. Michael, and in the east side a chapel of our Lady. The Captain and priest's lodgings be in the south side of St. Michael's Chapel." (Itin. VII. 118.) When this Captain was fixed there with a garrison, as we shall soon see when he was, the nuns were obliged to relinquish their cells to him and them. For this reason we have not a hint in all the ages afterwards of a nunnery here. Only the chapel was continued for the use of the garrison, while the church itself was still left to the monks. Such an union as this, of a monastery and a nunnery upon the summit of a pyramidal hill, and amid the sequestrations of solitude, carries a strange appearance with it to our Protestant suspiciousness; yet it was not very uncommon in the reign of popery. It seems to have been peculiarly calculated for that purpose for which both monastery and nunnery were generally calculated, to shew the triumph of faith over the impulses of sense, and to shew that triumph more conspicuously, by the association of monks and nuns in monastic vicinity to each other. "This little fortress," as Mr. Hals has told us before, " comprehendeth sufficient rooms and lodgings for the Captain, or Governor, and his soldiers to reside in," which I have supposed above " to have been the original habitations of the nuns and their Abbess; to which adjoining are several other houses, or cells, heretofore pertaining to the monks that dwell here, all admirable for their strength, buildings, and contrivance," and all probably therefore contemporary or nearly so.

P. 180. (*f*) This account of St. Michael's Mount is in a strain of intelligence and judiciousness much superior to the general tenor of Mr. Hals's writings. To it I wish to add some useful notices, in accompaniment of some that I have given before.

Upon the very crown and summit of this pyramidal hill, stands proudly eminent the church, stretching from east to west, and having a tower in the middle. It was built by Edward the Confessor, who was the first to consecrate the Mount to religion, and erected the church on the little plain at the top of it. Having done this, and erected habitations for the clergy attending it, he gave them, by charter still existing in recital, the whole of the Mount, and many lands beside. "Ego Edwardus, Dei gracia Anglorum Rex, dare volans pretium redemptionis animæ meæ vel parentum meorum, sub consensu et testimonio bonorum virorum, tradidi Sancto Michaeli Archangelo, in usum fratrum Deo servientium in eodem loco, Sanctum Michaelem," the church, "qui est juxta mare." He also gives them " totam terram de Venefire ;" and proceeds "portum addere qui vocatur Ruminella." Romney, in Kent. Then came Robert Earl of Mortaigne, the falsely reputed founder, merely to associate this church with another of the same appellation in Normandy, and to enlarge its endowments. In a new charter, equally as the old without a date, he, " habens in bello Sancti Michaelis vexillum," says, " do et concedo Montem Sancti Michaelis de Cornubiâ Deo et monachis ecclesiæ Sancti Michaelis de Periculo

Maris servientibus, cum dimidiâ terræ hidâ." But, as he adds, " postea autem ut certissime comperi, Beati Michaelis meritis monachorumque suffragiis michi a Deo ex propriâ conjuge mea filio concesso, auxi donum ipsi beato militiæ celestis principi, dedi et dono in Amaneth (Quere, where?) tres acras terræ, Travalaboth videlicet, Lismanoch, Trequaners, Carmailoc," &c. 2. And, finally, comes the Bishop of Exeter, in a charter dated expressly 1085, to free " ecclesiam Beati Michaelis Archangeli de Cornubiâ," from all episcopal jurisdiction. 3. Thus erected and thus privileged, the church remained till the day of William of Worcester, and he thus notes the dimensions of it: " Memorandum, longitudo ecclesiæ Montis Sancti Michaelis continet 30 steppys, latitudo continet 12 steppys." 4. Carew also speaks of it as " a chapel for devotion, builded by William Earl of Morton," (Carew so speaking with the multitude, when he ought to have given the building to the Confessor,) "and greatly haunted while folk endured (endeared) their merits by farre travailing." 5. Carew thus refers obscurely, perhaps unconsciously, to a particular privilege annexed to the church, which was given by one decree from Pope Gregory, and confirmed by another from Bishop Leofric. " Universis Sanctæ Matris ecclesiæ presentes literas inspecturis vel audituris salutem," cries the former, " noverit universitas vestra quod sanctissimus Papa Gregorius, anno ab incarnatione Domini millesimo septuagesimo," the very year, therefore, in which Earl Montaign gave this church to the other in Normandy, " ad ecclesiam Montis Sancti Michaelis, in comitatu Cornubiæ, gerens eximiæ devocionis affectum, piè concessit ecclesiæ predictæ, [et] omnibus fidelibus, qui illam cum suis beneficiis et elemosinis," (with alms and oblations, so that " folke endeared their merits," not merely " by farre travailing," but by a tax upon their purse,) " exepecierint seu visitaverint, tertiam partem penetenciarum suarum eis condonari," a third of all those acts being remitted, which penitents were enjoined to perform, in order to prove the sincerity of their penitence to God, and to themselves. The same privilege is repeated by the Bishop of Exeter in 1085, thus: " omnibus illis, qui illum ecclesiam suis cum beneficiis et elemosinis expetierint et visitaverint, tertiam partem penitentiarum condonamus." Yet, what is surprising, the privilege became nearly as much unknown afterwards as it is at present, and was therefore promulgated by the clergy of the church at the beginning of the fifteenth century: " Tota verba," adds the reciter, " in antiquis registris de novo," a little before William's visit, " in hâc ecclesiâ repertis, inventa," being then unknown to the very clergy themselves, and only discovered by the discovery of some registers equally unknown, " prout hic in valvis ecclesiæ publicè ponuntur," were exhibited to public view by being posted upon the folding-doors of the church. " Et quia pluribus istud est incognitum, ideo nos, in Christo Dei famuli et ministri hujus ecclesiæ, universitatem vestram qui regimen animarum possidetis," all the rectors and vicars of the kingdom, " ob mutuæ vicissitudinis obtentum requirimus et rogamus, quatenus ista publicetis in ecclesiis vestris, ut vestri subditi et subjecti ad majorem exoracionem devocionis attentius animentur, et locum istum gloriosius peregrinando frequentent ad dona et indulgencias predicta graciosè consequenda." From this republication of the privilege, undoubtedly, did the numerous resort of pilgrims to the church begin. Then too was formed assuredly that seat on the tower, which is so ridiculously described by Carew, as " a little without the castle—a bad seat in a craggy place—somewhat dangerous for access;" when it is only a chair, composed of stones, projecting from the two sides of the tower battlements, and uniting into a seat without the south-western angle, but elevated above the battlements on each side. It thus appears somewhat dangerous from the elevation or projection only, is an evident addition to the tower, and was assuredly made at this period for the pilgrims, that they might complete their devotions at the Mount by sitting in this St. Michael's Chair, as denominated, and by showing themselves as pilgrims to the country round. Hence, in an author * who alludes to customs without feeling the force of his allusion, we read this intimation:

> Who knowes not Michael's Mount and Chaire,
> The pilgrim's holy vaunt?

We thus find a reason for the construction of such a chair, that comports with all the purposes of the church on the tower of which it is constructed, and that shows it ministered equally with this to the uses of religion then predominant; making it not, as Carew most extravagantly makes it, "somewhat dangerous for access, and therefore holy for the adventure," but holy in itself, as on the church-tower, holy in its purposes, as the seat of the pilgrims, and doubly holy as the seat of accomplishment to all their vows, as the seat of invitation to all the country. And the whole church remains to this day, beaten by the rains and buffeted by the winds, yet a venerable monument of Saxon architecture.

This Mount appears decisively, from the charter of the Confessor, to have been in his time not surrounded with the sea during all the flood tide, and not accessible by land only during some hours of the ebb-tide, as it is at present. It was then not surrounded at all. It was only near the sea then. Thus the Confessor describes it expressly, as "Sanctum Michaelem qui est juxta mare." But as Worcestre adds, with a range back into the past that is very striking, yet is in general confirmed by the charter above, "the space of ground upon Mount St. Michael is two hundred cubits, surrounded with the ocean," at flood tide; "the place aforesaid was originally inclosed with a very thick wood, distant from the ocean six miles, affording the finest shelter for wild beasts."

* William of Worcester

THE EDITOR.

Nothing is known with any certainty respecting the ancient state of St. Michael's Mount.

It may have been the seat of a Celtic superstition somewhat similar to that imagined and described by Dr. William Borlase. Sir Christopher Hawkins has adduced many arguments for proving this semi-island to have been the Ictis of Diodorus Siculus; and its situation, united to its sea-port, may well have recommended such a place for a factory to the merchants of any civilized nation engaged in commercial transactions with people so rude as were the Britons of those remote times. The universal practice in our days, is to establish fortified stations under similar circumstances, since neither person or property can be effectually protected in any other way.

The earliest definite tradition of a Christian establishment dates with the pilgrimage of St. Kenna, in consequence of the appearance of the Arch-angel at that place. No particular circumstances are ever related of this extraordinary vision, neither as to the occasion nor as to the persons so eminently favoured as to behold the celestial glory, nor as to the time, nor of the exact spot, since it could not have taken place on the top of the tower, that building having been constructed in honour of the vision itself.

It may be remarked that lofty and elevated situations throughout Europe are dedicated to St. Michael, probably on account of the Archangel being uniformly painted with wings, and therefore tacitly imagined to have habits similar to birds; and perhaps the dedication of the largest of our domestic fowls to the celebration of his festival, may owe its origin to a similar analogy.

Saint Kenna is believed to have imparted the same identical virtue to the chair which overhangs the tower, as she bestowed on the celebrated well near Liskeard, and since no one obtains a seat in this chair without much resolution and steadiness of head, one may be inclined to anticipate the supposed effect with greater certainty from the achievement of sitting in St. Michael's chair, than from drinking water from St. Kenna's well. The time of St. Kenna's visitation is not accurately known. She is supposed to be the same St. Keyna, daughter of a prince of Brecknockshire, who lived a recluse life for many years near a town situated midway between Bristol and Bath, since called Cainsbarn, after her name, where she founded a monastery in the beginning of the sixth century, and cleaned the neighbourhood from snakes and vipers by converting them all into Cornua Ammonis, which have abounded there ever since, in testimony of her sanctity and of the fervour of her prayers.

The supposed ancient site of St. Michael's Mount, its being the hoary monk in a wood surrounded by forests, is deduced from arguments very similar to those which prove the miraculous power of St. Kenna in converting serpents into stones.

Trees have been found buried under the sand and silt in the Mount's Bay, as they are frequently found in every similar inlet of the sea on the southern coast of England. And the tradition, if a term so respectable may be applied to such vague conjectures, applies equally to Mount St. Michael; or they may have been derived from a common origin. See Le Grand Dictionaire Historique, par M. Moreri, Paris edition of 1188, with the Supplement of 1735. In the 5th folio volume of the Dictionary, p. 193, and in the 2d folio volume of the Supplement, p. 261, will be found these passages:

" Saint Michel ou Mont Saint Michel, en Latin Mons Sancti Michaelis in periculo Maris. Bourg de France en Normandie, avec une Abbaie celebre et un chateau. Sa situation est assez particuliere, sur un rocher qui s'etend au milieu d'une grand greve, que la mer couvre de son reflux. On dit qu' Augustin, evêque d'Avranches, qui vivait au commencement du huitieme siecle, y suit des chanoines apres une apparition de l'Archange Seint Michel.

"Ce mont s'appelloit le Mont de Tombe à cause de sa figure. On pretend qu'une foret occupoit autrefois sont le terrain depuis le mont jusques aux Paroisses de Tanis et d'Ardevon; que la mer a detruit cette foret, et qu'elle en a pris la place; et c'est de la, dit on, que le Mont Saint Michel est surnomme, 'Au peril de la mer,' Mons in periculo Maris."

The first authentic document relative to St. Michael's Mount is the charter of Saint Edward the Confessor, the original of which remained among the archives of Mount St. Michael.

In the recent edition of Dugdale's Monasticon Anglicanum, vol. vii. p. 988:

Priory of St. Michael's Mount, in Cornwall.—A priory of Benedictine monks was placed here by King Edward the Confessor. Before A.D. 1085, however, it was annexed by Robert Earl of Moreton and Cornwall, to the Abbey of St. Michael in Periculo Maris, in Normandy.

The following entry relating to the property of St. Michael's Priory, in Cornwall, occurs in the Domesday Survey:

"Terra Sancti Michaelis.—Ecclesia S. Michaelis tenet Treiwal, Brismar tenebat tempore regis Edwardi. Ibi sunt ii hidæ quæ numquam geldaverunt. Terra est viii car. Ibi est i. car. cum uno villano, et ii. bord. et x. acr. pasturæ. Val. xx. solid. De hiis ii. hid. abstulit Comes Moriton i. hidam. Val. xx. sol."

In Hampshire, Domesday, tom. i. fol. 43, there is another entry concerning St. Michael's Priory:

In Basingstoches Hund.—Ecclesia S. Michaelis de Monte tenet de lege unam ecclesiam cum i. hida et decima M. de Basingestoches. Ibi est presbyter et ii. villani et iiii.

bord. cum i. car. et molin. de xx. sol. et ii. acr. prati. Tot. val. iiii. lib. et v. sol.

Oliver, in his Historic Collections relating to the monasteries of Devon, p. 147, gives the following list of Priors of St. Michael's Mount:—

 Ralph de Carteret, admitted Dec. 21, 1260.
 Richard Perer, ... April 11, 1275.
 Geoffrey de Gernon, ... July 8, 1283,
 Peter de Cara Villa, ... Sept. 12, 1316.
 John Hardy, ... Oct. 3, 1349.
 John de Volant, ... April 24, 1362.
 Richard Auncell, ... Dec. 7, 1385.
 William Lambert, ... Oct. 1, 1410.

As the alien priories were suppressed by Henry V. who began his reign in 1413, William Lambert was probably the last Prior.

Bishop Tanner says, in his Notitia Monastica:—After the suppression of the alien priories, this was first given by King Henry VI. to King's College, Cambridge, and afterwards by King Edward IV. to the nunnery of Sion, in Middlesex. At the first seizure by King Edward III. the farm was rated but at 10*l.* per annum, but at the general dissolution by Henry VIII. the lands belonging to this house, as parcel of Sion Abbey, were valued at 110*l.* 12*s.* per annum.

The charter of Saint Edward may be thus translated:

"In the name of the holy and indivisible Trinity. I Edward, by the grace of God King of the English, willing to give the price of the redemption of my own soul, or of the souls of my parents, with the consent and attestation of good men, have delivered to St. Michael the Archangel, for the use of the brethren serving God in that place, Saint Michael, which is near the sea, with all its appendages, that is to say, with its towns, castles, lands, and other appurtenances. I have added, moreover, all the land of Vennefire, with its towns, villages, fields, meadows, and grounds, cultivated or uncultivated, with their proceeds.

And I have joined, as an addition to the things already given, the harbour called Ruminella, with all things belonging to it, that is, with mills and establishments for fisheries and with their proceeds.

"But if any one shall endeavour to interpose subtile impediments against these gifts, let him be made an anathema, and incur the perpetual anger of God.

"And that the authority of our donation may be held the more truly and firmly hereafter, I have, in confirming it, underwritten with my own hand, which many also of the witnesses have done.

    Signum Regis Edwardi ✠
      Roberti Archiepiscopi Rothomagensis ✠
      Herberti Episcopi Lexoviensis ✠
      Roberti Episcopi Constantiensis ✠
      Radulphi ✠
      Vinfredi ✠ Nigelli Vicecomitis.
      Anschitelli Choschet. Turstini.

The next charter:

"In the name of the holy and indivisible Trinity, I Robert, by the grace of God Earl of Moriton, influenced with the fire of divine love, supporting in battle the standard of St. Michael, do make known to all the sons of our holy mother church, that for the salvation of the souls of myself and of my wife, also for the salvation, the prosperity, and safety of the most glorious King William, and for obtaining the reward of eternal life, do give and grant Mount Saint Michael, of Cornwall, to God and to the monks serving (God) of the church of Saint Michael in danger of the sea; with half a hide of land, so unbound, and peaceable and free from all customs, complaints, and suits, as I hold them. And I appoint, the King my Lord consenting, that they may hold a market on every Friday. Lastly, as I have most certainly ascertained that a son has been given me from God by my wife, through the merits of the blessed Michael, by the prayers of the monks, I have increased the gift to him the blessed chief of the heavenly host. I have given and do give in Amaneth three acres of land; that is to say, Trevelaboth, Lismanoch, Trequaners, Carmailoc, my most pious Lord King William assenting, together with the Queen Mathilde, and their noble sons the Earl Robert, William Rufus, and Henry yet a boy, to be quiet and free from all pleas, complaints, and forfeits, so that the monks shall not answer in any matter to the King's justice, homicide alone excepted.

"And I Robert Earl of Moriton have made this donation, which William the glorious King of the English, and the Queen, and their children, have permitted and testified.

Signum Willielmi Regis ✠   Reginæ Mathildis ✠
Roberti Comitis ✠   Willielmi Rufi filii Regis ✠
Henrici Pueri ✠   Roberti Comitis Moritoni ✠
Matildis Comitissæ ✠   Willielmi filii eorum ✠

This charter is ratified and confirmed in the year one thousand and eighty-five from the Incarnation of our Lord.

Signum Liurici Essecestriæ Episcopi ✠"

Among several other charters there is one from Richard King of the Romans, granting to the Prior three annual fairs, to be holden near their Grange, now the Long Barn.

"Richard by the grace of God King of the Romans, and always Augustus, to the Bishops, Abbats, Priors, Earls, Barons, and to all holding free tenures, and to others his lieges in the county of Cornwall, health, and every good. May you all know that we, by this our present confirmation, have granted and confirmed to the Prior of the blessed Michael, in Cornwall, and to his successors, that they may have and hold, and for ever possess, the three fairs and three markets on their own proper ground in Marchadyon, near their Barn; which three fairs and three markets they have hitherto held by the concession of our predecessors Kings of England, in Marghasbigan, on ground belonging to others; that is to say, on the middle day in Lent, and on the following day; and on the eve of the blessed Michael, and on the following day; and on the eve of the blessed Michael in monte tumbæ, and on the following day, provided that these fairs and markets may not cause any damage or injury to other fairs or markets, in conformity with the laws and customs of this kingdom of England.

"In witness of all which things we have thought fit to certify this present confirmation with our royal seal."

There is also a bull of Pope Adrian, in the year 1155, confirming all their possessions to the Abbat and monks of Mount St. Michael, and among them Saint Michael's Mount, in Cornwall; which, previously to its subjugation, had been exempted from all episcopal interference by Liuricus Bishop of Exeter, as he states by the exhortation and command of his Lord, Pope Gregory, and in compliance with the wishes of the King, of the Queen, and of all the magnates in the realm. And he also grants a release from a third part of their penances to all such persons as may visit this church of St. Michael with oblations and alms.

The Mount appears never to have received a religious society after its suppression as an alien priory in the reign of King Henry the Fifth. At the period of the general dissolution it must have been let at an annual rent, for in the abstract roll preserved in the Augmentation Office this entry occurs under Syon Abbey: "Cornub.— S. Michael. ad Montem, Firma 26*l.* 13*s.* 4*d.*"

The history of St. Michael's Mount since its dissolution, as a parcel of Sion Abbey, is very far from being clear. It appears to have been granted at first for terms of years to different gentlemen of the neighbourhood. To Millington, supposed of Pengersick, in Breage; to Harris, of Kenegie, in Gulval; and perhaps jointly with Millington to a Billett or Bennett. A person of that name, half-deranged, who died about the middle of the last century, continued during the whole of his life to shoot rabbits on the Mount one day in the year by way of maintaining a supposed right, which, being utterly groundless, was humanely allowed to pass unobserved.

Queen Elizabeth, or King James I. appears to have granted the whole in fee to Robert Cecil, created Earl of Salisbury May 4, 1605. But the Mount was seised into his own hands by King Charles I. just at the breaking out of the civil war, probably on account of the great military importance of this hold, when William Cecil, son of the former, having subscribed the Declaration made at York, on the 13th of June, 1642, left the party of which the King was at the head, and joined the opposite party in London.

An order was soon after given to Sir Francis Basset, then Sheriff of Cornwall, to place the Mount in a state of defence, and to supply it with ammunition and provisions; and it is not improbable that a grant was made of the castle and Mount to Sir Francis Basset at once, in witness of his zeal displayed in the cause, and as some indemnity for the expenses he had incurred, the royalist party never having had any considerable sum of money at their command.

The Bassets having suffered extremely in their property by efforts made during the war, and by compositions afterwards, it was found convenient to sell St. Michael's Mount about the year 1660; when it was most fortunately purchased by Sir John St. Aubyn, in whose opulent family, and through five John St. Aubyns, it has descended to the present possessor of that name.

Every individual of this family has proved himself desirous of supporting, of maintaining, and of beautifying one of the most extrordinary spots in the whole world.

Including Dartmoor and the Scilly Islands, granite breaks out into six large but unequal masses, which, like the Appenines of Italy, extend a narrow promontory into the sea. St Michael's Mount presents a ridge of granite equally distinct with any of these great masses, and rises into a lofty cone, the base being surrounded by the killas, a peculiar schist, the chief metalliferous rock of Cornwall.

And here most of the curious phenomena are found which occur at the junction of these two rocks.

The buildings on the summit are grand and appropriate to the scenery, and venerable from their antiquity. The church, with its tower, completing the pyramidal figure of the whole, are supposed to date so far back as the reign of St. Edward. And a modern addition of two rooms on the eastern part of the building, made by the late Sir John Aubyn about the year 1750, is in complete harmony with the other parts, and adds to the general effect.

The inside of the castle, or priory, has been much decorated within a few years, and florid gothic ornaments have been added to the exterior; but opinions are much divided as to the accordance of these new parts with buildings to which Sir Walter Scott's line may be applied,

In Saxon strength the Abbey frown'd.

At the foot of the Mount a small pier existed from a time probably anterior to the Monastery itself, but in the early part of the last century a lease on lives was granted to Mr. George Blewett, the early associate and in some degree rival of the great Mr. Lemon. This gentleman rebuilt the pier on a very enlarged scale, and concentrated here almost the whole commerce of Penwith hundred, which has since his time gone to Penzance and Hayle.

St. Michael's Mount is said to be selected as the scene of many strange adventures, in Italian romances; while Cornwall is supposed to abound with enchanters, goblins, and other supernatural beings.

An English romance, once popular with the old and with the young, but now banished even from our nurseries, begins thus:

"In the days of King Arthur the Mount of Cornwall was kept by a monstrous giant." ma

Tasca Argo i Mini, e tascia Artu qui' suoi
Erronti, che di sogni empion le carte.

Marazion has certainly to boast of very great antiquity.

MARAZION. 215

It may have existed in the earliest times, if the Mount really afforded protection to the Eastern merchants, who sought the shores of Cornwall for its tin.

And the names Marazion and Marketjew cannot but excite an inclination to believe that in the Middle Ages this place may have been the resort of the most extraordinary people, who at all times have manifested a peculiar inclination for dealing in metals; it is moreover worthy of remark that all remains of places where tin has heretofore been smelted in the most simple manner, are invariably denominated Jew's Houses. Marazion must also have afforded shelter and entertainment to the crowds of pilgrims assembling at particular periods to adore the Shrine of St. Michael, and to participate in the indulgence granted by Liuricus Bishop of Exeter, on the exhortation of his Lord the Pope.

Marazion received a charter of incorporation from Queen Elizabeth, but the town, although beautifully situated, has not kept pace in the career of improvement with many others, and especially not with Penzance.

About the middle of the last century, which was the great epoch for the establishment of turnpike roads, as the beginning of this century will be considered for their improvement on principles of science and of general accommodation, a turnpike road was laid out from Falmouth, through Penryn and Helston, to the western of Marazion, by which a new entrance was opened from Penzance; and about the year 1775 a large castellated house was built at the western extremity of the town, by Mr. John Blewett, son of Mr. George Blewett, the very considerable merchant noticed above, in imitation of the house at Tregenna, near St. Ive's, built by Mr. Samuel Stephens a few years before, under the direction of Mr. Wood, an architect from Bath, who had constructed most of the splendid works in that city.

Mr. George Blewett, rising from the lowest origin, is said to have accumulated a hundred thousand pounds. On the death of his only son the property went to a nephew, and the whole has been dissipated.

The house was some time afterwards purchased by another Mr. Blewett, wholly unconnected with the former, who acquired a considerable fortune in the war: that has also entirely disappeared, and the house has passed into other hands.

Mr. Pascoe Grenfell, Commissary to the States of Holland, resided here during a long life, although he was originally of Penzance; and here was born his son Mr. Pascoe Grenfell, junior, well known throughout England as an active Member of Parliament, as a man of talent and of great liberality, commensurate to his almost unexampled success in commerce.

From Marazion also have sprung the family of Cole.

Captain Francis Cole would have risen to the most elevated station in the Navy if he had not been cut off by an early death.

Captain Christopher Cole most justly acquired the highest military reputation by his capture of Banda in the East Indies, with a force several times less numerous than the garrison which he overcame; and, having taken the place with such an union of courage, determined resolution, and of prudence, as would rival the exploits of chivalry, he acquired still greater glory by extending a truly heroic courtesy to the vanquished, protecting them in their persons, in their properties, and in the exercise of their religious and of their civil rights. Having settled, in consequence of his marriage, in Glamorganshire, he has had the honour of representing that county in Parliament.

The Reverend John Cole, D.D. attained the high situation of Rector of Exeter College, Oxford.

And the younger brother, Dr. Samuel Cole, is now Chaplain-general to the Navy.

The principal inhabitant at present is Mr. William Cornish, a very respectable merchant and a magistrate for the

ST. HILARY.

county; he married a daughter of the elder Captain Cole, and has a numerous family.

Treveneage seems to have been the principal seat in this parish. A branch of the Godolphins resided here, having acquired the property by a marriage with the heiress of an ancient family denominated Goverigon or Gavrigan, whose principal residence was in St. Colomb.

Katherine Godolphin, daughter and heiress of Francis Godolphin, Esq. of Treveneage, married John St. Aubyn, of Clowance, Esq. and was buried at St. Hilary, on the 13th of March 1662, as appears from an inscription on a monument to her memory in the church.

The barton of Treveneage was however sold, and after passing through Robinson, it was purchased, about the year 1665, by the family of Tredenham, of Tredenham, or Tredinham, in Probus.

Mr. Joseph Tredinham was Sheriff of Cornwall in 1665, and was knighted. One of his daughters, and eventually his coheiress, married Scobell of Menigwins, in St. Austell; and from a coheiress of Scobell this barton, together with an extensive manor, descended to the Hawkins's of Pennance, and from them to the late Sir Christopher Hawkins, of Trewithan in Probus, and of Trewinnard in St. Erth.

Tregembo, or Tregember, bears an appearance of considerable antiquity. Mr. Lysons says that it belonged to the family of Grosse, and that it passed by sales, through King to Penneck, in the year 1684.

The Pennecks were originally of Trescow in Breage, and advanced themselves in the world by the stewardship and patronage of the Godolphins. One of this family, the Reverend John Penneck, who died in 1724, was Chancellor of Exeter, and would probably have been advanced much higher in the church if the Marlborough and Godolphin administration had remained longer in the possession of power.

On this gentleman's decease, without children, his property devolved on the Reverend John Penneck, vicar of Gulval, who married —— Wroughton, and left two sons and two daughters; John, who succeeded him in the living of Gulval, and Charles, bred to the law, but who quitted that profession for the militia during the American War.

Mr. John Penneck died in 1789, and his brother in 1801; they were succeeded by their two sisters, who were, Catherine, married to the Reverend William Borlase, son and eventually sole heir of the Reverend Walter Borlase, LL.D. of Castlehorneck; and Ann, married to John Bingham Borlase, M.D. who had the honour of bestowing his early medical education on Sir Humphrey Davy. Each of these sisters left an only daughter. Ann, daughter of the eldest, married to the Reverend Mr. Peters; and Ann, daughter of the second, married to Captain Pascoe.

The manor of Tregurtha also belonged to the Pennecks, having been purchased in the early part of the last century; but this manor, together with a large portion of their other possessions, were sold by the two last brothers. This manor was bought jointly by Mr. Carne, of Penzance, and the late Mr. Thomas Grylls, of Helston. Tregembo still belongs to the two ladies.

Ennis, usually called Ninnis, was for some time a gentleman's seat, although it is now become a mere farm. Mr. Humphrey Millett, the last resident gentleman, had been a member of Exeter College. He married Mary, daughter of Mr. Sandys, of Helston, and dying early in life left two daughters his coheiresses. The eldest daughter, Mary, married Thomas Grylls, Esq. and the second daughter, Grace, married Charles Short, Esq. of Devonshire, Clerk of the Rules in the Court of King's Bench, and both have families. The widow married secondly George Trework, Esq. of Penzance.

Trevarthen has the appearance of a place respectable in former times. The freehold belongs to the Duke of Leeds, as heir of the Godolphins; but it was held for a long period of years on a lease for lives by one of the numerous branches of the family of Davies, now all extinct.

This parish has abounded in mines, especially in the manors of Treveneage and Tregurtha; but the most remarkable in its consequences was a mine called Whele Fortune, on Trowall or Truthwell, belonging to Lord Godolphin, as it enabled Mr. Lemon to move on the great scale which afterwards so eminently distinguished him; as it laid the foundation of Mr. Blewett's large fortune; and brought forward Captain Dewen, whose fortune descended on two daughters, one married to the Rev. George Borlase, Fellow of All Souls, and son of the historian; the other married to Mr. Keir, a gentleman in the profession of medicine.

The church is situated on a commanding elevation, and would be an imposing object throughout the whole neighbourhood, if it were not disfigured by an insignificant spire.

The church and churchyard contain several monuments to the Godolphins, Pennecks, Milletts, Blewetts, &c.

On a stone, now made the floor of a seat in the south east corner of St. Hilary church, is the following curious inscription to one of the Godolphins.

> Aquila quæ volucres cœli supereminet omnes,
> Et Caper e summis qui carpit montibus herbam,
> Quique tuum referens *Godolphin* nomen in undis
> Delphinus, piscesque regit, cursuque fatigat;
> Hæc bene te natum proavis insignia monstrant
> Per cœlum, et terras, et vasta per æquora claris,
> Et tua te virtus cunctis majoribus æquat.
> > Sic transit Gloria Mundi!
> > Et quæ modo candida Nix est,
> > Phœbo splendente, liquescit.
> > Et quæ modo florida vigent
> > Per amœnos Lilia campos,
> > Citius quam dicere possis,
> > Aspectu Solis eoi
> > Marcescunt; sic violentis
> > Fatorum legibus omnes
> > Cedunt, juvenesque senesque,

Sic qui modo floruit inter
Primos, generosus, et inter
Claros; quos vexit honoris
Summi ad fastigia virtus;
Nulli pietate secundus,
Godolphin morte peremptus,
Fatis succumbit iniquis.
Humana hinc discite quàm
Vita incerta et brevis!
Sic transit Gloria Mundi!

In connection with the church, one of those casual coincidences may be noticed, which continued to be remembered and cited for more than a century in this parish, and to obtain belief or discredit, as an interposition of Providence, according to the religious or the political opinions of those who heard or related it.

It seems that a Mr. Palmer held this living previously to the Restoration of King Charles II. and that he was one among the two thousand, who in obedience to the dictates of their consciences, from the fear of disgrace, or from political motives, refused, " In the church, chapel, or place of public worship belonging to their benefices or promotions, upon some Lord's Day before the Feast of St. Bartholomew, which should be in the year of our Lord God one thousand six hundred and sixty-two, openly, publickly, and solemnly to read the morning and evening prayer, appointed to be read by and according to the Book of Common Prayer, at the times thereby appointed, and after such reading thereof, and openly and publickly before the congregation there assembled, to declare their unfeigned assent to the use of all things in the said book contained and prescribed." See the Act of Uniformity, anno decimo tertio et quarto Caroli II. ch. 4.

In consequence of this refusal the two thousand incumbents were ejected without any provision or allowance whatever, so that many of them perished from actual want. Several thus ejected without doubt continued the exercise of their sacred functions among such as were desirous or willing to assist at them; and for this offence Mr. Palmer was called before magistrates appointed by the new government, who ordered his commitment to prison, when the ejected vicar is said to have addressed Mr Robinson, of Treveneage, one of the magistrates, in the words of Micaiah, " If thou return at all in peace, the Lord hath not spoken by me."

Within a short time after this vaticination Mr. Robinson met his death by the goring of his own bull.

It would be inexcusable in me if I were to leave this parish without noticing the late Vicar, from whose kindness I received information whenever it was asked, in those sciences which have afforded me uninterrupted entertainment and delight throughout the whole continuance of a protracted life.

The Reverend Malachy Hitchins was born in the parish of Gwenap, about the year 1740; possessed of hereditary claims to mathematical attainments as the nephew of Mr. Thomas Martyn, well known by his excellent map of Cornwall published about that time; a map then equalling if not surpassing the best county maps of England, and still almost unrivalled for minute and accurate topography, including the boundaries of parishes—the work of fifteen years labour.

I have not succeeded in acquiring any information respecting Mr. Hitchins in his early years, with the exception of a general report of his being then distinguished by the ability, accuracy, and diligence conspicuous in his future years.

These qualities, and probably his near connection with Mr. Martyn, recommended Mr. Hitchins as an assistant to Mr. Benjamin Donne in constructing a map of Devonshire, an occupation decisive of his future life, for at Bideford he became acquainted with Miss Hockin, whom he married, and acquiring with her an accession of fortune, he proceeded to Oxford, and became a member of Exeter College, with the view of obtaining orders. But Mr. Hitchins possessed talents and acquirements that could not admit of his remaining undistinguished at a place of learning. He was soon noticed by the mathematicians, and recommended to the Reverend Nevil Maskelyne, Astronomer Royal, to assist him at the Royal Observatory; and when Doctor Maskelyne went to St. Helena, in the year 1761, to observe the transit of Venus, and to ascertain, if it were possible, the parallax of Sirius, Mr. Hitchins had the whole care of the Observatory entrusted to his hands.

Another object of Doctor Maskelyne's voyage, and one eventually of by far the greatest importance, was to prove from actual experience that Longitudes at sea might be derived from observations on the moon. Tables founded on the theory of gravitation and of inertia, as laid down by SIR ISAAC NEWTON, had then been constructed by Tobias Mayer, of Gottingen, and communicated to Dr. Maskelyne in manuscript, representing the moon's place at all times in the heavens, within narrow limits; and the admirable instrument invented by Mr. John Hadley, by rendering the apparent contact of two objects, independent of all agitations of the instrument itself, enabled observers to ascertain the distance of the moon from the sun, or from a star, almost as accurately on board a ship as on the solid land. With these assistances the determination of a ship's longitude became an easy problem. The moon is converted into the hand of a clock, indicating by its distance from a particular star, the time at Greenwich Observatory made the first meridian. This distance is ascertained by Hadley's sextant, and after applying certain corrections for parallax and refraction, the time at Greenwich becomes known. The actual time at the place of observation is then determined from the altitude of some celestial body, and thus differences in the longitude required.

Doctor Maskelyne having fully verified the complete practicability of this method, procured throguh the Board of Longitude the publication of Mayer's tables, accompanied by a reward or premium, under an Act of Parliament, to his widow, of three thousand pounds; and soon afterwards the same eminent and patriotic astronomer devised and executed a work absolutely necessary for enabling ordinary persons to avail themselves of this important discovery, namely the Nautical Almanac, in which the sun's place is accurately given for the noon of each day, the place of the moon for noon and midnight of each day, and the true angular distance of the moon from the sun, and from certain stars for every third hour of the day and of the night throughout the year, together with the equation of time, the places of the planets, &c.: thus saving to observers perhaps ninety-nine parts out of a hundred of the calculations that were previously indispensible.

The labour of such a work must obviously require many hands, especially as without great care in constructing the original calculation, and in correcting the press, it would prove worse than useless. To ensure this accuracy, the most important parts were performed in duplicate by different persons, and the whole carefully collated and verified by the superior officer, called the Comparer, under the ultimate superintendence of the Astronomer Royal himself.

In constructing the first Nautical Almanac that appeared, for 1767, Mr. Hitchins performed the office of a computer; but for all the others, up to the period of his decease in 1809, he most advantageously, not only for this country but for the whole world, executed the office of comparer.

The Lunar tables are now carried to a degree of perfection far exceeding those of Mayer, and the Nautical Almanac has been enlarged and improved; but the glory of devising the work remains with Doctor Maskelyne, and perhaps scarcely a less degree of glory with Mr. Hitchins, for having conducted it with unrivalled accuracy for a period extending through so great a number of years.

During his residence at Greenwich Mr. Hitchins had received holy orders; and, as the office of comparer did not confine him to any particular place, he removed to Exeter, and soon obtained the vicarage of Hennock, to hold for a minor. He did not fail however of attracting attention from the clergy of the Cathedral, and about the year 1774 Bishop Keppell collated him to St Hilary, which had lapsed in consequence of a dispute between two of the numerous patrons claiming unsettled turns to the presentation. Here Mr. Hitchins resided respected and admired till the close of his life, on the 28th of March 1809; having been distinguished by the succeeding Bishop of Exeter, Dr. John Ross, who conferred on him the adjoining vicarage of Gwinear.

Mr. Hitchins had four sons and one daughter.

The eldest, Richard, was a Fellow of Exeter College, and died unmarried on a college living.

The second, Thomas, also a clergyman, married Miss Emma Grenfell, of Marazion; he served for many years a church near Plymouth, and has left several children.

The third, Malachy, inherited his father's genius with his name. He filled the office for some time that his father had occupied in the Royal Observatory; but ultimately preferring the law, he settled at Marazion, where he died at an early age in December 1802.

The fourth son, Fortescue, was also in the law, and settled at St. Ive's. He distinguished himself as a poet and as a writer, having taken a considerable share in compiling a History of Cornwall; but his life was also restricted to a narrow space.

The only daughter, Josepha, married William Millett, Esq. originally of Gurlin in St. Erth, and is now a widow with several sons.

Mr. Hitchins had his time too much occupied to allow of his composing any considerable work. He made one communication however to the Royal Society, and another to the Society of Antiquaries; besides these there are various minor publications, some bearing his name, and others the signature of Vatum Ultimus, alluding to his

ST. HILARY.

which is not uncommon in Cornwall, is probably derived not immediately from the Hebrew Prophet, but from St. Malachy, Archbishop of Armagh, who is said to have died in the arms of St. Bernard in the year 1148.

Mr. Hitchins was succeeded by the Reverend Thomas Pascoe, the present vicar.

The Parish Feast is celebrated on the Sunday nearest to the 13th of January, the day of the patron Saint.

St. Hilary measures 3228 statute acres.

And here it is right to state that all the measurements of parishes were made by Mr. Hitchins, from the boundaries laid down in his uncle's map, and that they are copied from a manuscript which he had the kindness to give me in Oct. 1805.

	£.	s.	d.
Annual value of the Real Property, as returned to Parliament in 1815	3322	0	0
Poor Rate in 1831	676	16	0

Population,—	in 1801,	in 1811,	in 1821,	in 1831,
	990	1248	1558	1728

giving an increase of $74\frac{1}{2}$ per cent in 30 years.

THE GEOLOGY, BY DR. BOASE.

This parish is similarly constituted to the adjacent parishes of St. Erth and Gwinear, being all situated on a line running north-east and south-west, between the large masses of granite of the Land's End and of Cambrea.

St. Michael's Mount, adjoining the shore of this parish, is an object of great attention to the geologist as well as to the tourist. It is composed almost entirely of granite, having only two small patches of slate, one on the western and the other on the eastern side; at these two places, and more particularly at the latter, the junction of the granite and of the slate may be seen, the slate being intersected with numerous granite veins. The granite of the Mount is not so large-grained as that of the Land's End; but the structure of the rock is no where better displayed than at this place on the southern side; where the whole mass is distinctly divided into large quadrangular blocks, and is traversed in a direction parallel to the divisions, by quartz veins, which contain crystals of mica, of apatite, and of topaz, and also the ores of tin, copper, and wolfram, the latter of which is the most abundant.

One most important geological fact is here beautifully exhibited. That the mineral composition of granite is altered in the vicinity of quartz veins, whether they are metalliferous or otherwise; approaching these veins the granite becomes more and more siliceous, until at length it gradually passes into the quartz, which forms the body (or matrix as it is called) of the veins. A fact difficult to reconcile with the generally received opinion, which assumes all veins to have been originally fissures, subsequently filled up from above or beneath.

HILL, NORTH.

HALS.

Is situate in the hundred of East, and hath upon the north Lewanack, east Lezant, south and west Linkynhorne. Under what district this parish was taxed in Domesday Roll I know not; however, in the Inquisition of the Bishops of Lincoln and Winchester, into the value of Cornish Benefices, 1294, " Ecclesia de Northill in decanatu de Estwellshire" was taxed £6; in Wolsey's Inquisition, 1521, £36. 6s. 8d. The patronage is in Darley; the incumbent Darley. The parish is rated to the 4s. per pound Land Tax, 1696, £211. 12s.

Trebatha, in this parish, which after the English-Cornish may be interpreted a town of baths, or washing fountains, otherwise the town of clubs or bats, is the dwelling of an old family of gentlemen surnamed Spour. The present possessor Henry Spour, Gent. that married Rhodes, and giveth for his arms, Gules, on a chevron Or, a rose of the first between two mullets or spur rowells Sable pierced. Now Charles Grylls, Esq. married the daughter and heir of Spour, relict of Bellot, of Bochin. She surviving her husband, without issue, as I am informed, is married to her cousin Rodd, and to him and his heirs hath conveyed all her lands.

Batt-in, Batt-en, in this parish, from which place was denominated an old family of gentlemen surnamed Battin, whose only daughter and heir, in the latter end of Queen Elizabeth's reign, was married to one Mr. Vincent, a barrister-at-law, that came down the Western Circuit with the judges, and so together with herself brought this barton into his family.

The late possessor, John Vincent, Gent. sometime Fellow of All Souls College in Oxford, originally descended, as I am informed, from the Vincents of Stoke Dabernon in Surrey, and giveth the same arms, viz. Azure, three quatrefoils Argent. His younger brother, Mr. Matthias Vincent, was bound or bred an apprentice with a merchant at London, and having but a small fortune to begin trade with, yet for his care and industry was so taken notice of in London that he was sent by the East India Company as one of their factors to Surat in the Mogul's country, where by his skill in factorage and merchandize, but chiefly by marriage with a Portugal merchant's daughter and heir, he obtained a great quantity of riches, goods, and chattels; whereupon he left his servile trade of a factor to others, and returned with his family and riches safely into England, temp. James II. by whom he was knighted, and in one of his Parliaments was chosen a burgess for the town of Lestwithell, and served in that capacity for some time, till an unlucky accident happened between him and his wife, or lady, who upon some real or feigned grounds grew jealous of his familiarity with another, privately eloped from him, carrying with her great quantities of his gold and jewels. He left issue by her two sons, lately living, though, as I am told, this estate for the most part is spent or consumed.

TONKIN.

Mr. Tonkin has not made any addition to the history of this parish.

THE EDITOR.

By far the principal place in this parish is Trebartha, now for three descents the residence of the very respectable family of Rodd.

Mrs. Grylls bequeathed her property to Mr. Francis Rodd, of Herefordshire, a Captain in the Guards, not as her relation but as her intended third husband. This gentleman was succeeded by his son Francis Rodd, for many years Colonel of the Cornwall Militia. He married one of the three coheiresses of Heale and Paynten, and left three sons, Francis Heale Rodd, Esq. the present possessor of Trebartha; the Rev. Edward Rodd, D.D. and Rector of St. Just in Roseland, heretofore Fellow of Exeter College, and Proctor of the University of Oxford in the year 1802; and Sir John Tremayne Rodd, an Admiral. Also two daughters, Jane and Harriet, the latter married to Mr. Fursdon, of Devonshire.

Trebartha is in many respects worthy of being reckoned among the first places in Cornwall. The scenery, grand in other respects, is rendered still more so by the addition of a mountain torrent; and the house has been greatly improved by the late proprietor and the present, who has chiefly resided there, highly respected as a magistrate, as a gentleman, and as the benefactor of his neighbourhood. Mr. Rodd was a Fellow of All Souls, and during the war he served, as his father had done before him, in the defence of his country.

Mr. Lysons says that the Lord of the Manor of Treveniel, which was passed from the Carews to the Spours, and from them to Rodd, claims by immemorial custom of the Mayor of Launceston the service of holding his stirrup whenever he shall mount his horse in that town in presence of the Duke of Cornwall; a claim, however, difficult to prove by any exercise of it, even within legal memory, and now rendered obsolete by disusage if that effect is ever produced.

The presentation to the living is in Mr. Rodd. The church is large, consisting of three entire ailes with a lofty tower, and placed on a commanding eminence. The interior is adorned with several splendid monuments of the present and former families resident at Trebartha.

The present rector is the Rev. E. Trelawny, instituted in 1828.

North-hill measures 6,815 statute acres.

	£.	s.	d.
Annual value of the Real Property, as returned to Parliament in 1815	5102	0	0
Poor Rate in 1831	531	8	0

Population, —	in 1801,	in 1811,	in 1821,	in 1831,
	782	803	1089	1155

giving an increase of nearly $4\frac{3}{4}$ per cent. in 30 years.

GEOLOGY, BY DR. BOASE.

The western half of this parish is situated on granite, and the eastern half on slate belonging to the porphyritic series. The rocks of both resemble those of the corresponding parts of Alternum.

HILL, SOUTH.

HALS.

Is situate in the hundred of East, and hath upon the north Linkynhorne, east Stoke Climsland, south Killaton, west St. Ive. At the time of the Domesday-tax this parish, I suppose, was rated under the jurisdiction of Stoke Climsland or Trewollea, or Trewoolea. In the Inquisition of the Bishops of Lincoln and Winchester aforesaid, 1294, Ecclesia de Sut Hill was rated cxiiis. ivd.; in Wolsey's Inquisition £38. The patronage in the King or Duke of Cornwall; the incumbent Trelawny, Dean of Exeter; and the parish rated to the 4s. per pound Land Tax, 1696, 139l. 4s.

Quere, whether Killington Church be not a daughter to or consolidated into this church?

Mana-ton, in this parish, gave name and origin to an old family of gentlemen, from thence surnamed de Manaton; the present possessor, Francis Manaton, Esq. Receiver-general of her Majesty's Land Tax, that married Huckmore, and giveth for his arms, Argent, on a bend Sable, three mullets of the Field.

TONKIN.

It is so called from its situation in respect to North Hill, and its church lying on a high hill. The patronage in Trelawny. The incumbent Mr. Hele Trelawny, who succeeded his kinsman Edward Trelawny, Dean of Exeter.

Manor of Kellyland. This is the chief estate in the parish, it is called Conylond by Mr. Carew, through mistake, in one place, as he rightly names it in another, and is there said to be held by the Baron of Stafford.

The manor of Manaton, which I take to signify Stony Hill, as corrupted from main, a stone, and doon, a hill, has been ever the seat, perhaps from before the Conquest, of the family of that name, though the head of it Francis Manaton, Esq. has lately removed to Kilworthy, near Tavistock, which fell to him on the death of his kinsman Henry Manaton, Esq. of that place, and of Harwood in Calstock. Since his removal the house here, which was ruinous, has been left to fall, which I should scarce have noticed had I not observed the old arms of this family painted on glass in the hall there, Sable, a saltire Vairy between twelve crosses pattee fitchy Or, within a border Argent; which they have changed for, Argent, a bend Sable charged with three mullets of the Field, their present bearing.

THE EDITOR.

Mr. Whitaker, in a note, suggests Manach Don, or Ton, the Monk's House, as the derivation for Manaton.

Mr. Lysons says that two thirds of the great manor of Calliland or Kalliland, passed from the baronial family of Stafford, by a coheiress, to Willoughby Lord Brook, and are now vested in Lord Clinton; the other third was in the Crown, and was granted by King Richard the Third to John Coryton, Esq. of Newton; that it belonged in 1620 to the Glanvilles, and is now vested in Richard Strode, Esq. and that Manaton is become the property of Sir William Call. Lord Clinton is patron of the rectory; which was called St. Sampson's de Southill, in honour no doubt of St. Sampson already mentioned, a native of Monmouthshire, and afterwards a Bishop in France.

The church is large, and placed on an elevated situation, and contains memorials of the Manaton family.

The Rev. John Trefusis, instituted in 1802, is the present rector.

Southill measures 3089 statute acres.

	£.	s.	d.
Annual value of the Real Property, as returned to Parliament in 1815 . .	2622	0	0
Poor Rate in 1831	507	10	0

Population,— | in 1801, | in 1811, | in 1821, | in 1831, |
| --- | --- | --- | --- |
| 447 | 466 | 534 | 530 |

giving an increase of $18\frac{1}{2}$ per cent. in 30 years.

GEOLOGY, BY DOCTOR BOASE.

The eastern part of this parish nearly touches the granite of Hingston Down. Like the adjoining parish of Callington, its rocks are felspathic; and they are intersected by beds of porphyry, and by numerous metalliferous veins. The rocks of the other parts of the parish are rather anomalous, being such as occur between the porphyritic and the calcareous series.

JACOBSTOW.

HALS.

Is situate in the hundred of Stratton, and hath upon the north Poundstock, east St. Mary Wick, west St. Gennis, south Otterham.

In the Domesday Tax, 1087, this parish passed under the jurisdiction of Pen-fon, or Pen-foun. In the inquisition of the Bishops of Lincoln and Winchester, 1294, Ecclesia de Jacobstow in decanatu de Trigmajorshire was valued vi$l$.; in Wolsey's Inquisition, 1521, and Valor Beneficiorum 19l.; the patronage in Elliot; the incumbent Holden; and the parish rated to the 4s. per pound Land Tax, 1696, 113l. 14s.

Pen-fon, now Penfowne aforesaid, i. e. head well, spring of water or fountain, gave name and original to an old family of gentlemen surnamed de Penfowne, who have lived here in good fame and reputation for many generations.

TONKIN.

I take St. Jacob to be the patron Saint of this parish, and not the patriarch Jacob, as some have imagined.

The termination Stowe comes from the Saxon, and means a home or a dwelling.

THE EDITOR.

Mr. Lysons mentions some few particulars respecting this parish. He says that Sawacott, or Southcot, is the sole village in the parish; and that a manor called Penhallam, having belonged to a Sir John Stowell in the reign of Queen Elizabeth, has passed through various hands, and that it had been finally purchased about the year 1802 by the Rev. Charles Dayman.

The barton of Berry Court has its mansion surrounded by a moat, indicative of ancient importance, but nothing seems to be known of its history.

In Wood's Athenæ Oxonienses may be found the following account of a native of this parish:

Degorie Wheare was born at Jacobstow in Cornwall; retired to the habitation of the Muses called Broadgate Hall (Pembroke College) in the beginning of the year 1592, aged 19; took the degrees in Arts, that of Master being completed in 1600; elected probationer fellow of Exeter College; and six years afterwards leaving that house, travelled into several countries beyond the seas, by which he obtained as well learning as experience.

At his return he was entertained by the Lord Chandois, and by him respected and exhibited to. After his death our author with his wife retired to Gloucester Hall, where Doctor Hawley, the Principal, demised to him lodgings; and there he became so well acquainted with Mr. Thomas Allen, that by his endeavours the learned Cambden made him his First Reader of his History Lecture which he founded in the University.

Soon after he was made Principal of the Hall, the which with his Lecture he kept to his dying day; and was esteemed by some a learned and genteel man, and by others a Calvinist.

Having entered at Oxford in the year 1592, aged, as his friend states, nineteen years, the date of his birth must be 1573; and it appears from the Fasti of Gloucester Hall, now Worcester College, that he died in 1647, aged therefore 74. His chief works are,

Prælectiones Hiemales de Ratione et Methodo Legendi Historias Civiles et Ecclesiasticas; this work has gone through several editions, and been translated into English.

234 ILLOGAN.

Oratio Auspicalis ubi Cathedram Historicam primum ascendit.

Parentatio Historica—Commemoratio Vitæ et Martis Gulielmi Camdeni, cum Imaginis Camdenianæ Dedicatione.

Lord St. German's (Eliot) is patron of the living, and the present rector is the Rev. John Glanville, instituted in 1822.

Jacobstow measures 4,206 statute acres.

	£.	s.	d.
Annual value of the Real Property, as returned to Parliament in 1815	2098	0	0
Poor Rate in 1831	270	6	0

Population,— { in 1801, 432 | in 1811, 489 | in 1821, 571 | in 1831, 638 }

giving an increase of 47⅔ per cent. in 30 years.

GEOLOGY, BY DR. BOASE.

This parish is entirely situated on the Dunstone rocks, mentioned under the heads of Boyton and St. Gennys. To the cursory observer few opportunities offer themselves here for studying the nature of the rocks; but perhaps many quarries or similar excavations may be known to those who are resident.

ILLOGAN.

HALS.

Is situate in the Hundred of Penwith, and hath upon the north the Irish sea, west Gwithian, south Camburne, east St. Agnes.

In the inquisition of the Bishops of Lincoln and Winchester 1294, Ecclesia Sancti Illogani was valued to first fruits £8. In Wolsey's inquisition 1521, by the same name, £22. 7s. 5d.; the patronage in Basset, the incumbent Basset; and the parish rated to the 4s. per pound Land Tax 1696, by the same name, £191. 16s.

ILLOGAN.

The lordship of Ty-hiddy, alias Ty-lud-y, in this parish, hath from the time of Henry the Third, how long before I know not, been the seat of the ancient and knightly family of the Bassets, whose first ancestor came out of Normandy with William the Conqueror 1066, and was posted in those parts a soldier under Robert Earl of Morton and Cornwall, of whose posterity (an officer or soldier 17th Edward II.) was William Basset, who was then possessed of £40 *per annum* in lands and rents in knight service. Carew's Surv. Corn. p. 51. William Basset, of Ty-hyddy, 3 Henry IV. held in that place and Trevalga, one knight's fee of Morton, (idem liber); John Bassett was Sheriff of Cornwall 28 Henry VI. when John Chudleigh was Sheriff of Devon; John Basset was Sheriff of Cornwall 13 Henry VII. when Peter Edgecomb was Sheriff of Devon; John Basset, Knight, was Sheriff of Cornwall 13 Henry VIII. when William Courtenay was Sheriff of Devon. The present possessor, Francis Basset, Esq that married the relict of Sir William Gerrard, Knight, and after her decease Pendarves, of Roscrowe family; his father Lucy, the inheritrix of Heale, of Bradinge; his grandfather, Sir Francis Basset, Anna, daughter of Sir Jonathan Trelawney, Knight. Sir Francis Basset's two younger brothers were bred soldiers; and in the unhappy wars between King Charles I. and his Parliament, were, for their valour and good conduct in his service, knighted, but by the unfortunate end and success of that Prince and his wars, afterwards lived and died under the pressure of misfortune.

And here I take it worth remembrance that Sir Francis Basset, Knight, aforesaid, in the beginning of the reign of King Charles II. in the morning about ten o'clock on Ty-hyddy downs, himself or his falconer let fly a goshawk or tassell to a heathpolt or heathcock, which they had there sprung or started on the wing, which birds of game and prey in a short while flew eastwards, over St. Agnes parish, and quite out of sight, so that they despaired of ever finding them again; but, the next day, before twelve o'clock, to their wonder and amazement, a person sent from the Mayor of Camelford, brought both to Ty-hyddy to Sir Francis; the hawk well and alive, with his varvells on his legs, whereon his owner's name aforesaid was inscribed, but the heathpolt was dead; which messenger gave this further account of this rare accident, that the day before, as near as could be computed, about a quartes or half an hour after ten o'clock in the morning, the said hawk, in the midst of Camelford town, struck down his game dead upon the spot; so that by computation their flight straight forward, only in half an hour's space, was at least thirty-two Cornish miles.

For what reason Mr. Carew, in his Survey of Cornwall, gives such a slighting relation of this famous family, I know not; his words be these: p. 154, Beyond Nants Mr. Basset possesseth Ty-hyddy, who married Godolphin, his father Coffyn, and giveth for his arms as aforesaid.

In this parish, at ——, liveth Reginald An-gove, Gent. i. e. Reginald the Smith, a sirname assumed in memory of his first ancestor, who was by trade and occupation a smith.

And of this sort of sirname in England, thus speaks Verstegan,

> From whence came smith, all be it Knight or 'Squire?
> But from the smith that forgeth in the fire.

This Reginald Angove is that subtle crafty tinner, whom common fame reports to have gotten a considerable estate by labouring, adventuring, and dealing in tin, both in the mines below and blowing houses above ground, by indirect arts and practices; for which, about the 8th of William and Mary, he was indicted before the jury of tinners (whereof the writer of these lines was summoned for one) amongst other things, for putting hard heads of false metal and lead in the midst of slabs of tin, melted and cast in his blowing-house, in testimony whereof some pieces or slabs thereof was cut in pieces, and the fallacy detected; whereupon the Grand Jury returned the bill of indictment, indorsed, Billa Vera. But on his trial there was given a verdict of acquittal.

Carne Bray. Upon the top of a very high rocky mountain in this parish, which takes a large view over the land from the north to the south sea, that is to say, from St. George's channel to the British ocean, and also towards the Land's End and Scilly islands, stands Castle Carne Bray, erected long before the art of guns was invented. It is situate upon the summit of a large, lofty, and tremendous rock, built four-square of lime and stone, about forty feet high and twenty feet square; wherein, as appears from the beam holes, windows, and chimneys, were two planchins, besides the leads of the top thereof, though now there are not to be seen either leads or beams, only the walls, windows, chimneys, and garrets thereof are still extant and uniform, which, maugre all the force of wind and weather, are likely to stand firm till the final consummation of all things. It hath but one way of access or entrance into it, through a little hole artificially cut in the rock, under the foundation of its wall, about four feet high; the other parts thereof being surrounded with inaccessible rocks, carnes, and downfalls. Some such castle or fortification Cæsar mentions in his Commentary at Uxelodunum, for Uchell-dun-en, i. e. the lofty fort or fortress [in Gallia]. I take this castle to be the Watch Tower mentioned by Orosius, opposite to such another in Gallicia; which Mr. Carew and Mr. Camden conjecture stood near St. Ive's. Near this castle, on the top of this mountain, are divers circular walls or fortifications, made of rocks and unwrought stones, after the British manner (see Gonwallo); and a never intermitting spring, or fountain of water, for the use of the inhabitants thereof. Probably this castle was built by some of the Brays of Cornwall, or those that came into England with William the Conqueror of that name, otherwise so called from the natural circumstances of the place, Carne.

In this parish also I take it stands another mountain, though of less magnitude, called Carne-Kye; but this place is much more famous and notable for the great quantities of tin that have been for many ages, and are still found and brought to land from the bottoms thereof, than for its appellation, to the great enriching its lords of the soil and adventurers.

There is no tradition or memory of the person who built this costly and tremendous castle aforesaid, or tower; or for what use it was made other than to dwell in it, comparatively above the middle region of the air in those parts, more than what is expressed in the name thereof, Bray's Castle. Undoubtedly whatever human creature it was that dwelt in it and possessed the same, he was a person that had unparalleled confidence in the strength thereof, for his safety and protection, such as never any person after his quitting ever attempted to enjoy for the pleasure of his five senses.

TONKIN.

Tehidy; this lordship of Tehidy has been for many ages in the possession of the ancient, famous, and knightly family of Bassets, whose ancestors came out of France with William the Conqueror, and were posted among the standing troops in this county under Robert Earl of Morton.

Most certainly they were possessed of this lordship some short while after the Conquest; and from hence have sprung many noble and famous men in their generation.

Then, after copying Mr. Hals, Mr. Tonkin goes on to say,

At Carnekye is a considerable tin-work, chiefly pertaining to the Bassets, out of which has been raised above a hundred thousand pounds worth of tin, to the no small profit of the adventurers and of that family.

At Nants or Nance (the valley) was the dwelling of an old and well-regarded family of gentlemen, the Trengoves of Warlegan, the name from Gove, a smith.

These gentlemen have returned to their ancient habitation of Trengoff, in the parish of Warlegan; and the present possessors are denominated Nance from the place, giving for their arms, Argent, a cross Sable.

Mr. Tonkin then adds,

Tehidy. The first owner that I meet with of this noble lordship was Dunstanville; and then Basset, who was his grandson or nephew. Reginald de Dunstanville was a Baron of the Realm in the time of King Henry the First, and I take him to be the person meant in Testa de Neville; ever since which this lordship has been in this ancient and noted family. I shall only add, that the family now residing here, are descended from George Basset, the third son of Sir John Basset, of Umberly in Devonshire, and of Tehidy, who had Tehidy for his portion.

Leland saith, " Basset hath a right goodly lordship called Tehidy by the Cornish. There was some time a park, now defaced." And well he might call it a right goodly lordship, since it hath the advowsons of three large parishes, this parish, Camborne, and Redruth, with the royalties of wrecks, &c. thereto belonging.

The present lord of the manor is John Pendarves Bassett, Esq. a minor, and at present a Gentleman Commoner of Queen's College, Oxford, who is heir in expectance to his mother of all the estate of Pendarves of Roscrow, and is likely to come into the estate of the greatest of his ancestors in this county, by means of this accession, and of a rich copper mine called the Pool, within this manor, which has been and is still productive of tin and copper very rich in the ore.

The arms of Basset are, Or, three bars wavy Gules; but sometimes these bars are Dancette and the field Argent, as they are painted in the church windows of Camborne and Redruth.

The castle and park wall are still standing; and I have been informed by several old men, particularly by the late Mr. Udy West, of Redruth, that all the rocky grounds under Carnbray Castle, and from thence to Porth-Treth, were covered with stout trees in their remembrance; so that squirrels (of which there were many) could leap from one tree to the other all the way. These were mostly destroyed in the Civil Wars, and the rest were cut down by the old Lady Basset, who had it in jointure, so that now there is not the least sign of any trees ever having grown there.

THE EDITOR.

All the attempts at etymology in relation to this parish have been omitted, on the ground of their not bearing even the slightest resemblance to probability.

It has been conjectured that Il-luggan may have some reference to St. Luke, as the parish feast takes place on the nearest Sunday to St. Luke's day, October the 18th. But Luggan, indicating an uncultivated or uninclosed tract of ground, would seem to bear a near relation to the state of this district at no remote period.

Mr. Whitaker adheres to Saint Illuggan on account of the parish being designated as Ecclesia Sancti Illogani by the Bishops of Lincoln and Winchester in 1294; and by Cardinal Wolsey. It has been already remarked that many of the missionaries from the learned and zealous Convents of Ireland, have left no other trace of their existence than the names of parishes where they are usually honoured as Saints; in the sense probably of Holy, and without implying the technical deification of the Church of Rome, borrowed from ancient Mythology. Saint Illuggan may have been one of those who converted the Celts of Cornwall; but in the total absence even of tradition, this must be a mere conjecture, and the name does not seem to bear any analogy to others established by unquestionable authority.

Every attempt to decipher Tehidy has utterly failed. Mr. Angowe, who has been brought forward by Mr. Hals in a manner not likely to acquire for him much respect

ILLOGAN.

from posterity, resided at Trevenson, and left a son, Mr. Abel Angowe. This gentleman was for some time a student at Oxford, but ultimately preferred the law as an attorney. He married Jane, daughter of Mr. Henry Phillips, of Carnequidden in Gulval, who lived but a very short time; and Mr. Angowe died in consequence of a fall from his horse about the year 1767. His large property became divided among a great many distant relations, and has almost entirely disappeared. The Angowes held Trevenson on lease for lives; the freehold being in the families of Basset and Praed. Mr. Thomas Kivell, steward to Lord Dunstanville, built a very excellent house there about the year 1800, which has been still further improved by his successor in the stewardship, Mr. Reynolds.

Menwinnion existed for centuries as a second house and appendage to Tehidy; but it is now reduced in size, and converted to a farm.

Few parishes in Cornwall have flourished in an equal degree with Illogan. It has abounded in the most productive mines of copper; the dense population consequent to these great sources of employment has covered the tracts formerly waste, with houses, with gardens, and with cultivated fields; and a safe harbour has been constructed at Portreath, for the reception of vessels engaged in the reciprocal trade of exporting annually more than a hundred thousand tons of copper ore to Swansea, and of bringing to Cornwall a still larger quantity of coal.

And lastly, on the 25th of October 1809, when a jubilee was held all over England, on the epoch of King George the Third commencing the fiftieth year of his reign, Lord Dunstanville laid the first bar of an iron tram road, for extending far into the country the facilities afforded by this harbour and port, which has since been done; notwithstanding a most illiberal attempt by persons interested in the trade on the opposite coast, to convert a local Act of Parliament for improving turnpike roads, the sole object of which must be to render the conveyance of individuals and of property less expensive and more commodious, into the means of obstructing this great improvement. See the Journals of the House of Commons for the year 1817, and particularly on the 16th of May.

But these, and all other improvements in Illogan, and its general prosperity, are mainly owing to the continued residence, during six centuries, of one of the most distinguished among those families, which, having entered England in hostile array, assimilated themselves to its laws, its customs, and its institutions; and have been found, in all succeeding ages, the foremost defenders of its liberties and of its independence.

The family of BASSET appears to have taken root in various parts of its adopted country. Some branches were probably Barons from the earliest times, some attained that dignity in subsequent periods; others were distinguished in the law, and all in arms; and what must not be omitted, the signature of Basset is found in the great charters of our liberties, at the ratification of Magna Charta more than six hundred years ago.

Mr. Hals brings down the family of Tehidy to Mr. John Pendarves Basset, whom he leaves a Gentleman Commoner of Queen's College, Oxford. This gentleman married Ann, the only daughter and heiress of Sir Edmund Prideaux, of Netherton in Devonshire, by Ann Hawkins, daughter of Mr. Philip Hawkins, of Pennance, and died of the small-pox in 1739, at the premature age of twenty-five. His brother, Mr. Francis Basset, then took possession of the estate; but, unexpectedly to all parties, the widow proved to be with child, and a son was born, who lived to be sixteen, when the uncle came a second time into possession. During this interval, the guardians of young Mr. Basset finished the splendid house at Tehidy, commenced by his father; but, notwithstanding this large expenditure, so great was the product of the mines, and so considerable were the rents of the estate, that Mrs. Basset is said to have acquired above a hundred thousand pounds from her son's personal effects; all of which was naturally left by her among her own relations.

Mr. Francis Basset then settled principally at Tehidy; married Margaret, daughter of Sir John St. Aubyn, and represented Penryn in Parliament. Mr. Basset had three sisters; one married to the Rev. John Collins, afterwards presented to the rectory of Redruth; Lucy, the second daughter, married Mr. John Enys, of Enys, where his great grandson John Samuel Enys, is now the representative of that ancient family; the third married Nicholas Sweet Archer, of Trelaske and of Truro.

Mr. Basset died in 1769, having only completed his fifty-fourth year, leaving two sons, the eldest called after his own name; and John, who became a clergyman, held the family living of Illogan, married Miss Wingfield, and has left one son.

There were also four daughters; one married Mr. John Rogers, of Penrose, the other three remained single.

Having now arrived at the period when Sir Francis Basset, jun. came into possession of the family estate, the Editor would have found it his most pleasing task to trace an outline, however slight, of this distinguished person, in his splendid career through public and through private life. If the topics for his commendation had been in the least degree doubtful, the Editor would, indeed, have distrusted his own power of discrimination in reference to one, whom he is proud to claim, as the most liberal, generous, warm-hearted, and disinterested friend that it has been his fortune to obtain in the whole course of a pilgrimage through life, now exceeding sixty-seven years; but recent events have made recollections painful, which used to be associated with every thing most agreeable to the human mind.

Mr. Basset received the earlier part of his education at Harrow; but about the period of his father's decease, he removed to Eton, where, in addition to useful and ornamental learning, these principles of honour and liberality identified with the character of a true English gentleman, are imbibed, practised, and wrought into habit at the early age when *sincerum est vas*. After which, one can truly say

> You may break, you may ruin the vase if you will,
> But the scent of the roses will hang round it still.

After a residence of five years, from twelve to seventeen, at Eton, Mr. Basset became a member of King's College, Cambridge; and after taking a degree, proceeded on the usual tour through France and Italy, accompanied by the Rev. William Sandys, who, being the son of a former Steward, had received his education for the express purpose of becoming tutor to Mr. John Pendarves Basset, who is stated above to have died at sixteen.

On his return to England, Mr. Basset found himself in possession of abilities, joined to energy of mind; of a large estate, accompanied by great accumulations from the mines; and in addition, of a local influence assuring his introduction to Parliament. Thus circumstanced, it was natural for him to take an active share in the politics of his country, especially at a time when party spirit had acquired a height never to be attained but in the midst of civil commotions.

The two first Princes of the German line had remained firmly united with the Whig aristocracy, to whom they mainly owed what was then denominated their legitimate or lawful crown, as distinguished from others acquired by conquest or usurpation, or derived from a succession founded on no other title than a mere continuance of possession; but the victory of Culloden having finally extinguished all hopes in those maintaining, or rather, one may suppose, professing to maintain, indefeasible hereditary right, and having apparently established the Whigs and the legitimate crown, proved nevertheless to be the cause of their separation, and of the removal of the Whig aristocracy from power at the next accession.

A mutual feeling naturally grew up, that time must transfer rights, popularly termed indefeasible, from one race to another, when no prospect of restoration remained; and the advisers of a young monarch might easily persuade him, that new friends, holding such tenets, would prove more acceptable supporters of their adopted crown than those who originally bestowed it on principles of limitation. Hence the parts imputed to Lord Bute and others, the re-action led by Mr. Wilkes, the letters of Junius, and the final separation of America.

From combinations of these and of other causes, Mr. Basset found Lord North first Minister of a Tory administration, and engaged in war with America, and with France, Spain, and Holland; he eagerly joined that party, and was subsequently hurried with it into the most fatal measure that had occurred up to that period, the well known and well remembered coalition.

But previously to this time, an event had taken place locally connected with Cornwall, equally honourable to him who conducted a large of body of miners to the relief of Plymouth, and to the miners themselves who volunteered their services.

In the latter part of August 1779, the combined fleets of France and Spain most unexpectedly steered into Plymouth Sound, and anchored nearer to the shore than the base of the present Breakwater.

After the splendid successes of the Seven Years' War, marine fortifications had been wholly neglected as utterly useless, as never to be wanted in future times; but in the sixteenth year after the peace of 1763, the course of events demonstrated, that a naval force may be re-established with much less effort, and in a shorter space of time, than had been fondly imagined; and perhaps it also proved, that military navies are not necessarily based on those used for mercantile purposes.

A well-founded alarm spread immediately throughout the whole country, that Plymouth was incompetent to sustain an attack; when instantly the Cornish miners, worthy of the reputation long enjoyed by their predecessors, rushed from all directions, and offered themselves as volunteers to assist in defending Plymouth, and to exert their skill and labour in perfecting the works; and Mr. Basset, acting as his ancestors had done before, immediately placed himself at their head. Thus a large and efficient force was, in the course of a few days, added to our most important western arsenal.

On this occasion a patent was conferred on Mr. Basset, creating him a Baronet; a gift rendered honourable by the cause for which it was bestowed.

Since the nautical events of this period have attracted but little attention from general historians, as they failed of producing any decisive result, it may be well to state the most prominent facts.

The English fleet had been detained at home by various causes, and especially by the court martial which honourably acquitted Admiral Keppel. It sailed, however, at last to prevent a junction of the French and Spanish fleets, but that junction had been effected; and the combined fleet appeared in Plymouth Sound, while the fleet of England was cruizing near Ushant, or in the Bay of Biscay.

Plymouth was undoubtedly open to their attack; and the individual having the civil government of the dock-yard, is said to have actually deliberated about taking the last desperate measure, for depriving the enemy of every advantage to be derived from acquiring such stores as might be consumed by fire.

The Ardent, a sixty-four gun ship of the line, arrived from Portsmouth; and not suspecting that a hostile fleet could appear upon our coast, and still less occupy our harbours, continued its course into the midst of the ships, and became a prize; but not without making a brave resistance, and endeavouring to escape by running ashore.

The combined fleet, instead of attacking Plymouth, sailed in quest of the adverse fleet, having manifestly taken their original course with the view of giving battle; and what must be mentioned to their honour, not a single act of wanton hostility was committed on any part of the coast.

Every thing remained in suspense; watch and ward was established at all points. The gentlemen in every parish assembled, such as had arms, to take hasty instructions in military evolutions, while no one ventured to whisper the extent of his apprehensions to others, or even to avow them in his own mind; when, on the last day of August, both fleets appeared between the Land's End and the Lizard. In the night, or in a fog, the fleets had passed each other; and the Editor remembers seeing the English fleet collected together in a close mass, making its way up the channel, to the amount of about forty sail of the line, pursued by the combined fleet of nearly double that number, in what is termed, line of battle a-head.

An action now seemed to be inevitable; but for some unknown cause, the combined fleet discontinued the pursuit and returned to Brest, while the English fleet anchored in Tor Bay.

On the dissolution of Parliament in 1784, Sir Francis Basset exerted himself to the utmost, and made large sacrifices of money in support of the unpopular coalition ministry, and he remained stedfast with that defeated party till the whole political hemisphere became changed in every aspect, by an event manifested in one country alone, but originating from causes long in action, and imperceptively working throughout an entire change of ancient institutions, with the very form and shape perhaps of civilized society as it previously stood.

The conflict of opinion which gave rise to the French Revolution, has but one parallel in the history of mankind; in the mental agitation, almost amounting to phrensy, which accompanied and urged forward the great change of religion three centuries before. That agitation and conflict still divides Europe, although with diminished violence; and possibly, therefore, an equal period may elapse before the questions, relative to civil government and social order, shall have received their final settlement, if, indeed, the period is ever to arrive.

Most of those in the dawn of youth possessed of eager minds and liberal sentiments, were borne along by the torrent of passions, excited by new systems, promising universal happiness, with increased wisdom and virtue; founded on plans for reconstructing human society, derived, it was said, from philosophical investigation, to be substituted in the place of patched and mended institutions, originating with savages in the forests of Scandinavia.

But Sir Francis Basset had the advantage of several years passed in active experience with the world. He had learnt that the human faculties are unequal to the formation of systems *a priori*, but must submit to follow the more humble course of adaptation, tentative experiment, and induction; and it was manifest that the new political reasoners had entirely omitted to consider the real nature of the ὕλη ἀμεταχείριστη forming the wide basis of society; or that they were devising plans not suited to the actual state of things, but to one which they fondly imagined was about to be.

Every page of history, moreover, might prove to those willing or desirous of obtaining information from what has actually past, that the crisis of change is invariably bad; and that objects, attained by the sacrifice of an existing generation, have very frequently proved of less value than those for which they had been substituted. Parties, from their very natures, are known to run into extremes; it is probable, therefore, that the leaders opposed to Mr. Pitt professed much greater admiration of the new principles than they really felt; such professions were, however, made; and Sir Francis Basset concurring in opinion with many of the wisest, the best informed, and of those most deeply interested in the welfare of the country, that the safety of the state was at issue, added his weight to what would now be termed the Conservative scale.

Sir Francis Basset, so distinguished by personal qualities and attainments, by the antiquity of his family, by the achievements of his ancestors, and by fortune, had long been designated in public opinion as a person proper to be placed in the House of Peers; and accordingly, on the 17th of July 1796, an hereditary seat in Parliament was bestowed on him by the King, together with the nominal Barony of Dunstanville, so called after Barons of that name, in the time of Henry the First, Henry the Second, Richard Cœur de Lion, John, and Henry the Third, who were equally connected with his family and with the reigning family of Plantagenet.

A second creation took place on the 7th of November in the following year, of Baron Basset, with a special remainder to his daughter in failure of male issue.

Lord Dunstanville has from this period continued to support the genuine character of a dignified English gentleman; discharging his parliamentary duties in the manner deemed most useful to the interests of his country; executing the office of a magistrate to the benefit, and to the entire satisfaction, of his neighbourhood; setting an example most worthy of general imitation, as the possessor of an extensive landed estate, and as a most liberal proprietor of mines. Kind and benevolent to every one, esteemed in the highest degree by his private friends and relations, and certainly placed by general acclamation, in regard to all these qualities and circumstances taken together, as by far the first man in the county which he has benefited and adorned.

The Editor has written this imperfect and inadequate sketch of Lord Dunstanville with a heavy heart; for although his countenance brightens at the presence of a friend, and memory still presents some images of things past by, and reason continues to discriminate the ideas brought into view, yet such are the ways of Providence, leading, as we hope, believe, and trust to universal good, that a wreck only remains of what used to excite our admiration, our respect, and our esteem.

Lord Dunstanville married, May the 16th 1780, Frances

Susanna, daughter of John Hippesley Cox, Esq. of Stone Easton in Somersetshire, who has left an only daughter, the Hon. Frances Basset. He married secondly, Harriet, daughter of Sir William Lemon.

Illoggan measures 8,028 statute acres.

Annual value of the Real Property, as returned to Parliament in 1815 . £. 11,334 *s.* 0 *d.* 0

Poor Rate in 1831 . . . . . . 1887 0 0

Population,— { in 1801, 2895 | in 1811, 4078 | in 1821, 5170 | in 1831, 6072 }

giving an increase of 110 per cent. very nearly, in 30 years.

The present rector, the Rev. George Treweeke, presented by Lord de Dunstanville in 1822.

GEOLOGY, BY DR. BOASE.

This extensive parish resembles that of Camborne in its geological structure. Its southern portion rests on granite, which at Carnarthen abounds in shorl; and at Carnkie it contains a bed of porphyry, with crystals of felspar and of shorl; and at the same place another bed, the basis of which more resembles compact shorl rock than it does compact felspar. Near Portreath, and from thence to Perth Towan, the slate appears to differ from that of Camborne; and at Perth Towan it contains short irregular veins of calcareous spar, as at Porthalla in St. Kevern, and at other places on the borders of the calcareous series.

ST. JOHN'S.

HALS.

Is situate in the hundred of East, and hath upon the north Anthony, east Maker, west Sheviock, south the British channel. The modern name John is derived from the tutelar guardian and patron of the Church, St. John the Evangelist. In the Domesday tax this parish was rated under the district or manor of Makertone. In the Inquisition into the value of Cornish benefices, made by the Bishops of Lincoln and Winchester 1294, Ecclesia Sancti Johannis, in decanatu de Eastwellshire, is valued xls. viii*d*. In Wolsey's Inquisition 12*l*. 4*s*. 4*d* ; the patronage in , the incumbent Tarr. The parish is rated to the 4*s*. per pound Land Tax 1696, 72*l*. 0*s*. 8*d*.

TONKIN.

The manor of Insworth,

A Peninsula on whose neck, says Mr. Carew, standeth an ancient house of the Champernons; and descended by his daughters and heirs to Fortescue, Monck, and Trevilian, three gentlemen of Devon. The site is naturally both pleasant and profitable; to which the owner, by his ingenious experiments, daily addeth an artificial surplusage. Mr. Tonkin then adds, this estate (as I am better informed) being in the parish of Maker, I shall there treat more fully of it.

Sir Richard Champernon, of Madberie in Devon, Knt. had by Catherine his wife, daughter of Ralph Daubeney, Knt. two sons, Richard and John. He died in 1418, and gave this place to the said John, who lived here, and left only one son, a Richard Champernon, who by his wife, the daughter and heir of Sir John Hamley, Knt. left three daughters, one of whom married Humphrey Monck, of Potheridge in Devon, Esq.

The said Sir John Champernon was Sheriff of Cornwall 24 Henry VI. 1445, as his son Richard in the first year of Edward IV. 1461.

THE EDITOR.

Mr. Hals has not gone into any particulars respecting this parish; but he has occupied several pages with the real and with the legendary histories of the Evangelist, to whom the Church is dedicated; these are omitted as unsuited to a local history.

Mr. Lysons says, that the manor of Tregenhawke, situated partly in this parish and partly in Rume, and feudatory to the manor of East Anthony, did belong to the family of Eliot, by whom it was alienated in 1635 to Richard Treville, merchant; and that from the Trevilles it passed by coheiresses to the families of Cross and Trelawny. The whole now belongs to Lord Graves, who has also the manor of Withroe, called in this parish Winnow.

The right of presentation is appendant to the honour of East Anthony.

An excavation in the cliff at Whitsand Bay is noticed as having been made by Mr. Luggan, the proprietor of a farm called Freathy, by way of exercise and amusement.

The church is, perhaps, of less dimensions than any other in Cornwall, being no more than fifty-six feet long by eighteen in breadth; it bears the appearance of antiquity, and is decorated by some monuments, one to the family of Beel, with their arms, Azure, three griffins' heads erased Argent.

This parish measures 872 statute acres.

	£.	d.	s
Annual value of the Real Property as returned to Parliament in 1815,	1,016	0	0
Poor Rate in 1831	108	19	0

Population,	in 1801,	in 1811,	in 1821,	in 1831
	110	143	178	150

giving an increase of about 36 per cent in 30 years.

Present rector, the Rev. William Rowe, instituted in 1808.

Dr. Boase says of the geology of this little parish, that its rocks are precisely similar to those of East Anthony, to which it adjoins; and may almost be considered as forming a part.

ST. ISSEY.

HALS.

Is situate in the hundred of Pedyr, and hath upon the north the channel of Padstow habour, south and east St. Breoch and part of St. Colomb, west little Pedyrick. In Domesday roll 20 William I. 1087, this district was taxed either under the jurisdiction of Polton or Burge, now Burgus (i. e. Turris). In the Inquisition of the Bishops of Lincoln and Winchester into the value of Cornish benefices, Ecclesia de Sancti Issei, in decanatu de Pedyr, is rated iiii*l.* vi*s.* viii*d.* Vicar ejusdem xlvi*s.* viii*d.* In Wolsey's Inquisition 9*l.*; the patronage in the Dean and Chapter of Exeter; the incumbent Harris, the rectory in Wright. The parish is rated to the 4*s.* in the pound Land Tax 1696, 161*l.*

There hath been for many ages in Cornwall, a certain sort of unlearned men called attornies, who have taken upon them to solve all questions, debts, damages, and difficulties whatsoever, by exciting or increasing them, under pretence of friendship and good council, who are often called upon to the assistance of men of lazy or weak understanding to their undoing.

For instance thereof, I well remember in this parish of St. Issey there had lived two brethren of the surname of Warne, who having some small disputes or controversies one with the other, not determined, concerning a tenement of land in fee, containing about fifty acres, at a place called ———; they appealed to two attornies, viz. Joseph Hawkey, of St. Colomb, and Degory King, of St. Breock in Pider, who run this their controversy so far in law and equity, that they were not able to pay the cost thereof as punctually as those attornies expected; thereupon they brought actions at law against their clients for the same, and at length obliged the two brothers of the Warnes aforesaid, to sell the inheritance of their lands aforesaid to their attornies, the one half thereof to Hawkey and the other moiety thereof to King, now in quiet possession thereof.

The inhabitants of this parish will tell you by tradition, that the tutelar guardian of this church is one St. Giggy, who in a place so called in this parish, hath yet extant a walled consecrated well, or spring of water, where heretofore he heard and judged cases of conscience for the cure of souls; but all further history of him is wanting, save that they tell me St. Issey is only a corruption of Giggy.

Hale-wyn in this parish (or Hall-wyn, the fair or white hill, as Hal is a hill, and Wyn or Gwyn white or fair. Goonwyn in Lelant the fair downs; Hale is a moor. Whitaker.) This lordship was from Edward the Fourth's days one of the dwellings of the Champernons, of Intsworth, near Saltash; and in this place they had a great and magnificent house, as appears from the walls and ruinous rubbish and downfalls thereof yet to be seen, as also their domestic chapel and burying place; in the glass windows of which chapel was lately to be seen this inscription: " Orate pro anima Domini Ricardi de Campo Arnulphi; " and beneath the same his paternal coat armour, viz. Gules, a saltire Varry, between twelve cross-crosslets Or; which shews that he derived his blood and bones from the Champernownes, of Clyst Champernowne in Devon. For the Champernownes of Umberleigh and North Taunton, near Modbury, gave for their armes, the one Gules, a saltire Varry; the other, Gules, a saltire Varry between twelve billets Argent. [The name is originally Latin, De Campo Arnulphi, then formed by the Norman French into Champernulph, and finally formed by them, or by the Cornish, into Champernown. Whitaker.]

Cannall-Lidgye in this parish is the voke lands of a considerable manor, now in several persons' hands; much of those lands being in possession of Boscawen as I take it; the high rents are in Hart. As part of the same, is the possession and birthplace of my very kind friend and neighbour Thomas Carthew, Esq. Barrister-at-Law, who by his indefatigable study and labour, first in the inferior practice of the law under Mr. Tregena, without being a perfect Latin grammarian, always using the English words for matters or things in his declarations, where he understood not the Latin; who was at length, by a mandamus from the Lord Keeper North, called to the bar, and the generous practice of the law for some years, when afterwards in the latter end of the reign of King William the Third, he had a call for being made a Sergeant-at-Law, under which circumstance he grew into such great fame and reputation that he is likely to make a considerable addition of riches to his paternal estate.

He married North, a relation to the Lord Keeper North aforesaid; his father, Baker, of Lanteglos, by Fowey; his grandfather Lawry; and giveth for his arms, Argent, a chevron Azure, between three ducks Proper. The name is local, compounded of Car-dew, or Car-thew, i. e. Rock Black in this parish. Long since the writing hereof, those his lands of Canaligye are all sold by Mr. Carthew's son and heir to two of the brothers of Trebilliocks.

Trevance in this parish, i. e. the town upon the rising or advanced land, is the dwelling of Richard Harris, Gent. that married Vivyan, of Tollskidy; his father Moyle.

Tre-vor-ike in this parish, [Pryce, in his Archæologia Cornu-Britannica says, Ick I take to signify either a creek, rivulet, or brook, as Trevorick, the town or the brook. Whitaker.] is the dwelling of William Cornish, Gent. that married Cornish, his father Tonkyn; originally descended from one William Cornish that settled here tempore Queen Mary, a Welshman. To this place belongs a sea-mill, a healing or slate stone quarry, and a lime kiln, commonly made in jointure to those gentlemen's wives, to win whom in marriage this argument amongst others was commonly used,

> She that will this Squire marry,
> Shall have the mill, the kill, and the quarry;

now all spent and wasted by ill conduct, and those lands sold to a relation of his surnamed Cornish, or some other.

At Carthew, or Legarike, in this parish, is a considerable lead or copper mine in the lands of Bearford or Bond; wherein many labouring tinners are much employed as miners, and reap much benefit thereby, as well as the lords of the lands or soil thereof.

TONKIN.

Mr. Tonkin has not any thing in addition to what is transcribed from Mr. Hals.

THE EDITOR.

The church of this parish is called in some ancient writings, Eglos-Crock and Nansant. The Dean and Chapter of Exeter are impropriators of the great tithes, and patrons of the vicarage. The church is very old, but decorated with a lofty tower; there are monuments to Mr. Thomas Carthew, and to some of the vicars. The church town is the largest village in this parish, and lies nearly midway between Padstow and Wade Bridge. Mr. Lysons says that the manor of St. Ide, extending from this parish into the adjacent parishes of Little Petherick, St. Ervan, Breock, Padstow, and Mawgan, belonged successively to the families of Hiwis, Coleshill, and Arundell, and at a later period to the Morices. It was purchased by the late Mr. Thomas Rawlings, of Padstow.

And Mr. Lysons adds that, Blayble, a small farm in St. Issey, now belonging to Mr. Richard Williams, who occupies it, was at an early period the seat of a branch of the Arundell family.

This parish measures 3,932 statute acres.

	£.	s.	d.
Annual value of the Real Property as returned to Parliament in 1815	2,050	0	0
Poor Rate in 1831	508	13	0

Population, — { in 1801, 522 | in 1811, 632 | in 1821, 660 | in 1831, 720

giving an increase of 38 per cent. in 30 years.

GEOLOGY, BY DR. BOASE.

Dr. Boase says, that St. Issey has the same geological structure as the adjacent parish of St. Breock.

ST. IVES.

HALS.

Is situate in the hundred of Penwith, and hath upon the east and north the Irish Sea, south Leland, west Tywednick; as for the modern name, it is taken from the tutelar guardian of the Church, which, as Mr. Camden tells us (upon what authority I know not) was one Iia, an Irish woman that preached the Gospel here. In the Domesday Tax, the 20th of William I. 1087, both the town and parish were taxed under the jurisdiction of Ludduham, now Lugian-lese manor, still extant here, formerly pertaining to the King or Earl of Cornwall, now to the Duke of Bolton, of whom the town of St. Ives' privileges are held; and the same manor is held, as I take it, of the Earl of Cornwall's Castle of Lancaster under certain rents.

In the Inquisition of the Bishops of Lincoln and Winchester into the value of the Cornish benefices 1294, " ecclesia de Lelant in decanatu de Penwith," is only taxed xxii*l.* xviiis. iiii*d.* without mention either of St. Ives or Tywednick, probably at that time they were neither erected or endowed; in Wolsey's Inquisition 1521, Ewny juxta Lelant and St. Ives are rated together 22*l*. 11*s*. 10½*d*.; St. Ewny, that is to say Tywednike, and St. Ives being consolidated in their mother church Lelant, did pass in presentation with it; the patronage in the Bishop of Exeter, who endowed them; the incumbent Hawkins, now Polkinhorn, the rectory in possession of Pitz; and the parish rated at 4*s*. per pound Land Tax 1696, 158*l*. 13*s*. 4*d*.

This town, as Mr. Camden saith, was formerly called Pendenis or Pendunes, the head fort, fortress, or fortified place; probably from the little island here, containing about six acres of ground, on which there stands the ruins of a little old fortification and a chapel, betwixt which island and the bending shore, or sea cliff, stands an indifferent safe road for ships to lie at anchor with some winds, which gives opportunity of trade and merchandize to the townsmen (whose town is situate thereon) and also for fishing, whereby they have much enriched themselves of late years.

The manor of Ludduham, formerly comprehending the parishes of Ludduham, Lelant, Tywednick, and St. Ives. now so many districts, is a lordship of great antiquity, and was privileged with the jurisdiction of a court leet before the Norman Conquest, for under that name it was then taxed (as aforesaid) though its now transnominated to Luggyan Lese; in which stands the borough of St. Ives, which claims the privileges thereof by prescription and tenure, all which are confirmed by a charter of incorporation from King Charles I. afterwards by another from King James II. by the name of the Mayor, Aldermen, and Burgesses, which consists of a Mayor, ten Aldermen, and eleven Common Councilmen; the Members of Parliament elected by freemen, alias scot and lot men free there, who sign the indenture; the arms of which borough is a cluster and branch of grapes or pomegranates; and the precept on the writs for electing Members of Parliament from the Sheriff, or removing any action at law depending in the court leet of St. Ives, the writ must be thus directed: Preposits et Burgensibus Burgi sui de St. Ives in Com. Cornub. salutem.

The chief inhabitants of this town are, Mr. Hitchins, Mr. Beer, Mr. Stephens, Mr. Hickes; in which town is held a market weekly on Saturdays, and a fair annually on Saturday before Advent Sunday.

Sir Francis Basset procured their first charter of incorporation, who, being a Burgess, gave a silver cup of 5*l.* value to this corporation for ever, with this inscription,

> If any discord doth arise,
> Within the borough of St. Ives,
> 'Tis my desire this cup of love,
> An instrument of peace may prove

Trenwith in this parish, was the voke lands of a considerable manor, privileged with a court leet before the Norman conquest, that heretofore extended itself over divers parishes; for by that name it was taxed in Domesday book, 20 William I. 1087, from which place was transnominated an ancient family of gentlemen, now in possession thereof, from that of Bayliff now to Trenwith, who have flourished here in good fame and reputation beyond the memory of man, since Henry VIII. The present possessor is Thomas Trenwith. Gent. that married Lanyon; and giveth for his arms, Argent, on a bend cotised Sable, three roses of the Field.

Those lands of Trenwith were of old pertaining to the Earls or Kings of Cornwall, afterwards to the Kings of England; and were held by the tenure of knight service by such as possessed them, if not from King Arthur's days, (see Dundagall) yet from William the Conqueror's, who, in imitation of him, gave bartons, manors, fields, large territories of land to his favourites, under the tenures of villeinage and knight service in capite, by means of which knight service those tenants were obliged to do him any necessary service, either in wars or to his royal person, for the performing whereof he took their oaths in public courts, both of homage and fealty; and by reason of this tenure he disposed of the bodies of their heirs in marriage as he listed, and retained in his custody and wardship their whole inheritance till they accomplished the age of twenty-one years; and by those examples other men of great possessions did the like. Those lands of Trenwith, tempore Henry IV. were held by that tenure in capite by Edmund Plantagenet, alias Beaufort, Marquess of Dorset, grandchild to John Duke of Lancaster, 21 Henry VI. 1442, consisting of four knights' fees, 3 Henry IV. (See Carew's Survey of Cornwall, p. 39). He was slain at the battle of St. Alban's 1450, on the part of Henry VI. against Richard Duke of York; as also was his son Henry on the same part after the battle of Hexham, and his brother Edmund after Tewkesbury 1471, beheaded by King Edward IV. and his whole estate confiscated to the Crown; from whence Bayliff, now Trenwith, purchased part of those lands, which still pays high rent to the Kings of England. In like manner Humphrey Plantagenet, fourth son of King Henry IV. held by the same tenure in Conerton, Binerton, Drineck, and Ludgian, four knight's fees of land in those places. He was impeached of treason at the Parliament held at St. Edmund's Bury in Suffolk; afterwards murdered; and those and all other his lands confiscated.

TONKIN.

This church is a vicarage, valued in the King's books, together with Lelant and Towednack, with which it passeth in presentation, at 22*l*. 11*s*. 10½*d*.; the collation in the Bishop of Exeter; the late incumbent Mr. Hawkins, now Polkinhorne. The sheaf in possession of Edward Noseworthy, Esq.

The town of St. Ives, in Mr. Carew's days, was of small value or consequence for wealth, buildings, or inhabitants; although it now be much altered in these particulars, and equals several other fellow corporations. Of old it hath been privileged by the Earls of Cornwall with the jurisdiction of a Court Leet, and with sending two Members to Parliament; also with fairs and a weekly market.

ST. IVES.   261

On the island (or peninsula) north of St. Ives, standeth the ruins of an old chapel, wherein God was duly worshipped by our ancestors the Britons, before the church of St. Ives was erected or endowed; betwixt which island and the shore is an indifferent roadstead with some winds for ships to lie at anchor.

This town is particularly famous for the art of catching fish; in which trade or occupation of late they have been attended with good success, to the great advancement of their wealth and reputation. The chief inhabitants of which place were Mr. Hitchins, Mr. Trevilion, Mr. Beare, &c. In this port his Majesty hath his Custom House collector, surveyor, comptroller, and waiters, both for sea and land.

Trenwith, in this parish, is the seat of an old family of gentlemen, from thence denominated de Trenwith.

THE EDITOR.

St. Ives has grown, since the time of Mr. Carew, into a place of considerable importance, participating in the general prosperity of the whole country; and deriving great local advantages from the extension of its fisheries, from the construction of a pier, and from the extraordinary increase of trade at the adjacent port of Hayle.

Fish of almost every kind, frequenting the coast of Cornwall, are taken at St. Ives; but the fishery absorbing all the others in its magnitude is the taking of pilchards.

Pilchards are taken in two different ways quite distinct from each other.

The first, most ancient, most certain, and therefore of greatest importance to the inhabitants of the neighbourhood, is called drifting.

Boats sail in the open sea, drawing after them a great number of nets appended to each other, provided with small leads and corks at the opposite sides, and extending in all to a very great length. The meshes of these nets are made of such a size as to admit the head of a pilchard to pass through them, but not the body; in consequence such fish as strike against the net are retained suspended by their gills, acting in the nature of a barb.

The second method is on a much more extensive scale, uncertain as to success; but occasionally giving fortunes to those concerned in carrying it on, by the gain of one prosperous year.

This method is founded entirely on the habit common to all the clupea genus of congregating in large shoals, and coming occasionally near the shore into shallow water, and into places where the ground is free from rocks; this latter circumstance is peculiarly favourable in the St. Ives Bay, and the ground is moreover covered to the depth of several feet by a fine sand, composed entirely of shells, reduced almost to a state of powder.

All the most favourable stations are occupied during the proper season of the year by large boats, having nets on board measuring four hundred and forty yards in length by twenty-seven yards in breadth, capable therefore of covering nearly two and an half statute acres. These nets are provided with very heavy weights at one of their sides, so as to sink them firmly on the ground, and with large corks to make them buoyant on the other. Two large boats and one smaller, as an attendant, are appropriated to each net; and when a shoal is discovered approaching, by a well-known change of colour and a ripple on the water, these boats, sometimes directed also by signals from the shore, move in opposite directions, extending the immense net to intercept the fish, and then to close it behind them. In this way a quantity sufficient to fill a thousand casks, after being pressed, have been frequently secured at one time, and on some occasions much more. The casks are hogsheads of fifty-four gallons, and contain about two thousand five hundred pilchards, so that the thousand hogsheads make two millions and a half secured by one net.

The fish are taken out of the sea by raising them to the surface of the water in smaller nets, used within the great net forming an artificial pond; and finally they are dipped up in baskets. The first net, called a seyne, frequently remaining in its original position for several days, or perhaps gently slided towards the shore.

Pilchards are preserved for exportation in the following manner: they are laid in regular heaps along the sides of walls sheltered by roofs to a height easily reached, and to a depth suited to the ordinary length of the arm, where they are almost concealed by the great quantity of salt strewed with them: three hundred and thirty-six pounds, or three great hundred weight of salt, being allowed for each pressed hogshead. In this state they remain thirty-six days, while oil continually oozing from them is received in pits; they are then rinced in water, and laid with great care in casks made purposely with open joints, where they receive a strong pressure through the medium of a long beam and weights; more oil is then collected, and the casks, closed up, are fitted for sale. Nine of these packages, independent of the wood, are said to weigh two tons; so that in their final state, the quantity of a thousand hogsheads, not unfrequently caught at one time, must weigh above two hundred and twenty tons.

The quantity of oil is very considerable, varying from two to five gallons from each hogshead, but of inferior quality. Pilchards thus cured are called fumados, which seems to imply their having been originally smoked like red herrings; their chief consumption takes place in Spain and Italy.

The pilchards used for home consumption are invariably picked; these are opened and washed, and then rubbed with salt, about seven pounds to the hundred, and preserved in jars or troughs.

The herring, pilchard, sprat, anchovy, and several other species, are arranged by icthyologists under the genus clupea; the herring and pilchard being adjacent to each other. The pilchard is rather less in size than the herring, has larger and firmer scales, and contains much more oil.

There is one discriminating circumstance quite obvious; the pilchard, suspended by its dorsal fin, remains in equilibrio, while the herring, under similar circumstances, dips towards its head.

The pier was built under the authority of an Act of Parliament passed in the year 1767, after a personal survey and a report from the celebrated Mr. Smeaton, which is printed in his works. This shelter from every wind has equally tended to improve the fishery, to increase the general trade of the place, and to protect vessels bound for Hayle; but the fishery is indebted in a still greater degree to another Act of Parliament, carried through the legislature by the late Mr. Humphry Mackworth Praed, who had the honour first of representing this place, and then the county.

A custom had existed time of mind, by which any boat provided with a seyne net, having taken possession of one of the favourable stations or stems, might retain it till the net had been used to inclose a shoal, or, according to the technical expression, had been shot; and this right extended from one season to another: persons in possession of a stem were therefore unwilling to lose it, except for a considerable prize, and small shoals were generally allowed to escape. By Mr. Praed's Act, so great and so beneficial a change was made, that, arranging the succession in an equitable manner, it allowed each boat to hold its stem but for twenty-four hours, and consequently every shoal, however small, was eagerly secured.

The nets are preserved for a long succession of years by steeping them in a decoction of oak bark as frequently as they are used; and, what would scarcely have been expected, the fish oil without this preservative, would destroy the twine in a very short time.

It seems that these nets must have been originally introduced from Dungarvon in Ireland, since they are still said to be braided according to the Dungarvon mesh, but no similar fishery is remembered at that place. Fish, however, of all kinds not only migrate through distant seas, but without any known cause, frequently leave one part of a coast and resort to another, returning after uncertain intervals to their former haunts.

There is one custom at St. Ives, of which the origin and specific meaning are entirely lost. So soon as shoals of pilchards are discovered in the bay, all the people, and more especially the children, run round the town shouting, HEVA ! HEVA ! with all their might.

St. Ives was distinguished in the last century by the birth and residence for some years of a very eminent scholar, the Rev. Jonathan Toup. His father, who died in 1721, was lecturer of that Town, as the church being a daughter church to Lelant, is entitled to service from the vicar only once in three weeks; his mother was the heiress of the family of Busvargus, long settled at Busvargus in St. Just.

He was born in 1713; and it is apprehended received the rudiments of classical learning from his father. He became a Commoner of Exeter College, Oxford, and having taken the usual degree of Bachelor of Arts, obtained Holy Orders in 1736. He was Curate of Philleigh in that year, and of Burian in 1738. He continued to pursue, with extraordinary diligence, the study of Greek. He became Rector of St. Martin's, near Looe in 1750, through some private interest; but the Vicarage of St. Merran and a Prebend in the Cathedral of Exeter in 1774, were procured from the Bishop of Exeter by his literary friend Doctor William Warburton, Bishop of Gloucester.

Mr. Toup took his Master of Arts degree at Cambridge in 1756, when he had advanced towards the middle of life, and apparently as a qualification for his second living.

His chief work is, perhaps, " Emendationes in Suidam; in quibus plurima loca Veterum Græcorum, Sophoclis et Aristophanis in primis, tum explicuntur tum emaculantur." These were printed in three parts, which came out in three volumes in the years 1760, 1764, and 1766; and were followed in 1775 by " Appendiculum Notarum in Suidam." All these have since been reprinted at Leipsic in four volumes octavo; and the whole has been recently incorporated into a most splendid and learned edition of Kusterus' Suidas, by the very Reverend Thomas Gaisford, D.D., Dean of Christ Church, and Regius Professor of Greek in the University of Oxford.

Mr. Toup gave also to the world by far the best edition that has appeared of Longinus He also assisted the celebrated Mr. Thomas Warton in his edition of Theocritus; and added, " Curæ posteriores, sive Appendicula Notarum atque Emendationum in Theocritum, Oxonii nuperrime publicatum." He also published a letter to Bishop Warburton under the title of, " Epistola Critica ad Virum celeberrimum Gulielmum (Warburton) Episcopum Glocestriensem."

Nothing in particular is remembered of Mr. Toup's private life. He died unmarried at the Rectory of St. Martin's in 1785; and the delegates of the Oxford press, in regard for so eminent a scholar, and in return for a present of MSS. made by his niece and executrix, have erected a monument to his memory in St. Martin's Church.

Another gentleman, although not a native of the town, may be noticed here.

Mr. John Knill was born in the eastern part of Cornwall, and served his clerkship as an attorney in Penzance, from thence he removed to the office of a London attorney, where having distinguished himself by application and intelligence, he was recommended to the Earl of Buckinghamshire, who at that time held the political interest of St. Ives, to be his local agent.

After residing for some time at St. Ives, Mr. Knill was sent on a mission to the West Indies, highly honourable to his abilities and to his character, with an authority for inspecting all the custom-houses and their establishments; and, if sufficient cause should appear, with power to suspend any one, however high, from his office.

Having executed the functions thus delegated with integrity and moderation, he returned to the collectorship at St. Ives, and engaged in a very anomalous undertaking, at that time sanctioned and encouraged by the government, which consisted in equipping small vessels to act as privateers against smugglers. In this species of warfare he is said to have been very successful; and on the breaking out of the Dutch war in the war with America, these vessels were ready to act their part in a practice most disgraceful to a civilized nation, and which every good, honourable, and humane man must hope will never again be repeated. In this way vessels laden with private property, wholly unprepared for resistance, utterly unacquainted with the nations being at war, were plundered and robbed of whatever they contained, and unoffending passengers were exposed to insult and violence.

Mr. Knill was hurried by the force of circumstances, contrary to his inclination and habits, and to his deep subsequent regret, into doing what others did, and participating in these unhallowed gains. The Editor understands, however, that he showed every kindness in his power to some objects of compassion who were made prisoners; and that he restored several articles of their more valued property at his own individual loss.

Soon after this time Mr. Knill took up the singular fancy of erecting a triangular pyramid on a hill overlooking St. Ives, with the intention of his being buried in a proper receptacle hollowed in the base; and he invested a sum of money in trust for the support of some half ludicrous and half serious dances and processions, to be repeated every fifth year.

He however, removed, to London, resided in Gray's Inn, was called to the bar, and became a bencher; and having departed this life on the 29th of March 1811, was buried, by the direction of his last will, in St. Andrew's church, Holborn. The monument is ornamental to the country: on one side of the pyramid are inscribed the words, "John Knill;" on a second, " I know that my Redeemer liveth ;" and on the third the word " Resurgam."

The monument stands on the Editor's land, and pays him sixpence a-year, secured on a farm of some value, with a power of distress.

Mr. Knill was undoubtedly a man of considerable talent. When the Earl of Buckinghamshire took the office of Lord Lieutenant of Ireland, he selected Mr. Knill for his private secretary; but not liking the bustle, nor perhaps the responsibility of this situation, he returned to St. Ives. His philanthropy and general kindness were known to all; but a variety of idle fancies and singularities, unworthy of his talents and experience in the world, are remembered, while the estimable qualities of his heart are perhaps forgotten.

An extraordinary event took place at St. Ives on the 17th of Feb. 1780.

Some time in the month of December preceding, a large body of troops had been embarked at New York for the attack on Charlestown in South Carolina; and in a public dispatch from Gen. Sir Henry Clinton, dated March the 9th, he says, " only one ship is missing, having on board a detachment of Hessians; and supposed to have borne away for the West Indies." The Editor has ascertained by particular inquiries, that the vessel alluded to in this dispatch nearly reached Charlestown, the place of its destination, having about two hundred and fifty German soldiers on board with provision suited to so short a voyage, when being run foul of by a ship of war in a gale of wind, and injured in the masts and bowsprit, the vessel could sail no other way than before the westerly wind, then blowing with violence; most fortunately the direction of the wind continued steadily in the same direction, and the passengers arrived safe, but nearly famished, at St. Ives on the day above-mentioned. St. Ives and the neighbourhood contended with each other in efforts, not merely to relieve the distress of these unfortunate persons, but to make them comfortable and happy;

the best attainable lodgings were provided for the private men, and the officers were daily invited to gentlemen's houses. Their sufferings as foreigners on behalf of England, had excited general compassion, heightened by the reflection that they were not engaged in maintaining any cause in which their country had an interest, that they were not volunteers, but had been purchased by this nation from an individual entrusted with unlimited power, for the good of a portion of mankind, which he had most basely abused for the sake of private gain, in a manner that must commit his name and memory to infamy, and to the execration of mankind; nor can the administration be freed from blame that hired these human beings at so much a-day, and agreed to give the Landgrave of Hesse Cassel a certain sum for every one killed, or missing, or lamed.

Mr. Hals and Mr. Tonkin have enumerated several names of families at St. Ives. In recent times, that of Stephens has acquired an undisputed superiority.

That family, although merchants up to the decease of Mr. John Stephens in 1764, had been long in possession of landed property in St. Ives; and the Editor has seen the original of the following receipt given at the accession of King James the First.

xxii⁰ die Octobris, An⁰ Dom¹ 1603.

Received of John Stephens of the Burrough of St. Ives in the Hundred of Penwith, within the county of Cornwall, Gen^t, for his composition with his Ma^{tes} Commissioners for his not appearing at the Coronation of our said Souvraigne Lord the King, for to receive the Order of Knighthood, according to his Highness' proclaymasion in that behalfe, the sum of sixteen pounds.

I saye received - - - - xvi^{li}

Fra. Godolphin, Coll.

Mr. John Stephens married Mary, one of the three daughters of Mr. Samuel Phillips, of Pendrea in Gulval.

This gentleman appears to have been very successful in his various concerns of merchandise and fisheries, as he added largely to his landed property by purchases in the immediate neighbourhood of St. Ives, and also in the parishes of Newlyn and St Enoder. He acted for many years as agent to the Earl of Buckinghamshire in managing the political concerns of the town; but at last broke off the connection by getting his son, Mr. Samuel Stephens, returned on a vacancy.

Mr. John Stephens had a numerous family; his eldest son went to Holland, according to the practice of those times, with the view of continuing his father's mercantile concerns; and the next son, Samuel, became a member of the University of Cambridge to prepare himself for the church, and probably with the expectation of obtaining Lelant and St. Ives, but the death of his elder brother caused this to be relinquished. He married Anne, daughter of Mr. Seaborn, of Bristol; and on his father's decease about the year 1764, he disposed of every thing connected with the trade and fishery of this place, and having abandoned the sect of Presbyterians, to which all his family and relations had been strongly attached, he went so far as to pull down the meeting-house, and to withdraw his support from its minister; proceedings well remembered to his disadvantage on subsequent occasions.

About the year 1774, Mr. Stephens commenced building his new house at Tregonna; and in that and in a subsequent year proved unsuccessful at a poll, and on a petition, for the representation of St. Ives. He died in March 1794, leaving three sons, John Stephens, Rector of Ludgvan; Samuel, to whom he devised a large portion of his estate; and Augustus, all of whom have died in the present year (1834); also three daughters, Anne, Maria, and Harriet. Mr. Samuel Stephens, the second son, married Betty, sole daughter of Capt. Wallis, the discoverer of Otaheite, and coheiress of the families of Hearle and Paynter. He represented St. Ives in two Parliaments, and died February the 25th, 1834, leaving five sons, and one daughter, married to the Rev. Charles William Davy.

Previously to the Act of Parliament of 1832, St. Ives sent two Members to Parliament; and the right of voting rested in persons paying scot and lot throughout the parish. It now sends one member in conjunction with Lelant and Towednack. The present representative is Mr. James Halse, probably related to the historian: this gentleman is among the most enterprising and successful adventurers in mines of the present day.

The situation of the town would seem to be most salubrious, and perhaps it is so in ordinary times; but few places have suffered more from occasional epidemics.

The Editor remembers to have heard dreadful traditionary accounts of the plague in 1647. No market was kept in the town for a considerable space of time; but instead of it, supplies were brought to the edge of two streams of water at Polmanter and at Longstone Downs, where provisions were deposited with their prices affixed, which the inhabitants took away, leaving their money in the streams. It it said, however, that the Stephens family having retired to a farm called Aire, which they possessed just out of the town, and having there cut off all communication with others, entirely escaped, although 535 died in the course of one summer, out of a population which could not at that period have exceeded treble the amount. In the spring of 1786, a fever raged with great violence, to which the reverend Mr. Lane, then lecturer, and Mrs. Lane fell victims within a few days of each other.

The whole inscription on the cup given by Sir Francis Basset is as follows:

> If any discord 'twixt my friends arise
> Within the borough of beloved St. Ives,
> It is desired this my cup of love,
> To everie one a peace-maker may prove,
> Then am I blest to have given a legacie,
> So like my harte unto posteritie.
>
> Francis Basset, A° 1640

The arms of the town are, Argent, an ivy bush overspreading the whole field Proper, evidently in allusion to the name; but this bearing has afforded an obvious joke throughout the neighbouring parishes at the expense of the Mayor.

The church is unusually large and handsome, with a fourth aile at the eastern end, and a lofty tower; and few prospects are equally beautiful with that of the town and bay from the hill near Tregenna.

The parish feast is celebrated at the same time as that of Lelant the mother church; and Lelant, Redruth, and Crowan, are said to honour St. Eury by holding their feasts on the nearest Sunday to her day, February 1st, but no trace of any such saint can be found.

The parish measures 1524 statute acres.

	£. s. d.
Annual value of the Real Property as returned to Parliament in 1815	5,560 0 0
Poor Rate in 1831	1,174 0 0

Population,	in 1801,	in 1811,	in 1821,	in 1831,
	2714	3281	3526	4776

giving an increase of 76 per cent. in 30 years.

GEOLOGY, BY DR. BOASE.

The north-eastern part of this parish is composed of compact and slaty felspar rocks, like those of St. Just in Penwith; the other part is situated on granite. Both these rocks are traversed by metalliferous veins, which have been for many ages the objects of mining speculations.

ST. JULYOT.

HALS.

Is situate in the hundred of Lesnewith, and hath upon the north St. Gennis, west St. George's Channel, south Lesnewith, east Otterham. As for the modern name, it is so called from its tutelar guardian and patron thereof, St. Julius, Pope of Rome and Confessor. In Domesday Tax, 20 William I. (1087), it was rated under the jurisdiction of Lesnewith or Otterham. In the taxation of benefices made by the Bishops of Lincoln and Winchester in Cornwall, 1294, ecclesia de Sancta Juliot, in decanatu de Major Trigshire (id est, before Stratton was dismembered from it) is rated xii$l$. Again, Capella de Sancta Julyot, xxvi$s$. viii$d$.; but where this latter Church or Chapel now stands, I am wholly ignorant; for in Wolsey's Inquisition, 1521, and Valor Beneficiorum, both are forgotten or omitted; the patronage is in Molesworth, and the parish rated to the 4s. per pound Land Tax, 1696, 66l. 16s.

TONKIN.

This parish is a donative, the patrons Sir John Molesworth and Mr. Rawle. The name is from St. Juliet, a virgin saint and martyr.

THE EDITOR.

Mr. Whitaker agrees in assigning to St. Juliet the honour of giving her name to this parish.

There seems to be some confusion in Mr. Hals' narrative

between the appropriations of the Rectory and of the Vicarage, which Mr. Whitaker endeavours to explain in the following note.

"Mr. Hals has confounded himself by the identity of names. The Rectory of St. Julyot is placed by the first Valor in the Deanery of Trig *Minor*, and the *Chapel* of St. Julyot is placed by it; and by the second in that of Trig *Major*. The former too is rated so high as 12*l.*, while the latter is only 26*s*. 8*d*. even at a period so much later. The former therefore is the only large living of Trig Minor that is unnoticed in the first Valor, Lanteglos, correspondently valued in the second at 34*l.* 11*s*. 3*d*. And the latter is the present St. Julyot, not a Rectory, but a mere Chapel in the first Valor, a mere Curacy Parochial in the second, once appropriated to the Abbey of Tavistock, and therefore having only 15*s*. certified value at present, the old allocation settled upon it by the Abbey."

Mr. Hals has given a very long history of Julius, Pope or Bishop of Rome, from the year 343 to 358, which is omitted.

Nor is there anything worth relating in the history or legend of St. Julyot. She is said to have suffered death, having been accused by a violent and wicked person who had previously taken from her by force some ample possessions. There is extant a sermon of St. Basil in praise of this saint, who is commemorated in the Rituale Romanum on the 30th of July.

The family of Rawle, settled for some time at Leskeard, are said to have originated from Hennot, in this parish. They, together with Molesworth of Pencarrow, are joint impropriators, and alternately nominate the perpetual curate.

St. Julyot measures 2276 statute acres.

	£.	s.	d.
Annual value of the Real Property as returned to Parliament in 1815.	1784	0	0
Poor Rate in 1831	143	18	0

Population,—{ in 1801, | in 1811, | in 1821, | in 1831,
              199 | 208 | 263 | 271

giving an increase of 36 per cent., in 30 years.

Present Vicar, the Rev. John Russell, instituted in 1810.

GEOLOGY, BY DR. BOASE.

The rocks of this parish are nearly allied to dunstone, into which they pass at Tresparret Downs; some of them, however, more nearly resemble the dark-coloured pyritous rocks of Forrabury.

ST. JUST, IN ROSELAND.

HALS.

Is situate in the hundred of Powdre, and hath upon the north King's Road and other parts of the Sea of Falmouth Harbour, east Phillery, south Gerans, west Anthony; the modern name of this parish and church is taken from the name of the saint to whom the same is dedicated, viz. St. Just; for in the Domesday Tax it was rated under the jurisdiction of Egles-ros, now Philley, or Tregarada, now Tregare in Gerance, both contiguous therewith. In the Inquisition of the Bishops of Lincoln and Winchester into the value of Cornish Benefices, 1294, ecclesia de Sancto Justo, in decanatu de Powdre, was rated at iiii*l*. vi*s*. viii*d*. This church was partly endowed by the Dean and Chapter of Exon, who received an annuity out of the same of xxx*s*., as appears from that Inquisition; and partly by the Prior and Convent of St. Mary de Val, or Vale, contiguous therewith, and St. Mary de Plym, its superior, who received annually out of it xiii*s*. iv*d*. In Wolsey's Inquisition it was valued at 37*l*. The patronage was formerly in the Prior of St. Mary de Val, now Antony (in right of their manor of St. Mary's, now St. Maws), annexed since the dissolution of that Priory, 26 Henry VIII, to the manor of Tolverne,

ST. JUST, IN ROSELAND.

afterwards in Arundell of Tolverne, now Tredinham; the incumbent Bedford. The parish rated to the 4s. per pound Land Tax, 1696, 172*l*. 13s. 4*d*.

In this parish, upon a cove or creek of Falmouth Harbour, stands the borough of St. Mawes, also St. Mary's, so called from the manor of land on which it is situate, heretofore pertaining to the Canons Regular of the Priory of St. Mary de Plym in Devon, both dedicated to the blessed Virgin Mary, and thence from her denominated St. Mary's. It is the yoke lands of two ancient manors, named Tolverne and Bohurra, privileged time out of mind with the jurisdiction of court leets, held before the Steward or Portreeve, who governs the same, and is annually chosen by the majority of the homage or tenants of the manor of Tolverne Court; the lords of which formerly were the Priors aforesaid, afterwards Arundell of Tolverne, now Tredinham as aforesaid. It sendeth two Members to sit in the Lower House of Parliament, who are chosen or elected by the freeholders or freemen of the said borough. It hath a weekly market, and an annual fair on Friday next after Luke's day; and giveth for its arms, a bend lozengy of six pieces ermine, between a castle in the sinister chief and a ship rigged without sails in the dexter.

The writ to remove an action at law depending in this Leet to a Superior Court, and the precept for election of Members of Parliament, must be thus directed: Præposito et Senescallo ville sue de St. Mawes alias St. Mary's in Com. Cornub. salutem.

At the north end of this borough, upon a well advanced promontory, stands the Castle of St. Mawes, alias St. Mary's, first built, fortified, and supplied with a small garrison of soldiers, by King Henry VIII. in his French wars, for defence of the harbour of Falmouth, against invasion of enemies; having now about thirty cannon, demy cannon, and culverins pertaining thereto (but scarcely so many soldiers of war). The Captain and Keeper whereof hath from the King 54*l.* 15*s.*; his Deputy 27*l.* 7*s.* 6*d.*; three Gunners, in all 72*l.*

After the dissolution of the Priory of St. Anthony, 26 Henry VIII., 1535, this Castle and the land whereon it stands, together with the government thereof, as I am informed, was given by that King to Sir Robert Le Greice, Knight, an Arragonist or Spaniard, whose son, in Queen Elizabeth's reign, sold the inheritance thereof to Hanniball Vyvyan, Esq. of Trelowarren, who thereupon was made Governor thereof; as some say after his decease, Sir Francis Vyvyan, Knight, his son; after his decease Sir Richard Vyvyan, Bart., his son; after his decease Sir Vyell Vyvyan, Bart., who was so far imposed upon by John Earl of Bath, by licence of King Charles II., as to sell the inheritance of the lands whereon this Castle stands, to him for 500*l.*; who forthwith transferred it over to Sir Joseph Tredinham, Knight, who then became Governor thereof, but was displaced by King William III., and the government thereof given to his Privy Councellor, the Right Honourable Hugh Boscawen, Esq., now in possession thereof at the writing of these lines.

There was a great controversy in Parliament, 4 James I., between Cotterell and Legrice, about Legrice's lands. See the Memoirs of Parliament, page 68, and modus tenendi Parliamentum.

During the interregnum of Cromwell, Sir Richard Vyvyan, as a person dissaffected to his government, was displaced from the gubernation of this Castle, and one Captain Rouse put in his place, which gentleman, as I have been informed, before the war broke out between King Charles I. and his Parliament, was of such low fortune in the world that he lived in a barn at Landrake, and lodged on straw, till he got a commission to be a Captain in the Parliament Army under the Earl of Essex, which brought him into money and credit; so that at length he was posted the Commander or Governor of this Castle, who behaved himself so very proud, grand, severe, and magisterial towards the neighbouring gentlemen of the royal party, that it gave occasion to John Trefusis, Esq., to make this short description of him in verse; which the Cavalier party, when they met to drink the King's health, would commonly sing in derision of the Governor, and called it their passado, viz.:

> In wealth Rouse abounds;
> He keepeth his hounds,
> Full fourteen couple and more.
> When he lived in a house
> With an owl and a mouse,
> Oh! they say he was wondrous poor.—Oh! they say.

Part of this barn aforesaid, tempore William III., as I am informed, was converted to a dwelling-house, the other part was made a Presbyterian meeting-house, by Mr. Robert Rouse of Wootton, son of the gentleman before mentioned, who with his family commonly on Sundays met there with great numbers of people of that profession, to hear the predicaments of their Priest. This Mr. Robert Rouse married Harrington of Somersetshire, and resided there during his father, the Governor, Rouse's life, with his wife, during which stay there he had by her one or two sons; and after his father's death, he came down to Wootton in this county.

As the Captain or Keeper of St. Mawes Castle hath a salary as aforesaid, so the Governor of its opposite Castle of Pendenis, hath yearly from the Crown 182*l*. 10*s*.; his Lieutenant-Governor 73*l*.; the Master Gunner 36*l*.; and two other Gunners 36*l*. each; and the like payments are made to the Governor and Lieutenant-Governor and Gunners of Scilly Castle and Islands.

TONKIN.

The patronage of this parish is in Sir Joseph Tredenham, in right of his manor of Tolvern.

A great part of this parish is included in the manor of

Tolvern, but as the capital place is in Philly I shall there treat of it.

Treveres; the town in the ways or roads, veres being the plural of ver or vere, a road, way or lane.

This place has been for several generations, by lease from the Arundells and the succeeding lords of Tolvern, the seat of the Jacks, the last of whom, Richard Jack, Esq. dying without issue, left this estate to his sister's only daughter, heiress of William Hooker, of Trelisick, in St. Ewe, Esq. and married to John Pomeray, Clerk.

Near this place lies Rosecossa, the woody valley, which I am told was formerly the seat of Sir John Rosecossa, who had here a large house and a chapel, but lately demolished. He left two daughters coheiresses, married to Trefry and Woollcumbe. This estate, with another called Tolcarne, that is the stone with a hole bored in it, have descended to Roger Woollcumbe, of Langford Hill, Esq. the present possessor of both.

THE EDITOR.

Mr. Hals has given a long history of St. Just, the companion of St. Austin, and his successor in the See of Canterbury, all of which is omitted. The parish is supposed to be under the patronage of St. Just, or Justus Archbishop of Lyons, about the year 350. This Saint, already a Bishop, began his career towards beatitude, by assisting St. Ambrose in his furious hostility against the Arians, and completed it by retiring into the deserts of Egypt, to prepare himself for the society of superior beings, through the favour of Him who is the author of all wisdom, of all knowledge, and of all benevolence, to be obtained by discarding or stupefying in solitude every kind affection, and every faculty of intelligence bestowed on him by the Almighty.

He is commemorated in the Roman Calendar on the second of September.

St. Mawes and its castle are by far the objects of greatest curiosity in this parish.

The shelter afforded for boats must at all times have rendered this place a resort of fishermen, but it acquired more importance and a name by the residence of St. Mawes, who seems to have come from Ireland with the other missionaries.

Accounts respecting him are extremely various. Some assimilate his history to that of St. Just, stating that he attained the episcopal dignity, and then, in compliance with the taste of that age, retired to an ascetic solitude; other legends represent him as a schoolmaster, and in early paintings he may be seen with the well-known emblem of scholastic authority in his hand.

The castle at St. Mawes was undoubtedly built by King Henry VIII. but a tradition universally believed in Cornwall is much less certain.

It is said that the King came to view the situation of his two projected castles of St. Mawes and Pendennis; that he passed two nights at Tolvorn, then a seat of the Arundells; and that he crossed the river from thence to Feock, at a passage that has ever since gone by his name. There is not, however, any trace of this journey to be found in histories of the times, nor in any public document.

The privilege of sending Members to Parliament was given to this village by Queen Elizabeth, in pursuance, probably, of the Tudor policy noticed under Michell; and if the creation of a close borough were the object really intended, it proved invariably successful up to the general disfranchisement of 1832.

This right of sending Members to Parliament, accompanied by the pageantry of maces and sergeants-at-arms, and combined with various personal advantages, could not fail of exciting feelings of envy and ridicule. In this instance the village of St. Mawes, extending in a single line of houses in the direction of the beach, has readily presented a topic, which was, to inquire whether the new mayor lived on the same side of the street as his predecessor.

ST. JUST, IN ROSELAND.

Corrack Road, the best anchorage for large vessels in all Falmouth harbour, lies off this parish, called by Mr. Hals King Road, but the popular appellation is St. Just, or Sainteast, Pool.

Mr. Lysons gives the following inscriptions, said to have been written by Leland, and cut in the castle walls.

" Henricus, Octavus Rex Angliæ, Franciæ, et Hiberniæ invictissimus, me posuit præsidium reipublicæ, terrorem hostibus.

> Imperio Henrici naves submittite vela,
> Semper honos, Henrice, tuus laudesque manebunt;
> Edwardus famâ referat factisque parentem,
> Gaudeat, Edwardo duce nunc, Cornubia felix.
>
> Semper vivat Aiâ Regis Henrici Octavi, qui anno XXXIVo sui regni hoc fieri fecit.
> Honora Henricum Octavum Angliæ, Franciæ, et Hiberniæ Regem excellentissimum.

The advowson of this parish has passed by succession from Tredinham, through Schobells, to Hawkins. The present incumbent is Edward Rodd, D.D. of Trebartha, late Fellow of Exeter College, Oxford, and Proctor of the University in 1802.

St. Just in Roseland measures 2340 statute acres.

	£.	s.	d.
Annual value of the Real Property, as returned to Parliament in 1815:	4714	0	0
Poor Rate in 1831	817	8	0

Population,	in 1801,	in 1811,	in 1821,	in 1831,
	1416	1639	1648	1558

giving an increase of 10 per cent in 30 years; there being a decrease of 90 in the last 10 years.

GEOLOGY, BY DOCTOR BOASE.

This parish, which forms the eastern shore of Falmouth harbour, is composed of the same rocks as the adjoining parishes of Filley, Gersons, and St. Anthony.

ST. JUST, near Penzance.

HALS.

Is situate in the hundred of Penwith, and hath upon the north-east Morsa, west St. George's Channel and Sennan, east Saneret, south Buryan. For the modern name, it is taken from the tutelar guardian to whom this church is dedicated, viz. St. Just the Roman, first Bishop of Rochester, afterwards Archbishop of Canterbury.

At the time of the Norman Conquest this district passed in tax, either under the jurisdiction of Buryan or Alverton. In the taxation of benefices made by the Bishops of Lincoln and Winchester, into the value of Cornish Benefices, 1294, ecclesia Sancti Justi in decanatu de Penwith is rated viii$l$.; in Wolsey's Inquisition, 1521, 11l. 11s. 0$\frac{1}{2}d$.; the patronage in the Crown; the incumbent Millet; the rectory in possession of Borlase, and the parish rated to the 4s. per pound Land Tax, 1696, by the name of St. Just, 133l. 7s.; which name is derived from the Latin words jus, justus, right, just, lawful, righteous, well-meaning, upright.

At Pen-dene, or Pen-dayn, in this parish, is the dwelling of John Borlase, Esq. Commissioner for the Peace, who married Lydia Harris, of Kenegye, and giveth the same arms as the Borlases of Borlase in St. Wenn and Newland; this gentleman's father greatly advanced his wealth by tin adventures, and is descended from the Borlases of Sythney, as I am informed.

Bray in this parish, situate on the Irish sea coast, gave name and original to an old family of gentlemen surnamed de Bray who by the tenure of knight service, held in this place two parts of a knight's fee of land, 3 Henry IV. Carew's Survey of Cornwall, p. 39.

I take the Lord Bray of Hampshire to be descended from this family. This place is now in the possession of that well-known quaker, John Ellis, Esq.

On the south side of this parish, upon a lofty hill, stands Chapel Carne Bray, that is to say Bray's spar-stone Chapel, and suitable to its name it is situate upon the top of the most astonishing burrow or tumulus of Carnes, or spar stones, that ever my eyes beheld; artificially laid together perhaps upon the bodies of human creatures, interred upon the mountain before the fifth century; on the top of which burrow of stones, which is about fifteen feet high from the ground, stands the chapel itself; which riseth about ten feet higher, well built with moor-stone and lime, with a window in the east, and a durns, or door, on the south of the same stones; the roof all well covered or arched over with large flat moor-stones, wrought with the hammer and strongly fastened together. The chapel being about ten feet broad and about fourteen feet long (as that on Roach Rock) on the outside; and round this chapel may be seen, the downfalls of many sparstone-stairs and walks, by which heretofore the people ascended to this chapel, and diverted themselves with a full prospect of the contiguous country by sea and land—St George's Channel, the British Ocean, and the Atlantic Sea towards the Scilly Islands, of which from hence in fair weather you may have a full view; which lands of Scilly seem to stand in equal height with this chapel, though the ground towards the Land's End, in St. Leucan and St. Lennan, on the sea-shore towards it, are at least eighty fathoms lower, or under it, as is the sea itself, betwixt that and the Scilly Islands. Such another chapel as this, though not built upon a burrow of stones, is to be seen on Mountague Hill, in Somersetshire, and dedicated to St. Michael the Archangel, for half a mile ascended up the hill upon stone stairs, embowed or arched over head right artificially. (See also Camden in Somerset.) Thus it appears that this tribe of Bray were heretofore men of great wealth, fame, and renown in those parts; since their name adheres not only to two local places in this parish, but divers others, as Castle Carne Bray in Luggan, Bray in Morvall, and many other places.

In this parish also was formerly St. Ewny's Chapel, now dilapidated; see Redruth and Lelant for more of this St. Ewny.

Those spar-stone monuments of Carne Bray Castle, and Chapel Carne Bray aforesaid, will I suppose perpetuate the name and memory of those Brays till the final consummation of all things, as aforesaid. Bray, in Battle Abbey Roll, is recorded to have come into England with William the Conqueror; but by the names of those local places and the fabrics aforesaid, it is probable they were here long before.

In this parish is a large flat stone, on which, as tradition says, seven Saxon Kings at one time and day, dined thereon, at such time as they came into Cornwall to see the Land's End thereof, and of Great Britain; which Kings are said to have been: 1. Ethelbert, 5th King of Kent; 2. Cissa, 2nd King of the South Saxons; 3. Kingills, 6th King of the West Saxons; 4. Sebert, 3d King of the East Saxons; 5. Ethelfred, 7th King of the Northumbers; 6. Penda, 5th King of the Mercians; and 7. Sigebert, 5th King of the East Angles; who all flourished about the year 600, and were all crowned heads, as Samuel Daniell in his Chronicle tells us. *

TONKIN

Has not any thing in addition to what is stated by Mr. Hals, except a description of Mayne Scriffer, or the "inscribed stone," which he ends by saying is really not in this parish, but in Madders, where he purposes to give a more full account of it.

THE EDITOR.

Pendeen claims the first attention of any place in this parish. It was for some ages the residences of the Bor-

---

* This is said by modern tradition to have happened at Mean, in the adjacent parish of Sannen. *Edit.*

lases, since removed to Castle Horneck, near Penzance. At Pendeen resided in the early part of his life Mr. John Borlase, sometime member for St. Ives. Here were born his two sons the Rev. Walter Borlase, LL.D. Vice Warden of the Stannaries; and the Rev. William Borlase, LL.D. by diploma from the university of Oxford, the justly celebrated writer of the Antiquities and of the Natural History of Cornwall.

Pendeen exhibits an excellent specimen of the large but comfortless houses, inhabited by gentlemen two centuries ago.

Near the house may be seen one of those very ancient excavations called vaus or faus. See Borlase's Antiquities, p. 293, 2d edit. 1769. They are conjectured to have been made for places of refuge in times when predatory descents on the coast were of frequent occurrence, and always causes of alarm. Yet the entrance could not be concealed, and the five kings of the Amorites had left an example, confirmed at no remote period by the cruel fate of a northern clan, proving the utter insecurity of such a retreat.

On the sea-shore below the house is a small cove, where boats and nets are kept for fishing; but so small is the shelter on this iron-bound coast, that the boats are drawn up by ropes or chains, and kept suspended during the winter, on the sloping surface of a steep cliff.

Some miles westward of Pendeen, and near the sea, is Botallock, the seat of the Usticks; one among the many families that resided for centuries in this remote peninsula, moderately endowed with gifts of fortune, but possessed of the honour and feelings of gentlemen.

This parish has been productive of tin from the most early periods; and Botallock would have elevated its proprietors in the scale of wealth, but times and manners had changed, so that the last Mr. Ustick of that place having spent his estate, and then got it redeemed by a productive mine, sold it at last to Admiral Boscawen, to whose grandson the property now belongs. The veins or lodes of tin having been wrought within the last fifty years to depths unattainable before the introduction of improved steam-engines, copper has, in very many instances, been found under the tin; and this has occurred at Botallock, where situated on the edge of a cliff, the workings with the steam-engines, whims, &c. present a spectacle more unique and more imposing than any other in Cornwall.

Further from the shore is Busvargus, the seat of an ancient family of the same name, the heiress of which was the mother of the Rev. Jonathan Toup, whose eminence as a scholar has been noticed under St. Ives. He died without issue in 1785; and the estate of Busvargus, having been settled on the children of his half-sister, is now the property of his niece, Mrs. Nicholas of Looe, the present representative of the Busvargus family.

The families of most distinction in latter times, inhabitants of St. Just, were Allan and Moddern, but both names are now extinct.

The great tithes appertained to the monastery of Glaseney, in Penryn. They now belong to Borlase.

The vicarage is in the presentation of the crown, and was held for many years by Doctor William Borlase, the historian.

And here perhaps the Editor may be allowed to mention the name of one whom he esteemed and admired, although his connection with Cornwall was so little permanent as to consist only of his serving the curacy of this parish.

The Reverend John Smyth, Fellow of Pembroke College, Oxford, received his title for deacon's orders from Doctor William Borlase, as vicar of St. Just, where he remained about six or seven years, till Cornwall lost one of its greatest ornaments.

Leaving St. Just, after Doctor Borlase's decease, he became the friend and assistant of the Reverend Sir Richard Kaye, Dean of Lincoln, and through his recommendation made the tour of Europe with Mr. Langley, a gentleman of Yorkshire. He then went back to College, and on a vacancy became tutor, and succeeded to the Headship; returning from a visit to Penzance, in 1809, he died in consequence of some local complaint at Exeter, where a monument has been placed to his memory in the Cathedral Church, with the following inscription:

Juxta conditur\
Joannes Smyth, S. T. P.\
Magister Collegii Pembrochiæ\
apud Oxonienses,\
Qui Academiam remeans, hac in Urbe,\
vi morbi grassantis, cito abreptus est,\
die 19 Octobris, A.D. 1809, ætatis suæ 66.\
Grata recordatione ejus in Collegiam beneficentiæ,\
in amicos comitatis et benevolentiæ,\
imo in omnes Φιλανθρωπιας,\
hoc marmor posuêre\
Successor ejus et Socii.

There is also a cenotaph in the Cathedral at Gloucester, a prebend of which church is annexed to the mastership of Pembroke College, by the liberality of Queen Anne.

Few men were ever more universally esteemed, or were more deserving of being so. His abilities and learning commanded respect; kindness, generosity, and benevolence endeared him to every friend; whilst good nature and convivial manners made him the favorite of each casual acquaintance.

To him the Editor is indebted for his good fortune in being himself a member of Pembroke College.

The parish feast is celebrated on the Sunday nearest to All Saints, November the first; but the church is known to claim for its patron St. Just, the companion of St. Austin, Bishop of Rochester, and afterwards Archbishop of Canterbury. Little is handed down to posterity of St. Just, but that little is entirely to his praise; at the command of Pope Gregory the Great, he undertook the perilous but successful service of converting the English Saxons; he attained the highest ecclesiastical dignity from the suffrages of those who had been brought by the labours of St. Austin and of his followers, within the pale of the church; and he obtained deserved commendation from Pope Boniface, either the third or fourth, who with one intermediate Pope, were the successors of St. Gregory, when the apostolic confirmation of his appointment to the metropolitan see was given, and himself honoured by the investure of a pall. He is stated in the Rubrics to have died on the 10th of November in the year 627.

Nothing seems to be more obvious, or to be more congenial to the human mind, than an annual celebration of particular events. Nature has completed in twelve months the most distinctly marked of her cycles. The seasons are renewed in the same order; and, if experience did not soon convince us of the contrary, we might be induced to think that our own existence in this world was destined to tread the same perpetual round.

Birth-days appear to have been celebrated in honour of living persons from times the most remote, either by nations, provinces, or private families, in proportion as their claims to attention were more or less wide. After the decease of those who have been supposed to confer benefits on mankind, " Quique sui memores alios fecere merendo," and more especially of those to whom nations owed their spiritual light and hopes, the days of such persons leaving this scene of trial, of sorrow, of anxiety, and of disappointment, to obtain their reward in Heaven, became epochs for uniting religious observance with joy and gladness. Churches were, therefore, dedicated to their memories and festivals instituted; but in England at least this instinctive propensity received the aid of a policy similar to that which, in still earlier periods, had fixed the Christian festivals on the very days previously occupied by the celebration of ancient superstition. Bede has preserved the following letter from Pope Gregory to St. Mellitus, who led a second band of missionaries into England, after the successful preaching of St. Austin, and became the first Bishop of London, where he is said to have founded the two Cathedrals, and finally to have attained the Archbishopric of Canterbury.

Historiæ Ecclesiasticæ Gentis Anglorum Libri Quinque, autore Sancto et venerabili Baeda. Lib. 2, ch. 30.

Exemplar Epistolæ quam Mellito Abbati Britanniam pergenti misit Sanctus Gregorius.

Abeuntaibus autem præfatis legatariis misit post eos beatus Pater Gregorius litteras memoratu dignas, in quibus apertè quàm studiosè erga salvationem nostræ gentis invigilaverit ostendit, ita scribens:

Dilectissimo filio Mellito Abbati GREGORIUS Servus Servorum Dei.

Post discessum congregationis nostræ, quæ tecum est, valde sumus suspensi redditi, quia nihil de prosperitate vestri itineris audisse nos contigit. Cum ergo Deus Omnipotens vos ad reverendissimum virum, Fratrem nostrum Augustinum Episcopum perduxerit, dicite ei quod diu mecum de causa Anglorum cogitans tractavi; videlicet quia Fana Idolorum destrui in eadem gente minime debeant, sed ipsa quæ in eis sunt Idola destruantur; Aqua benedicta fiat; in eisdem Fanis aspergatur; Altaria construantur; Reliquiæ ponantur, quia, si Fana eadem bene constructa sunt, necesse est ut a cultu Dæmonum in obsequio Veri Dei debeant commutari, ut dum gens ipsa eadem Fana sua non videt destrui, de corde errorem deponat, et Deum Verum cognoscens ac adorans, ad loca quæ consuevit familiariùs concurrat. *Et quia boves solent in sacrificio Dæmonum multos occidere, debet eis etiam, hac de re, aliqua sollemnitas immutari; ut Die Dedicationis, vel Natalitii sanctorum Martyrum, quorum illic Reliquiæ ponuntur, Tabernacula sibi, circa easdem Ecclesias, quæ ex Fanis commutatæ sunt, de ramis arborum faciant, et Religiosis convivis sollemnitatem celebrant.* Nec Diabolo jam animalia immolent; et, ad laudem Dei, in esu suo animalia occidant, et Donatori omnium de satietate sua gratias referant; ut dum eis aliqua exteriùs gaudia reservantur, ad interiora gaudia consentire faciliùs valeant. Nam duris mentibus simul omnia abscindere impossibile esse non dubium est; quia et is qui summum locum ascendere nititur gradibus vel passibus, non autem saltibus elevatur; sic Israelitico populo in Ægypto Dominus re quidem innotuit; sed tamen eis sacrificiorum usus, quæ Diabolo solebat exhibere, in cultu proprio reservavit, et eis in suo sacrificio animalia immolare præciperet, quatenus cor mutantes, aliud de sacrificio amitterent, aliud retinerent; ut etsi ipsa assent animalia quæ efferare consueverant, vero tamen Deo hæc et non Idolis immolantes jam sacrificia ipsa non essent.

Hæc igitur dilectionem tuam prædicto Fratri necesse est dicere, ut ipse in præsenti illic positus perpendet, qualiter omnia debeat dispensare.

Deus te incolumem custodiat, dilectissime Fili! Data die decima quinta kalendarum Juliarum, imperante Domino nostro Mauricio Tiberio piissimo Augusto, anno decimo novo; post consulatum ejusdem Domini anno decimo octavo; Indictione quarta. A. D. 601.

It may be presumed that the Jesuit missionaries to China and to Paraguay were not unacquainted with this letter from the Pope.

St. Just in Penwith measures 6,984 statute acres.

	£.	s.	d.
Annual value of the Real Property, as returned to Parliament in 1815	7776	0	0
Poor Rate in 1831	817	8	0

Population,— { in 1801, | in 1811, | in 1821, | in 1831,
               2779 | 3057 | 3666 | 4667

giving an increase of 68 per cent. in 30 years.

Present Vicar, the Rev. John Buller, presented by the Lord Chancellor in 1825.

This parish is called St. Juest as a distinction from the name of the parish in Roseland pronounced St. Jeast.

GEOLOGY, BY DR. BOASE.

This parish, with the exception of a narrow band of slate which skirts the coast from Pendeen Cove to Cape Cornwall, is situated entirely on granite. It has been long celebrated for its mines, which generally are placed on or near to the junction of the granite and the slate; and in consequence of the narrow limits of the latter rock, their workings often extend under the sea. Botallack mine is a noted instance of this description; and its steam engine and machinery, perched on the side of a steep rocky cliff, present one of the most picturesque objects in the country. St. Just has afforded specimens of by far the greater number of British minerals. Its slate has a basis of compact felspar, and exhibits many interesting varieties of this rock; but the most rare is that which abounds with disseminated garnets at Botallack. The principal lodes of this parish exhibit some peculiarities in their direction, and the little coves are generally covered with beds of diluvium, some of which are composed of large granitic pebbles and boulders, which appear to have once formed a beach, although at present they are elevated above high-water mark. St. Just abounds with so many interesting objects as to make it impossible to enumerate them in these short notices. Ample details may be found of all these productions in the Transactions of the Geological Society of Cornwall.

ST. KEYNE.

HALS.

Is situate in the hundred of West, and hath upon the east Leskeard and the Loo river, south Dulo, west Lanreth, north St. Pynnock; at the time of the Norman Conquest this district passed under the jurisdiction of Leskeard, and so in the Domesday Tax as part thereof. In the Inquisition into the value of Cornish benefices made by the Bishops of Lincoln and Winchester 1294, ecclesia de Kayne in decanatu de Westwellshire was rated xx*l.* In Wolsey's Inquisition, 1521, 5*l.* 18*s.* 6*d.* The patronage in   ; the Incumbent Doweringe; and the parish rated to the 4s. per pound Land Tax, 1696, 53l. 16s. by the name of St. Kain.

The presidual guardian of this church is one of those two holy women mentioned by writers as famous for their piety and supernatural facts; the one of the British blood, the other of Saxon race. That of the British is St. Kayne, daughter of Braghan, king and builder of the town of Brecknock in Wales, who flourished about the year 500; the which King Braghan had issue also twenty-three other daughters, all for the like reasons aforesaid entered into the catalogue or calendar of saints; and also two sons, St. Canock and St. Caddock, to whose honour and memory a chapel in Padstow parish was erected; and still, though disused from divine service, bearing his name. The other St. Kayne was born about the seventh century, upon the river Avon in Somersetshire, at a place which after her decease sprung up a town, still flourishing in fame and wealth, from her denominated Kainsham, i e. Kain's house, home, habitation, or dwelling. She is famous amongst agonal writers for miracle working, particularly for turning serpents into stones wheresoever she saw them, so that they had not power either to hurt man or beast; a woman very much wanted now in Cornwall, where adders or serpents abound to the great hurt of man and beast.

She is also highly praised by John Capgrave in his book of the English Saints, for her purity, piety, and chastity.

To one of these two women is also dedicated the vicarage church of Cainham, in Holderness hundred in York; as also Caynham vicarage church in Ludlow hundred in Salop.

In this parish at   lived some of the Coplestons of Colbrook in Devon, as I take it; which place descended to them by some of the heirs of Flemmen, Berkley, Turvey, Courtney, Bonvill, Pawlet, Chichester, Bridges, Graas, Hawley, Huish, Wiedbury, Fitzwalter, or some others, which they married with successively; and thereby obtained such a mighty estate in Cornwall and Devon that they were generally distinguished by the name of the " great Coplestons." But, alas! maugre all their great riches and wealth, the last John Great Coplestone, tempore Elizabeth, for killing his natural son and godson in discontent, was indicted at the assizes at Exeter, tried and found guilty of wilful murder, and sentenced to death for the same; and lay in gaol till he sold thirteen manors of land in Cornwall to obtain a reprieve or pardon; and left of legal issue only one son, named John, who had issue only two daughters that became his heirs; married to Bamphield and Elford, in whom the estate, name, and blood of those Coplestons is terminated, who gave for their arms, Argent, a chevron Gules, between three leopards' faces Azure. These gentlemen were hereditary esquires of the white spur, who, together with the Champernowns and the Carmenows, possessed and enjoyed the profits of their private estates in Devon and Cornwall, to that great degree, in former ages, that the like great riches was not then to be found in any other family for value in those counties, though now I know not of any lands in Cornwall remaining in those tribes, or any of those names now extant there.

TONKIN.

Camden, in Somersetshire, mentions Keine as a devout British Virgin, whom many of the last age, through an over credulous temper, believed to have changed serpents into stones, because they find sometimes in quarries some such little miracles of sporting nature. She is said to have been born on the banks of the river Avon in that county, at the place where after her decease sprung up a town, from her denominated Keynesham. She is famous among the agonal writers for her purity, piety, and charity, as also for many miracles, particularly for turning serpents into stones.

There was one other St. Keyne famous among the Britains of Wales, daughter to Brechanus, King, and namer of Brecknock Town. He had twenty-four daughters and two sons, all Saints.

It is possible, however, that both these St. Keynes may be one and the same.

THE EDITOR.

Mr. Lysons says, that the ancient name of this parish was Lametton, and that the manor still exists.

This manor he further states was the property of Sir Robert Tresilian, Lord Chief Justice of the King's Bench, attainted in the reign of King Richard the Second, by whom this portion of his property was bestowed on John Hawley, of Dartmouth, supposed to have married a daughter of the Chief Justice. His daughter and heiress brought it to the Coplestones.

In the reign of James the First it belonged to the Harrisons of Mount Radford in Devonshire, and from them it passed by marriage to the Rashleighs.

Mr. William Rashleigh, of Menabilly, is now the proprietor of the whole or nearly the whole of this parish, and in it of the celebrated well, which Mr. Carew notices in the following manner, p. 305, Lord Dunstanville's edit.

" Next I will relate to you another of the Cornish natural wonders, viz. Saint Keyne's Well; but lest you make wonder, first at the Saint before you notice the well, you must understand that this was not Kayne the Manqueller, but one of a gentler spirit and milder sex, to wit, a woman. He who caused the spring to be pictured added this rhyme for an explanation:

> In name, in shape, in quality,
>   This Well is very quaint;
> The name to lot of Kayne befell,
>   No over holy Saint.

> The shape, four trees of divers kind,
>   Withy, oak, elm, and ash,
> Make with their roots an arched roof,
>   Whose floor this spring doth wash.
>
> The quality, that man or wife,
>   Whose chance or choice attains,
> First of this sacred stream to drink,
>   Thereby the mastery gains.

Mr. Tonkin quotes this passage from Carew, and adds: "Did it retain this wondrous quality, as it does to this day the shape, I believe there would be to it a greater resort of both sexes than either to Bath or Tunbridge; for who would not be fond of attaining this longed-for sovereignty?" And Mr. Tonkin adds further, "since the writing of this the trees were blown down by a violent storm; and in their place Mr. Rashleigh, in whose land it is, has planted two oaks, an ash, and an elm, which thrive very well; but the wonderful arch is destroyed."

For a most interesting account of St. Keyne's Well, and of all that portion of Cornwall, the reader is referred to Mr. Bond's "Topographical and Historical Sketches of East and West Looe, and of the Neighbourhood," 1 vol. 8vo. 1823, printed by John Nichols and Son, No. 25, Parliament Street, Westminster.

Mr. Bond says that the trees were blown down by the great storm of November 1703, and that Mr. Philip Rashleigh, who succeeded his father in the property about that time, planted soon afterwards the trees which have now acquired their full growth, and probably equalled those which stood there before them.

Mr. Bond has also printed the beautiful as well as humorous lines composed by Mr. Southey, and referred to other verses on the same subject in the Gentleman's Magazine for June 1822, vol. xcii. i. p. 526.

Mr. Southey's lines cannot be too frequently reprinted.

SAINT KEYNE'S WELL.

By Robert Southey.

(From Carew's History of Cornwall.)

A well there is in the West Country,
  And a clearer one never was seen;
There is not a Wife in the West Country,
  But has heard of the Well of St. Keyne.

An oak and an elm tree stand behind,
  And beside does an ash-tree grow;
And a willow, from the bank above,
  Droops to the water below.

A trav'ller came to the Well of St. Keyne;
  Pleasant it was to his eye,
For from cock-crowing he had travelling been,
  And there was not a cloud in the sky.

He drank of the water so cool and clear,
  For thirsty and hot was he;
And he sat down upon a bank
  All under the willow tree.

There came a man from the neighbouring town,
  At the Well to fill his pail;
So on the well side he rested it,
  And bade the stranger hail.

" Now art thou a bachelor, stranger?" quoth he,
  " For if thou hast a wife,
The happiest draught thou hast drank to-day
  That ever thou didst in thy life.

" Or has your good woman, if one you have,
  In Cornwall ever been?
For, and if she have, I'll venture my life
  She has drank of the Well of St. Keyne."

"I left a good woman who never was here,"
 The stranger he made reply,
"But that my draught should be better for that,
 I pray you answer me why."

"St. Keyne," quoth the countryman, " many a time
 Drank of this crystal Well;
And before the angel summon'd her hence,
 She laid on the water a spell :—

"If the husband of this gifted Well
 Shall drink before his wife
A happy man thenceforth is he,
 For he shall be master for life.

"But if the wife should drink of it first,
 God help the husband then!"——
The stranger stoopt to the Well of St Keyne,
 And he drank of the water again ! !

"You drank of the Well, I warrant, betime?"
 He to the countryman said:
But the countryman smiled, as the stranger spoke,
 And sheepishly shook his head.

"I hasten'd, as soon as the wedding was done,
 And left my wife in the porch;
But i' faith! she had been wiser than me,—
 For she took a bottle to church."

 It is almost unnecessary to observe, that the stones said to originate from serpents petrified at the intercession of St. Keyne or St. Kenna, and supposed by Mr. Tonkin, according to the philosophy of his day, to be *Lusus Naturæ*, are the shells of extinct Nautili, called Cornua Ammonis, from their resemblance to the horns sculptured on the statues of Jupiter Ammon, found in abundance throughout the neighbourhood of Kainsham, and in most of the formations intermediate between the iron sand and red marle.

 Transforming serpents into stone, seems to have been an achievement as appropriate to Saints as was the encountering of dragons to knights errant. St. Hilda cleared her favourite Island from these venomous reptiles; and St. Patrick, more powerfully gifted, swept them from the whole of Ireland at once.

It was at last observed, with no small degree of wonder, that those metamorphosed snakes invariably wanted a head, and the times of fabricating legends having passed by, this phenomenon never received a solution from the cloister.

St. Brechan, the British Saint and King, the happy father of twenty-six children, all sainted like himself, is represented in the second plate of St. Neot's Church, in what is called the Young Women's Window, displaying these twenty-six Saints, small in stature, within a fold of his kingly robe.

This parish measures 769 statute acres.

	£.	s.	d.
Annual value of the Real Property, as returned to Parliament in 1815,	1,017	0	0
Poor Rate in 1831,	68	12	0

Population,—	in 1801,	in 1811,	in 1821,	in 1831,
	139	157	153	201

giving an increase of $44\frac{1}{2}$ per cent. in 30 years.

THE GEOLOGY, BY DR. BOASE.

This little parish is situated entirely on rocks of the calcareous series, like those of Dulo, one of the adjacent parishes.

KEY, or KEA.

HALS.

Is situate in the hundred of Powdre, and hath upon the north Kenwyn and Truro, and the sea channel thereof, south the Vale River and sea, west Feock. As for the modern name Keye, it signifies in British a hedge or mound, against sea or land, as sepes in Latin; from whence we have our English words key or keys, wharfs for exportation and importation of goods and merchandize over seas; no improper appellation to the circumstances of this place, where are several of that sort. It was taxed in the Domesday Book, 20 William I., 1087, by the name of Landegey, (and from thence the manor of Lan-digge in this parish, contiguous therewith, and surrounding the same, is denominated; now corrupted to Lansagey, alias Keye.) From whence it is plainly evident that before the Norman Conquest here was an endowed rectory church that received tithes or tenths, of the profits of the earth, predial or otherwise, towards the maintenance of the worship and service of God, and doubtless invested with that benefit by the Bishop of Bodmin or Cornwall, before that was united to Kirton and Exeter.

In the Inquisition of the Bishops of Lincoln and Winchester into the value of Cornish Benefices, 1294, ecclesia de Landigh in decanatu de Powdre was rated viii*l.* vi*s.* viiid. Vicar ejusdem xx*s.* In the grant of fifteenths, granted by the clergy to the King, the 24th Henry VI., 1447, the parish and church of Landege was rated £2. 7*s.*, Carew's Survey of Cornwall, p. 90. In Wolsey's Inquisition, 1521, Landegge was then rated together with Kenwyn, £16.; the patronage formerly in the Bishop of Cornwall that endowed them, now the Bishop of Exeter; the late incumbent Mitchell, now Borlase; and the parish rated to the 4*s.* per pound Land Tax, 1696, £171. 8*s.*

Nansa-Vallan, in this parish, is the dwelling of Charles Boscawen, Esq. Barrister-at-Law, second brother to the Right Honourable Hugh Boscawen, of Tregothnan, Esq. who for many years hath retired himself in this place in great esteem and respect of all that know him; doing good to all those that, for his counsel, hospitality, friendship, or charity, make addresses unto him; though he hath hitherto lived a bachelor's life, and whilst he lives I suppose ever will, with a kind of abhorrence of women and marriage. I take this place either to be part of or the voke lands of the manor of Blanchland, i. e. white land, formerly the lands of Albalanda, now Boscawen's of Tregothnan, the waste lands of which lordship is not only abounding in tin and tin mines, but for about twenty years last past hath yielded its owner about twenty thousand pounds out of its coppermines, though the waste or down lands in which it is found, is in many places scarce worth eighteen pence per acre.

Guddarne in this parish, part of Blanchland manor, by lease is the dwelling of Reginald Bauden, Gent. that married Pendarves, his father Paynter, his grandfather Trewoolla.

In this place of Guddarne, in my youth, I was showed by Mr. Bauden a brass or iron crock, containing about eight gallons; wherein, as he said, his father found by virtue of a dream of one Hendra, under Key Cross, in a tempestuous night of wind, thunder, lightning, and rain, so vast a quantity of gold and silver as not only advanced him from the rank of rack-renter to that of a freeholder, but from the distinction of a plebeian to that of a gentleman.

Kelleho, Kellyow, Killeyow, synonymous words in this parish, id est Hazell Copps, a place it seems heretofore notable for those sort of nut trees called hazells, one of the sweetest and best sorts of nuts this island affordeth, if left to grow full ripe and well saved. This place is the dwelling of John Hawes, Esq. that married Sprye, his father Vosper, and giveth for his arms, Azure, a fess wavy between three lions passant Or.

Trelogas, in this parish, is the dwelling of Robert White, Gent. that married Philips, of Poughill.

From this family was descended Mr. John White, linendraper in London, who having got much money by trading in tin, settled lands of ten pounds per annum beyond reprizes for ever, to be divided into four equal parts, between the poor inhabitants of the four ancient coinage towns in Cornwall, viz. Leskeard, Lestwithell, Truro, and Helston; to be distributed by the ministers and churchwardens of those churches on St. John's day yearly; the remainder, being forty shillings, to be divided into four equal parts between the four ministers of those churches, who on that day in their respective churches annually are to preach an anniversary sermon in remembrance of him for ever, of which elsewhere (see Truro.)

In this parish of Kea on the open downs, by the highway or street, are situate the four burrows, i.e. the four sepulchres, tumuli, or graves, after the British-Roman manner, to put those travellers that passed by in mind of mortality and death; one of them is called Burrow Bel-les, i. e. the far off, remote, broad or large burrow or sepulchre, (viz. on the confines of this parish) and suitable to its other names it is one of the broadest or largest burrows in those parts; into which some tinners, temp. William III. in hopes of finding money, pierced a hole or adit into the centre thereof, where, though they missed their expectations they found in the same two of the broadest and flat moor-stones as a cover, supported by three perpendicular stones of suitable strength or bigness, that they had seen in the adjacent country. In the vacant space, vault, or arch under those stones, they found decayed or broken pieces of the urn or ossilegium, and about a gallon of black matter and ashes, which doubtless was the gleanings or remains of that once famous human creature, before the fifth century interred here, with many thousands others, doubtless of less degree in the contiguous lands thereof, who had not money to raise such troublesome, laborious, and costly funeral monuments as those four burrows were, and still are.

Cur-Lyghon in this parish is now transnominated to Carlyon; and here for many descents lived the family from thence denominated Curlyghon, who were gentlemen of considerable fame, lands, and revenues in those parts, as appeared to me from several old Latin deeds, some bearing date 6 Henry V. (see Truro); from whence it came by marriage, descent, or purchase to Burleigh, and from him to Hawes, as I was informed.

TONKIN.

I take the name to be a corruption of Caius; and that St. Caius, Pope and kinsman to the Emperor Dioclesian, who suffered martyrdom under the said Emperor in 296, is the tutelar patron of this church, which is a daughter to Kenwyn, and passes in the same presentation, being valued with it in the King's Books at 16*l*. The patronage in the Bishop of Exeter. The incumbent Mr. Mitchell, the oldest clergyman now living in this county; who though aged, and his churches three miles apart from each other, regularly serves them both every Sunday; he is since dead, in 1731, and has been succeeded by the Reverend Walter Borlase, LL.D. and vicar of Maddern.

In this parish lies the extensive manor of Blanchland, latinized into Albalonda. This manor gave name to a considerable family, in which it continued for many descents. The last of them, Otho de Albalonda, had only one daughter and heir, Johanna, married in his lifetime to John Boscawen, of Tregothnon, in the 31st year of Edward III. and carried this rich inheritance into that family; in which it hath ever since continued, to their very great advantage, having within these fifty years brought them more money for copper than almost all the other mines in the county together, if the last twenty years are excepted, during which time great discoveries have been made in various other places. Neither are the wastrels of this manor destitute of good mines of tin; one of which, called the White Works, occasioned a law-suit between Mr. John Mayo, of Truro, owner of the tin bounds thereon, and Mr. Hugh Boscawen, lord of the soil, towards the latter end of the reign of Charles the Second.

Mr. Mayo claimed the farm or toll of the copper-ore,

as well as of the tin, in right of his bounds; but the suit was very justly determined in favour of Mr. Boscawen, as Lord of the Soil, for that the right of the tin as bounder was only by the custom of the Stannaries, and that no such custom could be pleaded for copper ore.

This one suit put an end to all disputes between the lords of the soil and the bounders, which otherwise would have been endless, and very much to the discouragement of copper mines; and there have not been wanting some designing people of late, who made application to King George II. then Prince of Wales, falsely representing that much tin ore was carried into Wales with the copper ore, and there separated from the copper, to his great loss of duties.

Guddern. This place hath been for several generations the seat, on lease from the family of Boscawen, of the Bowdens; perhaps ever since the Albalonda's time, although they were possessed of fair estates in fee elsewhere.

Reginald Bowden, Esq. is the present possessor.

Nansavallan. Avallan is an apple-tree, and the name signifies the valley of apple-trees. This I take to have been the chief seat of the Albalondas, as it hath been since of some of the Boscawens; and particularly of late years that of Charles Boscawen, Esq. a younger son to Hugh Boscawen, Esq. and sometime Member of Parliament for Tregony, and a Justice of the Peace. The arms of Albalonda were, Gules, three bends Argent; Mr. Bowden's, Azure, a chevron between seven griffins' heads couped Or, each head transfixed by a dagger, the pommel Or, the blade Proper.

Adjoining to Nansavallan is Kelliou, the groves, this name being the plural of Kelli, a grove. It was once the seat of a family of the same name, but whether they were of the same stock with the Kellios of Lanleke and Rosiline I am yet to learn. By a daughter and heir, this place, if I am not mistaken, came to Edward Vivian, Esq. a younger son to Vivian of Trenoweth, by whom he had only one daughter and heir Jane, married to John Howeis, of Redruth, whose great-grandson Reginald Howeis, Esq. is the present owner of it. He was Sheriff of Cornwall in the tenth year of George I. 1724, and hath married Susanna, the eldest daughter and coheir of Edward Harris, Esq.; and his brother Edward Howeis, Jane her younger sister, and both have issue. The family of Howeis, give for their arms, Azure, a fess wavy between three lions passant Or, armed and langued Gules.

Trevoster. This place is very pleasantly situated on Truro river, facing the town, from which it is but two miles distant by water. This was a seat of a younger branch of the Trevanion family, for here lived John Trevanion, youngest son of John Trevanion, of Carhays, Esq. which John Trevanion had by his wife, the daughter of   Holland, Esq. of Devonshire, a son of the same name, who married Marianne, the daughter of John Somaster, of Painsford, in Devon, Esq. by whom he had three daughters and coheiresses. Mary, married to Richard Trefusis, of Trefusis, Esq.; Joan, to William Bligh, of Botathon, Esq.; and Alice to Nicholas Boscawen, of Tregothnan, Esq.

Since that, Trevoster has been held on lease by one of the family of Davies, and now Mr. Howeis, of Killion, has a lease of it on lives.

All these estates before mentioned, I take to be within the manor of Blanchland, and I have passed by one place in it to the north-west of the Great Works, called Kelly freth: this was for several generations the seat, in lease from the Boscawens, of the Winters, a younger branch of that eminent family in Gloucestershire, and the family remained here till very lately, giving for their arms, Sable, a fess Ermine.

I don't know whether it be worth while to take notice of a place to the south of it, called Chase Water, which being on the great road between Truro and Redruth, and very near the Great Works, hath now several houses built in it.

The manor of Key, alias Landegay.

I take this to be the same with that called by Mr. Carew Landegy. I find this parish called Ecclesia de Landigay.

This manor was forfeited by Francis Tregion, Esq. with the rest of his estate, as may be seen in Probus.

About the 8th or 9th Charles I. this manor was given or sold for a small sum by the King to William Coryton, of Newton, Esq. in whose family it hath remained ever since. On the commons belonging to Guddern is a large barrow called Guddern Barrow, near which are several large moorstones; and also at no great distance is another barrow, called Craig Vrause, or the large barrow, remarkable for giving name to some good mines of tin and copper near it.

THE EDITOR.

All the legends of this parish concur in claiming for their patron Saint Kea, one of the great company of missionaries, and as the ludicrous, almost from a species of fatality, appears to have blended itself with these ancient tales, a large block of granite, hollow on one side, which happened to lie near the bank of the river, was for centuries pointed out as the boat used by St. Kea to waft himself from Ireland to the Cornish shore; and so currently was this story repeated, that, if persons went to sea in a vessel not adequate to the service, it was observed they might as well have made a voyage with St. Kea in his moorstone trough.

Mr. Hals having used a strange orthography for Nansavallan, and given as fanciful a derivation of the word; both are omitted, since Nans or Nance is known to be a vale; and Avallan may be proved to be the Celtic name of an apple, by referring to the History of Glastonbury. This seat of the Albalandas presented within fifty years one of the most venerable specimens in all that neighbourhood of the dwellings used by gentlemen of consideration in former times.

It was entirely surrounded and sheltered by large trees,

and at some little distance stood a wood more extensive than any one west of it; and both were conspicuous and pleasing objects from the whole district round Truro; but the *auri sacri fames* has swept away the whole, and the place is now become very little preferable to an open down. The Editor expresses himself with some feeling on this subject, having passed at Nanceavallan many happy weeks of his childhood; and fancied the wood an exact counterpart of that in which the favourite objects of infantine compassion perished from want of food, and were painfully covered over with leaves by the little bird, doubly consecrated by this effort of his kindness.

In the hands of the proprietor, the farm of Nanceavallan is however now improving, by extensive drainages, and by a system of husbandry, that cannot fail of extending the benefit derived from example to all the neighbourhood.

Killiow is now the seat of Mr. Robert Lovell Gwatkin, where he has built an almost entirely new house with extensive gardens and plantations, improved the land, and made the whole into a handsome modern residence.

To this gentleman the parish is also mainly indebted for a removal of the church.

Either cultivation began on the banks of the river, or a strong feeling of veneration was entertained for the spot where St. Kea landed from his granite trough, but so it happened that the church stood at one extremity of the parish, and that by far the least populous. Mr. Gwatkin led the way, and contributed largely towards constructing a new church much nearer to the great mass of the inhabitants; in this he was followed by other proprietors, and a spacious church is now in use for divine service between Killiow and Nanceavallan. Prayers, with a sermon suited to the occasion, were first given, after reading the Bishop's license, on the 3d of October 1802, being the feasten Sunday, to a congregation so large as almost to fill the churchyard as well as the church itself, which is decorated by Mrs. Gwatkin, niece of Sir Joshua Reynolds, with paintings which that great artist could not have failed to admire.

The tower alone remains to point out the site of the former church.

Mr. Reginald Haweis, mentioned as the possessor of Killiow by Hals, received his education as a Gentleman Commoner of Exeter College; but he spent the whole of the remainder of his life in retirement. One Oxford anecdote he used to relate with peculiar pleasure. It seems that he was selected to recite some Latin verses in the theatre, commemorating the victory of Blenheim, an event without parallel in the modern history of Europe till the year 1815. In the verses occurred this apostrophe, Quo, Tallarde! ruis? and as Mr. Haweis was actually pronouncing these words, the Duke of Marlborough with Marshal Tallard entered the theatre, amidst thunders of applause. But possibly the entrance of Marshal Tallard may be a mistake.

Mr. Reginald Haweis and his brother Edward, both stated to have families, died childless; and the estate devolved on Mr. David Haweis, the grandson of an uncle.

That uncle had been a beneficed clergyman, but was deprived with the two thousand turned out to poverty and to suffer persecution (see St. Hilary parish) on St. Bartholomew's day 1662; a day ill chosen by those who might recollect what happened on the same festival ninety years before.

This gentleman having a family, and being without support, found himself obliged to dispose of them in any way to procure their own maintenance, and his eldest son submitted to become a barber. His son was apprenticed to the same trade; and on him the estate devolved. He married a gentlewoman, Miss Kempe, of Roseland; but persevering in low habits of intemperance, the peculiar vice of that time, he died at an early age, leaving the property to his widow for her life, with the remainder to his sisters. They were married, and in stations not more elevated than his own; their husbands were ready to pursue a line of conduct similar to that which had cut short the 'squire's life; and in consequence, the whole reversionary interests were soon dissipated, with the exception of one subdivided portion, transmitted by a sister's daughter, who died early in life, to her only daughter, Mary Ann Jenkins, of whom it may be sufficient to say, that if the whole estate had devolved on her, it would have been in hands worthy of her best ancestors.

On the banks of the river, directly opposite to Tregothnan, the magnificent seat of Lord Falmouth, is a farm called Trelease, belonging to the Editor; for beauty of natural situation and for command of prospect, scarcely inferior to Tregothnan itself.

But if ancient romances could be relied on as authorities, the place most deserving of regard in this parish, or in the whole county, after Tintagell Castle, would be Carlian, since Thomas of Erceldowne, the celebrated northern poet of the twelfth century, universally known by the appellation of Thomas the Rhymer, describes Carlian as the birth-place of the renowned Sir Tristrem, Knight of the Round Table, companion of Arthur and the chief hero of chivalry, where all exceed not merely the prowess, but whatever the imagination can create in these degenerate times. Yet perhaps the armies and fleets of England may say,

> Taccia Argo i Mini, e taccio Artu che suoi
> Erranti, che di sogni empion le carte

Chase Water is now grown almost into a town. A chapel has recently been built there for the accommodation of a dense population; but in such wretched taste as to burlesque the worst imitation of Gothic.

The parish of Kea measures 7382 statute acres.

	£.	s.	d.
Annual value of the Real Property, as returned to Parliament in 1815	4306	0	0
Poor Rate in 1831	1254	7	0

Population,—	in 1801,	in 1811,	in 1821,	in 1831,
	2440	2766	3142	3837

giving an increase of 57 per cent. in 30 years.

In 1821 and in 1831 the population of Tregavethen is subjoined, 66—59.

The present Vicar of Kea is the Rev. George J. Cornish, collated by the Bishop of Exeter in 1828.

GEOLOGY, BY DR. BOASE.

The southern part of Kea is formed of the same rock as the adjoining parish of Feock; the northern part runs towards the granite, and is similar to the corresponding part of Gwennap; and, like it, has been much explored by mines.

Baldue, the Black Work, about a mile east of Chase Water, has produced great quantities of the sulphate of zinc, called by the miners Black Jack.

KELLINGTON, or CALLINGTON.

HALS.

Is situate in the hundred of Eastwellshire, and hath upon the north Stoke Clemsland and South Hill, east St. Dominick, south St. Mellin, west St. Eve.

At the time of the first inquisition into the value of Cornish benefices by the Bishops of Lincoln and Winchester, anno Dom. 1294, this church had no endowment, neither was it then consolidated into South Hill; but before Wolsey's inquisition 1521, they were both united, and were then valued for revenues at 38*l*. per annum; the patronage in the Duke of Cornwall, who endowed it; the incumbent Trelawnye; the town and parish rated to the 4*s*. per pound Land Tax 1696, 120*l*. 16*s*.

This church or chapel town bailiwick is now known by the name of the town, manor, and borough of Killiton, i. e. chapel town, privileged with the jurisdiction of a Court Leet, and sending two Members to sit in the Commons' House of Parliament, which are chosen by the tenants of the said manor that are freeholders; as also by a jury chosen out of them, is elected the Mayor or Portreeve that governs the said borough yearly; the arms of which are in a field, a wreathed flourish. This borough is also privileged with a weekly market on Wednesdays; and fairs yearly on April 23, September 8, and November 1.

The writ to remove an action at law depending in this town Court Leet, as also the precept for electing Members of Parliament, must be thus directed: Preposito et Burgensibus Burgi nostri de Killiton in com. Cornubiæ salutem; and for the same purpose, to remove an action at law depending in the Hundred Court Baron of this Bailiwick, the writ must be thus directed: Senescallo et Ballivo Hundredi et Libertatis nostri de Eastwellshire in comitatu Cornubiæ salutem.

Near this place is situate Hengiston Downs, the place mentioned by Roger Hoveden in his Latin Chronicle, which says, that in the year of our Lord 806 a great fleet of Danes arrived in West Wales, which some conjecture to be Cornwall, not North or South Wales (in all thirteen shires); especially for that he says, the Welsh joined in insurrection with them against Egbright thirteenth King of England or the West Saxons, by whom they were all overthrown at a place called, Hengiꞅ-ton-ƀun, i. e. Hengis-tondun; that is to say, Hengist's fenced, fortified or camp town, which some take to be Hengiston Downs aforesaid, which place in former ages so abounded with tin that it gave occasion to those rhimes, (neither is it at present altogether destitute thereof)

> Hengiston Downe well ywrought,
> Is worth London towne dear ybought.—Carew.

In this town or borough of Killington, for retirement and delight, lived Sir Edward Bray, Knight, originally descended, as tradition says, from the Brays of Bray, in St. Just in Cornwall, that came into England with William the Conqueror, otherwise from Ralph de Bray, Sheriff of Hampshire, third of King John.

KELLINGTON, OR CALLINGTON.

The Bray's arms were, in a field Argent, a chevron between three eagles' legs erased at the knees Sable. He gave also in a field Varry Purple and Argent, three bendlets Gules.

Sir Reginald Bray, Knight Banneret and of the Garter, Privy Councillor to King Henry VII. and Speaker of the House of Commons in his eleventh year, is noted to have made the usual protestation for himself to that King, without any petition for the liberty of the Commons, as is to be seen in modus tenendi Parliamentum: he was a brother of the Lord Bray, or descended from the same family. (See Camden in Hampshire.) Others will not allow those Brays to be of British, but of French descent, from the province of Bray in that country, and that they came into England with the Conqueror, and that the many places in Cornwall distinguished by the name of Bray were denominated from them after their coming into England: but of this query.

A Knight Banneret was made in the field or camp of war, under the King's standard, who was personally present, by cutting off the point of his standard, and making it a banner; after which they might display their particular arms in a banner in the King's army, and take place of Knights Bachelors.

TONKIN.

As for the name of this parish, which is a daughter church to South Hill, and has for its patron saint St. Nicholas, Bishop of Myra in Lycia, I take it to be Killy-Ton, the town in a grove of trees.

Then follows a long conjectural account of the lords of this manor, which is wholly uninteresting, and therefore omitted.

THE EDITOR.

Mr. Tonkin does not state on what authority he has assigned the town and parish to the care of St. Nicholas. The popularity of this saint is now, and always has been, so great as to render the fact of his being the patron very probable. He is held in the highest veneration throughout Russia.

St. Nicholas ran through the ordinary course of those days. He became a monk, succeeded to the abbacy of his convent; and when the clergy of Myra assembled to elect a Bishop, and almost agreed in their choice, they were divinely instructed to wait till the next day, and then to choose the person who first offered himself to their notice, on their opening the church-door. They obeyed; and in the morning St. Nicholas was led to the spot by an irresistible impulse. He assisted in overthrowing the Arians, under the direction of Constantine, at the Council of Nice. All these, however, were matters of frequent occurrence. The fame of St. Nicholas rests on something more unusual; and if the tale is of a date sufficiently early, it may have been the cause of his subsequent advancement, and of his having obtained an influence so great as to effect the change of his simple bishoprick into a metropolitan see, with thirty-six suffragans.

So very early was the *præcox ingenium* of this saint directed towards observances, then deemed most acceptable to the Divinity, that when an infant in arms he rigidly abstained, every Wednesday and Friday, and on all other days kept as fasts by the church, from touching his nurse's breast; for this truly wonderful ascetic achievement he has been deservedly accounted the peculiar patron of children, and more especially the preserver of their health.

He died in 342, and was buried in the Cathedral at Myra; but in the year 1087 his relics were forcibly taken from a country no longer Christian, and were enshrined in the Cathedral of St. Stephen at Bavi in Italy, where pilgrims have ever since resorted in great numbers to witness or to experience miraculous cures effected by his intercession with Almighty God.

His festival is kept on the 6th of December, and on this day the ludicrous or profane ceremony of the Boy Bishop used to be exhibited in most Cathedrals. At Salisbury a boy is represented on a monument, dressed in the habit of a bishop including the mitre; and this is said to have been occasioned by the lad dying in his mock pontificate.

Mr. Lysons states, that the manor of Callington has passed through various families, Ferrers, Champernowne, Willoughby, Dennis, and Rolle.

The heiress of Samuel Rolle brought it to Robert Walpole, Earl of Orford, son of Sir Robert Walpole; and on the death of his son George Walpole in 1791, *sine prole*, this property passed to Mr. Robert George William Trefusis, of Trefusis in Cornwall, together with the barony of Clinton, created by writ of summons to Parliament in the reign of Edward the First.

George Walpole, Earl of Orford, executed a deed by which, after reserving a life interest to himself, and a power of revocation never acted on, he settled the remainder in fee of all such property as came to him from his maternal relations, on the right heir of Samuel Rolle, son of Robert Rolle and Arabella Clinton, his ancestor, from whom the Barony had descended; but his legal adviser forgot a most important distinction between deeds and wills; a will not coming into action till after the testator's death, when Mr. Trefusis would have been the undoubted heir of Samuel Rolle; but the deed, being effective from the instant of its execution, vested the remainder in Mr. George Walpole himself, the then heir of Samuel Rolle; and on his decease carried the property which had vested in him by act of law, although in direct opposition to his wishes and intention, from the maternal line to that of his father. Fortunately, however, in this instance, the whole was under mortgage, which brought the cognizance of the affair into Chancery. Mr. Trefusis took possession unopposed; and proceedings to obtain the property in consequence of the mistake, were not commenced till after twenty years, when a solemn decision of the House of Lords declared that the interference came too late for disturbing matters in equity.

It is obvious that Mr. George Walpole should have settled the remainder in fee on such person as would be the heir of Samuel Rolle after his own decease, or perhaps in trustees for such person. Mr. Trefusis (Lord Clinton) has since disposed of the Callington property to Mr. Alexander Baring.

This town or village received a Tudor charter in the 27th year of Queen Elizabeth, and continued to fulfil the duties, for which the corporation was instituted, till 1832, when the privilege of sending Members to Parliament ceased to exist.

Callington parish measures 2387 statute acres.

	£.	s.	d.
Value of the Real Property, as returned to Parliament in 1815	4142	0	0
Poor Rate in 1831	950	17	0

Population,— { in 1801, 819 | in 1811, 938 | in 1821, 1321 | in 1831, 1388 } giving an increase of 69 per cent. in 30 years.

GEOLOGY, BY DR. BOASE.

The north-eastern part of this parish extends to the foot of Kitt Hill, the most elevated point in Hingston Down, which is composed of granite. The slate adjoining thereto resembles that which occurs in similar situations in the parishes of St. Austell and St. Blazey; and it has also been the scene of mining speculations. As the town of Callington is approached, the slate becomes of a darker

KENWYN. 315

blue, and passes into hornblende rock, which prevails in the other parts of this parish; but where quartz predominates, the land is barren. This rock, however, does not possess here a very marked character, nor is it frequently exposed to view; near St. Eve it appears to graduate into the calcareous series.

KENWYN.

HALS.

Is situate in the hundred of Powdre, and hath upon the north Peran Sabulo, and St. Allen, east St. Clement's, south Truro, west Kea.

In the Domesday tax 20 William I. 1087, this district was rated under the jurisdiction of Edles. In the Inquisition of the Bishops of Lincoln and Winchester, into the value of Cornish benefices, 1294, there is no such church as Kenwen named then in the hundred of Powdre; if it were then extant, at that time it had no endowment; however, I find in the 15th granted by the Clergy, the 24th Henry VI. 1447, the parish of Kenwen in Powdre was rated 2*l*. 19*s*.; in Wolsey's Inquisition, 1521, Landegge or Keyewis consolidated into Kenwen (the elder church into the younger) and rated as aforesaid 16*l*. The patronage in the Bishop of Exon, who endowed them; the incumbent Mitchell, and the parish of Kenwen rated to the 4*s*. per pound Land Tax 1696, 196*l*. 14*s*. 6*d*.

Near Edles, or Ideless, i. e. narrow breadth (formerly the voke lands of a considerable manor, taxed in Domesday Book as aforesaid, privileged then with the jurisdiction of a Court Leet) is yet to be seen the ruins and downfalls of St. Clare's consecrated and walled well; chapelwise built, by the Nuns of the nunnery-house of Poor Clares in Trurow, called An-hell, i. e. the hall; but yet, alas! as tradition saith, they were not so poor as their rule obligeth them to be, for in the walls of this well they had deposited or hid away considerable sums of money, which, by tradition or some dream, was discovered tempore James II. to some of the inhabitants of this parish, who one night pulled down the walls and totally defaced this chapel-well in quest thereof, and probably succeeded in their design and undertaking, for soon after some poor labourers in agriculture became rich farmers and landed men, and others. From this place was denominated a family of gentlemen, surnamed de Idless, whose heir was married to Hamley, tempore Edward III.

Trega-veth-an, in this parish, the grave town or dwelling, so called from the cemetery and free chapel yet extant here, of public use before the church of Kenwen was erected; which barton and manor for several descents was the lands of a Welch family of gentlemen surnamed de Langhairons; i. e. holy or sacred laws; till the latter end of the reign of King Charles II. when Mr. Langhairne sold this barton to Walter Vincent, Esq., barrister at law, and the manor to Mr. Bawden and others. The arms of Langhairne were Azure, a chevron between three escallops Or.

Chyn-coos in this parish, i. e. the wood-house, formerly surrounded with woods, is the dwelling of Thomas Hawes, Gent., that married Hawes of Kea, and Paynter; and giveth the same arms as the Hawses of Kea.

TONKIN.

The manor of Tregavethan.

This signifies the dwelling in the meadows, vethen being the same with bither, a meadow; and whoever sees the place will be soon convinced of the truth of this etymology.

Tregedick was lord of the manor and sometimes dwelt here, but having only one daughter and heir, the barton passed with her to — Langhairne, Esq., but the father having reserved the manor, he in consequence of some difference sold it. The Laughairnes, however, continued to reside on the barton in much esteem till the great Civil Wars, in which this family suffered so much as to be compelled to sell it; and it came at last into the possession of Henry Vincent, Gent., of Tresinsple, who let out the barton in leases to several tenants, so that it is now become a village, and little of the mansion or house left standing.

To the west of Tregavethan, or the high town, on the confines between this parish and those of St. Agnes and Perran in the Sands, are three great barrows, called the Three Barrows; and about a mile to the westward of these on very high ground are four barrows, one belonging to this manor and the other three to Lambourn in Perran. These barrows give name to the downs, and the great road from London to the Land's End passes between them. They were doubtless the burying places of some principal commanders, and probably Danes. To the left of Tregavethan and within the manor, is Roseworth, the Green Valley. This was once a seat of the family of Cosens; and here lived Nicholas Cosens, Esq. who was Sheriff of Cornwall in the year 1660. He dying without issue left it to his widow, and after his death it became the property of Samuel Enys, Esq. by purchase.

THE EDITOR.

Kenwyn may be said to include the old part of Truro, which occupies the mere extremity of a point or tongue of land stretching from this parish and enclosed between two rivers. The land immediately round the town is fertile, in a high state of cultivation, and decorated by trees and villas; but towards the Four Barrow Down and Chasewater, nothing can be more desolate than the barren commons studded with heaps of rubbish from deserted mines.

In this parish are situate two of the earliest establishments for smelting tin by means of coal, and on the largest scale of any in the county, Calenick and Cavedras; but of late years this business has taken an entirely new character; tin ores are sold, like those of copper, by public tender or ticketings, and smelting houses are constructed in some cases for the use of particular mines.

The manor of Newham formed part of the Bodregan property, and after the despoiling of Sir Henry Bodregan by King Henry VII. it was given to Trevanion, of whom it was purchased by the late Mr. Ralph Allen Daniell, sometime member for West Looe, by whom a handsome house has been built on the side of the river, half a mile below Truro; Bosvigo is also a gentleman's seat.

And at Comprigney, near Bosvigo, the Editor apprehends that several ancestors in succession of General Sir Hussey Vivian resided. Kenwyn church and tower, with an excellent glebe house adjacent, built about the year 1780, are very conspicuous objects, and command themselves a fine view of the town and river. The church is provided with a set of bells said to surpass all others in the country; and to have been placed there when ringing was a favourite amusement with the neighbouring gentlemen.

This parish measures 8,094 statute acres.

	£.	s.	d.
Annual value of the Real Property, as returned to Parliament in 1815 .	13,296	0	0
Poor Rate in 1831	2133	1	0

Population,—	in 1801, 4017	in 1811, 5000	in 1821, 6221	in 1831, 8492

giving an increase of 111 per cent. in 30 years.

GEOLOGY, BY DR. BOASE.

This large parish does not appear to offer anything peculiar in its geology, as Doctor Boase merely remarks that Kenwyn lies entirely on slate, which is of the same nature as that of St. Allen and St. Clement's.

ST. KEVERNE.

HALS.

Is situate in the hundred of Kerryer, and hath upon the north St. Martin's, east St. Anthony, west Ruan Minor, south the British Channel. As for the modern name, whether it be derived from the Saxon ᵹefopon, ᵹefopan, ᵹeuopan, i.e. Geferon, Geforan, Geuoran, synonymous words, signifying a fraternity, seers, equals, fellows, inspectors, with reference to the six, eight, or twelve men of this parish, who as a body politic, corporation, or fraternity, govern the same in joint or equal manner; or from the British Keveren, as schism, separation or division in church matters or religion (see Lhuyd upon Schisma); or from Kieran, a famous Bishop amongst the Britons about the fifth century, who perhaps was born in this place, and is the tutelar guardian and patron of this Church; and to him also is dedicated St. Kieran rectory, in decanatu Christianitatis in Exeter: of which every man may think as he please.

In the Inquisition made into the value of Cornish Benefices by the Bishops of Lincoln and Winchester, 1294, ecclesia Sancti Kierani, in decanatu de Kerryer, xxii*l*. viii*s*. iiii*d*. Vicar ejusdem iiii*l*. vi*s*. viii*d*. In Wolsey's Inquisition, 1521, 18*l*. 11*s*. 4*d*. The patronage in Bulteel; the Incumbent Gerry; the Rectory in possession of Heale; and the parish rated to the 4*s*. per pound Land Tax, 1696, by the name of St. Keverne, 310*l*. 16*s*. 4*d*.

Part of this new parish of St. Keverne, at the time of the Norman Conquest, was rated in the Domesday Book, 1087, under the jurisdiction of Treleage (i. e. Physician or Surgeon's Town, or the Law Town); it is now the possession of Robert Buggin, Esq. (id est, Bacon) who married Prudence, daughter of John Arundell of Trethall, Esq.; his father, Jane, the daughter of Sir Francis Vyvyan, Knight, a younger branch of Gatcomb House in Devon, originally descended from Zacharias Boggan, Gent., Mayor of Totness, A.D. 1550, whose ancestors were merchants of that town, and gave for their arms, Sable, a cocatrice displayed Argent, membered and taloned Gules.

Note further, that as ker, kerr, kyr, kir, signifies dear, beloved, choicely affectioned, in British, Cornish, and the Armorick languages, answerable to dilectus in Latin; so from thence proceeds Kerryer, a lover, or one dearly affectioned. See Floyd upon *dilectus*.

Tre-land in this parish (either the temple town, or a town notable for land) was another district or manor, taxed in Domesday Roll; and I take it, there are yet extant two tenements here called Tre-land Vear, and Tre-land Vean; i. e. the greater and less Tre-lands. One of those places, as I am informed, is the dwelling of John Hayme, Gent. (Saxon, i. e. a house, home, or covering; see also Verstegan upon this word) that married Tregose; his father Boggans.

In this parish is situate Condura and Tregarne, manors formerly pertaining to Condura, Earl of Cornwall.

Lanareh, also Lan-arth, in this parish is the dwelling of Sampson Sanns, Gent., that married Cood, which tenement or barton was formerly the lands of Kensham, who sold it to the present possessors.

This Mr. Sanns died without legal issue about the year 1696, and left his estate to his brother's son, John Sanns, that married Hamley of St. Neot, now in possession thereof, who in the month of January, in the afternoon, in the year 1702, with seven other persons, men and women of this parish, coming by sea from Falmouth town and harbour towards their own homes in a fishing boat of about five tons burden, without deck or covering, on a fair day; and having got off at sea about a league beyond the said harbour, and within two leagues of their dwelling to the west; suddenly there happened to arise a high and mighty storm of wind against them, which rose the rapid waves of the sea to that degree, that the boatmen or oarmen, with all their skill or strength, were not able to put the boat further forward without its being filled with water or swallowed up with the raging sea.

Whereupon, despairing of getting home to St. Keverne, they all resolved if possible to return back to Falmouth harbour before this tempestuous storm of wind that blew that way, or to run on shore on any other part of the country as they could. But, alas! they no sooner attempted those expedients, and turned their boat, but instantly the wind turned and thwarted their design. In this extremity they knew not what to do; both wind and water being thus outrageous against them: and that which added more to their calamity was, that, through their long toiling at sea, the light of the sun was past and night approached.

Then every person present being at their wit's end, called upon his God for pardon of their sins, and mercy upon their souls, as despairing of the preservation of their bodies from the merciless element of the seas; when at length, after much fervent prayers, tears, and cries, the watermen proposed, all other their endeavours failing, that the boat must be left to drive before the wind and sea, to such port or place as God in his infinite mercy and providence should guide it.

This course was taken, and the boat forthwith, by letting loose its helm, in a dark long night and most tremendous storm or hurricane, followed the current of the wind and waves all night; the passengers every minute casting out of the boat such water as the outrageous seas cast in upon her, least she might thereby be overwhelmed or filled therewith. At length the glimpse of daylight appeared, when they beheld themselves environed with the billows of the great ocean, without sight of either sun, moon, stars, or land. The storm still continuing all that day and the night after, also the third day and the night after, the boat and mariners in the same condition as aforesaid, when afterwards the fourth day in the morning, the wind and seas being somewhat abated of their fury and violence, about ten of the clock they discovered land, and forthwith rowed and steered the boat to the sea-shore thereof, where they arrived with the boat safely; which happened to be, as I was informed, on the coast of Normandy in France, about a hundred leagues distance from the place the boat first was driven off at sea. Which happened to be at such time as Queen Anne had wars with the French King. As soon as Mr. Sanns and his companions stept on land, they were met by three or four men with fusees, demanding what they were (as they judged, for they understood not French), to which they replied they were English; which one of them that understood the English tongue hearing, demanded the occasion of their coming there, and by what expedient they came over; the particulars of which hearing, as aforesaid, they were all astonished to hear of their hazardous passage, miraculous preservation, and to behold the boat, the instrument thereof next Providence.

Upon which discourse, a gentleman of the company asked Mr. Sanns what part of England he was born in, to which he replied Cornwall; and further interrogated him whether his name were not Sanns, to which he replied that it was; 'Why then,' said the gentleman, 'I know your person, and well remember the kindness you shewed me in my distress many years since at your house, when the ship in which I was, was cast away and lost on the coast of St. Kevern;' understanding which, after they embraced each other. Then, he demanded their arms and money, if any; whereupon Mr. Sanns having with him forty guineas that he had received at Falmouth for pilchards, the day before his boat was driven off at sea, he forthwith delivered it to his friend, who told him he and his companions must yield themselves prisoners of war; which accordingly they did, and Mr. Sanns was taken home to the gentleman's house. After which they were all examined concerning the premises before a justice of the peace, who finding matters as aforesaid, ordered that they should not be kept in custody as prisoners of war, but be all permitted to go at liberty and beg the alms of the people; whereupon they found extraordinary charity and favour amongst them, since they were not enemies, but persons by fate or Providence, brought there after an especial manner, and preserved from the violence of the seas by the great Maker and Protector of all things.

The news whereof forthwith not only flew over the country, but was transmitted to the cognizance of King Lewis XIV., who thereupon ordered that by the first transport ship for prisoners of war, they should all be sent home freely into England; which happening soon after, Mr. Sanns took his leave of his kind landlord, in whose house he had been dieted and entertained, and was content to leave the forty guineas aforesaid with him, as his recompence; but contrary to his expectation the gentleman gave the same to him again, saying he would take nothing of that kind at his hands, since God in such a wonderful manner had preserved him and his companions from the great danger of the seas. Whereupon, he presented five or six guineas to his wife, who after some reluctancy accepted thereof, and so they parted and went on board a transport ship, and safely landed at Portsmouth; and in about eight weeks after their departure from England, returned safe to St. Keverne, to the great joy and astonishment of their friends and relations, who concluded them all drowned long before.

And that the reader may not think those people's subsistance three nights and four days in their dangerous sea voyage, was as supernatural as their preservation, it must be remembered, that one of Mr. Sanns' companions being a woman that was an inn-keeper, had bought at Falmouth town before they departed thence, for to sell to her customers, twelve pennyworth of white bread and three or four gallons of brandy, which proved the material support of their lives. Matthew of Westminster, our Chronologer, tells us that about the year 900, Dusblan, Machreu and one Maxlium, in a boat made of one ox skin and a half, with seven days provisions, in two days and a night arrived miraculously into Cornwall from Ireland, at the Mount's Bay.

TONKIN.

Mr. Tonkin does not add any thing to Mr. Hals's narrative, except the single observation,
It takes its name from the famous St. Keven.

THE EDITOR.

St. Keverne's fame does not extend out of Cornwall. He must have been one of the Irish missionaries who crossed the seas in granite troughs, or in skiffs made of bullocks' hides. Tales were in circulation about mutual visits from St. Perran and St. Kevern, but they contain only vulgar incidents of modern fabrication.

The extraordinary escape of the passengers from Falmouth, is retained at the full length in which Mr. Hals relates it, as the narrative bears evident marks of authenticity, and the incidents are creditable to all the parties introduced.

This parish is amply provided with small harbours or coves affording shelter to boats, and the shore admits of using seine nets for taking pilchards. The principal of these harbours, Coverack, has been long noted for an extensive trade, still more lucrative than fishing; the other two are Porthoustock (Proustock) and Porthalla (Prala).

About seventy years since a large shoal of pilchards came into the cove at Porthoustock, while the seine boats were on the outside. One of these extended its net across the entrance and shut in the whole; but salt in sufficient quan-

ST. KEVERNE.

tity could not be procured for saving them, when the fishermen resolved on the hazardous expedient of sailing to France for a supply; the weather continued fine till their return, and they are reported to have prepared for exportation above a thousand hogsheads. The Church is situated on the highest ground in this whole district, having the addition of a spire instead of the lofty tower usual in Cornwall. The existing spire is of recent date, although probably on the model of that which was destroyed by lightning on the 28th of February 1770.

For a very accurate and able account of this thunder storm, which occurred during divine service, and seems to have been one of the most violent on record, see a paper in the 61st vol. of the Philosophical Transactions, p. 71, art. 8, 1771; (and vol. 13, p. 98, of the Abridgment,) by the Rev. Anthony Williams, then Vicar.

The spire was rent in pieces. The roof of the church almost entirely destroyed; large stones scattered over the floor, and small stones on the outside carried to a distance little short of a quarter of a mile. Mr. Williams himself was rendered insensible, the whole congregation, with very few exceptions, fell on the ground deprived of all recollection; but no life was lost, nor did any sustain a serious injury; about ten were slightly hurt.

In the church are several monuments; and in the churchyard stands a large sarcophagus, having sculptured on it the representation of a shipwreck, and military emblems, with the following inscription.

To the memory of Major-General H. G. C Cavendish,
Capt. S. C. Duckenfield, Lieut. the Hon. E. Waldegrave,
Sixty-one non-commissioned officers and privates
of the regiment,
who in returning from Spain in the Despatch transport
unhappily perished in Coverack Cove,
the 22nd of December 1809.

The ship was known to be very old and in bad repair; but, although the wind blew with some violence, it would have been a matter of no difficulty whatever to clear the Mein Egles, or Manacles Rocks. Seamen have therefore conjectured that the Captain kept near the shore for the purpose of stranding his vessel, to obtain the exaggerated value contracted for with the Government; and that in attempting this fraud, he fell on the rocks which caused the loss of every one on board.

Mr. Cavendish was a son of Lord George Cavendish, of East Bourn, Sussex, afterwards created Earl of Burlington.

The great tithes of this parish have been sold to the various proprietors of the land.

The tithes of fish belonged, however, to Mr. Matthew Wills of Helston, in right of his marriage with the only daughter of Mr. Tonkin of Trenance near Porthoustock. For some years they were of considerable value, but as all tithe of fish is allowed to be in this country the mere creature of custom, the custom then acted on was attacked at law, and after a trial, on which the celebrated Mr. Dunning attended by a special retainer, it was overturned. Trenance and the other property in St. Kevern are now possessed by his son, the Rev. Thomas Wills, Vicar of Wendron, for about fifty years.

Kilter, in this parish, was the birthplace and probably belonged to the individual of that name, who with Humphry Arundell and others, excited the common people to take arms against the government of King Edward VI. in 1549, by holding out those unattainable objects which have misled the ignorant to their own destruction in all ages and nations, in union with others certainly of a different description; one of which was the re-establishment of the Bloody Statute, or the Six Articles, by which every person refusing to acknowledge the King's supremacy over the church was adjudged to be hanged; and every one conscientiously disbelieving the real presence of Christ's body in consecrated bread and wine, was condemned to be burnt alive.

Lanarth has been for a considerable time the residence of the Sandys family. The Rev. Sampson Sandys lived there to a very advanced age. He was probably grandson to the gentleman whose wonderful escape to the coast of France is detailed by Mr. Hals under the name of Sanns, which the editor remembers to have heard was the original appellation of their family, till they adopted the name and cross-crosslets of the Sandys of Ombersley.

Mr. Sampson Sandys was succeeded at Lanarth by his nephew, Mr. William Sandys, a colonel in the army of the East India Company, who rebuilt the house, and greatly improved the place.

The rectory was, before the Reformation, appropriated to the Abbey of Beaulieu in Hampshire, founded by King John.

In the schedule of the property returned to King Henry the VIII. on its surrender, are the following entries, which may be found in the Augmentation Office.

Com. Cornub.

St. Kivion—Redd. Assis. lib. ten.	2	15	10
Redd. et Firm. ten. ad volunt'	8	2	4
Terr. dominic.	1	16	8
Tregonon, firma molend.	1	2	6
Opera autumpnal'	0	1	6
Perquis' cur'	1	7	2
Firma rector'	57	4	0
Helston redd. annual'	6	3	4

The reasons assigned for King John founding this magnificent Cistercian Abbey of Beaulieu, or De Bello Loco, are so curious, and so illustrative of the profligacy and weak superstition united in forming his character, that the Editor thinks it right to insert the following original, with a translation.

Anno sexto Regis Johannis idem Rex construxit quoddam Cœnobium ordinis Cisterciensis in Anglia, et Bellum Locum nominavit; quod quidem Cœnobium tali occasione narratur ab eo factum. Quia enim idem Rex versus Abbates, et alias personas ordinis Cisterciensis prænominatas, supra modum, sine causa, est iratus, et eosdem non mediocriter per ministros suos gravaret, ad quoddam Parliamentum, quod ipse apud Lincolniam tenuit, Abbates dicti ordinis venerunt, si quo modo Regis ejusdem gratiam et favorem potuissent aliquatenus invenire. Quibus visis, sicut crudelis animi erat, præcepit suis ut dictos Abbates sub pedibus equorum viliter conculcarent; Regis vero injustum tam facinorosum et inauditum hactenus mandatum ab aliquo principe Christiano, perficere nolentibus, hii Domini Abbates, jam fere desperantes de Regia benignitate, ad sua hospitia festinanter accesserunt. Nocte vero sequenti, cùm idem Rex Johannes in lecto suo dormiret, ei quod coram quodam Judice, prædictis Abbatibus illuc assistentibus, ductus fuerit: qui eisdem Abbatibus jusserat dictum regem supra dorsum suum cum flagellis et virgis verberare: quam quidem verberationem, mane vigilans, se sensisse dixit. Sompnium vero suum cuidam personæ ecclesiasticæ de curia sua narravit, qui dixit ei, quod Deus erga eum supra modum esset misericors, qui eum tam clementer et paternè in præsenti seculo dignatus est corripere, et eidem sua misteria revelare; et consuluit Regem ut pro Abbatibus dicti ordinis velociter mitteret, et ab eisdem de reatu suo veniam humiliter imploraret.

Rege siquidem acquiescente, pro eis, ut ad Regem venirent, missum est. Quod audientes per nuncium Regis, putaverunt se ab Anglia fore exterminandos; Deo tamen, qui suos non deserit, aliter disponente, cùm nunc ad conspectum Regis venissent, indignationem suam quam ergo eos habuit Rex remisit.

"In the sixth year of his reign King John founded a certain monastery of the Cistercian order in England, and gave it the name of Beaulieu; and the following account is given of the cause which induced the King to found this abbey.

"The King, without any just cause of offence, having taken the most violent and unbounded anger against the Abbats and others of the Cistercians, and having immoderately oppressed them through the medium of his officers, the Abbats of the said order came to a Parliament which the King held at Lincoln, to try if they might be able by some means to obtain a small share of the King's grace and favour. But when the King saw them, he became so cruelly disposed towards them, as to order that the said Abbats should, in the most disgustful manner, be trodden under the horses' feet; but his people being unwilling to execute a command so unjust, so atrocious, and hitherto unheard-of from any Christian prince, those Lord Abbats, now despairing of any kindness on the part of the King, hastily retired to their hostels. But in the following night, as the said King John lay sleeping on his bed, it seemed to him that he was brought before some judge, these Abbats standing by, whom the judge ordered to scourge him on the back with whips and rods; and when the King awoke in the morning, he declared that he actually felt the scourging. Having related his dream to a certain ecclesiastic of his court, this person assured him that God had been merciful to him beyond measure, by deigning thus kindly and paternally to correct him in this present life, and by revealing to him his mysteries; and he advised the King to send immediately for the Abbats of this order, and humbly to implore from them the pardon of his offence.

"The King consenting, a message was sent to them that they should come to the King; which they hearing from the messenger, thought that they should be banished from England: but God, who never deserts his servants, disposed things otherwise; so that when they came into the King's presence, he put away the anger which he had entertained against them."

There is not any trace of the advowson of the vicarage having belonged to this splendid abbey, which afforded sanctuary to Queen Margaret and Perkin Warbeck. It is now possessed either by Mr. Pascoe, the present incumbent, or by his family.

Mr. Lysons has given the descents and alienation of various manors or farms of little general interest.

St. Keven measures 8792 statute acres.

	£.	s.	d.
Annual value of the Real Property, as returned to Parliament in 1815 .	10,433	0	0
Poor Rate in 1831	1,310	17	0

Population,—{ in 1801, | in 1811, | in 1821, | in 1831, 2104 | 2242 | 2505 | 2437

giving an increase of about 16 per cent. in 30 years.

The Rev. James Pascoe was instituted to the vicarage in 1817.

GEOLOGY, BY DR. BOASE.

There are few spots that have excited greater geological interest than the serpentine tract of the Lizard, and no part of it will be found more instructive than this parish.

By far the greater part of St. Kevern rests on magnesian rocks; but north of a line drawn from Porthalla, nearly due west to Goonhilly Downs, the rocks belong to the calcareous series. The latter rocks may be seen on the coast from Porthalla to the Nare Point, and will be found to resemble the series between Gorran and the Dodman Point. On the left side of Porthalla Cove the blue slate abounds in veins and in irregular nodules of calcspar; and at low-water-mark a more compact variety is exposed, which evidently forms the passage into the black limestone, loose fragments of which are sometimes found on the shore. In a small creek within the Nare near Bostowda, is a large patch of conglomerate, the pebbles and fragments of which have been derived from the rocks which line the banks of the river Hellas as high up as Gweek; but which bear no resemblance to the rock of the immediate vicinity. This is the most decided instance of a fragmentary rock in Cornwall.

The hollow occupied by the little stream which discharges itself at Porthalla divides the calcareous shale from a rock of totally different nature, videlicet serpentine, several varieties of which form the neck of land stretching thence to Dranna Point.

At Porthoustock a glossy lamellar rock, already noticed as joining the serpentine at Cadgwith, forms each side of the cove; but here, on proceeding to the Manacles Point it may be seen passing into diallage rock: the latter extends so far as Coverack, and also inland to the foot of Goonhilly Downs. At Coverack the diallage rock appears to pass into serpentine; but here again, as at Porthalla, the junction is a concrete. The varieties of serpentine near Coverack Pier are numerous, and several of them may be seen passing into each other, which in other parts of the Lizard district form large and apparently independent masses. From Coverack to Kennick Cove the cliffs are very bold, and display different kinds of serpentine and diallage rocks, and at Blockhead a large stratum of indurated steatite, beautifully marked with brown arborescent figures on a yellow ground. At Kennick Cove, red and olive green serpentine, abounding in scales of diallage, and traversed by numerous veins of asbestos, talc, and calcareous spar, are exposed to view on a grand scale; and at Gwinter, a little north of the cove, diallage rock is accompanied by layers of beautiful violet-coloured jade, or compact felspar, containing large plates of diallage as metalloide as at Coverack.

It may be noticed here, that all the uncultivated land extending over serpentine formation, is clothed with the most beautiful of European heaths; the Erica Vagans of Linnæus, so named on account of its being found in various parts of the world on particular spots. Hudson named it "Multiflora" from its splendid inflorescense; and Dr. Withering, with some others, didyma, with reference to double antheræ on each flower. This heath bounds itself almost within a yard to the limits of the magnesian earths.

ST. KEW.

HALS.

Is situate in the hundred of Trigg, and hath upon the north Endellyan, east St. Eath, south St. Mabyn, west Egleshayle and Minver. In the Domesday Tax, 20 William I. 1087, this parish was rated by the name of Languit, or Lan-cuit; that is to say, the Church or Temple Wood, or a church or temple in a wood; not unsuitable to the former circumstances thereof, surrounded with copse trees and oak woods; from whence it appears here was an endowed church or temple of that name before the Norman Conquest, implied in the word Lan. In the Inquisitions of the Bishops of Lincoln and Winchester into the value of Cornish benefices 1294, it was rated by the name of Lan-owe, i. e. my Church or Temple, or the Egge Church or Temple, for owe is an egg, in decanatu de Minor Trigshire viii*l.* xins. iiiid. Vicar ejusdem xls. In Wolsey's Inquisition 1501, by the name of St. Kuet, i. e. holy, sacred, or consecrated wood, 19*l.* 10*s.* The patronage, formerly in the priory of Bodman, who endowed it, now Tregagle. The incumbent Nation; the rectory or sheafe in possession of Tregagle; and the parish rated to the 4s. per pound Land Tax 1696, by the name of St. Kewe 356*l.* 15*s.* 10*d.*

The manor and barton of Lanew in this parish, was formerly the lands of the Beavills of Gwarnack or Killygarth; by one of whose heirs, as I am informed, it came in marriage to the Grenvills of Stowe; and was entailed, together with the barton of Bryn, and other lands, upon the issue of the said Beavill, by Grenvill to be begotten.

Now it happened, tempore Charles I., that Sir Bevill Grenvill, being much encumbered with the debts of his ancestors, in order to free the same, sold for a valuable consideration this manor of Lanow and barton of Bryn to William

Noye, Esq. Attorney-general to King Charles I. the which William Noye and his heirs quietly enjoyed the same for about thirty years' space, till King Charles II. returned from his exile beyond the seas, and was restored to his dominions 1660; at which time Sir John Grenvill, Knt. afterwards created Earl of Bath, (son of the said Sir Bevill Grenvill) then also in exile with the said King beyond the seas, came back to his native country with the said King; and some time after delivered leases of ejectment, on writs of ejection, firme formedon, or right, to the tenants of Humphrey Noye, Esq. then in possession thereof, son of the said Attorney-general Noye, and brought down a venire facias and trial for the same, at Lanceston assizes, where, on the issue, the verdict passed for the said Earl of Bath; and after judgment was entered up and recorded thereupon, writs for possession were sued forth, and his lordship became seised of those lands, and forced the tenants thereof to double their accustomed rent, on condition of holding their leases. Afterwards Noye's son aforesaid, files his bill in chancery, suggesting the wrong he had received by this verdict at law, whereby he lost his lands and purchase money, which matter coming to a hearing on bill and answer, an issue was directed out of Chancery to try once more this title at common law, on which Noye proved Sir Beavill Grenvill to be tenant in tail for those lands, and that he levying a fine thereon, *come ceo qui il eit de son done*, according to due form of law, with deeds declaring the same to be for the use of the said William Noye, his heirs and assigns for ever, that was a sufficient dock of the entail, and bar to the son and heir of the said Sir Beavill Grenvill, whereupon the sense and judgment of the Court then was, that according to law the verdict must be for Noye: as accordingly it then passed. Notwithstanding which, a cross bill was filed by the Earl of Bath against Noye, about the premises, praying a writ of injunction for stopping further proceedings at common law; whereupon his lordship still kept possession, and Noye grew weary of this controversy, who, otherwise, was a man much depressed with debt, and therefore an unequal contester with the then great Earl of Bath; wherefore he sold his title to those lands in dispute to Mr. Christopher Davies, of Burnewall in Buryan, who revived Noye's drooping case and title to the premises, and delivered ejectments to the Earl of Bath's tenants, then in possession thereof, and accordingly brought down a trial at Lanceston upon that plea and demise, tempore James II., when it was manifest his lordship relied more on his privilege as a Peer or Baron of this Realm than the right or justice of the merits of his case, for he served all the council, officers, and attornies of the court at that assizes with writs of privilege, so that no person was permitted to speak or act publicly on the part or title of Noye or Davies; but the case or trial was immerged or was swallowed up without due course or form of law, so that Mr. Davies was only permitted to plead his case himself, which he did with so much judgment, sense, law, and equity, as the Court admired at it, being no lawyer. But, alas! he wanted instruction in the grand point in such cases, to have cried out a merger or emerger, and the verdict must have been for him or Noye the second time.

After which bad success, and for that Mr. Davies was threatened to be sued on the statute of *scandalum magnatum*, for words said to be spoken by him reflective on his lordship's honour and reputation, he was terrified into a composition or agreement with the said Earl, by the end of Hilary term then next ensuing, for the consideration of 500*l.* to levy a fine *sur cognizance de droit*, with proclamation on those lands, with deeds declaring the uses thereof to be only to the proper use and behoof of the said Earl of Bath, his heirs and assigns for ever, as accordingly was performed, and so this controversy ended. But, alas! when too late it appeared further, that when Mr. Davies had sold his title to this manor of Lanow as aforesaid, that there were two tenements of Mr. Noye's paternal estate whilst he was in possession thereof, after his purchase from

Grenvill, that he had annexed to the said manor, situate in this parish, and worth 900*l.*, which Mr. Davies ignorantly debarred himself of, to his greater loss. See Withell parish for Bryn, the lands of Bevill and Grenvill.

Bo-Kelly in this parish was the dwelling of the genteel family surnamed Carn-sew, i. e. dry, sterile, or barren spar-stone, or rock; perhaps so called from the local place of Carnsew in Mabe, altogether under such circumstances; otherwise Mr. Carew tells us the name of those gentlemen was Carn-deaw, i. e. black spar-stone or rock. William Carnsew of this house was sheriff of Cornwall 18 Edward IV.; William Carnsew was Sheriff of Cornwall 3 Henry VIII.

Richard Carnsew, Esq. afterwards knighted, was Sheriff of Cornwall 17 Charles I. 1642, whose heir George Carnsew, as I am told, sold it to Tregagle, and is now by lease in possession of John Nicholls, of Trewane, Esq. The two only daughters and heirs of Sir Richard Carnsew, of Tregarne, were married to Prideaux, of Fewborough, and Godolphin of the younger house, whose arms were, Sable, a goat passant Argent, attired Or.

Tre-havar-ike, alias Tre-ar-ike, gave name and original to an old family of gentlemen, from thence surnamed de Trehauarike, whose sole inheritrix was married to Cavall, tempore Henry VII. who, out of a supposed allusion to this name, as appears from the glass windows of this house, gave a calf for their arms, viz. Argent, a calf passant Gules; whereas Leugh is a calf in British-Cornish, and Cavall is a bee-hive, cradle, or flasket. They gave also, Azure, three sails of a ship Argent; for that, as tradition saith, one of this family was admiral of a squadron of ships at sea, under King Henry VI. against the French; finally, about the year 1612, the two sole daughters and heirs of those Cavalls were married to Vivian, of Trenowth in St. Colomb, and Hore of Trenowth in St. Ewan. Upon the division of Cavall's lands, this barton and manor fell to Vivian's share, whose grandson Thomas Vivian, Esq.

sold this barton to John Peter, of Treater, gentleman, for 2,100*l*.; and the manor to other persons, now in possession thereof, about the year 1700.

At the top of those lands is a field called the Dower Park, i. e. the water field, where a spring or pool of water commonly stands, which gives the spring, or original of the aforesaid riveret of water, from whence Trehavarike is denominated.

At Tregeare in this parish, and Resurra in St. Minver, was the seat of the Penkivells, gentlemen of ancient descent, and heretofore of great revenues, now comparatively extinct.

Pen-pons in this parish, now Pen-pont, synonymous words, signifies the head bridge, or the bridge at the head or top of the sea in this place, according to the natural and artificial circumstances thereof, which was the voke lands of an ancient and extensive manor, privileged with the jurisdiction of a court leet before the Norman Conquest: for by the name of Penpont it was rated in the Domesday Tax 20 William I. 1087; from whence was denominated an ancient family of gentlemen now extinct, surnamed Penpons, whose sole inheritrix was married to Arundell of Tolverne, tempore Queen Mary, from whose heirs and assigns it came to Cole and Arscott of Devon, and others, now in possession thereof. By the inquisition 12 Edward III. it was rated for twenty-one Cornish acres, before the judges Solomon de Ross and others, at Lanceston, that is to say, 1260 statute acres. I take the tenure of this manor to be either customary or copyhold lands; near which is still extant Chappell Amble, or Ambhull, i. e. the dull, blockish, or ignorant chapel or chaplain, a free chapel, where the Bishop never visited.

In this parish at Middle Amble is the dwelling of Jonathan Webber, Gent. (id est, in Saxon, a weaver, so called from his first ancestor, who was of that trade or occupation,) who married Williams, and giveth for his arms, Gules, on a chevron engrailed Or, charged with three annulets or round plates Azure, pierced in the middle, Or, between three round plates or platters, two in chief and one in the base, Argent. This family, as it branched downwards to the year 1640, had married with Mathew of the said parish of St. Kew, who gave for his arms, Sable, a crane Argent, legged and beaked Gules; also with Prewbody and Polwhele. This arms of Webber, consisting of four colours in its field and in its charge, is a ridiculous or contemptible bearing, as heralds tell us all such bearings are.

Note further that Mr. Carew, in his Survey of Cornwall, A. D. 1602, tells us, p. 55, that John, the son of Thomas, living at Pendarves, took up the name of John Thomas Pendarves, and that Richard his younger brother took up the name of Richard Thomas Pendarves; and that Trengone, living at Nance, took up the name of Nance; and Bonython, living at Carclew in Milor, took up the name of Carclew; and for the same reason two brothers of the Thomases, living at Carnsew in Mabe, another at Roscrow in Milor or Gluvias, took up the names of Carnsew and Roscrow; as did also one of them living at Caweth in Mabe, take up the name of Caweth; and in further testimony thereof, give one and the same coat armour as Thomas did, viz. in a field Argent, a chevron between three talbots Sable, though Pendarves gives a different arms from that of Thomas. See Cambourne. Query, whether Carnsew of Bokelly does not derive his name from Carnsew? i. e. dry rock, in Mabe parish.

TONKIN.

This parish takes its present name from the patron saint Kew, which, says the author of the English Dictionary, 8vo. London, 1691, is certainly the same with Kebius the Briton. The impropriator of the sheaf and patron of the vicarage, is at present Robert Croker, Esq. by purchase from Mr. John Tregeagle. The incumbent, Mr. Edward Stephens, Mr. Croker's nephew.

The ancient name of this parish was Lanow.

THE EDITOR.

If Saint Kebius is really the patron of this parish, and has given it his name somewhat disguised in the sound of St. Kew, he has the unusual felicity of being honoured in his own country. Doctor Borlase states, on the authority of Archbishop Usher, (Antiquities of Cornwall, 2d ed. p. 369.) " About the middle of the fourth century, Solomon Duke of Cornwall seems to have been a Christian; for his son Kebius was ordained a Bishop by Hilarius, Bishop of Poictiers, in France; and afterwards returned into his own country to exercise that high function."

Saint Kebius, however, stands in the Roman Calendar on the 26th of April; but the parish feast is kept (I believe) on the nearest Sunday to the 25th of July, the day of Saint James the Apostle.

This parish is one of the most fertile in Cornwall, as well for corn as for grass. The church is situated in a pleasant valley; and near it is Skinden, for many years the residence of Mr. Joseph Bennet, a clergyman, but without preferment; and after his decease, of Mr. Clode, a native of Camelford, who having risen to the situation of a major in the East India Company's army, returned with a fortune, and purchased this place; it now belongs to his sister Mrs. Braddon.

The principal seat in St. Kew was in former times Trewane, the residence of an ancient and opulent family the Nichollses. The house, partly converted into a farmhouse and partly in ruins, appears in a style of grandeur quite unusual in the houses of this county. It is believed to have been built before the Civil Wars. These four descents are recorded in the Heraldic Visitation of 1620.

John Nicholls—His son and heir, John Nicholls, married Catharine, daughter of John Trowbrigge, of Trowbridge in Devon.—Their son John Nicholls married to Elizabeth Fortescue, of Fallowpit in Devon;—and their son, the fourth John Nicholls, aged seven years, with other children. The granddaughter, or great-granddaughter, from these last recorded, became an heiress possessed of the whole property, and married Mr. Glynn, of Glynn; but being left a widow, and childless by the death of her only son, she devised her estate in certain portions, to Mr. Glynn, of Helston, with the whole of Trewane; and to Mr. Bennet her steward, father of the Rev. Joseph Bennet, who built or improved Skisden. The arms of Nicholls, of Trewane, were, Sable, three pheons Argent.

The rectorial tithes of this parish belonged to the priory of Plympton in Devonshire, and now belong to Molesworth of Pencarrow. The advowson has passed by purchase with their other property, from Mahon to Pitt and Glanville.

The church contains some monuments and painted glass. Mr. Hals has given the details of a law suit, which may tend to reconcile the admirers of olden times to those in which they live; nor can the Editor, who is the descendant and heir-at-law of Attorney-general Noye, and of his son Colonel Humphrey Noye, be supposed to entertain much respect for the memory of the Earl of Bath.

St. Kew measures 6343 statute acres.

	£.	s.	d.
Annual value of the Real Property, as returned to Parliament in 1815	8598	0	0
Roor Rate in 1831	1029	6	0

Population,—
in 1801,	in 1811,	in 1821,	in 1831,
1095	1113	1218	1316

giving an increase of 20 per cent. in 30 years.

The Rev. John Pomeroy was presented to the vicarage in 1777 by W. Pitt, Esq.

GEOLOGY, BY DR. BOASE.

Doctor Boase says of the geology of this parish, that the northern part resembles Endellion, and that the southern part is similar to Egloshale and Helland.

KILKHAMPTON.

HALS.

Is situate in the hundred of Stratton, and hath upon the north Morwinstow, west St. George's channel, south Stratton and Poughill, east part of the county of Devon. For the modern name, it is derived from the church, compound of Saxon-British Kirk or Kilk-hampton, i. e. church home or habitation town, answerable to church town in English. In the Domesday Tax, 20 William I. (1087), this district was taxed under the jurisdiction of Orcett, of which more under. In the Inquisition made into the value of Cornish Benefices, in decanatu de Major Triggshire, ecclesia de Kilkhampton was rated xiiii*l*. xiii*s*. viii*d*. In Wolsey's Inquisition, 1521, 26*l*. 3*s*. 10½*d*.; the patronage in the Earl of Bath; the incumbent Corringdon; and the parish rated to the 4*s*. per pound Land Tax, 1696, 352*l*. 10*s*.

Stowe for many ages hath been the seat of that famous and knightly family now Earls of Bath.

[Mr. Hals goes on with a long account of this family in the early Norman times, apparently without much authority, and quite unconnected with Cornwall.

I shall therefore select particular passages, more especially as a genealogy in sufficient detail is given by Mr. Lysons.]

KILKHAMPTON. 341

It appears that the Grenvilles settled near Bideford, where they are stated to have held knights' fees under the Crown, and also under the honour of Gloucester; and Sir Theobald Grenville in the latter part of the reign of King Edward the Third, was the principal founder and promoter of building the bridge at Bideford; John Grandison was then Lord Bishop of Exeter, who caused it to be proclaimed in his Cathedral, and throughout all other churches in Devon and Cornwall, that all persons whatsoever that would promote or encourage such a work should partake of all spiritual blessings for ever. Sir Richard Gurnard or Gurney was then parish priest of Bideford, who it seems was admonished in his sleep to undertake this work, as Bishop Bronscomb was to build Glasney College in Cornwall; the Goldneys, Octanetts, and most other families of note in Cornwall and Devon (as Risdon's Manuscript informs us) were benefactors to this work, which bridge was finished tempore Richard II., assisted by a bull of indulgencies from Rome.

John Grenvill of Bideford, that married Burghert, was the first Sheriff of Devon of this family, 15 Richard II., son of Sir Theobald. Thomas Grenvill, that married Gilbert, was the first Sheriff of Cornwall of this family, 21 Edward IV., 1480, also the first of Henry VII., 1485, and probably the first of those gentlemen that settled at Stowe, for at such time as he was Sheriff of Cornwall, 21 Edward IV., one George Grenvill was Sheriff of Devon.

One Robert Grenvill was Sheriff of Cornwall the 2nd, 10th, and 14th Henry VIII. Richard Grenvill was Sheriff of Cornwall 36 Henry VIII. Richard Grenvill was Sheriff of Devon 18 of Elizabeth. Bernard Grenvill was Sheriff of Devon 38 of Elizabeth.

Roger, younger son of Sir Richard Grenvill that married Bonvill of Killigarth, who in the Mary Rose frigate, 37 Henry VIII., 1545, commanded by Sir George Carew, Knight, with more than four hundred men besides, after they had for several days fought the French fleet off the Isle of Wight under the command of the Lord Dambolt, Admiral of France, with great victory and success, unfortunately afterwards as the said ship passed out of the harbour of Portsmouth into the sea, by the neglect and carelessness of the gunner and mariners, one of which had left the cannon or ordnance untrigged or chained, and the latter having left the under port or gun-holes open, by means whereof, when the ship turned upon her lee, the guns fell all on that side of the ship and bore the port-holes under water, so that the sea in an instant abundantly flowing in through those port-holes filled her with water, whereof she sunk into the deep (in the sight of King Henry himself), whereby the captain and all his men were suddenly and violently drowned in the sea.

Of his father, Sir Richard Grenvill, the elder, thus speaks Mr. Carew in his Survey of Cornwall, "he interlaced his home magistracy with martial employments abroad, whereof the King testified his good liking by his liberality." Again, his son, the second Sir Richard, after his travel and following the wars under the Emperor Maximilian against the Turks, for which his name is recorded by sundry foreign writers, and his undertaking to people Virginia and Ireland, made so glorious a conclusion in her Majesty's ship the Revenge, of which he had charge as Captain, and of the whole fleet as Vice-Admiral, that it seemed thereby, when he found none other to compare withal in his life, he strived through a virtuous envy to exceed it in his death; a victorious loss for the realm, and of which the Spaniard may say, with Pyrrhus, that many such conquests would beget his utter overthrow. Lastly, his son John took hold of every martial occasion that was ministered him, until, in service against her Highness' enemies, under the command of Sir Walter Raleigh, the ocean became his bed of honour. Thus Mr. Carew, page 62. See also Baker's Chronicle in the latter end of the reign of Queen Elizabeth.

Sir Beville Grenvill, son of Bernard, by Beville's heir of Killigarth in Talland, was a gentleman of such urbanity, valour, and integrity in those parts, that my commendations cannot make the least addition thereto, nor I think that of a more florid or abler pen; who, as his duty obliged, engaged himself, his life and fortune, on the part and behalf of King Charles I.; and being first a horse Colonel in the militia for this County, was afterwards obliged to head or lead those soldiers he had raised in Cornwall, by virtue of the King's Commission, under command of Sir Ralph Hopton, Knight, his General in the west, from Launceston into Somersetshire, at a place called Lansdowne, five miles from Bristol, where Hopton with the King's army met and gave battle to the Parliament forces under command of Sir William Waller; in which engagement Sir Beville Grenvill, Knight, charging boldly in the head of his troop, was unfortunately slain, the 5th of July 1643.

Orcot, now Orchard, in this parish, was the jurisdiction under which Kilkhampton was taxed in Domesday Roll, 1087; from which place, I take it, was denominated the family surnamed de Orchard, now in possession thereof; particularly Charles Orchard, gentleman, steward to Sir John Rolle of Stevenston. This gentleman was sheriff of Cornwall about the year 1703.

Mr. Hals' concluding part of this parish is lost.

TONKIN.

Mr. Tonkin has merely copied from Mr. Hals.

THE EDITOR.

The following extract from Mr. Lysons's Cornwall is the best account that the Editor can give of the distinguished family of Grenville.

The manor of Kilkhampton is supposed to have belonged to the Grenville family from nearly the time of the Conquest; Dugdale says, that they were seated here in the reign of William Rufus. Richard de Grenville, who came over with William the Conqueror, is said in the pedigrees of the family to have been a younger brother of Robert Fitzhamon, Earl of Carbill, Lord of Thurigny and Grenville, in France and Normandy, and to have been lineally descended from Rollo, Duke of Normandy. It is on record that Richard de Grenville held certain knights' fees at Bideford, in Devonshire, in the reign of Henry II. We have not found any record of the Grenville possessions at Kilkhampton of an earlier date than the *quo warranto* roll before mentioned; but it appears that it had at that time been long in the family: they continued to reside at Stowe, in this parish, for many generations, and frequently served the office of sheriff for the county. William Grenville, or Grenfield (as the name was at that early period generally written), son of Sir Theobald, became archbishop of York, and distinguished himself as an able statesman: he died in 1315. Sir Richard Grenville, son of Roger, (who was himself a captain in the navy, and lost his life, as Carew tells us, in the unfortunate Mary-Rose) was a celebrated military and naval commander in the reign of Queen Elizabeth. He first distinguished himself in the wars under the Emperor Maximilian against the Turks, for which his name is recorded by several foreign writers. In the year 1591, being then Vice-Admiral of England, he was sent in the Revenge, with a squadron of seven ships, to intercept the Spanish galleons; when, falling in with the enemy's fleet, consisting of fifty-two sail, near the Terceira Islands, he repulsed them fifteen times in a continued fight, till his powder was all spent; his ship, which sunk before it arrived in port, was reduced to a hulk, and himself covered with wounds, of which he died two days afterwards, on board the vessel of the Spanish commander. Sir Richard's grandson was the brave and loyal Sir Beville Grenville. This distinguished officer was one of king Charles's generals in the West, and shared the glories of the successful compaign in Cornwall, in the autumn of 1642; in the summer of the following year he lost his life at the battle of Lansdowne, near Bath. Sir Richard Grenville, who had been created a Baronet in 1631, was, after his brother's death, made General of all the King's forces in the West. He was an active and zealous officer, and so particularly obnoxious to the Parliamentary party, that he was perpetually the subject of abuse to their journalists, who seldom spoke of him but by the appellation of *Skellum* Grenville. During the dissensions between the civil power and the military in 1645, Sir Richard Grenville was superseded and imprisoned by the advice of Sir Edward Hyde, afterwards Earl of Clarendon. That noble author gives a very unamiable character of Sir Richard, who is represented as having been in the highest degree oppressive, tyrannical, and unprincipled; but other writers attribute much of this to the personal enmity which subsisted between them. Sir Richard Grenville died, in reduced circumstances, at Ghent, in the year 1658, leaving no male issue; the title became extinct. Sir John Grenville, son of the brave Sir Beville, succeeded to the Kilkhampton estates: at a very early age he had a command in his father's regiment, and was left for dead in the field at Tewkesbury. He was appointed Governor of Scilly Islands when they revolted from the Parliament, and was one of the chief instruments in effecting the restoration of King Charles II. He gave the living of Kilkhampton to Nicholas Monk, and employed him to influence his brother (the General) in favour of the exiled Monarch; having succeeded in his negociations, he had the satisfaction of being the bearer of the King's letters to General Monk and to the Parliament. In April 1661 Sir John Grenville was created Lord Grenville of Kilkhampton and Bideford, Viscount Lansdowne, and Earl of Bath. On the death of his grandson, under age, in 1711, these titles became extinct; and the Kilkhampton estates passed to his aunt and coheiress Grace Grenville, who married George Lord Carteret, and was afterwards (being then a widow) by King George the First created Countess of Granville, with remainder to her son John, who inherited that title and the Kilkhampton estate. On the death of Robert the second Earl of Granville, in 1776, that title became extinct, and the Kilkhampton estate passed, under his will, to his nephew Henry Frederick Thynne, second son of Lord Viscount Weymouth, who had married his sister Louisa. Mr. Thynne was created Lord Carteret in 1784, and is the present possessor of Kilkhampton; the remainder of which, as well as the title of Carteret, is vested in Lord George Thynne, second son of the Marquis of Bath.

John Grenville, Earl of Bath, in the reign of Charles II. built a magnificient mansion at Stowe in this parish, of which scarcely a vestige remains. It stood on an eminence, overlooking a well-wooded valley; but not a tree near it, says Dr. Borlase, to shelter it from the north-west. That writer speaks of it as by far the noblest house in the west of England, and says that the kitchen-offices, fitted up for a dwelling-house, made no contemptible figure. It is a singular circumstance, that the cedar wainscot which had been brought out of a Spanish prize, and used by the Earl of Bath for fitting up the chapel in this mansion, was purchased by Lord Cobham at the time of its demolition (the house being then sold piecemeal), and applied to the same purpose at Stowe, the magnificent seat of the noble family of Grenville in Buckinghamshire, where it still remains. Defoe, in his Tour through Great Britain, speaking of Stowe in Cornwall, says that the carving of the chapel was the work of Michael Chuke, and not inferior to Gibbons

Ilcombe, now a farm-house belonging to Lord Carteret, is described by Norden as the residence of a younger branch of the Grenvilles.

Alderscombe, formerly a seat of the Orchards, is the property of the Rev. Thomas Hooper Morrison, nephew of the late Paul Orchard, Esq. of Hartland Abbey.

Elmsworthy, some time a seat of the Westlakes, is now a farm house, the property of Mr. Galsworthy, of Hartland. The last of the Westlakes died in very indigent circumstances about the year 1772, having been reduced to the situation of a parish pauper. It is a singular circumstance, that he was twice pricked for Sheriff after he was an inhabitant of the poor-house. In the parish church are monuments of the Grenville family, and memorials of the Orchards of Alderscombe, the Westlakes of Elmsworthy, and the Waddons of Tonacombe in Morwinstow. On the monument of Sir Beville Grenville, which is surrounded by military trophies, is the following inscription: " Here lyes all that was mortal of the most noble and truly valiant Sir Beville Grenville, of Stowe in the county of Cornwall, Earl of Corbill and Lord of Thorigny and Granville in France and Normandy, descended in a direct line from Robert, second son of the warlike Rollo, first Duke of Normandy; who, after having obtained divers signal victories over the Rebels in the West, was at length slain with many wounds at the battle of Lansdowne July 5, 1643. He married the most virtuous lady, Grace, daughter of Sir George Smith, of the county of Devon, by whom he had many sons, eminent for their loyalty and firm adherence to the Crown and Church; and several daughters, remarkable examples of true piety. He was indeed an excellent person, whose activity, interest, and reputation was the foundation of what had been done in Cornwall, and his temper and affection so public that no accident which happened could make any impressions on him, and his example kept others from taking any thing ill, or at least seeming to do so; in a word, a brighter courage and a gentler disposition were never married together to make the most cheerful and innocent conversation. Vide Lord Clarendon's History of the Rebellion.

"To the immortal memory of his renowned grandfather this monument was erected by the Right Honorable George Lord Lansdowne, Treasurer of the Household to Queen Anne, and one of Her Majesty's most Honorable Privy Council, &c. in the year 1714.

> " Thus slain thy valiant ancestor did lye,
> When his one bark a navy did defy,
> When now encompass'd round the victor stood,
> And bath'd his pinnace in his conquering blood,
> 'Till, all his purple current dried and spent,
> He fell, and made the waves his monument.
> Where shall the next famed Grenville's ashes stand?
> Thy grandsire fills the seas, and thou the land.
>   MARTIN LLEWELLIN."
> Vide Oxford University Verses, printed 1643.

Sir Beville Granville was forty-eight years of age at the time of his death, as appears by the following record of his birth in the parish register at Kilkhampton:

" Bevell, the sonne of the worshipful Bernarde Greynville, Esquire, was borne and baptized at Brinn in Cornwall, Ao. Dni. 1595."

In the margin, " Marche 1595, borne the 23d day, baptized the 25th day of Marche."

His brother Sir Richard's baptism is thus entered, " Richard, the son of Barnard Granevile, Esq. baptized 26 June 1600."

Lord Carteret is patron of the rectory of Kilkhampton. In the registers of the see of Exeter, mention is made of a chapel at Brightley in this parish, dedicated to St. Catharine.—Thus far from Mr. Lysons.

All the accounts and traditions of Sir Beville Granville represent him as a hero bordering on romance, as the rival of Sir Philip Sidney, and of Lord Herbert of Cherbury. He fell, however, into all the political errors of that age, by attaching himself to the existing form of Government, not because it appeared, on the whole, to prove most conducive to human happiness, but from some fanciful, superstitious, or blasphemous analogy it was supposed to bear with the Divine administration of the universe. Then he concurred with those who thought it expedient and right to destroy the resemblance, by limiting that which, on the supposition, should exist without restraint or control; and entertaining that opinion, he nevertheless endeavoured to prove by arguments, and still more powerfully by his arms at Stratton and at Bath, that no resistance could in any case be lawfully exercised against the individual who happened to hold the chief magistracy from the accident of his birth. Such glaring inconsistencies were, however, almost obscured by the splendour of undaunted courage, of disinterested generosity, and, by adherence to principles honestly entertained, however erroneous or contradictory.

It would be unfair to the memory of Sir Beville Granville not to insert his letter to Sir John Trelawny, recently printed in the Memorials of John Hampden, 2 vols. 8vo., by George Grenville Nugent Temple, Lord Nugent, vol. 2, p. 195.

Most Honourable Sir,

I have in many kinds had trial of your nobleness, but in none more than in this singular expression of your kind care and love. I give also your excellent Lady humble thanks for respect unto my poor Woman, who hath been long a faithful much obliged servant of your Ladyes. But Sir! for my journey, it is fixed. I cannot contain myself within my doors, when the King of England's standard waves in the field upon so just occasion. The cause being such as must make all those that die in it little inferior to martyrs. And for my own part, I desire to acquire an honest name, or an honourable grave. I never loved my life or ease so much as to shun such an occasion; which if I should, I were unworthy of the profession I have held, or to succeed those ancestors of mine, who have so many of them in several ages sacrificed their lives for their country. Sir, the barbarous and implacable enemy, notwithstanding His Majesty's gracious proceedings with them, do continue their insolences and rebellion in the highest degree, and are united in a body of great strength; so as you may expect, if they be not prevented and mastered near their own homes, they will be troublesome in yours, and in the remotest places ere long.

I am not without the consideration, as you lovingly advise, of my wife and family; and as for her, I must acknowledge, she hath ever drawn so evenly in the yoke with me, as she hath never prest before, or hung behind me, nor ever opposed or resisted my will. And yet truly I have not, in this or any thing else, endeavoured to walk in the way of power with her, but of reason; and though her love will submit to either, yet truly my respect will not suffer me to urge her with power, unless I can convince with reason. So much for that, whereof I am willing to be accomptable unto so good a friend.

I have no suit unto you in mine own behalf, but for your prayers and good wishes; and that if I live to come home again, you would please to continue me in the number of your servants.

I shall give a true relation unto my very noble friend Mr. Moyle, of your and his Aunt's loving respects to him, which he hath good reason to be thankful for. And so I beseech God to send you and your noble family all health and happiness, and while I live I am, Sir,

Your unfeigned loving and faithful servant,

BEVILLE GRANVILLE.

With the death of Sir Beville Granville, in the moment of victory at Lansdown, the splendour of this family seems to have fallen under a temporary eclipse.

His brother is represented by Hyde, the partial historian of these civil wars, as unworthy of the character supposed to distinguish Cavaliers.

John Grenville, his eldest son, created Earl of Bath, appears to have been rapacious and oppressive.

But all this was amply compensated by the subsequent conduct of his son and heir Charles Grenville, who served with honour in the continental wars, and participated with John Sobieski in the preservation of Christendom under the walls of Vienna in 1683.

George Grenville, son of Barnard Grenville, brother to the first Earl of Bath, is known to every one by his literary attainments and by his talents for poetry. This gentleman had the honour of being elected member for the county of Cornwall, with Mr. John Trevanion, after the great contest of 1710, amidst shouts of

> Grenville and Trevanion as sound as a Bell,
> For the Queen, the Church, and Sacheverel.

In the following year an hereditary seat in Parliament was bestowed on him, with the appellation of Lord Lansdown, and he was succeeded in the representation of Cornwall by Sir Richard Vyvyan.

Lord Lansdown suffered imprisonment after the accession of George I. and retired from public life. His genuine works in prose and verse were collected in 2 vols. 4to., London 1732. He died, sine prole, in 1734.

The old house at Stowe was taken down by John Grenville the first Earl of Bath, and a superb mansion erected in its place, partly, as it is said, at the national expense; having the internal decorations suited to the size and magnificence of the exterior; but soon after the decease of his grandson in 1711, when the property passed into a female line, this house was taken down and the materials of all kinds sold.

It used to be said that almost every gentleman's seat in Cornwall had received embellishments from Stowe. Mr. Prideaux' house at Padstow received an entire staircase, and some carved wainscot has, by a singular fate, found its way to Stowe, in Buckinghamshire.

Alderscombe, in this parish, was for many years held on lease for lives by the family of Cottell.

Mr. Alexander Cottell, about the year 1720, having

served his clerkship in Penzance, as an attorney, married Sarah Phillips, one of the daughters of Mr. Samuel Phillips, of Pendrea. There is a monument to her memory in the church, stating her decease on the 7th of August, 1727, in her thirtieth year, with the arms of Cottell, Or, a bend Gu. This gentleman married again and dissipated his whole property.

The church is one of the finest in Cornwall, containing splendid monuments; and under, is a most spacious vault belonging to the Glanville family.

It is perhaps worth noticing that here, while he served the curacy, Mr. Hervey composed his Meditations among the Tombs.

Kilkhampton measures 7,234 statute acres.

	£.	s.	d.
Annual value of the Real Property as returned to Parliament in 1815,	3,959	0	0
Poor Rate in 1831	792	5	0

Population,— | in 1801, | in 1811, | in 1821, | in 1831 |
|---|---|---|---|
| 808 | 852 | 1,024 | 1,126 |

giving an increase of 39 per cent in 30 years.

Present Rector, the Rev. John Davis, presented by Lord Carteret in 1810.

GEOLOGY, BY DOCTOR BOASE.

Doctor Boase says of the geology of this parish, that Kilkhampton is entirely situated on the dunstone, which forms the substratum throughout the north-eastern part of Cornwall.

LADOCK, COMMONLY PRONOUNCED LASSICK.

HALS.

The manuscript relating to this parish is lost.

TONKIN.

Ladock is in the hundred of Powder, and confines on

the west to St. Erme, on the north to St. Enodor, on the east to St. Stephan's in Branwell, on the south to St. Probus.

This parish takes its name from Saint Ladoca, whom I take to be an Irish Saint; and probably she came over with St. Breage.

This parish is a rectory, valued in the King's Books at £18. The patronage in Kelland Courtenay, and Thomas Pitt, Esqrs. Governor Pitt, grandfather of Mr. Thomas Pitt, purchased this alternate right of the Lady Mahon, together with all the Mahon property in Cornwall. The incumbent Mr. Wm. Wood.

The manor of Nansoath, in this parish, signifies the fat (i. e. fertile) valley, the name being compounded of nans, a valley, and soath or soa, fat, tallow, &c.

To the north of Nansoath is Hay. This was the seat of the Randyls, and was sold to Mr. William Tregea, of Lambrigan, who did not keep it long, but parted with it to Richard Bone, Gent. who dying without being ever married, left it by will, with several other estates, to his kinsman Richard Bone, Gent. who now lives there, and hath married Anne, the daughter of Mr. John Andrew, of Trethurfe, by whom he has issue. Mr. Randyll's arms were, Gules, on a cross Argent, three mullets pierced Sable. Mr. Bone's are, Ermine, a fess indented Sable.

Joining with Hay is Boswaydel, usually called Boswidle, which I take to signify a house in an open place, or one easy to be seen from.

The manor of Bedocke or Bessake. Francis Tregian, Esq. forfeited this manor, with his other lands (see Probus). To the east of this is the church and rectory house; and the manor of Trethurfe or Tretherf. This was anciently, perhaps before the Norman Conquest, the seat of a very eminent family of the same name, who gave for their arms, Azure, a buck's head cabouched Argent. John Tretherfe was one of the Knights returned to Parliament for this county in the 15th year of King Henry VI. Reginald Trethurf married Margery, the second daughter and coheir of John St. Aubyn, Esq. by Catharine his wife, the daughter and heir of Sir Robert Challons, of Challons Legh in Devonshire, as appears by a bill in the Treasury, of 7 Henry VI.

THE EDITOR.

In the Taxation of Ecclesiastical Benefices by the Bishops of Lincoln and Winchester, under the authority of Pope Nicholas, will be found:

	Taxatio.	Decima.
Ecclesia de Sancto Ladoca	£6 0 0	0 12 0
In Wolsey's Valuation, Ladocke	18 0 0	1 16 0

Besides the church town there is one considerable village in this parish called Bedock or Besock, after the manor of which it forms a part.

Mr. Pitt not only acquired the alternate presentation to this rectory by purchase from the family of Mahon, as is stated by Mr. Tonkin, but also the manor of Ladock, which had previously belonged to the Carminows and Courtenays. The barton of Trethurfe has passed by the heiresses of Kelland Courtenay to the families of Poyntz and Boyle. The barton of Nansaugh is the property and the residence of Mr. Andrews.

Hay, noticed by Mr. Tonkin as belonging to Mr. Richard Bone, came by purchase to the Hearles of Penryn, and in the division of the lands belonging to that family, it has fallen to Mrs. Stephens, of Tregenna.

The manor of Bessake was acquired by Mr. Francis Tregian, son of the gentleman from whom it had been seized, but soon afterwards it passed by sale to the Arundells, from them by gift to the Moncktons, who have added the name of Arundell; and finally Robert Monckton Arundell, Viscount Galway, sold it in 1780 to the late Sir Christopher Hawkins.

The Rev. John Eliot, rector of this parish, and of Truro,

who died in 1760, founded two exhibitions at Exeter College for young men from Truro school.

The vale, extending from north to south quite across this parish, is one of the most beautiful in Cornwall: it was, however, little known beyond the immediate neighbourhood, till the line of road forming the great communication from Falmouth, and the whole western part of the county, with London, was carried through it in the year 1830. The church and tower, which are handsome in themselves, stand on a commanding situation, and are seen to great advantage from the new road.

Ladock measures 4,859 statute acres.

	£.	s.	d.
Annual value of the Real Property, as returned to Parliament in 1815	4,566	0	0
Poor Rate in 1831	310	2	0

Population,	in 1801,	in 1811,	in 1821,	in 1831,
	542	651	806*	761

giving an increase of 40 per cent. in 30 years.

GEOLOGY, BY DR. BOASE.

This parish is entirely situated on rocks belonging to the slate series; its northern corner, however, approaches very near to the boundary of the granite.

Its different kinds of slates are the same as those of the adjacent parishes of St. Enoder and St. Erme; the rocks of its northern and eastern boundaries resembling those of

---

* This parish presents a very singular anomaly in respect to its Population Return It would obviously occur that the 8 might possibly have stood for a 7 in the place of hundreds in the return for 1821; but that return at large, as printed by the House of Commons, has

Families employed in Agriculture	Families employed in Trades, &c.	Other families.	Males.	Females.	In all.
90	19	15	418	388	806

This gives however 6⅓ for each family

If the rate of increase had continued for the last ten years, as it did in the former twenty, the final number would have been 983, with an increase at the rate of 81 per cent in 30 years.

St. Enoder, the southern part corresponding to those of St. Erme.

Most of the vallies have been excavated for stream tin, and these have yielded some of the largest pieces of gold that have been found in Cornwall.

LAMORAN.

HALS.

The manuscript relating to this parish is lost.

TONKIN.

Lamoran is in the hundred of Powder, and hath on the west and north St. Michael Penkivell; on the east Cornelly; on the south the river Fale, between it and Ruan Lanyhorn.

The right name of this parish is Lan Morun, the church of St. Morun, to whom it is dedicated; but as to who St. Morun was I must plead ignorance, except that I believe him to have been one of those who came from Ireland in the fifth century.

This parish is a rectory, valued in the King's Book at £6. The patronage is in Sir John Molesworth, in right of the manor of Lanmoran, to which it belongs.

The incumbent Mr. Samuel Ley.

This little parish hath but one manor in it, and that is called by its own name.

THE EDITOR.

In the valuation of Pope Nicholas the taxation is £1, the tenths nothing.

LAMORAN.

This parish has but two villages, the Church Town and Tregenna.

The manor of Lamoran, including the whole parish, has passed through various families; Halep and Trevenor, from that family by coheiresses to Roscarrack and Chamond, then Vermans and Sparks, and Molesworths, from whom by purchase, it passed to Boscawen. The advowson is an appendage to the manor.

The church is said to be most curiously situated on the edge of the river, and with a tower more venerable than itself, at a certain distance from it.

The church has some monuments to the Vermans. Their old manor house is fallen into decay.

This parish measures 1130 statute acres.

	£.	s.	d.
Annual value of the Real Property, as returned to Parliament in 1815	895	0	0
Poor Rate in 1831	25	3	0

Population,—	in 1801,	in 1811,	in 1821,	in 1831,
	78	94	93	96

giving an increase of 23 per cent in 30 years.

THE GEOLOGY, BY DR. BOASE.

The geology of this little parish is precisely the same as that of Filley, of the lower part of Kea, and of other parishes situated around the numerous creeks communicating with Falmouth harbour.

Present Rector, the Rev. William Curgerven, presented in 1803 by the Earl of Falmouth.

LENDAWEDNACK, or LANDEWEDNACK.

HALS.

The manuscript relating to this parish is lost.

TONKIN.

Landawednack lies in that part of the hundred of Kerrier which is called Meneage. It hath to the west, south, and east, the English Channel, to the north Ruan Major and Grade.

The name signifies the church of St. Wednack, or Wynnock; (although Mr. Carew, I know not on what authority, calls it St. Landy,) to whom is likewise dedicated Towednack, in the hundred of Penwith, and St. Winnow. It is a rectory, valued in the King's Book at £11. 16s. 8d. The patronage in the heirs of George Robinson, Esq.

The manor of Lizard, so called from the famous Point of that name, which is a part of it. This manor was one of those given to the Earl of Morton.

THE EDITOR.

This parish has but two villages. The Church Town and an assemblage of small houses near the Point, and called Lizard, or Lizard Town.

Mr. Lysons says, that the very extensive manor of Tretheves, Lucies, and Rosswick, extends over a great part of this parish, and into Ruan Minor and Grade: it belonged to the Carminows, then to the Reskymers, and to Robinson, by whom it was sold in 1768 to Mr. Thomas Fonnereau, after whose death it was purchased by the late Sir Christopher Hawkins.

Mr. Fonnereau came into Cornwall as an adventurer, and chiefly for the purpose of constructing Lighthouses on the Lizard Point, under one of the improvident grants which were frequently made in those times.

A single lighthouse stands on St. Agnes Island at Scilly, and three, forming a triangle, on the rocks of Guernsey. Two towers were therefore built on the Lizard, that each Point might be distinct from the others, and experience has proved their utility to be very great. For many years after their construction the lights consisted of coal fires in

LANDEWEDNACK. 359

each lantern, after the manner of a smith's forge, and urged in a similar way by bellows; but the blowing could not be always maintained, and when that had been intermitted for a short time the lights nearly disappeared.

Since the expiration of the grant made to the first projector, the affairs have been under the intelligent, scientific, and liberal management of the Trinity House. They have substituted large Argand lamps, each placed in the focus of a parabolic mirror, plated with burnished silver; and these cast a continued and steady light, visible in clear weather to the extremity of the horizon.

Latitude of the Lizard flagstaff 49° 57' 55".8; longitude west from Greenwich 5° 11' 17".7. From the Trigonometrical Survey.

In Mr. Lax's Table, the Western Light House is stated to have latitude 49° 57' 44", and longitude 5° 1' 15".

This parish measures 1,843 statute acres

Annual value of the Real Property, as returned to Parliament in 1815 . £1,187 s. 0 d. 0

Poor Rate in 1831 . . . . . 126 4 0

Population,— { in 1801, 244 | in 1811, 303 | in 1821, 387 | in 1831, 406 }

giving an increase of 66 per cent. in 30 years.

Present Rector, the Rev. H. T. Coulson, presented in 1827 by Henry Coulson, Esq.

GEOLOGY, BY DR. BOASE.

By far the greater part of this parish is composed of serpentine, which is generally of the red variety, with dark-coloured and shining scales of diallage.

South of a line drawn east and west, a little north of the church, across the peninsula of the Lizard, the rocks are for the most part schistose, and are covered with a deep soil, which is exceedingly productive.

The cliffs around this part of the parish are very interesting, and if minutely scrutinized would probably throw some additional light on the nature and position of the serpentine. To this end it would be necessary to make the survey from the sea, which could only be effected occasionally, and under very favourable circumstances.

At Perranbonse Cove, near the church, the slate is a variety of schistose diallage rock, such as has been already described at Cadgwith.

Near the lighthouses the cliff is formed of a glossy decomposing talcose slate, which has been called by some geologists Micaceous schist, but talc appears to be the characteristic mineral, as it is present in a distinct form throughout the veins, with nodules of quartz abounding in this slate.

At Hensall Cove the blue slate is much intermixed with calcareous spar in various forms, resembling the slate adjoining the calc shists, and blue limestones at Veryan, Padstow, and some other parts of Cornwall.

The Editor would take the liberty of adding that in this parish veins of steatite run through the serpentine formation; and that considerable quantities have been raised by the late Mr. Wedgwood from some veins larger than the others, and near the cliff. The soft and unctuous qualities of this substance gave it the popular name of soap rock. Thin veins of native copper traverse also the serpentine formation; but never in sufficient quantities to bear the expense of mining. In some places specimens of semi-transparent serpentine are found shot through by branches of native copper, forming what has been termed dendrites.

At Kynans Cove the assemblage of rocks possesses such an extraordinary degree of beauty and magnificence as to render it one of the spots most worthy of attention on the whole coast. The interest excited by the general effect is heightened, on a more close inspection, by natural caverns, and the intervals between the rocks are perpetually varied in their appearance by the swell and by the subsidence of waves from the sea.

This spot possesses further interest to a botanist by the production of some rare plants. The asparagus officinalis, the beta maritima, the carduus acoulis, rare in Cornwall, and some others.

Doctor Borlase records some instances of great longevity in this parish, but such generally occur in all dry and unconfined districts, more especially when they are somewhat elevated above the ordinary level of alluvial countries.

A manufactory has been recently established for producing ornamented trifles from the beautifully coloured and variegated serpentine of this district, and with so much success that vases have been turned in lathes, exceeding a foot in height, and they hope to polish chimney-pieces on a large scale.

LANDRAKE.

HALS.

The manuscript relating to this perish is lost.

TONKIN.

Landrake is situate in the hundred of East, and hath to the west St. Germans; to the north Quethiock; to the east Pillaton, Botus Fleming and St. Stephan's; to the south St. Erney.

This church, in A. D. 1291, the 20th Edward I., is valued at £4. 13s. 4d. being then appropriated to the Priory of St. Germans; the vicarage at £10.

The vicarage is valued by Wolsey at £18. 12s. 4d. The patronage in Lord Hobart, as heir to Sir John Maynard.

The manor of Lanrake, as the parish should also be written, is reckoned to be the very best in the county. It was valued in the 1st year of Edward I. at £100, which no

LANDRAKE.

other estate came up to but Sheviock and Pawton, which last however was valued at £120.

THE EDITOR.

There seems to be but little of importance connected with this parish. The extensive manor of Lanrake is said by Mr. Lysons to have belonged at an early period to the family of St. Margaret, and in the seventeenth century to have belonged to Sergeant Maynard, from whom it passed by marriage to the family of Hobart, and from that to Edgecumbe. This manor includes the advowson of the vicarage; and the impropriation of the great tithes belonged also to Sergeant Maynard, having been a part of the endowments taken from the Priory of St. Germans.

The church town is rather a large village, and the church and tower are of the form and size common throughout Cornwall. The church contains several monuments.

In this parish is another village, called Wotton Cross, and part of a third called Tidiford, where a small river, navigable for barges, and communicating with the Tamar at Hamoaze, divides Landrake from St. Germans.

The facility of water communication has established some trade at Tidiford, but it is chiefly remarkable by the great quantities of Plymouth limestone burnt there for manure.

The system of using lime in agriculture does not date further back in this district than the early part, or perhaps than the middle, of the last century; and it is supposed at the least to have doubled the value of all the land, and in consequence to have increased the population, improved the country, and largely added to all the sources of honest industry and employment.

Wotton, as a seat of the Courtenays, must have been in former times a place of some consequence. It belonged to the family of Blake, the heiress of which family has married Francis Dogherty, Esq.

St. Erney.

The little parish of St. Erney, being in fact a part of Landrake, except that its church still exists as a chapel supported by a local rate, is not noticed by Mr. Hals under the letter E, and his account of it is therefore lost, with this part of his manuscript.

TONKIN.

St. Erney, St. Erna, or St. Erne, stands in the hundred of East, and hath upon the north Landrake, upon the south St. Germans Creek, upon the west St. Germans, upon the east Botus-Fleming.

San Erna in the Cernawish tongue signifies holy hour, with reference to, I apprehend, the time set apart for the celebration of divine service. In the Saxon and Kernawish combined, San Erna is an holy or sacred eagle; and if so, I take it, the name must be construed as relating to the person that officiates at divine service, who, as an eagle, ascends up to heaven for metaphysical or supernatural mysteries—as St. John the Evangelist, whose similitude is an eagle. In this sense we have Eagle vicarage in Graffo hundred, Lincolnshire.

This is a daughter church to Landrake.

THE EDITOR.

Mr. Lysons notices the manor of Trelugan, of which Wotton in Landrake seems to be the barton; and also the manor of Markwell, which he says belonged to Thomas Earl of Lancaster, attainted in the reign of Edward II. Then to the Bodrugans, and after the attaint of Henry de Bodrugan, in the reign of Henry VII. it was granted to Sir John Paulet, and descended to the late Duke of Bolton.

Mr. Lysons states, that this being a daughter church to Landrake, is entitled to service but once a month; it is probably entitled once in three weeks, which is the general custom or canon.

| Landrake measures | . | . | 2217 | } statute acres. |
| St. Erney | . | . | . | 881 |

3098

	£.	s.	d.
Annual value of the Real Property in both parishes as returned to Parliament in 1815	5818	0	0
Poor Rate in both parishes 1831 .	459	2	0

| Population of both parishes. | in 1801, 613 | in 1811, 768 | in 1821, 841 | in 1831, 872 |

giving an increase of 42 per cent in 30 years.

Rector of Landrake, the Rev. Wymond Cory, presented in 1802 by the Countess of Mount Edgecombe; of St. Erney, the Rev. H. Molesworth, presented in 1823 by Lord de Dunstanville.

GEOLOGY, BY DOCTOR BOASE.

St. Erney consists principally of a blue slate or calcareous schist, and it probably also contains limestone, as is the case in St. Germans, the two parishes being separated only by a small creek.

Landrake. This parish is entirely constituted of rocks belonging to the calcareous series, like those of the adjacent parishes, St. Erney and St. Germans.

LANDULPH, or LANDILIP.

HALS.

The manuscript relating to this parish is lost.

TONKIN.

Landulph is in the hundred of East. To the west of it is Pillaton and Botus-Fleming, to the north St. Dominick, to the east and south the river Tamar.

This signifies the church of Dilp.

It is a rectory, valued in the King's Books at £20. 3s. 6d. The Duke of Cornwall patron.

This church was valued in the time of Pope Nicholas at £4, having never been appropriated, the prior of St. Germans receiving out of the rectory a pension of £8; and if I understand the entries rightly, the same did the abbat of Tavistock.

THE EDITOR.

The church of Landulph is situated almost on the margin of the shore, and looks directly down the river. It contains monuments of the Lowers, but it has one monument of extraordinary interest, to the memory of Theodore Paleologus, descended from the last Emperors of Greece, or as they styled themselves in the single city of Constantinople, Emperors of Rome.

A very ample account of all that can be collected with respect to this personage, has been given by the present learned and ingenious rector Mr. Francis Vyvyan Jago Arundell, in a communication to the Society of Antiquaries, in 1815.

" In the parish church of Landulph, in the eastern extremity of Cornwall, is a small brass tablet fixed against the wall, with the following inscription :—

' Here lyeth the body of Theodore Paleologus, of Pesaro in Italye, descended from ye Imperyal lyne of ye last Christian emperors of Greece, being the sonne of Camilio, ye sonne of Prosper, the sonne of Theodoro, the sonne of John, ye sonne of Thomas, second brother of Constantine Paleologus, the 8th of that name, and last of y^t lyne y^t rayned in Constantinople until subdued by the Turks, who married w^t Mary, ye daughter of William Balls, of Hadlye in Souffolke, Gent. and had issue 5 children, Theodore, John, Ferdinando, Maria, and Dorothy; and departed this life at Clyfton, ye 21st of Jan^y, 1636.'

" Above the inscription are the imperial arms proper, of

the empire of Greece—an eagle displayed with two heads, the two legs resting upon two gates; the imperial crown over the whole, and between the gates a crescent for difference as second son.

" The Paleologus dynasty were descended from the imperial race of the Comneni; and the first of the family was Michael Paleologus about 1270; to whom succeeded Andronicus the First and Second, John I., and Emmanuel, who died 1425, leaving six sons. The eldest, John II., who was associated with his father in the government during his lifetime, succeeded him. Andronicus, the second son, had the principality of Thessalonica, and died of a leprosy soon after the sale of that city to the Venetians. Some fortunate incidents had restored Peloponnesus, or the Morea, to the empire; and in his more prosperous days Emmanuel had fortified the narrow isthmus of six miles with a stone wall and 153 towers. The wall was overthrown upon the first blast of the Ottomans; the fertile peninsula might have been sufficient for the four younger brothers, Theodore and Constantine, Demetrius and Thomas, but they wasted in domestic contests the remains of their strength, and the least successful of the rivals were reduced to a life of dependance in the Byzantine palace. On the death of John II., who survived four years the Hungarian crusade, the royal family by the death of Andronicus, and the monastic profession of Isidore (or Theodore), was reduced to three princes, Constantine, Demetrius, and Thomas. Of these, the first and last were far distant in the Morea; but Demetrius, who possessed the domain of Selybria, was in the suburbs at the head of a party. His ambition was not chilled with the public distress, and his conspiracy with the Turks and the schismatics had already disturbed the peace of the country. He would have supplanted his brother, and ascended the throne, but for his mother and the great men, who prevented him. His younger brother, the despot Thomas, also accidentally returning to the capital, asserted the cause of Constantine, who was crowned emperor.

"Demetrius and Thomas now divided the Morea between them; but, though they had taken a solemn oath never to violate the agreement, differences soon arose, and Thomas took up arms to drive Demetrius out of his possessions; Demetrius hereupon retired to Asan, his wife's brother, by whose means he obtained succours from Amurat, and compelled Thomas to submit the matters in dispute to the emperor's (Constantine's) arbitration. But that prince refusing to deliver to his brother the territories that fell to his share, Mohammed ordered Thuraken, his governor in the Morea, to assist Demetrius, and demolish the wall that shut up that country. Hereupon Thomas gave him the city of Kalamata, in lieu of the territory of the Skortians, which he detained. Immediately on this event, Mohammed besieged and took Constantinople, in defence of which Constantine was slain.

"The dissensions of the two brothers may be considered a principal cause of the fall of the Greek empire.

"After the capture of Constantinople, Mohammed makes war on Demetrius and Thomas, under pretence of recovering the tribute due to him from them as despots of the Morea; but he is obliged to retire, and soon after comes to agreement with them. At this time the Albanians, Thomas's subjects, revolt, and attack Pattras, a city of Achaia, where Thomas resided, but are repulsed; they would have been, however, ultimately successful, had not Mohammed sent his general Thuraken to their assistance.

"The two brothers again falling out, and endeavouring to supplant each other, Mohammed takes advantage of it, and in 1458 sends an order to the despots of the Morea to pay three years' arrears of ten thousand ducats tribute, or quit the country. In spring following, he marched to attack the Morea, and reduced Corinth, without using force. At the first news of his appearance, Thomas, one of the despots, retired to Italy with his wife and children; and Demetrius, the other, submitted of his own accord to the Soltân, who carried him away to Constantinople.

"Such is the account given in the Universal History from Dukas. The relation of Khalcondylas in the same work is more particular, as well as more favourable to the character of Thomas: 'Prince Thomas having retired from Pylos, repaired to the island of Korfu, where he left his family, and set sail for Italy; at the same time he sent an ambassador to know if Mohammed would give him a great extent of country along the sea coast in exchange for the city of Epidamnum. The Soltân, by way of answer, put the envoy in irons, but soon after sent him back. Thomas arriving at Rome 1461, was lodged in the Pope's palace, and had a pension of three thousand livres for his other expenses.'

"Rycaut, in his History, gives a still higher character of Thomas: 'Thomas getting into the castle of Salmenica, defended the same against the infidels a whole year, when, despairing of relief, he escaped into Italy, where the Pope allowed him a pension till the day of his death.' Of him Mahomet gave this character: 'That he had found many slaves, but never a man in the Grecian province besides Prince Thomas.'

"But Gibbon has a very contemptible account of the ultimate fate of this unfortunate family. He says, that Demetrius died at Constantinople in a monastic habit, and abject slavery; that the misery of Thomas was prolonged by a pension of six thousand ducats from the Pope and cardinals; that he died leaving two sons, Andrew and Manuel, who were educated in Italy; that Manuel the younger returned to Constantinople, where he was maintained by the Soltân, and died, leaving a son, who was lost in the habit and religion of a Turkish slave. The elder brother, Andrew, contemptible to his enemies, and burthensome to his friends, was degraded by the baseness of his life and marriage, and sold his title to the empires of Constantinople and Trebizond to Charles VIII. in 1494, who assumed the purple and title of Augustus. And in a note he says, from Du Cange, that the Palæologi of Montferrat were not extinct till the next century, but they had forgotten their Greek origin and kindred.

" So degrading is the account this historian gives us of the remains of this celebrated family. It is a grateful task to endeavour to prove his representation in some respects incorrect and undeserved; as we shall then be authorised to hesitate upon what he tells us as to the rest, and to put a more liberal construction upon the whole.

" From the inscription at Landulph it is clear Thomas had *three sons*: the third, called *John*, whose family, though we have no particular mention of them, remained in Italy, at Rome probably, and Pesaro, till the time of Theodore. From the inscription it is also certain that this family was not extinct in 1636, and perhaps some of the descendants are still living in England at this moment.

" The imputation thrown on the *Montferrat* Paleologi certainly does not apply to this branch, that they had forgotten their Greek origin and kindred; on the contrary, the inscription proves, from the accuracy of the pedigrees and the arms with the difference of second brother, that the family of Theodore Paleologus, had neither forgotten their Greek origin nor high descent, but still gloried in them, and were scrupulously exact in perpetuating the same.

" The names of Theodore and John occurring in this pedigree, and continued in the family of Theodore, are still stronger evidences. Camillo, Prosper, and Ferdinando, were probably acquired on their connection with Italian families.

"It would be absurd to make any conjectures as to the history of Theodore's predecessors, as we have no documents to warrant any conjecture. If we hazard any opinion at all, we may suppose, that when, in 1464, the Venetians under Vetorio Capelli warred against the Turks and attacked *Pattras*, Thomas's former residence, he probably joined them, perhaps fell there; and in the frequent wars which afterwards occurred between those powers, John, Theodore, Prosper, and Camillo, were probably not idle spectators, but joined against the common enemy, as well from a recollection of former wrongs, as a hope to regain some part of their ancient possessions. Indeed, their settlement at Pesaro might have been whilst the duchy of Urbino belonged to the Venetians, and in consideration of the part they took in those wars.

"Theodore Paleologus was born, we may infer from the inscription, at *Pesaro*. Of his mother we know nothing; his father was called *Camillo*. The time of his birth is also uncertain; though, from his marriage in 1615, *then a widower*, we may suppose him to be then about forty, which carries back his birth to 1575.

"Theodore's removal from Italy, and settlement in England, must have been either compulsive or voluntary. If the former, it was probably either on account,

"1. Of his religion; or,

"2. From other causes.

"As to the first, the Paleologus family, from the time of John II., were reconciled to and in union with the Latin church; and to this circumstance is probably to be attributed the protection afterwards afforded to Thomas by the Pope, perhaps through the interest of Cardinal Isidore, the resident nuncio at Constantinople. But the Greek church still differed very materially in many points from the Latin; and though Gregory XIII. founded a college at Rome for the education of the Greek children in the sciences and religion, (and here perhaps Theodore was educated), yet we find him opposing what he called the errors of the Greeks; and in particular, on his alteration of the calendar he is much incensed against them for refusing to receive it. And again, in the pontificate of Clement VIII. we find him particularly anxious to reform the Greek church, and much enraged at being imposed on by a pretended embassy from the metropolitan of Russia, which proved to be a forgery. If Theodore, as is most probable, was still of the Greek Church, these circumstances might have induced the Pope to withdraw the protection and support hitherto afforded to the family.—But if,

2. To other causes, is to be attributed Theodore's departure from Italy, it was perhaps from the rigid decree of *Sixtus* the Fifth, (about the year 1585), prohibiting foreigners from living at Rome, unless they brought a certificate that they were able by some trade or profession to maintain their families. If Theodore's family were then at Rome, and in dependance on the papacy, perhaps Sixtus might enforce this decree to rid himself of a family whose high descent he possibly regarded with a jealous eye, recollecting the meanness of his own origin. Or, the severe famine, which in 1590 afflicted all the ecclesiastical state, might oblige Theodore, among others, to emigrate to another country.

" If, on the other hand, Theodore's departure from Italy was voluntary, as is most probable, it might be from having formed some acquaintance, either with natives of this country, or with foreigners who were coming hither.

"About the same time that the Greek college was founded at Rome, (and where we may imagine Theodore to have had his education), another was founded called the Scotch college, for children of refugees from Scotland and England. Here we may suppose Theodore to have had some acquaintance; nor is it unlikely that when the jubilee in 1601 attracted a vast assemblage of persons from all countries to Rome, some one of these might have prevailed on Theodore to return to England with them. In the same year 1601, the Duke of Braciano, a neighbouring state to Pesaro, came to England, or rather Scotland, on a visit to the King of the Scots his relation. Did Theodore accompany him? Again, we may suppose him to have volunteered in the war against the Turks under Rodolph II. in whose army were many Englishmen, and in particular Sir Thomas Arundel, whose namesake, and probably friend, Thomas Arundel, resided at Clifton, the subsequent residence of

Theodore. Did he come over with him? If not, we may lastly imagine he came here through Sir Henry Killigrew, ambassador about this time to the Venetians or Genoese. The connection between the Arundel, Killigrew, and Lower families, give the most plausibility to the two last conjectures.

" But whatever may be our conjectures as to Theodore's removal from Italy, we know that in 1615 he was actually in England, at Hadley in Suffolk, and (then a widower) married Mary, daughter of William Balls, of that town. No traces of the Balls family remain at present, either from tradition or otherwise, except the register of Theodore's marriage; and even here, Mr. Wilkins, the minister, who has favoured me with a copy of this register, says that it is too mutilated and imperfect to decipher accurately the name of Paleologus.

"The issue of this marriage, as the monument tells us, were five children, Theodoro, John, Ferdinando, Maria, and Dorothy, all of whom must have been born before Theodore left the eastern part of the kingdom; for the register of Landulph, perfect till the year 1629, makes no mention whatever of the name. He could not therefore have settled at Clifton in Landulph earlier than 1622 or 1623.

"Clifton, a few years before this, in 1600, was the mansion of the Arundels; but in 1630, Sir Nicholas Lower, a Cornish gentleman, who married Sir Henry Killigrew's daughter, was living at Clifton. Between these two dates Paleologus must have come here; and what is more particular, he died at Clifton in 1636, at the very time that Clifton was the residence of Sir Nicholas Lower.

" I have made repeated inquiries of the old people of the parish, but not the slightest tradition remains respecting him; and here again conjecture must supply the place of fact. When Theodore came to Clifton, he came with his family, for by the register it appears one of his daughters married in the parish, and the other died here unmarried.

There must then have been some connection either between the Arundel or Lower families and himself.

"As to the first supposition, if it is probable he came into England with Sir Thomas Arundel from the battles in Hungary, we may suppose Sir Thomas recommended him to Landulph, as from its vicinity to the sea and warmth of climate, more nearly resembling the climate and situation of Pesaro than any other place in the kingdom. In this case we may suppose him to have taken Clifton for a term, and as the house appears to have been originally divided into two, the subsequent occupier, Sir Nicholas Lower and Paleologus, might be both living at Clifton at the same time, unconnected with each other.

"The more probable supposition, however, is, that he settled at Clifton from the connection that subsisted between Sir Henry Killigrew (who, I feel strongly inclined to believe, brought him to England) and Sir Nicholas Lower. Sir Nicholas Lower married Sir Henry's daughter, and as they were now advanced in life, without any family, the society of Paleologus and his children might be desirable to them; particularly when we recollect that this was the time when the Greek language was so much in fashion in England, that even ladies studied it most zealously; that Lady Killigrew was one of the learned daughters of Sir Anthony Cooke, celebrated for her literary attainments, and particularly her knowledge of Greek; and it is reasonable to suppose her daughter, Lady Lower, wife of Sir Nicholas, was brought up with the same fondness for the classic languages; and where could she expect to find so able an instructor as a descendant of the first family in the Greek empire; or what place could be more suited to classical pursuits than the retirement of a country mansion, such as Clifton.

"On the 21st of January 1636, as appears by the monument, Theodore Paleologus died at Clifton, Sir Nicholas and Lady Lower being still alive; of whom the latter died in 1638, and Sir Nicholas in 1655.

"The Landulph register, perfect from 1540 to 1628, has then a great chasm till the year 1649; and during this interval all the entries that would have been probably most interesting to our inquiries were made.

"Some little time since I examined the duplicates of parish registers, deposited in the room of archives in Exeter cathedral; and after a laborious search among the registers of two centuries, thrown promiscuously together without arrangement as to either parishes or dates, and those for the most part obliterated by the damp, I had the good fortune to recover the Landulph register for the year 1636, which had the following entry:

"'Theodore Palleologus was buryed the 20th daye of October.'

"By the monument Theodore is said to have died the 21st of January 1636; from the register it appears he was buried October 20, 1636. It can hardly be supposed the body was kept from January till October, and the difficulty is increased from the knowledge, that by the mode of calculation in use at that time, the year commenced at Ladyday; so that, if he died January 21, 1636, the 20th of October following must have been in 1637.

"The body, if it remained any considerable time uninterred, would have been inclosed in a lead coffin; but this was not the case, for about twenty years ago, when the vault was accidentally opened, the coffin of Paleologus was seen, a single oak coffin; and curiosity prompting to lift the lid, the body of Paleologus was discovered, and in so perfect a state as to ascertain him to have been in stature much above the common height, his countenance of an oval form, much lengthened, and strongly marked by an aqueline nose, and a very white beard reaching low on the breast.

"Of the five children left by him, no traces remain of two sons, John and Ferdinando. Whether they joined the brothers of Sir Nicholas Lower, who were distinguished cavaliers on the king's side in the unhappy wars that distracted the country soon after the death of Theodore, and in which Major Lower gallantly fell; or whether the miserable state of England induced them again to re-visit Italy, cannot be ascertained.

"Theodore was a sailor, and served on board the Charles II. Captain Gibson. He died at sea 1693, as appears by a will and power in the Commons, obligingly communicated to me by Francis Townsend, Esq. Windsor Herald. This is dated August 1, 1693, and solely in favour of his wife Martha. If he had any children they are not named in it. The signature is Theodore Paleologey; and though described simply as mariner, it should seem he was possessed of landed estate, as there are four witnesses, Charles Gibson, commander, J. Wright, John Corneth, Richard Roberts.

"Mary Paleologus died at Landulph unmarried in 1674; and her sister Dorothy was married in 1656 to William Arundel, the grandson probably of Alexander Arundel, of Clifton. This marriage is registered at Landulph and St. Mellion, as solemnised in both parishes; the entry at the latter is, ' Dorothea Paleologus de stirpe Imperatorum.' Soon after their marriage they settled in St. Dominick, an adjoining parish, the registers of which having been accidentally destroyed, it is impossible now to determine if they had any issue, though it seems highly probable. They were both buried at Landulph, Dorothy in 1681, and her husband in 1684; and as some years after, a Mary Arundel was married to Francis Lee, the imperial blood perhaps still flows in the bargemen of Cargreen !"

The manor of Landulph is traced back to the family of D'Alneto, from whom it passed to the Courtenays, and fell to the Crown on the attainder of Henry Courtenay, Marquis of Exeter, in 1539, soon after which it was annexed to the duchy of Cornwall.

The manor of Glebridge has passed through various families, and is now the property of Mr. Bluett.

But the principal place in this parish was Clifton. Sir John Arundell is said to have built the house about the year 1500. It is believed to have afterwards belonged to the Killigrews, as it passed in succession to Sir Nicholas Lower and Sir Reginald Mahon, who married the daughters of Sir Henry Killigrew. The former died without issue; and it was ultimately sold with the other property of the Mahons to Pitt.

The Lowers had their principal seat at St. Winnow, and were eminent during several successions. Some of this family were distinguished by their proficiency in science, and by their friendships with scientific men. This has been very recently made prominent in a work that cannot receive too much commendation, either for the accuracy, the ability, or for the industry displayed by its author. The Life of Dr. Bradley, by Stephen Peter Rigaud, M.A. Savilian Professor of Astronomy in Oxford, and Director of the Radcliffe Observatory, 1 vol. 4to. 1832.

Landulph measures 1564 statute acres.

	£.	s.	d.
Annual value of the Real Property as returned to Parliament in 1815 .	3596	0	0
Poor Rate in 1831	363	0	0

Population,—	in 1801,	in 1811,	in 1821,	in 1831,
	529	590	579	570

giving an increase of not quite 8 per cent. in 30 years.

Present Rector, the Rev. F. V. Jago, F.S.A. presented by the Prince of Wales, as Duke of Cornwall in 1805.

GEOLOGY, BY DR. BOASE.

Doctor Boase says of the geology of this parish, that it is situated like the last on the calcareous series, and that its rocks are similar.

LANEAST.

HALS.

The manuscript relating to this parish is lost.

LANEAST.

TONKIN.

Laneast is in the hundred of East. To the west of it is St. Clether, to the north Egloskerry, to the east Trewren, to the south Alternun.

This parish taketh its name from its situation to the east of St. Clether.

It is an impropriation, belonging formerly to the Priory of Launceston. The great tithes are at present in the hands of the Earl of Radnor (Robarts); and the small tithes, out of which seven pounds a-year are paid for the supply of the cure, are in the possession of Mr. Arthur Squire and Mr. King.

THE EDITOR.

This parish contains three villages, the Church Town, Badgall, and Trespearn.

The principal or only seat is Tregeare, belonging to the family of Baron.

The late Mr. Jaspar Baron either rebuilt or greatly improved the house. This gentleman was for some time a member of Pembroke College, Oxford, but did not proceed to a degree. He died in early life, leaving a son and a daughter. The son became a member of Wadham College, Oxford. He died unmarried, and still earlier than his father. The sister, heiress of the very considerable property possessed by this family, has married a son of the late Mr. Christopher Lethbridge, of Madford in Launceston.

The great tithes now belong to Mr. George Bennett, and the impropriate vicarage to Mr. Baron and Mr. Cook.

This parish measures 2111 statute acres.

	£.	s.	d.
Annual value of the Real Property as returned to Parliament in 1815,	851	0	0
Poor Rate in 1831	148	19	0

Population, — { in 1801, 179 | in 1811, 149 | in 1821, 229 | in 1831, 279 }

giving an increase of 56 per cent. in 30 years.

THE GEOLOGY, BY DR. BOASE.

The geology of this parish is precisely similar to that of the adjacent parish of St. Clether.

The northern part is situated on that range of downs which extends from Launceston to the British Channel. These downs consist principally of varieties of dunstone, which are sometimes felspathic; but in general they are very siliceous, and even quartzoze. They are interesting in an economical point of view, as containing extensive deposits of the ores of manganese. A mine of this substance has been long worked at Letcot in Laneast. The ores occur in a lode or cross course of capel, running north-east and south-west; the lode is about twelve fathoms in width, and is composed of siliceous materials, or rather varieties of compact felspar, in which silex greatly predominates. The ore is arranged throughout the substances of the lode in veins and branches. In the latter form it was originally discovered, not many feet below the surface, and in such abundance that it was obtained at a very trifling cost, for the hardness and tenacity of the capel permitted the ore to be followed in all its ramifications without needing support: and the result of these operations has been to produce a large chasm, with curiously irregular and indented sides.

LANHIDROCK.

HALS.

The manuscript relating to this parish is lost.

TONKIN.

Lanhidrock is in the hundred of Pider; hath to the west

Lanivet; to the north Bodmin; to the east Fowey river, between it and St. Winnow; to the south, Lanlivery.

This parish takes its name from St. Hidrock, and is the church of St. Hidrock.

This probably may be the manor that in Domesday is called the Lanredock; and if so, it is one of the manors given by William the Conqueror to Robert Earl of Morton, with the Earldom of Cornwall.

In the year sixteen hundred and .... John Lord Robarts, being disgusted on some occasion or other with the town of Truro, left his barony-house there, and new built a large one in this place, quadrangularwise, to which he added afterwards a noble gate-house, and enclosed a very handsome park, well-wooded, and watered by the river Fowey.

This noble lord was afterwards, in 1662, made Lord Privy Seal, in the place of William Lord Say, deceased. In Sept. 1669 he was made Lord Lieutenant of Ireland, but continued there no longer than the May following; and about this time he received the honour of being made Custos Rotulorum of Cornwall. In 1679, July 20, he was created Earl of Falmouth and Viscount Bodmin, but he kept the title of Falmouth only six days, when he got it changed to that of Radnor. In October of the same year he was made Lord President of the Council, in the room of Anthony Ashley Cooper, Earl of Shaftesbury. He was twice married, 1st. to the Lady Lucy Rich, daughter of Robert Rich, Earl of Warwick, by whom he had issue Robert Lord Viscount Bodmin. He married, secondly, a daughter of John Smith, Esq. of Kent, a lady of great beauty, who, it is said, was to have married his eldest son the Lord Bodmin; for which reason there was never a good understanding between the father and son. By her he had several children, the eldest of which was Francis Robarts, a very ingenious man, and a great mathematician, author of several small works. He was twice married, first to Penelope, daughter of Sir Courtenay Pole, of Devonshire, by whom he had no issue; secondly, to the Lady

Ann Fitzgerald, daughter of the Earl of Kildare, and widow of Mr. William Boscawen, of Tregothnan. The said John Robarts, Earl of Radnor, died at his house in Chelsea, very aged, July 17, 1685, and was brought to Lanhidrock, where he had constructed a vault for himself and family, and was succeeded by his grandson Charles Bodville Robarts.

Robert Robarts, Lord Bodmin, his father, was much esteemed by King Charles the Second, for his bright, lively parts and ready wit. He was sent Ambassador to the King of Denmark in July 1679-80, but died soon after his return. Charles Bodville Robarts, second Earl of Radnor, married Mary, the daughter and heir of Sir John Cutler, by whom he acquired a great accession of fortune, but no issue. He succeeded the Earl of Bath as Lord Lieutenant of Cornwall, and he was also Lord Warden of the Stanneries. He was succeeded by his nephew Mr. Henry Robarts.

Trefry, that is, the house on the hill, (for bre, bray, vre, fray, are synonymous terms, indicating a hill or a mountain,) adjoins Lanhidrock, and was formerly a barton belonging to the Trefrys of Fowey; although they took not their name from this place, but from Trefry in Linkinhorne. It now belongs to the Earl of Radnor, who keeps it as a domain to Lanhidrock. The Earl of Radnor's arms are, Azure, three estoiles, and a chief wavy Or; the crest, a lion rampant Or, holding a flaming sword Proper, the pommel Or; supporters, two goats Argent, with a ducal coronet round their necks Or; the motto, "QUÆ SUPRA;" which coat was thus given by John Robarts Earl of Radnor, but for what reason I cannot tell, since the arms of the family granted to Sir Richard Robarts, afterwards Baron Truro, by the celebrated William Camden, Clarencieux King-at-Arms, were, Azure, on a chevron Argent three mullets Sable, as may be seen in their house at Truro, and also in the church.

THE EDITOR.

Henry Robarts, the third Earl of Radnor, in possession of the property when Mr. Tonkin wrote, was succeeded by his cousin John Robarts, son of Francis Robarts, youngest son of John Robarts, the first Earl of Radnor; and with him, who died in 1764, the family became extinct in the male line; and the estate reverted to a sister's son of Henry Robarts, who had married Thomas Hunt, Esq. of Mellington in Cheshire.

Mr. George Hunt, the eldest son of this marriage, resided occasionally at Lanhidrock, and represented Bodmin in several Parliaments. This gentleman never married, and he was succeeded by his brother's daughter, Anna Maria, now (1834) the widow of the Hon. Charles Bagnal Agar: left with an only son, who has assumed the name of Robarts.

It is obvious that all families, to whatever degrees of elevation they may afterwards ascend, must at some period or another have emerged from the ordinary fortunes of mankind. At the time of the Norman Conquest, hundreds started forth at once by successful warfare and confiscation; others have risen or fallen by the chances of civil war, favouritism, marriages, adventures, or speculation in foreign countries, by professions, or commerce; these last have recently been more efficacious for ordinary individuals and families than force of arms.

The family of Robarts, illustrious as it has since been, derives its origin entirely from trade, and that too conducted in the town of Truro, now indeed, and for a century past, a place of opulence, and connected with a productive mining district, where several ample fortunes have been acquired; but in the reign of the Tudors it could have been no more than an obscure place in a remote province.

There is nothing known of any particularly fortunate occurrence which might have heaped wealth on this family;

they probably accumulated patiently through several generations from father to son, when the rate of interest on all capital gave a facility to the increase of wealth unknown at the present day. That the family made their progress in the world after this manner, is evinced by the nature of the possessions transmitted to their heirs. Extensive on the whole, but instead of being made up of large masses, like those acquired in feudal times, it mainly consists of small pieces of land scattered over the country, on which the successful merchant or dealer lent his superfluous money on mortgage, and afterwards entered into possession or foreclosed.

The first Lord Robarts, created a Baron through the influence of George Villiers Duke of Buckingham, with King James the First,* who emerged from Truro, and built or improved the house at Lanhidrock, and planted in all probability the magnificent avenues, must have been a man worthy of his high fortune.

The editor remembers the house, a complete square, with a superb barbican in front, united to the house, or rather castle, by two lofty walls.

These walls were first taken down, and then the front, by Mr. George Hunt, which he replaced by green palisades. This gentleman had the reputation of being a classical scholar, and he travelled into the south of Europe, where Taste once fixed her abode, and where she still lingers or loves often to return; but according to all the opinions now entertained, he never met her in his walks, nor profited by the contemplation of her works. Perhaps in his youth the prejudice had not disappeared which confined all the elegance and beauty of architecture to upright pillars with horizontal cornices, and esteemed the word Gothic as of the same import with barbarous, and inviting destruction wherever it was applied.

This parish was heretofore a complete impropriation to the priory at Bodmin, in respect to small tithes as well as the great; and being situated so near the monastery, it was

---

* See Nichols's Progresses, &c. of King James, iii, 230.

LANHIDROCK. 383

probably served from thence, and considered as exempt from the canon enjoining the residence of some spiritual person on all benefices, and it has continued a donative to the present time. Mr. Tonkin conjectures that the parish is dedicated to a Saint Hydrock, or Hidrock. No such name is to be found; but it may belong to the list of missionaries.

The Editor remembers to have heard as facts, from an old lady of Bodmin, who died many years before the words 'political economy,' were pronounced in England, that the last Lord Radnor kept house at Lanhidrock in the style of ancient baronial magnificence; that a bullock was killed every week, and a sheep every day; and that whatever remained over-night of meat, of broken bread, or of certain allowed quantities of beer, were on the morning distributed at the gate; and that in consequence the whole neighbourhood became idle, depraved, and vicious, to such a degree as to force itself on the notice of every one, and to produce a full conviction of the utter destruction that must ensue if it were possible that such mistaken liberality could be common.

The manor of Lanhidrock belonged in former times to the Glynns, of Glynn. Mr. Lysons says that it passed from them as a marriage portion to the family of Lyttleton, and from them by a heiress to Trenance; and that in the year 1620 Lyttleton Trenance, Esq. sold it to Sir Richard Roberts, afterwards created Lord Truro. Mr. Tonkin has stated that this gentleman built the house; but the whole place has the appearance of much greater antiquity: that he improved and decorated the building, and perhaps added the barbican and the connecting walls, is very probable.

Lanhidrock measures 1659 statute acres.

	£.	s.	d.
Annual value of the Real Property as returned to Parliament in 1815	1213	0	0
Poor Rate in 1831	137	6	0

Population, —	in 1801,	in 1811,	in 1821,	in 1831,
	187	235	251	239

giving an increase of 28 per cent. in 30 years.

GEOLOGY, BY DR. BOASE.

The south-western corner of this parish touches on the granite; the rest is composed of rocks belonging to the porphyritic series, being principally varieties of compact and schistose felspar rocks, containing mica or horneblende, or a mineral of an intermediate nature, not easily discriminated.

LANIVET.

HALS.

The manuscript relating to this parish is lost.

TONKIN.

Lanivet, in the hundred of Pider, hath to the west Withiel, to the north and east Bodmin and Lanhydrock, to the south St. Roach, Luxilian, and Lanlivery.

This parish is a rectory, valued in the King's books at 24l. The patronage in Kelland Courtenay, Esq. and the heirs of Anthony Nicholl, Esq. of Penrose, *alternis vicibus*. The incumbent Mr. Vasnoom.

A. D. 1291, 20th Edward the First (the valuation of Pope Nicholas) this Church is rated at 8l. having never been appropriated.

In treating of the estates of this parish, I shall begin with Tremere, the great town, called in Domesday book Tremer, being one of the numerous manors in this county given by William the Conqueror to his half brother, Robert Earl of Morton, with the Earldom of Cornwall. Mr. Carew calls it Tremore.

It had formerly owners of the same name, who, I suppose, held it in vassalage under the Earls of Cornwall;

LANIVET.

they gave for their arms, Argent, three reap-hooks conjoined in the blades Sable. The last of whom was John Tremere, Esq. of this place, who left two daughters and heirs; Alice, married to Geoffrey St. Aubyn, of Clowance, Esq. which Alice, as appears by the inscription on her husband's tomb-stone in Crowan church, died the 1st of May 1400.

And ....

This place hath been for several generations the seat of the Courtenays, whom I take to be a younger branch of those of Trethurfe, to whom they have at length been heirs; for the present owner's grandfather, Humphry Courtenay, Esq. during many years, and up to his decease, Representative in Parliament for the borough of Michell, married the daughter of Sir Peter Courtenay, of Trethurfe, and eventually sole heiress to her brother William Courtenay.

Their son, William Courtenay, married the daughter of —— Kelland, of Peynsford in Devonshire, and their son Kelland Courtenay, Esq. is the present possessor, 1734; Member of Parliament for Truro; he has two daughters, both as yet unmarried.

THE EDITOR.

On the decease of Mr. Charles Courtenay, son of the last-mentioned Kelland Courtenay in 1761, all the property devolved on his two sisters; one of whom married William Poyntz, Esq. of Berkshire, and the other Edmund Boyle, Earl of Cork.

Tremere, with much of the other property, has been sold; and Mr. William Stephen Poyntz has acquired the Boyle share of what remains.

This extensive parish contains several villages. The Church Town, Bodwanick, Bokiddick, Lamorick, St. Inganger, Trebell, Tregullan, Tremoore, and Woodly, with a part of St. Lawrence, the locality of an ancient incorporated lazar-house.

The church and tower may be considered as handsome models of western ecclesiastic architecture, where all are superior to the average of other districts. This tower, as well as the adjoining one of Roach, are without the usual ornament of pinnacles.

In the church are some monuments; one to the memory of Mr. Richard Courtenay and Thomasin his wife, dated in 1632, is remarkable for its simplicity and quaintness of its inscription:

> They lived and died both in Tremere,
> God hath their souls, their bones lie here,
> Richard with Thomsen his loved wife,
> Lived sixty-one years—then ended life.

The advowson of this parish was purchased about the middle of the last century by Mr. Phillipps, a substantial yeoman of Roach; and the Editor has heard for a thousand pounds. It now belongs to his great-grandson, the Reverend William Phillipps, who is the Rector.

This parish possesses the curious and interesting remains of a convent or female monastery, dedicated to St. Bennet.

Very little is known of its history. The remote, and in former times almost inaccessible, situation of Cornwall, and perhaps the frequent insurrections during the reign of Henry the Seventh and of Edward the Sixth, have involved the history of its religious institution in a greater obscurity than what hangs over any other part of England.

This nunnery is believed to have been a cell to some foreign convent; and it is not certainly known whether it was entirely suppressed by Henry the Fifth, or whether, as some have conjectured, it became attached to the priory of Bodmin, and remained a parcel of that house till the general dissolution.

It belonged for a considerable period to the Courtenays

of Tremere, and in a state of repair, for there is a tradition of its having made some defence in the great Civil War, till cannon were used against it.

It was sold in the year 1710; and about ten years afterwards became the property of Mr. Grose, a farmer of the parish. His son or grandson, about the year 1775, built a new house on the farm, when some remains of a beautiful cloister, which the Editor faintly remembers, afforded a ready supply of materials. It is said, that Mr. George Hunt, of Lanhidrock, more impressed by the elegance of these ruins than by the splendour of his own house, interfered to the extent of remonstrance for their preservation; but when the proprietor replied that he would willingly spare them, if the difference of expense for getting stone from a neighbouring quarry were paid him, nothing further was done.

The mere site of the building has been purchased within twenty years by the Rev. Francis Vyvyan Jago Arundell, Rector of Landulph; and in the present year this sequestered spot—scarcely visible in any direction at the distance of half a mile, inclosed in a deep vale, and surrounded by trees more lofty than its half-ruined tower; the appropriate retreat of those who choose their lot—

> The world forgetting, by the world forgot,
> Where round some mould'ring tow'r pale ivy creeps,
> And low-brow'd rocks hang nodding o'er the deeps;

—is by the progress of recent improvement laid open to public view, and above all to the inspection of strangers. A hill so steep as to be dangerous for carriages, and extending to a mile in length, has been avoided, by conducting the London road through this valley, which, after an interval, perhaps, of a thousand years from the time when it was devoted to superstitious observances, directly opposed to the benevolence inseparable from the Author of all Good, and congenial only to the demon of evil, has at last become subservient to general utility.

This parish is possessed of certain lands, some within its

own limits, but others at considerable distances in other parishes. These are held by twelve feoffees, called the twelve men of the parish, a species of select vestry, which existed in all large parishes in Cornwall down to the early part of the last century, till it was tacitly done away by those improvident or insane acts of the legislature, made no doubt in conformity with the existing prejudices of the times, which have generated a rapidly increasing tribe of lazzaroni, threatening, if their progress cannot now be checked, most infallibly to reduce this once flourishing country, the favoured seat of arts, of science, of morals, and of legitimate refinement, to a state of vice and of degradation, worse than that of savages in their primeval condition of wandering hunters.

The rents are applied to the support of a school, and to some specific charities, and the surplus given in aid of the poor rate.

Mr. Lysons says, that these lands belonged to Credys in Padstow, a cell to St. Bennet's. This does not, however, seem to be very probable, considering the nature of St. Bennet's foundation. It is more likely that the lands were the immediate possession of this convent; and no such place as Credys is noticed by Tanner.

The history of Lanivet would here close, but the Editor hopes that he may be allowed to bestow a few lines on the Reverend John Lake, Rector of this parish more than thirty years; possessed of learning, piety, and benevolence,

In wit a man, simplicity a child.

He was educated in Truro, according to a custom evidently derived from Catholic times, in the acquirement of some classical knowledge, and then placed in an inferior line of business at Leskeard, where at that period resided Mr. Heydon as schoolmaster, an ornament to his country by every species of learning and of acquirement. Here Mr. Lake, forgetful of his having married early in life, and of a growing family, devoted his time to assisting Mr. Heydon, and in obtaining knowledge from his conversation, till on a sudden he found himself deprived of his wife, left with two daughters, and his business failed.

Thus circumstanced, Mr. Lake placed the two daughters with his father; and having collected a hundred and thirty pounds, he proceeded to Oxford, became a member of Magdalen Hall, and contrived, on this scanty supply, to keep terms and to obtain orders. He then returned into Cornwall, served the curacy of Roach, and there married the daughter or sister of Mr. Phillipps, who had purchased the advowson of Lanivet; and a vacancy occurring in the course of a few years, he obtained the rectory.

Here he again became a widower, and married a third time Miss Bridget Hoblin, of Bodmin, by whom he had two sons. The eldest became a Fellow of Wadham, and the other of Exeter College. Both his daughters were dead; and in May 1805, Mr. Lake departed this life, having completed his 76th year, in peace with all men, having been pious without fanaticism, and to the utmost of his power, a practiser of the good doctrines which he taught.

His widow was left with a competence; and his sons were advanced by their merits and their talents into situations at once honourable and lucrative; but permanent happiness in this world was not to be their lot. William went to sea, and was lost with Admiral Reynolds in a first rate ship of the line; and the second, after struggling with a consumption, expired in his mother's arms.

Lanivet measures 4690 statute acres.

	£.	s.	d.
Annual value of the Real Property, as returned to Parliament in 1815	4086	0	0
Poor Rate in 1831	375	12	0

Population,	in 1801,	in 1811,	in 1821,	in 1831,
	513	687	803	922

giving an increase of 80 per cent. in 30 years.

GEOLOGY, BY DR. BOASE.

The southern part of the parish reposes on granite; and proceeding northward, the next portion is composed of rocks of the porphyritic series, which are again succeeded by those of the calcareous series. The middle portion is by far the most extensive, the other two occupying only a narrow part, on the extreme southern and northern parts of the parish. The middle, or porphyritic series, presents the most interesting phenomena.

Lanivet Hill is covered with large boulders and projecting torrs of massive rock, which have the appearance of granite; but on examination it proves to be a felspar rock. The greater part of this hill is composed of lamellar and slatey varieties of the same kind of rock, as may be seen in the rubbish of the numerous shafts that occur on the side of this hill. On the road to Bodmin, near the boundary of the parish, is a very interesting elvan course. The upper part of it is completely decomposed, resembling a mass of prepared China clay; the perfect rock is a greenish yellow compact felspar, with disseminated grains of quartz; it bears the same relation to the porcelainous granite of this and of the adjoining parishes, that the hard porphyritic elvans do to the common Cornish granite, near which they generally occur.

LANLIVERY.

HALS.

The manuscript relating to this parish is lost.

TONKIN.

Lanlivery is situate in the hundred of Powder, and hath to the west Luxilian, to the north Lanivet and Lanhidrock; to the east Lestwithiel and the river Fowey; between it and St. Winnow, to the south, Tywardreth and Golant.

LANLIVERY.

The name Lanlivery signifies the church of bucks; for livrou in Cornish is the plural of levar, or livar, a buck; but for what reason I cannot so much as guess. This parish is sometimes called Lanvorch, the church of St. Vorch, to whom it is dedicated.

It is a vicarage, valued in the King's books at 13*l*. 6*s*. 8*d*. The patron, Walter Kendall, of Pelyn, Esq.; the incumbent, his father, Mr. Archdeacon Nicholas Kendall.

In 1291, the 20th of Edw. I. this church was valued at 9*l*. 11*s*. 8*d*. for the rectory, and the vicarage at 15*s*. being the appropriate to the priory of Trewardreath.

Since the writing of the above I have thought upon another etymology, which I believe to be the true one; that this name is no other than a softening of Lan-le-Vorch, St. Vorch's church-place, which is a very easy and natural alteration.

THE EDITOR.

The church and town of Llanlivery are very conspicuous objects for miles round, and especially from the Plymouth or great southern road.

The church contains various monuments to the family of Kendall. This family were originally of Treworgy, in the parish of Dulo, but have long resided at Pelyn, in this parish. The house is beautifully situated in a small wooded valley, joining in a transverse course the river Fowey, about a mile below Lestwithiel. There appears to be a vague tradition of some religious establishment having existed here, dedicated to St. Chad, or Ceada, the patron of Lichfield, Worcester, and Shrewsbury. No trace, however, can be found of any such establishment; and it is probable that these tales frequently rest on no more solid foundation that the casual residence of some monk or anchorite, or perhaps on the dedication of a domestic chapel. There still exists at Pelin a small summer house, considered as under the protection of this saint; and an inscription records the festivities and friendly meetings of four gentlemen annually on the 2d of March, to commemorate the day, when, according to the legend, this Saint expired amid a company of angels, singing hymns for the solace of his dying moments, and for joy of such an accession to the heavenly mansions.

The inscription is as follows, under a portrait of the Saint:

> Friend, within these walls St. Chad you see,
> A place made sacred to his memory,
> For here four friends did meet upon this day,
> And heads, and hands, and hearts together lay;
> And never dying friendship's knot to tye,
> And call this place St Chad's Society.
> March 2, 1694.

The glory of this parish, however, is Restormel Castle, but these buildings have been so amply described by almost every writer on Cornish antiquities, that it would be idle to repeat what has been so often done. It presents one of the finest objects in the whole country.

Richard, King of the Romans, is believed to have kept court here, and in his more commodious habitation at Lestwithiel, and he was the last who exercised even the semblance of independent authority. The earldom and dukedom of Cornwall have, since his time, done no more than afford a revenue and bestow a name, like the shadows of a shade, with which the private gentlemen, holding hereditary seats in Parliament at the present time, continue to decorate themselves, by assuming the verbal denominations of offices extinct above three centuries, and which habit alone enables us to pronounce, as applicable to them, without a smile; but which offices, like the ancient earldom of Cornwall, while they had any existence, conferred real feudal sovereignty, proportionate to their different degrees.

The palace at Lestwithiel has degenerated into a prison for the stannary courts; and that town no longer witnessing the county election, nor holding any of its own, may still boast of its being in some degree at the head of a duchy jurisdiction.

There is a handsome seat almost at the foot of Restormel Hill now called Restormel, but formerly Trinity. It seems to have been built after leases of the park were granted by the Crown. It has passed through various hands, and finally into those of the Edgecumbe family, who have been supposed desirous, up to very recent times, of acquiring all species of property, and, most of all, gentlemen's residences, situated near Lestwithiel.

The late Mr. Francis Gregor lived here in 1790, when he was first elected member for the county, and it is at present held under Lord Mount Edgecumbe by Mr. Francis Hext, a gentleman of ancient family and ample fortune, and universally esteemed.

This parish measures 5,951 statute acres.

	£.	s.	d.
Annual value of the Real Property as returned to Parliament in 1815,	5,232	0	0
Poor Rates in 1831	622	17	0

Population, —	in 1801,	in 1811,	in 1821,	in 1831
	778	965	1,318	1,687

giving an increase of 117 per cent in 30 years.

Present Vicar, the Rev. Nicholas Kendall, instituted in 1815.

GEOLOGY, BY DR. BOASE.

A gently undulating line, drawn north and south through this parish, a little to the eastward of the church, would divide it into two parts; of which, the western is the larger, and rests entirely on granite; the eastern division on schistose rock. Both of which exactly resemble those of St. Blazey, already described.

LANREATH.

HALS.

The manuscript relating to this parish is lost.

LANREATH.

TONKIN.

Lanreath is situate in the hundred of West, and hath to the west St. Veep, to the east Duloe, to the south Pelynt. This parish, in the taxation of Pope Nicholas, is called Lanraithow, by Mr. Carew Lanrethon, and the same in the King's book.

Rhaith is in old British a law; Rhaithow the law; so that it signifieth the church of laws, or of the laws, according to this etymology, which I will not venture to say is a true one, but it is the best that I can give at present.

This church is a rectory, valued in the King's book at 32*l*. The presentation in John Francis Buller, Esq. by purchase from the late Charles Grills, Esq. The incumbent, Mr. Richard Grills, only brother of the late patron.*

As I take Court to be the head place of this manor, from whence it is so called, to have been the chief seat of these Seriseauxes, I shall here insert what I find of them.

Richard de Seriseaux or Cereseaux, junior, was one of the men-at-arms who had 40*l*. in rent of lands 17th Edward II. (Carew, p. 139, Lord Dunstanville's edition).

Richard de Cereseaux, I suppose father to the former, was one of those that had 20*l*. per annum of lands or rent, or more, 25 Edward I., and was summoned to attend the King, and to go into parts beyond sea.

Richard Sargeaux, son, I believe, of the former, was Sheriff of this county the 12th of Richard II. A.D. 1389. This I take to be the same person with that Richard de Seriseaux who sold his estate in the 3d of Henry IV. He held lands also in Kelland and Kilkoid in the hundred of Trigg. Carew, p. 126.†

---

* Mr. Grills dying in 1735, has been succeeded by Mr. Heal Trelawney, on the presentation of Mr. Butler.

The parish is printed Laurayton in the Taxatio Ecclesiastica Papæ Nicholai; but the u and n may have been easily mistaken in the manuscript.

It is rated in the Taxation 6*l*. 6*s*. 8*d*. Decimæ 12*s*. 8*d*.

† Carew says, p. 125 of Lord Dunstanville's edition, Richard de Seriseaux ten 3 parv. feod. de Mort. in Lanrethan, Kilgather, et Lansalwys. THE EDITOR.

This Sir Richard Ceriseaux or Sergieaux, for he was knighted, had one only daughter and heiress, called Alice, who first was married to Sir Guy St. Alban, Knt. and secondly, to Richard de Vere, Earl of Oxford; and, thirdly, to Sir Nicholas Throwley, Knt. By the first she had issue; and the last Earl of Oxford of the Veres, Aubrey de Vere, who died in 1702, quartered her arms, Argent, a saltire Sable, between twelve cherries slipped Proper; from whence I guess that Sergiaux was only by way of abbreviation, their coat alluding to his name, *cerise* being in French a cherry. This Sir Richard Ceriseaux must have lived to a great age, since his great-grandson, Geffrey St. Aubin, Esq. was Sheriff of Cornwall but ten years after him, in 22d Richard II. A.D. 1399, or, I rather suppose, that this Sir Richard Ceriseaux may have left a son, who was the Sheriff, and that upon his death, without issue, Alice his sister became the heir.

THE EDITOR.

It appears from Mr. Lysons's researches, that the manor of Lanreath, with the barton of Court, passed from the Serjeaux to Pashleys, Chudleys, and Chamonds, from which last they were carried by heiresses to Trevanion and Grylls.

William Grylls, of Tavistock, is said in a pedigree of that family to have married the widow of Knight, and to have settled at Court in Lanreath; perhaps this lady was the coheiress of Chamond.

Their son, Charles Grylls, bred to the higher department of the law, married Agnes, daughter of Charles Tubb, Esq. and by this marriage a very considerable property was acquired in the parish of St. Neot, where one of the painted windows, the sixth, had been given by the Tubbs; but where their descendant the Reverend Richard Gerveys Grylls has, with equal taste and munificence, raised the splendid decorations of this church to a degree of perfection exceeding that of their original state, although they are some of the most curious and beautiful specimens of the arts and of the piety of former times, that have escaped the fury of passions excited by great changes in religion and in civil government. See Mr. Hedgeland's coloured prints of the sixteen windows, with descriptions of each, and the life of St. Neot, from Capgrove, 1 vol. 4to.; printed for the Author, No. 6, Claremont-place, Brunswick-square, and sold by Nichols and Son, Parliament-street, London, price 2*l*. 2*s*.

The church, which is a fine one with a lofty tower, yet almost obscured by trees, has a monument recording the decease of Charles Grylls, Esq. on the 2d of March 1612, and of Alice his wife on the 13th of June 1607.

Their son, John Grylls, took a part in the Civil War, as indeed every Cornish gentleman was obliged to do, on one side or the other; for in Cornwall, which might well have been conjectured likely to remain almost free from actual conflicts, two considerable armies were routed in pitched battles, and two still larger were forced to capitulate.

This gentleman was knighted by King Charles the First on the field of battle. He married Grace, daughter and coheiress of William Bear, Esq. A monument in Lanreath church testifies that he was buried there on the 30th day of September 1649.

Their eldest son, Charles, resided on his estate in this parish, and married a lady of the family of Mahon.

John, his son and heir, resided also at Court; he married Elizabeth, daughter and sole heiress of Richard Gerveys, Esq.

Charles, their eldest son, married Mary, daughter of Edmund Spoure, Esq. of Trebartha, but died without issue. This gentleman sold the manor of Lanreath, with the barton of Court and the advowson of the living appended, to Mr. Buller, of Morval. His brother, the Reverend Richard Grylls, held the living till his decease in 1735; and succeeded his elder brother as heir of the family property.

His son, Richard Grylls, settled at Helston, where he married Cordelia, daughter, and eventually heiress, of Thomas Glynn, Esq. descended from the Glynns, of Glynn.

Their son is the Reverend Richard Gerveys Grylls. It would be presumptuous in the Editor to attempt any particular praise of this gentleman, universally esteemed and respected.

The manor of Botelett is stated by Mr. Lysons to have belonged at an early period to the family of Botreaux, the last of whom, Lord Botreaux, died in the year 1462, leaving an only daughter, who married Robert Lord Hungerford.

It has in more recent times belonged to the families of Roberts and Treville. It became divided by coheiresses of the latter between Trelawny and Cross; and the latter half has passed to the family of Lethbridge in Somersetshire. The manor of Treyer is also stated by Mr. Lysons to have been the joint property of Rashleigh and Glynn; but in consequence of an exchange to be now Mr. Glynn's solely; and that Trewen, a seat of the Dandys, and Trecan, a seat of the Lowers, are now farm-houses.

Lanreath measures 4353 statute acres.

	£.	s.	d.
Annual value of the Real Property, as returned to Parliament in 1815 .	3110	0	0
Poor Rate in 1831	485	8	0

Population,— | in 1801, | in 1811, | in 1821, | in 1831, |
| --- | --- | --- | --- |
| 478 | 548 | 629 | 651 |

giving an increase of 36 per cent. in 30 years.

Present Rector, the Rev. Stephen Puddicombe, presented by John Buller, Esq. in 1827.

GEOLOGY, BY DR. BOASE.

This parish is entirely situated within the calcareous series; its rocks are similar to those of Boconnock and Duloe.

LANSALLOS.

HALS.

The manuscript relating to this parish is lost.

TONKIN.

Lansallos is in the hundred of West, and hath to the west Lanteglos juxta Fowey, to the north and east Pelynt and Tallant, to the south the English Channel.

This church is a rectory, valued in the King's book at 18*l*. The patronage in Thomas Long, Esq. as heir to the Speccots. The incumbent Cummin.[*] The church was valued for Pope Nicholas in 1291 at 5*l*. 6*s*. 8*d*. and the tenths 10*s*. 8*d*. under the name of Lansalewys, having never been appropriated.

Richard de Seriseaux held (3 Henry IV.) three small fees de Mort. in Lanrethon, Kilgather, et Lansalwys. (See Carew, p. 125, Lord de Dunstanville's edition, quoted in Lanreath). But however this may be, it is quite certain that the family of Boligh had been possessed of property here long before that time, for here lived John Boligh, who married the daughter of Killigarth. He was succeeded by his eldest son William Boligh, who by Avice, the daughter of Richard Pentine, had issue a son, of his own name, which last William, by Isabel, the daughter of William Bodrigan, afterwards married to Ralph Vivian, had issue one sole daughter and heir, married to John Kelliow, who brought with her this manor, which continued the principal seat of this family, although they have sometimes lived at Lanleke in South Pederwyn, and sometimes at Rosesilian in St. Biazey. Here they flourished in good esteem, having married the heiresses of

[*] Died in 1730, or a few years afterwards.

Leveddon, Trehawke, and Trefusis of Landew, and matched into several considerable families of this county, until such time as Christopher Kelliow, of Lanlake, Esq. having first mortgaged it to pay the debts of the family, at last sold the property outright to John Speccot, of Penheale, Esq.; and this is gone with the rest, or with the major part of Col. Speccot's estate, as he devised it by will, to Thomas Long, of Penheale, Esq. who is the present lord of this manor.

The arms of Kelliow, Or, a chevron between two cinquefoils and a mullet pierced Sable.

This manor is one of those given by William the Conqueror to the Earl of Morton.

THE EDITOR.

This church is situated on very high ground; and one of the stations for the great trigonometrical survey was chosen immediately by it. When the latitude and longitude were determined, latitude, $50°\ 20'\ 25.7''$; longitude, $4°\ 32'\ 45.7'$; in time, 18m. 11s. west of Greenwich. Besides the church town, this parish contains three villages, Tregavethick, Tregou, and Trenewan.

The manor of Lansallas has been traced by Mr. Tonkin to Mr. Thomas Long, of Penheale.

Mr. Long left three daughters, as has been noticed under Egloskerry. One of these ladies married Mr. Charles Phillipps, of Camelford, Lieutenant-Colonel of the Cornwall Militia, and Member for Camelford. Neither of the sisters had any family; and on a division of the property, this manor came to Mr. Phillipps, who left it jointly to his two brothers, Jonathan Phillipps, a Captain in the Militia, and the Reverend William Phillipps, Rector of Lanteglos by Camelford. The former gave his share of this manor to his sister's daughter, married to her relation Mr. Winsloe, directing them to take the name of Phillipps; the latter gave his portion to his sister's son, Mr. John Phillipps Carpenter, of Mount Tavy, from whom the shares have respectively descended to Thomas Phillipps, Esq. of Landue, and to John Carpenter, Esq. of Mount Tavy.

Mr. Lysons mentions the manor of Raphel, formerly Rathwell, which belonged to the family of Hywis, and was sold to Speccot; and has followed the great manor of Lansallas, to which the rectory is appended.

The manor of Tregavithick belonged to the family of Avery, but has been purchased by the Rev. Joshua Howell.

The manor of Polvethan belongs to Mr. Rashleigh, of Menabilly.

The most remarkable place, situated partly in this parish, is Polperro, a small town lying on a cove, rendered secure for coasting vessels by a double pier, and affording an admirable staking for the fisheries. It was also distinguished for a precarious trade, occasionally heaping great wealth on individuals, but in general taking it away more rapidly than it accumulated.

Hinc apicem rapax
Fortuna, cum stridore acuto
Sustulit, hic posuisse gaudet.

Quem dies vidit veniens superbum,
Hunc dies vidit fugiens jacentem.

This is, however, at an end, or greatly diminished. The situation of the place is romantic and wild, so that an excursion from Fowey, along the cliffs to Looe, through Polperro, is one of the most interesting on the whole coast of Cornwall.

This parish measures 2774 statute acres.

	£.	s.	d.
Annual value of the Real Property as returned to Parliament in 1815	3218	0	0
Poor Rate in 1831	616	18	0

Population,—	in 1801,	in 1811,	in 1821,	in 1831,
	847	804	880	884

giving an increase of little more than 4 per cent. in 30 years.

Present Rector, the Rev. William Rawlins, jun. instituted in 1822; son of the Vicar of Padstow.

THE GEOLOGY, BY DR. BOASE.

The rocks of this parish belong to the calcareous series. A little north-west of the church a copper mine has been worked; among the rubbish of which a fine blue slate is very abundant, but which appears to differ from the rocks at the surface, merely by those having acquired a red colour from further oxidation of the iron. The strata near the coast dip landward at an angle of about 45º, being broken here and there by narrow gorges, through which the rivulets flow into the sea. At Polperro the scenery is very fine; and the narrow entrance into the harbour, which seems to indicate some great catastrophe, is an object much interest to the speculative geologist.

LANTEGLOS, juxta CAMELFORD.

HALS.

The manuscript relating to this parish is lost.

TONKIN.

Lanteglos by Camelford is situate in the hundred of Lesnewith; and hath to the west St. Teath; to the north Tintagell; to the east Davidstow; to the south Advent alias St. Anne, and Michaelstow.

This parish is a rectory, valued in the King's Book, together with Advent, at 34*l*. 11*s*. 2*d*. The patronage in the Duke of Cornwall. The incumbent Dr. Lombard.

This parish is wholly within the manor of Helstone in Trigg, so termed to distinguish it from that in the west called Helstone in Kerrier, they both having the same lord, that is the Duke of Cornwall. This parish is now said to be in the hundred of Lesnewith; yet formerly, when the three northern hundreds of Trigg, Lesnewith, and Stratton composed but two, Trigg Major and Trigg Minor, it was in the hundred of Trigg Minor, in which deanery it is still reckoned as to the ecclesiastical jurisdiction.

The manor takes its name from its once chief place, though now but a village, about a mile to the west of Camelford. Here, I suppose, the Duke had a castle; for there were two parks, which, though now disparked, do still retain the name. They are adjoining to this village; the one called the Deer Park, and the other Hellesbury Park, the walls of which are still standing; and the latter of the two is of large extent, formerly well wooded, and watered by the river Alan, being a place exceedingly well fitted for country sports; and no doubt, when the Earls of Cornwall held their Court at Tintagel Castle, this place was in much repute, not being five miles distant from it.

These two parks are now held by a lease of three lives from the Duke of Cornwall, by Mr. Nicholas Dennithorne of St. Agnes.

I next come to the town of Camelford, so called from the ford here over the Alan; "called also," saith Mr. Camden, " Comb Alan and Camel from its winding channel, for Cam with them implies as much."

At the head of this river Alan is seated Camelford, otherwise written Galleford,— a little village, formerly called Kambton, in the opinion of Leland, who tells us that Arthur, the British Hector, was slain here. For, as he adds, pieces of armour, rings, and brass furniture for horses, are sometimes digged up here by the countrymen; and, after so many ages, the tradition of a bloody victory in this place is still preserved. There are also extant some verses of a middle age poet, about " Camels" running with blood after the battle of Arthur against Mordred.

In the mean time, not to deny the truth of this story concerning Arthur, I have read in Marianus, mentioned also in the Saxon Chronicle, of a bloody battle here between the Britons and Saxons in the year 820, so that the place may seem to be sacred to Mars. And if it be true that Arthur was killed here, the same shore both gave him his first breath and deprived him of his last. Harrison also saith, that to this day men that do eare (till) the ground there, do oft plough up bones of a large size, and great store of armour; or else it may be (as I rather conjecture) that the Romans had some field or castra there about, for not long since (and in the remembrance of men) a brass pot full of Roman coins was found there, as I have often heard.

To these Mr. Carew adds (p. 288, Lord de Dunstanville's edition) "Camelford, a market and fair, but not fair town, fetcheth his derivation from the river Camel, which runneth through it, and that from the Cornish word Cam, in English crooked, as Cam from the often winding stream. The same is incorporated with a mayoralty, and nameth burgesses to Parliament; yet steppeth little before the meanest sort of boroughs for store of inhabitants, or the inhabitants' store. Upon the river of Camel, near to Camelford, was that last dismal battle stricken between the noble King Arthur and his treacherous nephew Mordred, wherein the one took his death, and the other his death-wound. For testimony whereof, the old folk thereabouts will shew you a stone, bearing Arthur's name, though now depraved to Atry." Then follows what is before quoted out of Mr. Camden.

Mr. Willis, in his Notitia Parliamentaria, says, Camelford was created a borough by Richard Earl of Cornwall, who, when King of the Romans, by his charter made this place a free borough, and granted the burgesses a Friday market, and a fair on the eve, day, and morrow of St. Swithin, all which liberties were confirmed by his brother King Henry the Third, by his charter, dated at Westminster June the 12th, 1259, and in the 44th year of his reign, as appears from an inspeximus in Queen Mary's time, of confirmation of liberties to Camelford, in whose reign this poor borough was encouraged to send burgesses to Parliament, which it had begun to do in the preceding reign of Edward the Sixth. The present charter of incorporation is said to be granted by King Charles the First; and the manor of the borough to be held by the corporation of the duchy of Cornwall to which it belongs. It is governed by a mayor and eight burgesses or aldermen, who with ten freemen, elect the members of Parliament.

The corporation, which is doubtless ancient, enjoys the tolls of the markets and fairs, with an estate also of 15*l.* per annum, which helps to support the dignity of otherwise a very mean magistracy. All these revenues are reputed worth about 80*l.* per annum. The seal of arms pretended to by this town, seems to be in imitation of the device of Oxford, for as the arms of that city are an ox passant over a river, so this has a camel.*

Here is only one street of ordinary building, of not above fifty or sixty houses, all of which are in the parish of Lanteglos; to the church of which place, distant about a mile, the inhabitants repair to hear divine service. There was formerly a chapel, which is reported to have been converted into a dwelling-house: it is not known to what saint this chapel was dedicated.

Dodridge's History of the Duchy of Cornwall tells us, that the chief rent payable to the said Duchy by this borough, is 4*l.* 5*s.* 4*d.*

THE EDITOR.

The manor of Helston in Trigg is of very considerable extent. Mr. Lysons says, that the ancient site or barton

---

* The device used for arms by the City of Oxford, has evidently been derived from a corruption of Ouse Ford into Oxford, which has also given rise to the tale of the Empress Matilda escaping from thence on an Ox's back.

The Saxons or Normans, unacquainted with the Celtic language, mistook cam or camel for the name of an animal of which they had read in the Gospels.

of the manor is supposed to have been at Michaelstow Beacon, called St. Syth's, where vestiges remain of a camp. Besides the town of Camelford, this parish abounds in villages: Fenterwarson, Fooda, Helston, Trefrew, Treegoodwell, Tremagenna, Trevia, and Trewalder.

At Fentonwoon in this parish was born Capt. Wallis, celebrated for his voyage round the world and the discovery of Otaheite.

The right of voting for members of Parliament having been declared by a Committee of the House of Commons, reported on the 10th of November 1796, "to be in the freemen, being inhabitants and paying scot and lot; and that the capital burgessess as such, have not the right," it became important to acquire as much as possible of the property within the borough to secure political influence; and after various sales and transfers, Lord Darlington at last succeeded in acquiring the whole.

The civil corporation hold the manor, mentioned by Mr. Tonkin to have been given by Charles the First, in the capacity of lord of the manor; but the freemen are persons presented by the homage in the Lord's Court. It is almost needless to add that, when the whole property came into a single hand, and that residence with the payment of scot and lot were requisite to complete the power of voting in one presented by the homage, the Borough became what is well understood by the term "quite close," and that it continued so till its extinction in 1832, since which the property has been sold in parcels.

When Mr. Thomas Pitt, of Boconnock, received in 1784 the grant of an hereditary seat in Parliament, and it became necessary, according to the established custom, to create an imaginary office for the purpose of bestowing on him a new appellation, Camelford was feigned to be a barony.

Mr. Macpherson, the author, editor, or paraphraser of Ossian, represented this borough in several Parliaments. This gentleman made a considerable figure in his day, and excited universal attention, chiefly from his publishing what are called the Poems of Ossian. He is now perhaps best remembered by his correspondence with Doctor Johnson, who argued with the force always exerted by his mighty genius, against the authenticity of this work; and Mr. Macpherson, probably unable to meet the reasoning, attempted to establish his case by recurring to a practice almost as obsolete as the achievements of his supposed heroes, which was by reviving the ordeal or wager of battle, as the best mode of ascertaining truth; and with this view, according to the modern phrase, he wrote a challenge to Doctor Johnson, and obtained the following answer:

" Mr. James Macpherson,

" I have received your foolish and impudent letter. Any violence offered me I shall do my best to repel; and what I cannot do for myself, the law shall do for me. I hope I never shall be deterred from detecting what I think a cheat by the menaces of a ruffian. What would you have me retract? I thought your book an imposture, and I think so still. For this opinion I have given my reasons to the public, which I here dare you to refute. Your rage I defy. Your abilities, since your Homer, are not so formidable; and what I hear of your morals, inclines me to pay regard, not to what you shall say, but to what you shall prove.

" You may print this if you will.   SAM. JOHNSON."

The living was held for many years by the Rev. William Phillipps, whom the Editor recollects residing at Camelford, and universally respected for his placid manners and benevolent disposition. A handsome monument has been placed to his memory in the church, by John Phillipps Carpenter, Esq. of Mount Tavy, his nephew and devisee, which records his decease on the 20th day of April 1794, aged 70.

Mr. Phillipps's immediate predecessor was Daniel Lombard, Doctor of Divinity, son of a Protestant clergyman in France, one of those who were constrained to abandon their country by the persecution raised in the name of Lewis the Fourteenth, by a Jesuite Confessor to the King and his mistress, the widow of a buffoon. He received the early part of his education at the Merchant-Taylors' School in London, and proceeded from thence to St. John's College, Oxford, where he obtained a fellowship, and took his degree of Doctor in Divinity. But Lombard never assimilated himself to the manners nor the society of England. He spent much time abroad, and especially in Germany, where he became known either to King George the Second, or, what is more probable, as a scholar and a divine to Queen Caroline: from them he obtained this living.

In Germany he most fortunately became acquainted also, with a Cornish gentleman, then serving with distinction in the army, but distinguished still more by his abilities, learning, and taste. This gentleman (Mr. Gregor) frequently received Doctor Lombard at Trewarthenick, and carried on with him a correspondence on literary subjects, which is still preserved, and appears to have been his chief friend and main support in a situation of complete banishment from all other associates of his studies or of his amusements; for it appears, from one of his letters, that in former times, he had been admitted a member of what would now be termed a club, with several branches of the reigning family at a German court.

All accounts agree in representing Doctor Lombard as a man of profound ecclesiastical and school learning; but at the same time wholly unacquainted with the ways of the world in which he was destined to live, or with the discoveries of modern science. Innumerable anecdotes were current about him half a century ago; of these two may serve as specimens.

He proceeded from London to take possession of his parish, mounted on one horse himself and his servant on another, driving a third laden with such articles as appeared to be indispensible in a country where he supposed nothing could be procured; thus attended, he followed the great road, then passing through Camelford, but inquiring in a foreign accent for Lan-te-glos juxta Camèl-ford, he proceeded nearly to the Land's End without obtaining the least information as to where his parish lay.

The other evinces that he had not condescended to pay any attention to the general classifications of Natural History, although Aristotle or Pliny might have communicated a sufficient store of knowledge in respect to animals, without his recurring to modern authors. Having observed a hen surrounded by a large brood of chickens, Doctor Lombard expressed his utter astonishment and surprise that so small an animal could possibly afford milk in sufficient quantity for the sustenance of such a numerous offspring.

He died at Camelford Dec. 14, 1746; and left a valuable library for the use of his successors.

This parish measures 3562 statute acres.

	£.	s.	d.
Annual value of the Real Property, as returned to Parliament in 1815	4,141	0	0
Poor Rate in 1831	662	14	0

| Population. | in 1801, 912 | in 1811, 1100 | in 1821, 1256 | in 1831, 1359 |

giving an increase of 49 per cent. in 30 years.

Present Rector, the Rev. Coryndon Luxmoore, presented in 1794, by the Prince of Wales.

GEOLOGY, BY DR. BOASE.

This parish no where rests on granite, although it approaches very near to it. Its southern part is composed of massive schistose rocks like those of Advent, and is also traversed by beds of elvan, which very nearly resemble granite. Its northern part consists of rocks of the calcareous series, among which are slates of an excellent quality for roofing.

LANTEGLOS, juxta FOWEY.

HALS.

The manuscript relating to this parish is lost.

TONKIN.

Lanteglos, near Fowey, is situate in the hundred of West; and hath to the west Fowey Harbour, to the north St. Veep, to the east Plynt and Lansallas, to the south the English Channel.

It is a vicarage, valued in the King's books at 14*l*. 7*s*. 6*d*. The patronage in Mr. Thomas Pitt (late Mohun). The incumbent was the Rev. Mr. Henry Sutton, lately deceased.

The first place of note in this parish is the manor of Hall. Hall signifies a moor, as Mr. Carew truly observes; and so by its situation it seemeth formerly to have been. This place was for many generations the seat of the Fitz-Williams, a family of special note in this county. Gervasius filius Wilhelmi Fitz-William, held five knights' fees in the reign of Richard the First.

Robertus, filius Willielmi Fitz-William, impotens Miles, Coronator Domini Regis, (Carew, p. 139, Lord Dunstanville's edition, Edw. II. A.D. 1324), an office much regarded in those days.

Sir John, son of William Fitz-William, and Robert, I believe his brother, were two of those who held 20*l*. per annum of land as rent or more, 25 Edward I.; and had summons to attend the king in parts beyond the sea.

Sir John Fitz-William, mentioned above, had only one daughter and heir, Elizabeth, married to Reginald de Mohun, fourth son to John Lord Mohun, of Dunster Castle in Somersetshire, whereof some of his ancestors had been Lords, which John Lord Mohun died in the fourth year of Edward the Third, leaving his grandson John de Mohun his heir; so that I take John de Mohun, named among the knights 17 Edward the Second, to be the same with him married to Elizabeth Fitz-William, and the dates agree.

They say that this Sir Reginald de Mohun, coming into Fowey harbour with a company of soldiers bound for Ireand, landign there, let fly a hawk at some game, which killed it in the garden of Hall, where Sir John Mohun going for his hawk, and being a very handsome personable young gentleman (qualities which his descendants retained to the last) the young lady fell in love with him; and having a great fortune, the match was soon made up between them by the consent of their friends on both sides. I shall add no more of this place, than that it continued to be the chief seat of the Mohuns till the reign of King Charles the First, when they removed to Boconnock; some time after which, Warwick Lord Mohun sold the barton only to Mr. Kekewich, whose seat it has been ever since. Peter Kekewich, Esq. his son, took to wife the daughter of William Williams, of Bodenick; and dying soon after 1720, left a son, now residing at Hall. The arms of Kekewich are, Argent, two lions in bend passant Sable, cotised Gules. The arms of Fitz-William were, Or, three bends Azure.

The manor of Hall continued in the family of Mohun till the general sale to Mr. Pitt; and Mr. Thomas Pitt is the present lord of this manor.

Hall, from its pleasant situation, has been called View Hall; but as this was an addition of latter years, so is it now lost, and the place has returned to its ancient plain name. Mr. Carew hath a long description of the walk here (P. 310), which is still in being, but much neglected; and also of a remarkable fagot, or rather a piece of wood, belonging to the Earls of Devon, and carefully kept here; but this fagot is, I suppose, now lost. There is but little left of the old house, which I believe was destroyed in the Civil Wars, which may have inclined the Lord Mohun to part with it.

Under Hall, and adjoining to it, is Bodenick; that is,

the house on the water, suitable to its situation. It is but an indifferent place, consisting of one long street on a very steep hill, through which is the highway, and at the bottom of it the passage over the river to Fowey. There is but one good house in the place, and in that the late Mr. William Williams lived, and got a good estate by merchandizing.

The manor of Lamellin, that is the Mill Place, from a mill there, lies on the side of a creek between Bodenick and Polruan. " At the head of this little Pill," says Leland, is a chapel of St. Wilow, and by it is a place called Lamellin, lately belonging to Lamelin, now to Trelawney by heir general. John Trelawney, of Pool, Esq. married Margery, only daughter and heir of Thomas Lamellin, Esq. ever since which this manor hath been in this family, who some time resided here. The present lord of this manor being Sir John Trelawney, Baronet.

The arms of Lamellin were, Argent, a bull's head passant Sable, the horns and hoofs Or.

THE EDITOR.

The church is situated between hills, and therefore but little seen; it contains monuments to the Mohuns and to others. It was rated in the valuation of Pope Nicholas at 10*l*. 13s. 4*d*.

There is a popular tradition, that in the year 1644, just before the surrender of the infantry commanded by Lord Essex, King Charles the First was walking on the terrace at Hall, described by Mr. Carew, when a shot was fired, which missed him, but killed a fisherman almost by his side. The tradition adds, of course, that the ball was aimed at the King by some one who knew him, but that must be uncertain.

Polruan, a place in this parish, having some pretensions still to be called a town, has been wholly omitted by Mr. Tonkin, and probably was so by Mr. Hals, from whose work the greater part of Mr. Tonkin's manuscript is copied. This place is without doubt of great antiquity; and seems in former times, when vessels required much less depth of water than they do at present, to have been the principal station in Fowey harbour. Pol means exactly the same as the English word pool, and may possibly be the original theme; Ruan has been ascertained in several instances to signify Roman. Polruan is, therefore, in all probability, the Roman pool or haven. This place, with a small district round it, forming in some respects a hamlet within the parish of Lanteglos, shared in the elective franchise of Fowey, where all residents paying scot and lot were entitled to vote till the act of 1832 swept it all away.

Tales are related of Polruan having been an independent corporate town, and of its having sent Members to Parliament, while Fowey was a mere village; but such traditions are prevalent in all places under similar circumstances, and they have not here any sanction whatever from authentic sources.

In the Taxatio Ecclesiastica Papæ Nicholai, the three adjacent parishes, printed Lansalewys, Lanteglos, and St. Wepy, have this, App'a. Hosp. de Brugg. want.; and Mr. Lysons states, that this church was given by Robert de Boyton, in the reign of Edward the First, to the hospital of *St. James* at Bridgewater.

The name is inadvertently wrong; for in the Valor Ecclesiasticus, 26 Henry VIII. preserved in the Augmentation Office, is the following entry in the return from the Hospitale *Sancti Johannis* de Brugwalter.

Lanteglos, rector 20*l.*

The great tithes and the presentation to the vicarage, came into the possession of the Mohuns, and were sold with their other property to Pitt.

There is also extant the appropriation of this church to the hospital by Peter Quiril, Bishop of Exeter from 1280 to 1292.

" Omnibus, &c. Petrus miseratione divina Exon. Episcopus salutem, &c. Ecclesiam de Lanteglos, juxta Fawy, cum capella S. Salvatoris, juribus et pertinentiis omnibus; quæ quidem ecclesia cum prædicta capella de advocatione Magistri et Fratrum prædicti Hospitalis existit; præfatis Magistro et Fratribus ac eorum successoribus, ad pauperum et infirmorum sustentationem, capituli nostri prædicti unanimi accedente consensu, appropriamus, &c.

"Dat. Exon. in crastino S. Marcæ Evangelistæ, anno gratiæ MCCLXXXIIII et consecrationis nostræ anno quarto."

Lanteglos by Fowey measures 2773 statute acres.

	£.	s.	d.
Annual value of the Real Property, as returned to Parliament in 1815:	4146	0	0
Poor Rate in 1831	548	13	0

Population,— { in 1801, 678 | in 1811, 859 | in 1821, 973 | in 1831, 1208

giving an increase of 78 per cent. in 30 years.

Present Vicar, the Rev. W. Hocker, instituted in 1806.

GEOLOGY, BY DOCTOR BOASE.

The geology of this parish is the same as that of the southern part of the parish of Fowey.

LANCELLS, LAUNCELLS, LAWNCELLS.

HALS.

The manuscript relating to this parish is lost.

TONKIN.

Lancells is situate in the hundred of Stratton, having to the west Stratton, to the north Kilkhampton, to the east the river Tamar, running between it and Devonshire, to the south Marham church and Bridgerule. This church is so called from its being a cell to the abbey of Hartland in Devonshire. The patronage in Paul Orchard, Esq. by purchase from Francis Basset, Esq.

It is a vicarage valued in the King's Book at 10*l.* 10*s.* 8*d.*

The incumbent, Mr. Thomas, brother-in-law to Mr. Paul Orchard.

In 1291, 20th of Edward I. this church was valued for Pope Nicholas at 7*l*. 15*s*. for the rectory, 15*s*. for the vicarage, and 15*s*. 6*d*. for the tenths; it being then appropriated to the abbey of Hartland, as was

The manor of Lancells. After the dissolution of Hartland abbey, this estate came to Sir John Chamond, who made it his chief residence. Mr. Carew says, he was a man learned in the common law, and knighted at the Sepulchre (that is of our Saviour at Jerusalem). He had a park of fallow deer at this place, which Norden notices, as I suppose the abbats of Hartland had before him. It seems to have been to Sir John Chamond a country seat and a place of retirement. He was Sheriff of Cornwall in the 20th year of Henry VIII. and again in the 28th year.

His son, Richard Chamond, Esq. was three times Sheriff of Cornwall, 35th of Henry VIII. 2d of Edward VI. and 4th of Elizabeth. He received, says Mr. Carew, at God's hands, an extraordinary favour of long life. He served the office of a justice of the peace almost sixty years; he knew above fifty several judges of the western circuit. He was uncle and great-uncle to at least three hundred; wherein yet his uncle and neighbour, Master Greynville, parson of Kilkhampton, did exceed him. He married one of the daughters and heirs of Trevenner, and by her saw five sons and two daughters, the youngest oustepping forty years.

This Mr. Chamond was knight of the shire 14th Elizabeth, as also before in the 2d and 3d of Philip and Mary.

He had an elder brother, called Thomas, whose two daughters and heirs carried part of the lands to Tripcony and Trevanion, with whom they matched. Master Chamond beareth, Argent, a chevron between three flowers-de-luce Gules. And so far Mr. Carew; where note that part of the lands so carried off, contained those in the parish of St. Gorran, lately in the possession of Charles Trevanion, of Tregarthyn, Esq.

LAUNCELLS.

THE EDITOR.

Here was a cell of Austin Canons, dependent on the abbey of Hartland, distant from it but a few miles, although in the county of Devon.

The following entries are found in the Augmentation Office, in the roll 32d Henry VIII.:

Payment from Lancells to the Abbey of Hartland.

	£.	s.	d.
Lancells—Redd' liber' ten'	5	18	4
Custum' ten'	16	8	$5\frac{3}{4}$
Perquis' cur'	0	1	3
	£22	8	$0\frac{3}{4}$

Nothing seems to be known about the foundation of this small religious establishment.

Hartland is said to have been founded before the Conquest, for secular priests, by Githa, the wife of Earl Godwin; but in the time of King Henry the Second, Geoffrey de Dinam, by the authority of that King, and of Bartholomew Bishop of Exeter, and by the assistance of Richard Archdeacon of Poictiers, changed the establishment of Seculars into an abbey of Austin Canons.

The patronage of this abbey remained in the family of the founder, Geoffrey de Dinam, till the general dissolution; and the abbats were accordingly named alternately by Fitzwarren, by Touche, by Carew, and by Arundell, in consequence of their having married the four daughters and coheiresses of the founder.

Mr. Lysons gives a very ample detail of the descent of property in this parish.

The barton of Lancells was leased by King Henry VIII. to John Chamond, and became the seat of that family. The freehold has been for a considerable time in the family of Orchard. It is now the seat by lease of Mr. Joseph Hawkey, in right of his wife, widow of the Rev. Cadwallader Jones.

The manor of Norton Rolle has the bailiffry of the hundred of Stratton annexed as an appendage.

This manor has passed from the Rolls to Trefusis.

The manor of Yellow Leigh is the property and the residence of Mrs. Mary Harris.

The manor of Thorlibear belonged to the Arundells of Trerice, and has passed by inheritance to Acland.

The manor of Mitchell Morton, extending into several other parishes, belonged to a family of Smith, and became divided among coheiresses.

Two thirds, having passed through different hands by purchase, became the property of Wrey J'Ans, Esq. and have descended to his daughters. The remaining third, with the barton and the advowson of the living, having been for many years in the family of Orchard, now belong to the Reverend F. H. Morrison, heir of the late Mr. Paul Orchard.

Tre Yeo, said to have been the ancient seat of the Yeos, is now the property and residence of Robert Kingdon, Esq.

The church stands in a vale, about a mile and a half from Stratton. It has a handsome marble altar-piece and several monuments; one of considerable size, and decorated, to the memory of John Chamond, who died in 1624.

Scarcely any traces are to be seen of Lancells House, the splendid residence of the Chamonds

This parish measures 5610 statute acres.

	£.	s.	d.
Annual value of the Real Property, as returned to Parliament in 1815 . . .	3920	0	0
Poor Rate in 1831	637	13	0

Population,— | in 1801, | in 1811, | in 1821, | in 1831 |
| --- | --- | --- | --- |
| 647 | 672 | 891 | 848 |

giving an increase of 31 per cent. in 30 years.

Present Vicar, the Rev. Henry Bourchier Wrey, presented by L. W. Buck, Esq. in 1825.

GEOLOGY, BY DR. BOASE.

This parish is situated entirely on the dunstone of the

northern parts of Cornwall and Devon; for a more particular account of which, reference has already been given under the head of Boyton.

LANCESTON, or LAUNCESTON,

ST. MARY MAGDALEN PARISH.

HALS.

The manuscript relating to Lanceston is lost.

TONKIN.

Lanceston is situated in the hundred of East, and is bounded to the south by South Pederwyn, as likewise to the west, to the north by St. Thomas, to the east by St. Stephan's and Lawhitton.

It is well known that this town and parish took their name from an ancient priory and church here, now demolished, dedicated to St. Stephan, being called by the Cornish Lan Stephadon, the church of Stephan.

The present church is dedicated to St. Mary Magdalen, and is not valued in the King's Book.

As for what Mr. Carew says, that the Cornish men called it Lesteeven, that is no other than an abbreviation of Lan Stephan.

But before I go on with the account of this town and parish, it will be necessary to observe, that, although Norden (whose authority is indeed of no great weight, even in the description of those things which he had seen himself, and gives draughts of, which for the most part are very erroneous) with many others, call this town, or rather castle, here Dunhevet; yet it is most certain that the ancient town of Dunhevet stood at about half a mile distance to the south-south-west of the present town of Lanceston, in a moorish piece of ground facing the west, at the bottom of the hill on which Mr. Samuel Line has built his pleasure house and inclosed a bowling-green, (from whence is a a very pretty prospect of the vale under it to the east, and the course of the river Tamar) being parcel of the commons belonging to the freemen of Lanceston. I went on purpose to view the ruins of the said town this present year 1731, having before this been led aside by the vulgar opinion, of which every boy I found in the town could satisfy me to the contrary. On the place where the said ruins appear are three wells, which I suppose are from the same spring, being pretty close together; and are, (as I take it) the head of that small river which runs by Tresmorrow, Lanleke, Landew, &c. below which it hath a handsome stone bridge, and soon after falls into the Tamar. So that the said town had, in this respect, the advantage of the new one, as being well supplied with water, which is much wanting in this last. By the ruins it doth not appear to have been of very considerable bigness; though indeed there be no judging well of it, by reason that all the stones of any value have been from time to time carried off to build the present town, and the rest employed to make small inclosures of meadows there.

This place fell to decay, I suppose, on William Earl of Morton building a castle, or rather repairing the old one and putting it in the present form, in the beginning of the Norman times; for, by tradition, this castle has been, from remote antiquity, a seat of the Princes of Cornwall. This William Earl of Morton being also Earl of Cornwall by descent from his father Robert, who was half-brother by his mother to William the Conqueror, drew over the inhabitants of Dunhevet to this place, by granting great privileges to this his chief seat in this county.

But before we go on with the history of this town, let us see what Leland, Camden, and Carew say of it.

Leland.—" After that I had passed over Aterey, I went up by the hill through the long suburbs until I came to the town wall and gate, and so passed through the town, ascending the hill until I came to the very top of it, where be the market-place and the parish church of St. Stephan, lately re-edified. The large and ancient castle of Launceston standeth on the knappe of the hill by south, a little from the parish church. Much of this castle yet standeth; and the moles that the keep standeth on are large, and of a terrible height; and the arx of it having three several wards, is the strongest, but not the biggest, that ever I saw in any ancient work in England. There is a little pirle of water that serveth the high part of Launceston. The priory of Launceston standeth in the south-west part of the suburb of the town, under the root of the hill by a fair wood side; and through this wood runneth a pirle of water coming out of a hill thereby, and serveth all the offices of the place. In the church I marked two notable tombs, one of Prior Horton and another of Prior Stephan; one also told me that Mabilia, a countess, was buried there in the chapter house; one William Warwist, Bishop of Excester, erected this priory, and was afterwards buried at Plympton priory, that he also erected. Warwist, for the erection of Launceston priory, suppressed the collegiate church of St. Stephan, having Prebendaries; and gave the best part of the lands to Launceston priory, and took the residue himself. There yet standeth a church of St. Stephan, about half a mile from Launceston, on a hill, where the collegiate church was. Gawen Carew hath the custody of the priory. There is also a chapel by west-north-west, a little out of Launceston, dedicated to St. Catharine; it is now profaned." So far Leland.

Mr. Carew is more particular (p. 274 Lord Dunstanville's edition). "Those buildings, commonly known by the name of Launston, and written Lanceston, are by the Cornish men called Lesteevan (Lez in Cornish signifieth broad, and these are scatteringly erected) and were anciently termed Lanstaphadon, by interpretation Saint Stephan's Church: they consist of two boroughs, Downevet and Newport; that, perhaps, so called, of down-yielding, as having a steep hill; this, of its newer erection. With these, join the parishes of St. Thomas and St. Stephan. The parish church of Launceston itself fetches its title of dedication from Mary Magdalen, whose image is curiously hewed in a side wall, and the whole church fairly built.

"The town was first founded, saith Mr. Hooker, by Eadulphus, brother to Alpsius Duke of Devon and Cornwall; and by its being girded with a wall, argueth in times past to have carried some value.

"A new increase of wealth expresseth itself in the inhabitants' late repaired and enlarged buildings. They are governed by a mayor and his scarlet-robed brethren; and reap benefit by their fairs and markets, and the county assizes. The statute of 32d Henry VIII. which took order touching sanctuaries, endowed this town with the privilege of one; but I find it not turned to any use.

"To the town there is adjoinant in site, but sequestered in jurisdiction, an ancient castle, whose steep rocky-footed keep hath its top environed with a treble wall; and in regard thereof, men say, was called Castle Terrible. The base court compriseth a decayed chapel, a large hall for holding the shire assizes, the constable's dwelling-house, and the common gaol.

"About sixty years past (i. e. about 1540) there were found certain leather coins in the castle wall, whose fair stamp and strong substance till then resisted the assault of time as they would now of covetousness.

"A little without the town were founded a friary, and anno 1128 an abbey, furthered by Reginald Earl of Cornwall." Thus far Mr. Carew.

Having now done with what former writers have said of this place, I come to give my account of it; and herein I shall begin with

THE CASTLE.

This is seated to the west-south-west of the town, so that you have a full prospect of it from the western road. Below the wall is a large and deep graff, which formerly surrounded it, and is still very visible on the western side; the rest being taken up partly by the highway, and partly by gardens and buildings, which on the eastern side come home along to the castle walls. The west gate is in a manner all in ruins; neither are there any remains of the chapel, the hall, or the constable's house, there being now no other building remaining therein but the house which now serveth for the common gaol; whereas the old one, as the townsmen say, was over the north-east gate, which is still kept in good repair, though no one lives in it.

At the north-east end stands the keep, on a high tapered mount, which I once thought was artificial, though I am now satisfied to the contrary, there being a quarry of stones almost at the very top of it; though there has been some art used nevertheless to bring it to the form that it now has. A covered way formerly led you by steps of stone of an easy ascent, to the top of it, which steps are now carried off as well as the roof, and the whole in a ruinous condition; and truly it moveth compassion to see the woful plight of this so pleasant a seat, accommodated with a fine park, formerly well wooded, with a small rivulet of water running through it. The whole being now held for lease on lives by Hugh Piper, Esq. who by virtue thereof is likewise constable of the castle and keeper of the gaol, the which was granted to his grandfather Sir Hugh Piper, Knt. together with the lieutenant-governorship of Plymouth by King Charles the Second, as a reward for his sufferings and exemplary bravery in the Civil Wars, in one of the battles during which the said Sir Hugh Piper was left for dead in a field for a whole night; being found the next morning, he was put into a warm bed, and carefully looked to. He lived after this to a good old age, as may be seen by the inscription on his monument in the church.

I had forgotten to say anything of Mr. Willis's account of this borough, which I shall therefore now insert.

Robert Earl of Morton, and his successors Earls of Cornwall, having their chief residence at this castle, the town increased much in buildings and riches, and had certain privileges and liberties conferred upon it.

There were burgesses inhabiting or belonging to the castle of this town in the reign of King Henry the Second, and the reign of King Henry the Third. The town was by its then lord, Richard Earl of Poictiers and of Cornwall, the King's brother,* made a free borough, who granted to it by his charter, without date, power to choose their own bailiffs, who were to answer the farm of the borough, which was to himself 100*l*.; to the prior of St. Stephan 65*s*. 10*d*.; and to the lepers of St. Leonard, of Lanceston, 100*s*. of his alms. He granted them also to erect a guild of merchants in the said borough to hold of him and his heirs, which privileges (as may be seen by divers charters and letters patent of the Kings of England, reciting by inspeximus) were frequently confirmed, and with additional liberties. And in the 10th year of Richard the Second, upon the petition of these burgesses, complaining that the last assizes and sessions had been detained from them and held at Lostwithiel, the King grants that these should be kept no where else in the county of Cornwall but at Launceston.

This Prince's father* had, on his being created Duke of Cornwall, inter alia, the castle, borough, and honor of Launceston, assigned to him and the heirs of his body, eldest sons of the Kings of England, in whom accordingly this manor has been vested ever since; and is now held in fee farm by the heir-apparent to the Crown of England, being by birth Duke of Cornwall.

The corporation consists of a mayor, recorder, and eight aldermen, who, with the free burgesses, being in number

* King of the Romans. Ed. † The Black Prince. Ed.

about 130, elect the members of Parliament. Its present establishment of incorporation is owing to a charter of Queen Mary, A. D. 1555. At the last Visitation of the Heralds, held on the 27th of Sept. 1620, the entries were,

Thomas Morton, mayor, Sir Anthony Rous, Knt. recorder; John Genis, Richard Estcot, Arthur Pinard, Nicholas Baker, Hugh Vigures, Henry Cary, George Hext, Orwald Cooke, aldermen; and Philip King, town clerk.

Mr. Willis goes on to say, That this was an ancient market town, may be seen by the Pipe Rolls in King John's time, in whose reign the men of Launceston gave a fine of five marks to change the market from the Lord's Day, whereon it was formerly kept, to Thursday, although it hath since undergone a second alteration, and is now kept on Saturdays.

THE EDITOR.

No one can approach Launceston, and more especially from the eastward, without being struck by the magnificent remains of the ancient castle.

Mr. Edward King, in the third volume of his Munimenta Antiqua, treats much at large of the fortresses erected in remote times throughout Cornwall; and he particularly dwells on this at Launceston, assigning to it the most remote antiquity on account of its not bearing any resemblance to castles built by the Romans, Saxons, Danes, or Normans, and from its agreement with various of the Phœnician, Syrian, and Median castles, and especially with those in Asia Minor.

Mr. King says, the keep (unlike all Norman keeps) instead of being of great diameter and spacious, is very small, although there was evidently space enough on the top of the rock to have made it as large as Norman magnificence could demand, had it been erected, as some have hastily conjectured, by that people. It is only eighteen feet and a half in diameter within, and it is quite round. On the contrary, Trematon, in the same county, which may with good reason be concluded to have been built by Robert Earl of Morton, is a true Norman structure; and there cannot be a greater contrast than there is between it and Launceston. Like Tunbridge castle, it is placed, not on a high natural rock, but on an artificial mound, and is no les than sixty feet in diameter on the inside. See Dr. Borlase's Antiquities, 2d ed. p. 354.

The wall of the keep at Launceston is exceedingly strong, being at least ten feet thick; and within its thickness is a staircase, ascending up from one side of the passage of the doorway, without any winding, excepting that of the mere curvature of the wall itself.

The present height is thirty-two feet, the upper part being somewhat broken down; and it contained, as its only apartments, a sort of dungeon on the ground, which had no light at all, and two rooms over it, one above the other. The lowermost of these, or the room immediately above the dungeon, was nearly as dismal and dark as the dungeon itself, and appears obviously, therefore, to have been intended merely to be used as a place for store, or a sort of treasury; but in the uppermost apartment there appear to have been two large windows (now broken down) commanding a most extensive view, one to the east and another to the west; and also a fire-hearth, with a passage for the smoke carried up through the thickness of the wall towards the north, all which plainly indicate this room to have been intended as a sort of state apartment for the actual residence of the chieftain.

Such is this tower; and its close surrounding works are no less extraordinary, for we find it encompassed by a second munition still stronger than itself.

About six feet, or a little more, from its outside, is an encircling wall twelve feet thick, and nearly equal in height with the floor of the uppermost apartment of all.

Beyond this second wall is again a second surrounding

area in like manner with the first, only six feet wide, and which was further inclosed by a third encircling wall, forming a sort of parapet.

Beyond all these was an external wall with a deep ditch.

Mr. King then goes on to compare this castle with ancient descriptions of those in the east, and satisfies himself of their identity.

Respecting the name, Dun or Doon, is unquestionably a hill, and thence derivatively a fortress; but no plausible conjecture has been formed in regard to the second syllable.

A similar observation may be made respecting the name of the town. Lan occurs as a prefix, in the sense of indicating a church, eleven times in Cornwall; but it seems difficult to derive " ceston" from Stephan. Yet if the Celtic pronunciation of Stephan was really Staveton, Lanstaveton may have easily glided, through Saxon pronunciation and misapprehension of the terminating syllable into Lanceston.

The priory of Launceston appears to have been a foundation of no small magnitude. The list of its possessions, in the Augmentation Office, exhibit a considerable revenue; and Leland describes its church with handsome monuments: not a trace remains. No one more sincerely rejoices at the downfall of superstition, originating in ages of darkness, than the Editor of this work, and above all at the approaching annihilation throughout Europe of monastic institutions, promised by the regular and steady current of events; but the sudden and indiscriminating devastations of the sixteenth century, sweeping every thing before them like whirlwinds, destroying for the mere sake of wanton destruction, or at the very best—from a desire of obliterating all former remembrances; these stamp on the mind very different impressions; and when it is felt that the storm was urged forwards by the fury of an individual, by the avarice of those occupying the highest stations, and by the purposely inflamed passions of the multitude, it is impossible not to experience the forebodings of Scipio on the fall of Carthage; and to exclaim with him

$$\text{Εσσεται ημαρ όταν ποτ' ολωλη Ιλιος ιρη,}$$
$$\text{Και Πριαμος, και λαος ευμελιω Πριαμοιο.}$$

The registers and cartularies of this monastery have disappeared; for these were systematically destroyed. Fragments, however, exist in ancient transcripts; some, formerly in the possession of William Griffith, and referred to by Bishop Tanner, are now preserved in the Lansdowne Collection. Among these the following document may be found relative to the foundation of the priory by William Warlewast, Bishop of Exeter, from 1150 to 1159:—Noscat præsentis temporis ætas, quod Radulfus Ecclesiæ sancti Stephani de Launcestone decanus decanatum mihi Willielmo Episcopo reddidit. Et ego canonicis regularibus, quos in eadem constitui, totum dedi. Testes sunt,

> Osbertus, Abbas de Tavistoca.
> Gofridus, Prior Plymptoniæ.
> Will. de Augo, Archidiaconus Cornubiæ.
> Clarenbaldus, Capellanus Regis.
> Magister Odo.

The charter from King Henry the Third, also extant, is a fair specimen of the times, and contains some local descriptions of property:—

Henricus Rex Angliæ, &c. salutem. Inspeximus cartam Domini Johannis Regis Patris nostri in hæc verba.

Johannes Dei gratia Rex Angliæ, &c. salutem. Sciatis nos concessisse, dedisse, et hac presenti charta confirmasse Deo et Ecclesiæ Sancti Stephani de Lanstaveton et canonicis ibidem Deo servientibus, pro salute animæ nostræ, et pro anima Henrici Regis Patris nostri, et pro animabus omnium antecessorum et successorum nostrorum, viginti solidatas terræ in manerio nostro de Climerston, et preterea viginti nummatas terræ in eodem manerio. Scilicet, dimidiam acram, quam Eggerus de Holrode tenet. Hæ autem sunt metæ terrarum illarum. Scilicet, a termino terræ

Radulphi Pitlenam sicut rivus descendit in magnam aquam de Eny, et usque ad terminum terræ prædicti Eggeri de Holrode, ex parte orientis et meridiei. Item ex parte occidentis et septentrionis a Wideslade, sicut rivus currit et descendit in magnam aquam de Eny in terram de Climerston et terram de Treuris. Et preter hoc dimidiam acram terræ in Norton quam Warinus tenet. Confirmamus etiam eisdem canonicis omnia subscripta, sicut eis rationabiliter data sunt. Scilicet, ex dono Richardi de Raddon unam virgatam terræ, quæ vocatur Trewenta, quietam et liberam ob omni servitio, præter quindecim denarios, quos reddere debet ad Tidlaton, de quadam consuetudine, quæ vocatur Motiled. Et ex dono Roberti filii Alkitilli, concessu comitis Reginaldi domini sui, terram quæ vocatur Trenchicot. Et ex dono comitis Reginaldi partem Hamelini presbiteri de Capella de Castello, cum omnibus libertatibus et rebus parti illi pertinentibus. Et quadraginta solidos per annum de firma de Castello de Dunheved, et Ecclesiam Sancti Andreæ de Stratton, cum pertinentiis suis; et unam carucatam terræ de dominico manerii de Stratton, juxta alteram terram ejusdem ecclesiæ, cum quadam area Salmarii Elfordiæ, salvo dignitate capellæ nostræ de Castello de Lanstaveton; et Molendinum quod est sub Castello de Dunheved, cum eisdem pertinentiis, et consuetudinibus, quas habebat dum erat in manu Comitis Reginaldi; et terram de Karnedon, quæ est membrum de Kidlacton. Ita quidem quod de reliqua parte ipsius manerii de Kidlacton perficiatur eis tantum; quod bene et plenarie habeant centum solidatas terræ, sicut Comes Baldewinus de Redevers eis concessit et assignavit, et carta sua confirmavit; et ex dono Osberti de Bikesleya viginti solidatas terræ in manerio de Treuris, scilicet villam quæ vocatur Tregof, et terram quæ fuit Luffe, et terram Warnii juxta pontem; et unam acram in villa quæ vacatur Carsbroc, cum hominibus et omnibus quæ ad præfatas terras pertinent; et partem nemoris apud orientem, sicut via dividit usque ad aquam; et ex dono Bernardi Clerici duas acras terræ, quas tres homines tenent et reddunt Deo et Ecclesiæ Sancti Stephani, inde quinque solidos annuatim, quæ sunt subtus viam Trebursi; et ex dono Willielmi de Henemerdon totam terram de Pech. Hæc quidem omnia cum omnibus pertinentiis suis concessimus eis et confirmavimus dum essemus Comes Moreton, sicut ea rationabiliter possident, et sicut cartæ Donatorum suorum testantur.

Datum per manum H. Cantuariensis Archiepiscopi cancellarii nostri, vigesimo octavo die Junii, apud Aurivallem *anno regni nostri primo* (1199).

Nos igitus has donationes, &c. confirmamus, &c. Insuper concedimus et confirmamus eisdem canonicis et eorum successoribus, pro nobis et hæredibus nostris, donationem quam Reginaldus Regis Filius, consul Cornubiæ, eis fecit in incrementum Ecclesiæ suæ de Lanstaveton, de Ecclesia de Leskeret, et de Ecclesia de Lankinhorn, in die translationis Reliquiarum et canonicorum ipsius Ecclesiæ de villa de Lanstaveton ad vadum, sicut carta ipsius Reginaldi Regis filii, quam inde habent, rationabiliter testatur.

Hiis testibus,
    H. de Burgo, comite Kantii, Justiciario Angliæ.
    Philippo de Albiniaco.
    Thoma Basset.
    Willielmo Basset.

VALOR ECCLESIASTICUS 26 HEN. VIII.

Prioratus de Launceston.

Unde Willielmus Warwest, quondam Episcopus Exon. est Fundator.

	£.	s.	d.
Summa Valoris tam Spiritualium quam Temporalium Prioratus prædicti	392	11	2¼
Reprisa	38	10	3
Valet clarè ultra repris' per ann'	£354	0	11¼

LANCESTON, OR LAUNCESTON.

ABSTRACT FROM THE AUGMENTATION OFFICE.

Nuper Prioratus de Launceston.

Com. Cornub.		£.	s.	d.
Launceston.	Scit' cum Terris d'nicalibus	15	19	6
Launceston lande cum Burg' de Newporte				
	Reddit' assis' - -	118	5	7
Launceston lande.	Redd' Lib' Ten' -	0	3	5
	Firm' - - -	10	0	0
Bradford.	Redd' Lib' Ten' -	0	14	7
	Co'ven' Ten' - -	6	8	1½
	Perquis' Curiæ -	0	3	6
Canedon Prior'	Redd. Lib' Ten' -	3	9	7½
	Co'ven' Ten' - -	12	0	6
	Perquis' Curiæ -	1	11	10½
Clymysland.	Redd' Lib' Ten' -	0	8	0
	Conven' Ten' - -	6	13	9
Treworthgy.	Red' Lib' Ten' - -	4	13	7
	Ten' custum' quam conven't Ten' - -	3	17	0
	Perquis' Curiæ - -	0	6	2
Stratton.	Red' Lib' Ten' -	1	2	0
	Conven' Ten' - -	6	5	8
	Perquis' Curiæ -	0	3	3
Tottysdone.	Redd' Lib' Ten' -	0	9	5
	Conven' Ten' (Lib' cum')	1	0	0
	Perquis' Curiæ -	3	12	8
Estwaye.	Redd' Lib' Ten' -	2	10	0
	Cust' et Con' Ten' -	0	9	7
	Perquis' Curiæ -	1	8	4
Boyton.	Redd' Lib' Ten' -	1	3	11
	Co'ven' Ten' - -	6	16	5
Bradryche.	Terr' d'nical' -	8	11	0
Boyton.	Perquis' Curiæ -	0	7	2
Buclawrenbucke.	Red' Lib' Ten' -	0	1	6
	Conven' Ten' - -	19	15	6¼
	Perquis' Curiæ -	0	2	20

LANCESTON, OR LAUNCESTON.

			£.	s.	d.
Bonealvey.	Red' Lib' Ten' -	-	1	6	11
	Conven' Ten' -	-	6	4	6
	Perquis' Curiæ -	-	0	6	2
Halgh land.	Red' Lib' Ten'	-	1	6	9
	Ten' ad val' -	-	0	3	5
	Perquis' Curiæ	-	0	9	8
Treworell.	Red' Lib' Ten' -	-	1	4	10
	Conven' Ten' -	-	0	2	0
Beyworthye.	Pensio -	-	0	10	0
Ayssheby.	Pensio -	-	0	2	0
Deweston.	Pensio -	-	0	5	0
Loffyngeo.	Pensio -	-	0	2	0
S. Egid'	Pensio -	-	0	2	0
Tresmare.	Pensio -	-	0	1	8
South Siddenham.	Pensio -	-	0	1	0
Lyskerde.	Pensio -	-	5	0	0
Talland.	Pensio -	-	2	0	0
Bridgeruell.	Pensio -	-	0	3	0
Lynkinhorne.	Pensio -	-	1	6	8
Lanest.	Pensio -	-	0	3	4
Lescard.	Decim' -	-	25	0	0
Talland.	Decim' -	-	10	0	0
Wulryngton.	Rector'	-	21	9	4
Egloskery.	Rector'	-	21	8	0
Poughill.	Rector'	-	7	0	0
Stratton.	Rector'	-	11	0	0
S. Genefre.	Rector'	-	11	0	0
Lawanyke.	Rector'	-	10	0	0
Launceston.	Rector' S' Thomæ	-	6	0	0
Lanest.	Rector'	-	5	0	0
Inlett.	Rector'	-	6	0	0
Lankynhorne.	Rector'	-	18	0	0
Launceston.	Rector' B. Mar' Magd'		3	13	4
S' Steph' cum Tresmore.	Rector'	-	13	0	0
Tynnyherne.	Portio Xme -	-	0	6	8
Tamerton.	Rector'	-	9	13	4

Launceston, defended by its Acropolis, and important as a frontier town, probably remained in all respects the capital of Cornwall so long as that little state retained its separate existence. Lestwithiel afterwards became the residence of its nominal Earls, took from Launceston the sheriffs' court, and acquired the technical appellation of the county town.

The assizes, however, continued at Launceston, and the quarter sessions were opened there; and then, for the convenience of the western population, adjourned to Truro. Here also was the only county gaol; till at last the inconvenience and expense became so great, that about the year 1780, a new, extensive, and commodious gaol, with every recent improvement, was constructed at Bodmin, where the summer assizes had been removed under the authority of an act of Parliament 1st Geo. I. c. 45, rendered necessary by the charter of King Richard II.

But Launceston, only two miles from the boundary of Cornwall, and so remote from the mining districts, which comprehend the great masses of population and of litigible property, as to render a journey there in one day impossible, has been long considered wholly unfitted for the holding of any court having jurisdiction throughout the county; while on the other hand judges and counsel feared to extend their winter's progress over the bad roads and hills of Cornwall. The roads are now improved, and the hills are avoided; and in this year (1834) an order has been made for holding both assizes in future at the town adjacent to the prison, nearly in the centre of the county, and where an increased inducement will be afforded for providing the accommodation requisite on such occasions.

Launceston itself has received more improvement than almost any other place as a thoroughfare; the great London road crossing it from east to west, and one of considerable importance from north to south.

The exit from the east gate was about ten years ago made safe, and even convenient, from being dangerous in a very high degree; and in the present year (1834) a road from the north has been wound round the castle at a very easy ascent, and avoided altogether a hill so steep as almost to prohibit the use of wheeled carriages.

Launceston not only sent two Members to Parliament; but the long street, or suburb extending from the foot of the hill at the north gate, sent two members more under the name of Newport. By the act of Parliament of 1832, they are both included in a district, returning one member. Launceston is so amply described by recent writers of the county history, that it would be useless to repeat what they have given. The general view of the place is magnificent: and especially from the new iron bridge, completed this year, across the Tamar at Polston.

The parish of St. Mary Magdalen measures 1090 statute acres. The present Minister is the Rev. John Rowe, appointed by the Corporation in 1808,

	£.	s.	d.
Annual value of the Real Property, as returned to Parliament in 1815	3900	0	0
Poor Rate in 1831	736	0	0

Population,—
in 1801,	in 1811,	in 1821,	in 1831,
1483	1758	2183	2231

giving an increase of 50 per cent. in 30 years.

GEOLOGY, BY DR. BOASE.

Doctor Boase observes on the geology, that clayslate, calcareous schist, limestone, and other rocks belonging to the calcareous series, constitute the substrature of this parish.

It is quite obvious that the conical mound supporting the keep, as well as the whole extent of the base court, are composed of eminences favourable for defence but improved by art, being scarped in some places and elevated in others.

END OF VOLUME II.

CPSIA information can be obtained
at www.ICGtesting.com
Printed in the USA
LVHW080251100522
718387LV00008B/162